ISLAND TO ABBEY

Survival and Sanctuary

in the Books

of

Elsie J Oxenham

1907 to 1959

by

STELLA WARING

and

SHEILA RAY

Girls Gone By Publishers

Published by

Girls Gone By Publishers
4 Rock Terrace
Coleford
Bath
Somerset
BA3 5NF

First Edition privately published 1985
Second Edition privately published 1996
This revised edition published by Girls Gone By Publishers 2006
Text © Stella Waring and Sheila Ray 2006
Design and Layout © Girls Gone By Publishers 2006

The authors assert their moral rights.

Edited by Adrianne Fitzpatrick and Laura Hicks

Typeset in England by PCS Typesetting
Printed in England by Antony Rowe Limited

ISBN 1-904417-80-9

Eleanor reddened suddenly, and turned and sat gazing across the lower Downs.

From the short story 'Dicky's Dilemma', published in *The British Girl's Annual* for 1927.

Contents

FOREWORD

We began this study in the summer of 1981 and completed the first version, written for the enjoyment of ourselves and our EJO friends, early in 1985. In the early 1980s there was no *Abbey Chronicle* and little appreciation of how widespread the interest in the books of Elsie Jeanette Oxenham would become in the twenty years since then. The study was written in a very informal way, covering the books in the order in which they were published. As there was never any serious possibility of publishing the study, we worked out the overall plan as we went along and little was done in the way of revision.

We are indebted to many people who have helped and encouraged us along the way. The late Regina Glick of Leeds generously lent us those EJO books that neither of us owned and her interest and enthusiasm kept us going in the early days. We also owe an enormous debt to Monica Godfrey, without whose work on EJO we should not have been able to start from the point we chose in 1981. We were also helped along by the interest of Mary Irwin, Helen McClelland and the late Mabel Esther Allan. More recently, and particularly in connection with this version, we have appreciated the interest of Mary Cadogan.

Andrea Polden, then a librarian at the Library Association Library, which was part of the British Library, generously gave us copies of some of EJO's books and lent us letters that EJO had written on condition that she was allowed to make a copy of the study for the library. This was made available through the national library network and many people borrowed it.

In 1996 Ruth Allen, then editor of *The Abbey Chronicle*, suggested that if a good quality master copy could be produced, additional copies could be made for those people who would like their own. Diane Moore very kindly volunteered to make the master copy. Revisions were kept to a minimum and that edition was completed in July, 1997.

Then, in February 2003, Clarissa Cridland and Ann Mackie-Hunter wrote to us and said that Girls Gone By would like to publish it. How could we refuse? For this edition we have not changed our ideas to any significant extent, but the text has been fully revised and reorganised. We have removed the need for reference numbers in the text to make for easier reading; we have included more information about the EJO places that we have visited ourselves.

The GGBP edition of Monica Godfrey's *The World of Elsie Jeanette Oxenham and her Books* was not published until after we had begun work on this latest version of our study, which was originally based on her 1979 pamphlet. We have, however, related our references to the new edition, in which we found the details of first editions (Appendix 3) and information about the short stories (Appendix 5) particularly useful.

We would like to thank Wendy Dunkerley very much for allowing us to use the two family photographs of her aunt on the cover. Special thanks are also due to Edna Golder for her pictorial map 'The World of the Abbey Girls'. The late Olga

Lock-Kendell, who was the first 'researcher' for the Society and whose enthusiasm encouraged its foundation, inspired some of the research that is reflected in this new edition.

In addition to all the people already mentioned we would like to say a general thank you to the members of the EJO Appreciation Society and to the writers of articles in *The Abbey Chronicle*. Their views have not always been taken on board but have inevitably influenced us. Doreen Litchfield, Chris Keyes, Gillian Priestman, Kate Kirman, Jennifer Hignall, Primrose Lockwood and Margaret Perry generously shared their knowledge of EJO sites with us.

We are delighted to have four pages of colour reproductions of dustwrappers and pay tribute to the publishers of those and of the many black and white illustrations used in the text.

Finally we would like to thank Clarissa and Ann and the other members of the production team for all their work on the production of *Island to Abbey*.

Stella Waring and Sheila Ray
March, 2006

Chapter 1

INTRODUCTION

'Many adults still enthusiastically collect her books', as Mary Cadogan wrote in the first edition of *Twentieth-Century Children's Writers,* in 1978. 'The titles everyone is after are those of thirties author Elsie J Oxenham,' said the writer of an article in the *Daily Telegraph* in 1981. Although Elsie Jeanette Oxenham is mentioned in most of the post-war standard reference books about children's literature, and Lynette Muir had contributed an article about her to the *Junior Bookshelf* in 1966, little was known about her until Monica Godfrey published a pamphlet, *Elsie J Oxenham and Her Books*, in 1979. Perhaps, we thought in the early 1980s when we began our study of her work, she was too busy writing her books, of which there are nearly a hundred, to have much private life, apart from her involvement with those activities, such as the Camp Fire movement and folk dancing, which play an important part in her books, and her visits to the many places that she describes in her books. The situation since then has been transformed.

EJO, as she is affectionately known amongst her admirers, is one of the authors known as 'The Big Three', the other two being Elinor M Brent-Dyer and Dorita Fairlie Bruce. All three belong to the same generation of women writers and knew and dedicated books to each other. It is worth noting, however, that, whereas EBD's books about the Chalet School went into paperback in the 1960s and stayed in print until the end of the century, and DFB's stories of Dimsie were updated and republished in hardback in the 1980s, EJO's work, apart from a few of the Abbey books that appeared in very much abridged Children's Press editions until the early 1970s, was not reprinted in either hardback or paperback until the twenty-first century when Girls Gone By Publishers (GGBP) began to produce the rarer titles in new editions aimed mainly at adult collectors.

Why did publishers in the late-twentieth century feel that EJO's work would no longer appeal to schoolgirls? There are some strictly practical reasons why it was not reprinted in the way that the works of EBD and DFB were. EJO's books were published by a number of different publishers—Collins, Muller and Chambers amongst others—so she lacked the advantage that EBD had in having Chambers, who published all the Chalet School books, firmly behind her, willing to support a fan club with a newsletter for its members and ensuring that the paperback rights were sold to a suitable publisher. Nor had she produced a short, virtually self-contained series of seven or eight books that a new publisher might take on, as John Goodchild did in the case of DFB's Dimsie books.

However, it is also fair to say that EJO's books seem somewhat old-fashioned when compared with those of her fellow writers. Unlike them, she virtually ignored the Second World War, perhaps because she had learned how references to the First World War had dated her earlier books, but also because by 1938 she had created such a romanticised and complex world of her own that the events of the 1939–45 war would have blown her chronicle well off course.

EJO's books, although they include male characters, are unlikely to have been read by boys; their appeal is totally female. Why do they continue to exercise such an extraordinary appeal for middle-aged and elderly women and even attract some younger women and girls, for whom they cannot have the nostalgic appeal of books read when young? Two reasons spring to mind. First, she portrays a society in which women are important and play a leading role, and secondly, she interlinked the majority of her books.

Although the male historians of children's literature such as Geoffrey Trease, Frank Eyre and Marcus Crouch are content with relatively brief mentions of EJO, both Mary Cadogan and Patricia Craig in *You're a Brick, Angela!* and Gillian Avery in *Childhood's Pattern*, both published in the 1970s, discuss the intensity of the personal relationships

between the female characters and remark on what were at that time coming to be recognised as feminist attitudes. EJO's books hover between an acceptance of the traditional female role, with almost all the girls marrying and most of them having large families, and an encouragement to independence, with careers, albeit often glamorous ones, being considered 'a good thing'. With the rise of the feminist movement, this aspect of EJO's work was to be even more fully explored in Rosemary Auchmuty's books, *A World of Girls* and *A World of Women*, both published in the 1990s.

The second reason for their continuing appeal is the way in which EJO's books are interlinked. A handful stand on their own—the rest are linked to each other, however tenuously— sometimes by just one character. For schoolgirl readers in the 1930s and '40s one of the disadvantages was that, because the books were produced by a variety of publishers, none of them contained a complete list of books about the Abbey, in either reading or any other order. Identifying and then tracking them down in libraries or bookshops was straightforward in the case of the Chalet School and Dimsie books; doing the same for the Abbey books was impossible. It was only as an adult that Monica Godfrey had the skills and resources that enabled her to identify all the books and work out their relationship to each other, producing a list for which every other Abbey fan has good cause to be grateful.

At the centre of EJO's work are the books about the Abbey and the Hamlet Club. These have, as Lynette Muir pointed out in her article, all the appeal of the Arthurian romance:

The construction of the series is exactly similar to the medieval romance cycle. A number of permanent characters alternate with individual girls, who appear for one book then vanish again, their story complete. They are drawn to the Abbey and the Hamlet Club as knights in the old romances were drawn to the Court of King Arthur and the Fellowship of the Round Table.

Margery Fisher also emphasises the romantic appeal in her entry for Joan and Joy Shirley in *Who's Who in Children's Literature.* When the reader first meets them, the cousins are living in the Cistercian Abbey of Grace Dieu, where Joan's mother is the caretaker:

To anyone who read the book in girlhood the impression that remains is one of colour—in the description of old stone and ancient glass and of elaborate embroidered robes of the Queens elected year after year by the Club ...

Significantly, Joan and Joy embody recurring themes in the Oxenham books. Joan sacrifices her chance to go school to her cousin Joy who, she feels, needs the chance more, but all comes right in the end when Joy turns out to be an heiress, and the two never lack for money again. The combination of Puritan attitudes and unostentatious wealth probably had an overwhelming fascination for a generation of women who grew up during the 1930s and '40s. All that has happened since Monica Godfrey's pamphlet was published in 1979, however, demonstrates that the appeal is even wider than that.

The pages of the *Abbey Chronicle,* the thrice-yearly journal launched by Monica Godfrey, with encouragement from Olga Lock-Kendell, in 1989, bear witness to the wide range of interests developed by members of what has become known as the EJO Appreciation Society as a result of their reading of this author. Flourishing groups of enthusiasts, with similar interests, are also to be found in Australia, New Zealand and South Africa.

When we first started work on the study which has now become, over twenty years later, this book, one intention was to establish the reason for the appeal of EJO's work for what we thought was probably a fairly small group of middle-aged, well educated women. The other was to show how the books relate to each other, and it was for the latter reason that we decided to look at the books in the order in which they were published. As we worked our way from *Goblin Island* (1907) to *Two Queens at the Abbey* (1959), it became clear that two major themes—survival, represented by an island, and sanctuary, presented by an abbey—appear in much of EJO's work.

Daniel Defoe's *Robinson Crusoe,* one of the earliest English novels, which has inspired many authors since it first appeared in 1719, describes a very different kind of survival from that experienced by most of EJO's characters. She comes nearest to the desert island story in her two historical novels set in North Wales, *Mistress Nanciebel* and *The Girls of Gwynfa*, where the heroines are involved in finding shelter and food in order to survive. They have to apply the same sort of techniques as Robinson Crusoe and all his many fictional successors have had to do to make life possible. Many of EJO's other books, however, have central characters who are orphans or penniless or, at the very least, in financial difficulties, but manage to survive through their own determination and efforts—

and, it must be admitted, a certain amount of luck.

A lot of problems are solved by the acquisition of money, but many survive both physical difficulties or difficulties in their relationship. Illnesses and broken bones, as far as the central characters are concerned, are cured or repaired by the end of the final chapter. The Marchwood twins, Elizabeth and Margaret, are perhaps the best examples of characters who survive a series of accidents, often introduced to move the story on or provide a catalyst for the action.

Those characters who experience problems in their lives, particularly the loss of close relatives or misunderstandings with friends, generally find some kind of sanctuary, sometimes quite literally in an abbey.

Most of the books are romances and have happy or satisfactory endings. Many of them are Cinderella stories, the fairy-tale version of survival, telling of a deserving character who undergoes hardship but emerges from it with money and, frequently, a handsome husband. Those women who do not get married are rewarded with a satisfying career—as a successful writer, for preference.

These various elements—survival, sanctuary and romance—will be examined in the chapters that follow.

Chapter 2

THE EARLY YEARS:
GOBLIN ISLAND TO THE HAMLET CLUB

Elsie Jeanette Oxenham was born in 1880 and published her first book, *Goblin Island*, in 1907 when she was 27. Writing was very much part of her background for her father was William Dunkerley, a journalist, who adopted the name of John Oxenham and under this pseudonym published many romances and enough poetry to establish himself as at least one of the minor War Poets.

Elsie, his eldest daughter, adopted the same surname as her father as her pseudonym and in fact *Goblin Island* reminds one of some of her father's stories. It appears to be partly autobiographical, probably much romanticised, and is not specifically for children (in fact none of her books really was), although it could be read and enjoyed, as her later books were, by girls in their teens. Sheila recalls that around 1940, when she was ten and in her first year at secondary school, she borrowed it from the class library and was quite unable to get through it, although she was attracted by the title and made several attempts to read it.

Goblin Island, like EJO's next two books, was published by Collins. It is set in Scotland, in an area familiar to the Dunkerley children. Mrs Dunkerley was Scottish, and the children often went with her to spend their holidays in Dunoon, where their grandmother had a holiday home. Unusually, the story is written in the first person, and this, together with the plot, suggests that at this stage EJO was unsure of her audience. The writer of the story introduces herself as the Girl and her father as the Author; because she helped her father with his stories, she too tried to write stories. This habit of naming people by descriptions of their roles, with the initial letter in capitals, was one that that was to endure—in a later book EJO introduced herself into an Abbey story as the 'Writing Person'.

In the first chapter of *Goblin Island* the heroine, Jean or 'the Girl', is portrayed as a constant companion to her father. They live in London, so that her father can 'keep in touch with people' and 'be near his publishers', but generally spend the summer months in the country, 'most often in Scotland'. EJO has disposed of most of the rest of her real-life family of three sisters and two brothers, retaining just one brother, Donald, who is training to be a doctor. *Goblin Island* tells the story of the romance between Donald and Peggy Colquhoun. The Colquhoun family own Strongarra, the house which Jean and her father take for the summer; the family consists of Malcolm, the eldest boy, who is also training to be a doctor, Peggy, slightly younger (20), Jack (12), Jill (12), Sheila or Red Riding Hood (10) and Robin or Boy Blue (6). Two more children drowned in a boating accident, their mother died when Robin was born and their father more recently, a year or two before the story opens.

Various motifs and themes that were to occur in later books are to be found in this first book, apart from large families and parents who have died early deaths—Jean's mother is also dead, and mothers in particular seem to die early, perhaps reflecting the difficulty which EJO found in portraying the mother-daughter relationship.

Jean and her father, for no apparent reason, look after Marjory or 'the Mystery', an invalid girl of twelve. Marjory Lesley has had an accident two years previously and is a cripple, although it is hoped that she will outgrow her injury in due course. Her parents have gone off to Australia on a long sea voyage for the sake of Mrs Lesley's health (if mothers are not actually dead, they are often weaklings, required to live abroad or to go on long sea voyages), and have left Marjory with the Maxwells. Just why it seems suitable to leave her with a male friend of her father's and a girl of about twenty is anybody's guess. Marjory's main role is to lie in her room and develop a secret relationship with Jack and Jill Colquhoun.

Jack and Jill are bitterly opposed to the Girl and the Author, whom they regard as interlopers, and much of the story is taken up with this one-sided feud. Because of a shortage of money (temporary, as their fortune is restored by the end of the book), the Colquhouns have had to move out of the big house into a cottage on an island in the loch, and let the house to the Maxwells. The Colquhouns' lawyer, Mr Sinclair, is also a good friend, and the friendly family lawyer was a character who was to appear over and over again in EJO's books, a necessary one since so many young people find themselves heirs or heiresses to substantial fortunes while they are still in their teens.

Apart from the atmosphere of general affluence and the strict division between the main characters and the servant class, there is one interesting hint of what was to come in the 'Abbey' books. Marjory's mother, although an invalid to the extent that she and her husband are prepared to take off for Australia leaving their crippled daughter to be looked after by friends, has been in the habit of making all Marjory's dresses. When Marjory is secretly visited by Jack and Jill, the latter admires the intricate embroidery on Marjory's dress and discovers that it represents oak leaves and tiny acorns, ivy leaves and blackberries. Marjory says she also has a dress with 'roses and buds and leaves' and another 'with primroses and blue and white violets'. This foreshadows the point that is made in the early Abbey books about the dresses of the maids of honour being embroidered with the floral emblems of their queens.

Goblin Island has a strong sense of place although the names are disguised. We are told that Strongarra is 'two hours journey from a great city'—presumably Glasgow. Evidence from later books confirms that EJO set this one on Loch Lomond. Jean, who tells Peggy and Marjory that one day she is going to write a book, is undoubtedly a romanticised portrait of the person EJO saw herself to be. Although in reality it seems to have been her sister Erica who was her father's helpmate, EJO perhaps liked to imagine herself in the favoured role. Be that as it may, Jean's remark—and the choice of Jean's name of course reflects her own middle name of 'Jeanette'—might have been made by EJO herself, for write books she certainly did.

A Princess in Tatters was published by Collins in 1908 and, like her previous book, is set in Scotland—on 'Loch Ruel', which is evidently Loch Riddon, into which the real River Ruel flows. Once again it is an area that EJO knows and loves, and her detailed descriptions reflect this. It is the particular beauty of the area that brings Bernard Raby there on a painting expedition, as a result of which he meets the 'Princess in Tatters'. This is a Cinderella story, but the girl of the title is a determined young lady with a will of her own and is not above a spot of mischief in her own right.

There have to be a plot and a villain here. Neither were EJO's strong points and, as this is her first published attempt at both, it is not surprising that the plot becomes rather involved and that the not entirely convincing villain is conveniently killed in a shooting accident. His name is Duncan Munro, and in his youth, while working as an engineer on the steamers which connect Glasgow with the lochs—these steamers have almost a role of their own in EJO's Scottish books—he met and married Helen Morrison, 'the bonniest lass in Glenaroon'. Unfortunately Helen died when their baby daughter Eilidh (Gaelic for Helen) was born, and in despair Duncan went away, leaving his daughter to the care of his wife's sister. This would be comprehensible, but his villainy lies in the fact that he never returned and did nothing about supporting his daughter financially.

By the time the book opens, Eilidh is eleven. Her

Jack and Hill took an oar each. (*Goblin Island*)

aunt had died when she was five and she has since been looked after by a poor family with seven small children. She helps with the work, looks after the babies and goes to school when it is possible or convenient. Her father, meanwhile, has been to America, become a millionaire (most of EJO's Americans are millionaires, which is interesting when you remember that her father's venture did not succeed), and married Miss Isabel Raby who 'though not rich was well-born' and who, almost certainly, married him for his money. They have two daughters, and the only way in which Duncan Munro acknowledges the existence of his eldest daughter is by his aversion to the name Helen and a curt dismissal of the beauties of Loch Ruel.

One idea that is presented here, and is to occur again and again in the books, is that it is quite acceptable to marry money, especially for the good you can do with it, so long as you also marry for love. Isabel Raby is firmly condemned by her stepbrother and sisters for this and also for a certain condescension towards those less fortunate than herself. She patronises her artist brother Bernard, but he, fortunately, takes it very tolerantly. He is a very attractive character and it seems a pity that EJO didn't use him again. He is more realistic than her average young man, which may be the reason.

In the book he is the connecting factor. On a painting visit to Loch Ruel, made in spite of Duncan Munro's comment that it's 'very dreary and out-of-the-way, and always raining', he discovers Eilidh Munro. At first he just wants to paint her, but as he meets and talks to her he becomes interested in her as a child in poor circumstances whom he would like to help, and finally he discovers that she is Duncan Munro's guilty secret. He rushes off to confront Munro with his guilt. We only have a report of this scene—EJO surely felt herself unequal to it—and Bernard is very easily deceived by Munro's seeming acquiescence to the request that he should provide for Eilidh. But Mollie Raby, Bernard's sister, the first of the 'dedicated teachers', is suspicious of a Sunday visit to London to see a solicitor, and, of course, Munro has done no such thing. Instead, he had made an underhand attempt to obtain the proofs of Eilidh's identity, with a view, presumably, to destroying them. The inference made is that he was afraid to face his wife with the existence of this child of his first marriage who is 'absolutely ignorant and untrained'.

His plan is foiled and Mollie Raby becomes Eilidh's teacher and guardian. Mollie also has the beginning of a romance of her own, after an unpleasant incident in a railway

Loch Riddon, 2001

carriage when she is saved from an undesirable character with designs on her watch. By a coincidence, her rescuer is also going to Loch Ruel to be tutor to a young aristocrat, Lord Larry, with whom Eilidh has already had several encounters and got into mischief. Mollie Raby and Jack Kerr are still only good friends at the end of this book, but they are to reappear. With the character of Lord Larry we have the first expression of EJO's views on the responsibilities laid upon those of noble birth. Larry is a spoiled, selfish boy who never considers the effect of his actions on other people. Eilidh considers that, for a lord, he is 'no better than other laddies', and implies that he ought to be.

Before the end of the book Duncan Munro is killed in a shooting accident. Although his wife has been given many clues to Eilidh's story, we are not present when she hears it— he told her on his deathbed—and we never really know her reactions to the news. Eilidh Munro remains the first of EJO's 'wild untrained girls' who become heiresses to fortunes and have to be educated to fit their position in life. The obvious Cinderella story is here redeemed by the character of its heroine, a mixture of domestic philosopher and mischievous fairy. She is possessed of all the domestic virtues and has a seeking mind as well. Like the young Colquhouns she uses the soft West of Scotland speech, which other characters in the stories often find charming but which teachers strive to eliminate.

At first sight it is difficult to see how even adolescent girls in 1909, when it was published by Collins, could have been impressed by EJO's next book, *The Conquest of Christina*. In this book, perhaps more than in any other, the moral problem is laid on so thick that it seems tedious to the modern reader and can hardly have failed to exasperate the early ones. The conquest of Christina is, in fact, Christina's conquest of herself, which is not achieved without a great deal of repeated, Lancelot-Gobbo-type dialogue. Christina, because she dislikes the idea of a group of children she doesn't know coming to share her home and her life, destroys a letter written to her elder brother, who stands in loco parentis to her. To a modern reader it may seem a much more serious offence than the book ever makes it; there is something here of the idea that story-book children of that period do get away with things for which real-life children would have been severely punished.

The underlying theme of the book is the way in which Christina can never come to terms with what she has done until she confesses and is forgiven. This is a theme that recurs in the books but is never treated so heavily again. The 'heavy morality' is redeemed by the setting of the book and by the other characters. Christina lives with her brother and his wife and their delicate twins at Criccieth on the coast of Wales. This time no attempt is made to change the names of the places, and any girl reader who had spent holidays in North Wales would remember and recognise Beddgelert, the little train at Blaenau Ffestiniog, Aberglaslyn and many other places.

Lovely Myfanwy, the Lady of the Sweet Peas, and her beautiful flowers—not to speak of her romance with Alec Carruth—provides a real 'dream heroine', and her flowers, always given to friends and used by Christina as an introduction to her nephews and nieces, take their place of importance in this story as flowers will continue to do throughout EJO's work. So often, in later books, flowers are used to introduce people, to bring colour and beauty into lives that are otherwise dull and drab. The picture of Jen sweeping into a drab London office with hands full of violets and shaking Mary-Dorothy out of her apathetic dreams is one of which we are continually reminded in later books.

Then there are the other children, the sons and daughters of Christina's older half-sister

Criccieth as seen from the castle, 1990

who, because their parents have to go abroad and because Christina destroyed the letter asking if they could come and stay, have to come and live, not in the happy young household where Christina herself lives, but with an elderly Uncle who is both nervous and strict. Winifred, Bill, Polly-Joan, Taffy and Dimity, not forgetting Dimity's 'dear Monk', are real and interesting children, in spite of their high moral tone. They are very distinct in character and are surely children her readers would recognise or identify with, depending on their ages. Perhaps it was for the people and places that readers enjoyed *The Conquest of Christina.*

For the setting of her next two books EJO stayed in the same area of North Wales but used the Lleyn Peninsula, which is described in loving detail. It is safe to assume that she must have spent at least one holiday there around this time, and all the places that she mentions can easily be identified on a map. It also seems likely that her interest in astronomy was aroused at this time, since star names are mentioned briefly in *The Girl Who Wouldn't Make Friends* (when Gwyneth has told Robin the names of the stars which can be seen), and star-lore is a central feature of Gilbert's courtship in *Mistress Nanciebel.*

The Girl Who Wouldn't Make Friends was published by Nelson in 1909. Robin, or, to give her her full name, Robertina Brent, is not exactly a Cinderella character, but she comes unexpectedly into a rich inheritance when Robert Quellyn, who had been in love with her mother and for whom she is named, dies leaving her his estate in the Lleyn Peninsula. The reason for the bequest is, on the face of it, explained, although how Robert Quellyn has come by it in the first place is not. His incompetence in not providing for Gwyneth, his adopted daughter, is also rather glossed over. Robert Quellyn's father had been a sailor, as is the father of Gwyneth's friend, Ivor Lloyd. Jim Carradale, an erstwhile neighbour of the Brents in London, is another sailor, and throughout EJO's books this career recurs—one thinks of Jandy Mac's husband, Littlejan's husband, Bill and Roddy Kane, and Angus in *Strangers at the Abbey*. The details are vague, but the general impression is created, not only that it is a respectable career, but also that it is a fairly paying one. It also has the advantage of getting inconvenient male characters out of the way, putting them into dangerous situations, and introducing hints of far distant and romantic places.

When the letter telling Robin of her inheritance arrives, Mr Brent is away on business in India, so Mrs Brent, Robin and her two brothers, one younger and one older, travel up to Plas Quellyn to view the estate. Robin's character is a Cinderella type in that she is deserving of her good fortune and only under the greatest provocation does she remind her brothers of the fact that the property is hers. Unlike Christina she does not have to conquer her faults, and in fact she develops little in the course of this book. The two brothers are much more strongly drawn. Cuthbert, the elder, is passionately interested in medicine (another of EJO's favourite male careers, of course), an interest which leads him positively to ill-treat the puppy at Plas Quellyn, while Dicky, the younger, is rather impetuous and given to saying whatever he thinks, a habit which can embarrass his elders on occasion.

Gwyneth fach, the girl of the title, is a much more interesting character than Robin, and she does develop. She does not resent the fact that the property has not been left to her, as she might well have done, but is upset when she discovers that her temporary guardian, another Gwyneth, the younger sister of Robert's young wife, who predeceased him, has asked the Brents to look after her. She causes Robin to have an accident and this brings her up with a start, after which she quickly reforms, becomes friends with Robin in particular and at the end of the book is adopted by the Brents, who welcome her as their 'second girl. You know we always wanted one.'

The off-centre romance, characteristic of EJO's earlier books, is to be found here. In Chapter 3 Jim Carradale turns up at the Brents' London home, having been away serving in the navy in the China seas for five years. His function is to court and, in due course, to marry guardian Gwyneth or Gwyneth fawr, and also to provide assistance when the children, now united with Gwyneth fach and her friend Ivor Lloyd (whom she later marries), become involved with criminals planning to steal the Quellyn pictures.

The conflict of the story is provided by Gwyneth fach's resentment of the Brents, her retreat to a hiding place and the attempt of the children to find that hiding place, which turns out to be the basement room of an old ruined tower in the grounds of Plas Quellyn. A climax is provided by the planned burglary, inevitably foiled by the children who employ the techniques of medieval siege warfare, with boiling water instead of boiling oil. The descriptions of the children at play in the surroundings of Plas Quellyn have definite overtones of the novels of E Nesbit, which also date from the first decade of the twentieth century, and, to a lesser extent, of *The Secret Garden* by Frances Hodgson Burnett (1911). An element of suspense comes with Mr Brent's illness, which seems introduced largely to get Mrs Brent out of the way so that the children can get on with having adventures unimpeded by her presence. This is not the last time that Mr Brent's well-being is to be sacrificed for the sake of the plot.

The pre-war period of the book's publication is reflected in the fact that Gwyneth fach, aged twelve, drives a car all over the Lleyn Peninsula, in the reliable postal services and in the existence of a railway across central Wales to Pwllheli by the side of Lake Bala. Since it nowadays, in the twenty-first century, takes the train just over two hours to travel up the coast from Machynlleth to Pwllheli, the speed and convenience of the trains in 1909 is something to marvel at!

The faces of the two Gwyneths (the Welsh fach and fawr mean little and big) and the dead Margaret, his wife, have been used by Robert Quellyn in his pictures based on the events and incidents of the *Mabinogion,* the legendary history of Wales. In the early chapters, when Robin reads the *Mabinogion* and Mrs Brent takes the children to the gallery in London to see the pictures, these stories loom large, and the reader could learn quite a lot about the traditional legends of Wales, as she could about the Welsh language. This insistence on the Welsh language and culture in 1909 at a time when 'anglicisation' was still the official policy reflects not only EJO's sympathy for the minority culture but also, perhaps, the growing influence of Lloyd George, whose roots were in this part of the world and who was rapidly gaining ascendancy in British politics at this period. *The Girl Who Wouldn't Make Friends* reflects EJO's interest in romance, in colour and in folklore and legend.

The Gwyneths were sitting beside the low doorway.
(*The Girl Who Wouldn't Make Friends*)

In 1910 EJO returned to the Lleyn Peninsula for the background of the first of her two historical novels, *Mistress Nanciebel*, published by Hodder and Stoughton. As Monica Godfrey shows, both she and Dorita Fairlie Bruce wrote historical novels followed by modern stories in which characters from the early books appear as ancestors. And certainly, in EJO's later books, the Seymours of Summerton and a modern Nancybell do make their appearance. Monica Godfrey also tells us that EJO said she 'deliberately stressed the Puritan and Quaker side because everyone else writes about the more romantic Cavaliers'.

Considering the date of its publication, the moral idea/theme in *Mistress Nanciebel* is surely an unusual one for the time. It seems unlikely that it was reprinted during the years 1914–18, when the idea that it was a man's first duty to fight for his country was, if other books, including EJO's own, are to be believed, very high in the minds of patriotic schoolgirls. Some of EJO's ideas may well come from her knowledge of the faith and history of the Society of Friends, but in this book she has taken just one facet of their beliefs—that for a man to fight other men is wrong and that a man is not bound to obey an order from a higher authority to do something which is against his conscience.

In *The Later Stuarts*, George Clarke writes: 'When the early Quakers maintained that no war was lawful for Christians, they used not only Biblical arguments, but objection of morality and common sense.' He quotes Robert Barclay, who, writing at the time, warned 'not only against rendering evil for evil' but also against going 'awarring one against another, whom we never saw and with whom we never had any contests, nor anything to do; being moreover altogether ignorant of the cause of the war, but only that the magistrates of the nations ferment quarrels one against another, the causes whereof are for the most part unknown to the soldiers that fight, as well as upon whose side that right or wrong is.'

Mistress Nanciebel is set in seventeenth-century England at the time of the Restoration of King Charles II. EJO gets her dates right—the Plague, the Fire and the Dutch War are all exactly accounted for, and her heroine shares the King's birthday. Nanciebel's father, Sir John Seymour of Summerton, has a clear sympathy for those of Puritan beliefs, but does not seem to have suffered for it. He has a handsome house and a place at court. Now, however, he has made himself unpopular by writing and speaking against war with the Dutch, and there is also a barely spoken threat that, if he comes to a public trial, the fact that he has helped and encouraged proscribed Puritan preachers and attended forbidden services may well come to light and he will suffer for it

When the story opens, Nanciebel, the protected and cherished elder daughter, has remained at home while her father and brother have gone to London to answer to the King for Sir John's ideas. Nanciebel has no idea of any threat to her happy, ordered world, and when the truth is revealed it comes as a shock. The news is brought by a lady from the court, Lady Llety, who, we are allowed to infer, has 'some influence' with the King. Since the King is Charles II, this is possibly intended to tell us that she is one of his mistresses. (This would, of course, not have been clear to her readers, though later girls may have made just that inference. History teachers in the 1940s and after were more explicit than those in the teens of the century).

Sir John Seymour, when brought face to face with the King, has maintained his belief that for a man to kill another is wrong, even if he has been ordered to do so by his King. When reminded that 'it is man's nature to wish to fight', he insisted that there was no lack of other opponents—disease, poverty, ignorance, 'nature and wild beasts, and the difficulties of unknown lands'. Such a dangerous idealist can, clearly, not be allowed to go around infecting people with his ideas at such a time, and only Lady Llety's influence has saved him from death or imprisonment. She has suggested that he should be put to the test, so the King proposes to land him on some wild, foreign shore, with no money or resources, to see how he will fend for himself, putting his ideas into practice.

John Seymour accepts this offer, with the full support of his elder son, Gilbert, and of Nanciebel herself, who is to go with them, in spite of protests and arguments from friends and enemies alike. Her preparations for going are both naïve and practical. She outfits herself with suitable clothes, with help from her Quaker maid, Constancy, but takes one pretty dress, just in case. The Seymours' exile is complicated by the addition of Captain

Mistress Nanciebel

Blaise Morgan, a nominee of the King, who must go with them to see that they do not cheat. He goes, much against his will because, as a soldier, he considers that Seymour and his son are mere cowards who won't fight because they dare not.

The wild, lonely foreign shore on which they are abandoned very quickly turns out to be Wales—we are back on the Lleyn Peninsula. Sir John Seymour knows his geography and reasons it out at an early stage. Meantime Nanciebel has to cope with black Welsh cattle and cooking without utensils over an open fire. But this would, perhaps, have been less of a hardship for a seventeenth-century housewife who had no gas or electricity to cry for. In fact, the Seymours really have it very easy; it takes them barely a week to find someone who speaks English and to find work for themselves on a nearby estate.

Perhaps the intention here is that the contest is rather one of ideas than a physical struggle between man and his environment. The Seymours establish themselves, Sir John and Gilbert working in the fields, and Nanciebel keeping house and making friends with a young Welsh girl called Marsli. Meanwhile, Blaise Morgan, at first angry and contemptuous, anxious to provoke Gilbert and amazed when Gilbert controls his own temper, slowly learns to understand and appreciate John Seymour's ideas and, in the end, to share them. The final test and proof is made when the plague comes to the village and the Seymours go down to fight it, to nurse the sick and organise the villagers so that the maximum life is saved. In the end, of course, they all live happily ever after; a converted Blaise Morgan marries Nanciebel and Gilbert finds a Welsh bride.

Once again we have a story set in Wales where places and scenery are recognisable and her Welsh language, we are told, is correct. From a note that prefaces the book and explains that to the best of her knowledge 'the family of the Madryns of Madryn has been extinct for about two hundred and fifty years', it would seem that EJO had done some research into the area she was writing about.

Again we have importance laid on flowers and gardens, but perhaps the most important 'first' in the book is the introduction of folk songs. Nanciebel has quite a repertoire, and she sings them all the time. Perhaps it was the song of *Lord Lovel and Lady Nanciebel* that gave EJO the idea for her heroine's name. Since it is not easy, even now, to put a date to folk songs, it does not seem worthwhile trying to find out if Nanciebel's repertoire is at all anachronistic. EJO's readers would probably know *Barbara Allen* and *O Whaur hae ye been a' the day?*, but they were unlikely to have heard of *Alison Gross*. We know that EJO's enthusiasm for folk songs came before her joining the English Folk Dance Society, which was only founded in 1911. Perhaps she had seen and used Cecil Sharp's book of traditional songs, so we can surely trust her here. Certainly there are at least half a dozen songs, of which the words are quoted in part or in full, and Nanciebel's singing plays a part in the story.

For the setting of her sixth published book, *A Holiday Queen*, EJO returned to Scotland, to the area around Dunoon on the Firth of Clyde. As well as Dunoon, Greenock and Rothesay are mentioned as places to which people go; most of the families in the story have their base in Glasgow, but spend the summer months on the lochside. One minor place name that appears in the story is Cove—the handicapped boy, Nigel Scott, is made Marquis of Cove. This is on Loch Long and not far from Knockderry Castle, which appears to satisfy the requirements for Morven, the estate at the centre of the story. There is one mystifying thing about this book—the dedication to 'the members of Queen Lexa's Chinese meeting'.

Lexa (Alexina) Stewart is the perfect EJO heroine. She is only thirteen, but is successful, attractive, popular and well-adjusted, with just one flaw which gives rise to the conflict in the book. Her relationship with Jim MacFarlane is handled with great skill in a book for young people; all the tensions of a sexual relationship are there, when Lexa's jealousy of Jim's cousin Monica Howard is aroused, but no sexuality is hinted at. There is some simple psychology, a preparation for the reader for whom sexual relationships are still in the future. Lexa puts her finger on the problem when she says: 'Too much toffee makes me sick.'

It is no longer enough for EJO to confer princess status on her heroine. Lexa is a queen who on the first page declares: 'I'd like to be head girl in a big school, and order the others about … I'd be a very good Queen, but I would like to be a *Queen*.' It is possible to see here a hint of the 'Queen of the Hamlet Club' role—in the later Abbey books the Queen is seen as carrying out some of the more attractive functions of a head girl: making new pupils feel at home, looking after the little ones, sacrificing herself for the good of her 'subjects'. The responsibility of this self-appointed role is emphasised, and Miss Sparrow utters a warning at an early stage. Another hint of the Hamlet Club is to be found in the bronze medals, which are the badges supplied to the members of Queen Lexa's Band.

Lexa lives with her grandfather in Glasgow and is sent to his estate at Morven for the summer because the doctor has recommended a few months in the country to help her to recover from the after-effects of scarlet fever. Her father is another sailor—in fact, an explorer, who is away with his wife 'looking for the South Pole'. (This is an interesting comment on contemporary events—the book was published in 1910. Amundsen reached the South Pole in December 1911, and Captain Scott a month later in January 1912, so there must have been interest in the idea of reaching the South Pole for a year or so before the achievement.) Lexa's father has been abroad on expeditions before, which is what suggests that he is an explorer rather than a sailor, and has brought back 'rare specimens' of trees which are now flourishing in the grounds of Morven. Lexa has a governess, but the governess is given a holiday for the summer and Lexa is accompanied to Morven by Miss Sparrow, who is the daughter of a friend of the family. Miss Sparrow (which is not her real name) could be

EJO's way of writing herself into this story. Miss Sparrow's lifestyle could well have been EJO's ideal—living in a nice, well-staffed house in lovely surroundings, looking after an untroublesome girl, able, when Lexa is engaged with meetings of the Band, to go to her room and write. There is a man in the offing (he goes off to Canada during the course of the book), but marriage is said to be at least two safe years away.

The class distinctions have the overtones of a fairy tale. We hear about the wealthy upper class to which Lexa and her friends obviously belong, and about the proletariat whose role is to serve or to be done good to, but nothing about the people in between. Morven, which Lexa's grandfather says he never cared for, is 'a big stone house, with long straight windows and towers and turrets and battlements like a castle'. When Lexa, her grandfather and Miss Sparrow arrive in April, there is a big wood fire in the entrance hall; this tends to be a feature symbolic of luxury in EJO's books and is later to be found at Broadway End. Lexa's grandfather, although at one point moved to say that she has been 'a very expensive young lady lately', gives her everything she wants, and at the end she is hostess at a splendid evening party. During this the comment is made, since it is an early Halloween party, that 'there is no lack of apples at Morven'. In fact one doesn't feel that there is much lack of anything! Lexa has a yacht, a bicycle, a pony trap, tickets for the steamer; when they arrive at Morven, a landau meets them at the pier; when her mother and father arrive back from their expedition, nearly at the end of the book, they arrive in a Rolls—although apparently in the early editions it was a carriage.

Those who are done good to range from the MacTaggart family (Mr MacTaggart and Granny Mac are in charge of the estate; their son is away exploring with Lexa's father, while his wife lives at the lodge with five subservient children, who open gates, open the door and generally wait on the Band) through Lizzie and Willie, who are 'barefoot … ragged and untidy' and live in a cottage, and all the local schoolchildren, to the Glasgow slum children who are brought to Morven on a trip with money raised by Miss Sparrow through her writing. The MacTaggart children demonstrate EJO's preoccupation with 'J' names—Janet, Jim, John, Joanna and Jo. Janet, the eldest, is lent books by Lexa, is devoted to her, and 'when she was a little older she was going to be Miss Lexa's maid and never leave her'.

The haves and have-nots are distinguished by their speech. Lexa, Jim and the rest of the Band speak pure English while the have-nots are given the broadest of Scottish accents. This device is found in many books: the wealthy characters, with whom the reader is invited to identify, speak the Queen's English, while the loyal servants are given regional accents.

The boy characters are stereotypes. Even Jim appears to be waiting to be old enough to step into a romantic, Buchan-type adventure story, and his character is manipulated for the purposes of the plot. He is honourable and courteous, and Lexa likes him, but when Monica arrives he fails to understand Lexa's resentment of his apparent neglect of her, and then, to show up Lexa's capabilities, he behaves like a complete fool in the running of the Band, totally incompetent. When Lexa cycles out to where she knows Jim and Rob Cameron are fishing, to try and make peace, Rob speaks and behaves like a mini-minor Buchan character. After making a welcoming remark and inviting Lexa to admire their catch, he 'remembered the last meeting and felt suddenly awkward and in the way. "I'm going down to look at the boat," he stammered, and hurried away and left them together.'

Even more significant is Jim's behaviour—'Jim the polite, Jim the gentlemanly, neither rose nor took off his hat.'

The boys generally have an olde-worlde, mature approach to the girls. They enter into Lexa's make-believe kingdom, into the use of the titles she bestows upon them, and they allow her to boss them around to her heart's content; but they also believe that girls should be pretty and protected. Their behaviour is usually that of mature young men rather than that of thirteen year olds; perhaps they are behaving in a way that women and girls would like boys of nine to thirteen to behave rather than in a way that real boys of that age might—and this is perhaps one of the attractions of the story for the female reader.

The girls are much more interesting characters, despite the roles apparently envisaged for them by the boys. This can be seen most clearly in the case of the MacGregor twins, Roy and Isabella, known as Tibbie. Roy is the liveliest and perhaps the most convincing boy character (although even he is properly respectful to Queen Lexa), and he and Tibbie are constantly sparring. Tibbie frequently takes the lead and provokes her brother. It is Tibbie who is anxious to see the road under water, which leads them into 'mischief at midnight', and who suggests they take the yacht out without Mr MacTaggart, which leads to a wrecking in the storm. As Roy says, 'Tib's always up to something and she generally makes a mess of it.' Apart from Lexa herself, Tibbie, Monica, Nanny and Isabel all come over as distinct characters in comparison with the male stereotypes.

It is the progression of the relationship between Jim and Lexa that moves the story forward, and Monica and Nanny (Jim's younger sister) develop as characters in order to provide this progression. It is completely in keeping with Nanny's style that she would spy on Jim and Lexa and then reveal the secret of the hiding place to Monica—she is portrayed as a busy-body gossip right from her first appearance. Monica is an academic and gifted version of Lexa, and Lexa continues to like her—the fault which causes the rift is clearly Jim's, combined with the flaw of jealousy in Lexa's own character. The shy Isabel provides the raison d'être of the late evening talks between Jim and Lexa, while Tibbie (and Roy) are the ones to whom Lexa turns for solace during the period of bad weather and when she believes herself to be forsaken by Jim. At the other end of the social scale, Janet MacTaggart and Lizzie come over as positive characters. Although Tibbie complains, when Jim won't allow her to speak, 'It's as bad as the Suffragettes. "Votes for Women", Captain', thus providing another reference to the contemporary world, one feels that the girls are well able to look after themselves.

The adults, apart from the folksy ones, Miss Sparrow and the wealthy Mr Stewart, are shadowy and, in the case of mothers, elegant—for example, Mrs MacFarlane presiding over her 'at homes'.

The story has worn remarkably well. It is sometimes difficult to believe that Edward VII was still on the throne when it was written, although Lexa's name may have been chosen as an echo of the Queen's. The girls are extremely active, walking, hill-climbing, cycling, sailing and fishing. There is no suggestion that they are hampered by long skirts, although Lexa and Nanny are both said to be wearing white, as a matter of course, on a Sunday. Land transport takes the form of carriages, carts and bicycles. Although at one point Nanny and Monica are described as driving to Morven in a car, when Nanny is seen off the vehicle is described as the waiting 'carriage'. In *The Girl Who Wouldn't Make Friends* cars are seen as a novelty; here, a couple of years later, they are not perhaps a novelty, but not all that common either. Again the postal service is amazingly reliable—and fast. Communications posted in the evening can be relied upon to arrive first thing the next morning. Here in the country there is no second delivery to individual houses, and letters must be fetched from the post office if necessary, but one feels that telephones would have saved a lot of the misunderstandings that take place in this particular book.

It is easy to see the appeal of *A Holiday Queen*—there is an element of adventure, but it is the tension of the relationship between Lexa and Jim which makes the story, and that this takes place against a background of wealth and beneficence of yesteryear gives it the nostalgia element which made *Upstairs, Downstairs* and *Brideshead Revisited* so popular with television viewers in the 1970s and '80s.

Although by outsiders EJO is thought of as a writer of school stories, it was not until her seventh book, *Rosaly's New School,* published in 1913, that she actually wrote a story in which school played a major part. For this she also moved to a new publisher, Chambers, who were later to become associated with Elinor Brent-Dyer's still famous school stories, and

one can speculate that EJO may well have introduced Elinor Brent-Dyer to Chambers, who published the latter's first book, *Gerry Goes to School*, in 1922. EBD later appeared to borrow the idea of a school linked to a sanatorium from EJO, and Monica Godfrey has commented on EJO's slight coolness towards EBD as being understandable. There is an interesting link between *Rosaly's New School* and EBD in the name of one of the central characters, Malvina. The only other place in which we have come across this name is in the work of EBD—Joey Bettany suggests it as a name for her first niece, and this suggestion is much mocked, not only at the time but also in later books about the Chalet School.

Rosaly's New School appeared three years after *A Holiday Queen,* at a time when the girls' school story was just beginning to establish itself. Although L T Meade had published girls' school stories in the late nineteenth century, it is Angela Brazil who is often regarded as the real 'mother' of this genre, and she did not publish her first school story, *The Fortunes of Philippa*, until 1906. This, like *Rosaly's New School*, has quite a large element of home life in it.

Rosaly's New School is set on the North Yorkshire moors, in the area around Goathland. One can assume that EJO had recently visited the area and had, as usual, quickly absorbed the topography in some detail. Local beauty spots are mentioned; the local people are given broad Yorkshire accents, although the girls, the staff and the professional people speak pure English—apart from Malvina, who has a transatlantic twang and vocabulary. It is surprising that there is no mention of folk dancing here, as the north east is an area particularly connected with sword dancing. Sleights lies within the area covered by the story and is actually mentioned, while Flamborough, another place which gives its name to sword dancing, lies only twenty or thirty miles to the south. This may be because the tradition had died out and was only to be revived by the encouragement of the EFDS, which had at this date only recently been founded.

At the beginning of the story the Redworth children—Ruth (15), Ronald (14), Rosaly (11), Rona (8) and Richie (6) are living with their aunt at Moorside Manor near Goathland. The girls have a governess, Ronald has a tutor, and responsibility for them is shared by a lawyer/guardian, Mr Dalby, who lives in the village during the summer. Their life is shattered by the news that the Manor has been inherited by a Canadian girl, Malvina Dougal, the stepdaughter of their father's elder brother, who had been cut off with a shilling and gone abroad. The children's grandfather later repented, and it seems largely accidental that Malvina has inherited the property, particularly as the title, a baronetcy, goes to Ronald. It is generally agreed that what has happened is unfortunate and unjust, but that it is now necessary for the Redworths to be educated properly so that they can earn their own livings. The aunt goes off to the south coast for the sake of her health, and arrangements are made for Ronald to go to school in Scarborough and for Richie to live with the Dalbys. The girls are sent to a school that has just moved from Whitby to new buildings near Goathland, buildings in which Rosaly happens to have taken a great interest.

Rosaly is one of three central characters. She is only eleven, and is a very young eleven year old—her use of the words 'norful' and 'norfully' is indicative of her rather childish way of speaking. The centre of the story is shared by Ruth, her elder sister, and Malvina Dougal, the heiress, who, although only fifteen, are much more mature and at times seem like the young women of EJO's earlier books.

Rosaly is a very attractive character and the best developed of the three. She has always been on her own, since Ruth and Ronald have been close friends and have tended to exclude her from their activities, while Rona and Richie have always played together. (We see in the Redworth family the preoccupation with 'R' names—even Rosaly's dog is called Rough—which was to culminate in the names of the Kane family.) However, Rosaly is very generous and when first Rona and then Ruth turn to her after they go to school, she accepts their friendship eagerly. She is also very kind to Andrew Mackintosh, a boy whom she meets in the first few pages and who is left with his aunt, Miss Ingleton, the headmistress of the school, when his missionary-doctor parents return to China. Rosaly is bouncy and resilient; she takes her punishments philosophically, particularly the knitting which wrongdoers are required to do for the local fishermen under matron's supervision, she is always ready to contribute to the discussion or conversation, and at the end performs a heroic deed when she gallops back over the misty moors to bring news that she and two other missing children are safe.

The more adult and gracious qualities of EJO's earlier heroines are to be found in Malvina (also known as Vina or Malvie), the Canadian heiress. She also is very generous; she does not give away to the adults the facts behind her lack of welcome when she, her aunt and cousin arrive at Moorside Manor (Ruth and Ronald have suppressed her telegram announcing her arrival, and Ronald has misdirected her at Whitby station), and she is determined to return the Manor to the Redworths as soon as she comes of age. It must be said in passing that she is not short of money, as her stepfather was wealthy in his own right, and she has been travelling in Europe for two years. Malvina, like Rosaly, is attractive and outspoken and wins the hearts of all those who meet her. There is even a hint of romance in the attention that Hubert Dalby pays to her. Malvina is always in control of any situation in which she finds herself. Although she is kind and generous, she also does exactly as she likes. Much is made of the fact that she sometimes wears breeches and rides astride, rather daring perhaps in the years before the First World War. Her freshness and outspoken nature are fairly typical of the girl who comes from the outposts of Empire to join an English school in the early years of the twentieth century. She may be the first of her kind to do this, but she is by no means the last!

Ruth, although the same age as Malvina, is much less mature—not surprisingly, in view of the difference in their upbringings. Ruth and Ronald are both determined not to seek Malvina's charity, and Ruth won't allow the girls at school to know that she is from the Manor. She avoids meeting Malvina for as long as she can. Miss Ingleton, while sympathetic to her situation, appeals to her, suggesting that the situation is a trial of character, and Ruth at last decides to rise above her immediate feelings, to confess her part in suppressing the telegram and to make friends with Malvina. As someone whose character develops in the course of the story, Ruth is perhaps the most interesting of the three girls.

Ronald has no redeeming features, and one feels that he scarcely deserves the Manor that will one day be his, although this fact is not dwelt upon. In this he foreshadows the young Earl of Kentisbury, Geoff. He is very much Ruth's friend but loses interest in her affairs as soon as he gets to school; he is not only involved in the suppression of the telegram but also deliberately misdirects Malvina to Egton Bridge station, a mistake which involves Malvina's party in a steep hill-climb, a slow experience in the days of carriages. Ronald is given no chance to repent, whereas Ruth soon begins to have misgivings about their behaviour toward Malvina.

There are many links with EJO's other books. The form colours (violet, green, pink, brown, blue—dark for the upper form, pale for the lower) show EJO's interest in colour that was later to be given full rein in the colours chosen by the Hamlet Club Queens. The school is never named, although we are told in great detail about the colours and furnishings in the new buildings—this failure to name the school was something that was to happen in later books. The school in the Abbey series, for example, is always known as Miss Macey's, and to some extent this reflects the period at which EJO was writing—many small schools were known by the name of the headmistress.

At one point, when the other girls are being introduced, Gladys explains that Dorothy and Margery are twins, and adds: 'Did you ever know twins that weren't called Dorothy and Margery? You haven't noticed it? Well they always are, you know.' Nearly thirty years later Maidlin's twins were to be named Marjory, for her mother-in-law, and Dorothy, for Mary-Dorothy.

The idea of the usurping heiress, which is at the centre of *Rosaly's New School*, was one that appealed to EJO. She had, of course, already used it in *The Girl Who Wouldn't Make Friends*, although there the situation is resolved by sharing; she was to use it again in a similar way for Jandy Mac, although Jandy Mac, after going through all the agony, discovers that in fact she has never inherited the Abbey property. Other ideas have been used before. Rupert, the son who has been cut off with a shilling and then made his fortune in Canada, echoes Duncan Munro doing likewise in America. The destruction of the telegram telling of Malvina's arrival is a repetition of Christina's destruction of the important letter.

The plot is not without flaw—Andrew, for example, is in a good position to reveal the secret of the Redworths to the rest of the school, and the fact that he does not do so, even accidentally, is never explained. Nevertheless, EJO manages to weave the familiar ingredients into an appealing and readable story, the strength of which probably lies in the three central characters, Rosaly, Ruth and Malvina, who between them provide someone for every reader to empathise with, and in the detailed Yorkshire setting.

Schoolgirls and Scouts

In *Schoolgirls and Scouts*, first published by Collins in 1914, we are once again in Scotland and among the lochs of the West Coast. The Glenleny estate that is at the centre of the story evidently lies on the western shore of the Gare Loch, between the Loch Avie of *Goblin Island* and the Morven estate of the *Holiday Queen*. As well as familiar places we meet a number of familiar characters from other books. Here, for the first time, we find an example of the interconnecting of EJO's books by the introduction of characters from previous works. We meet again Jill Colquhoun from *Goblin Island*, Monica Howard and the *Holiday Queen* and her Band, and Eilidh Munro, the *Princess in Tatters*, with her family, her governess Mollie Raby, and Lord Larry and his tutor Bill Kerr. It is as though in *Schoolgirls and Scouts* EJO is drawing together characters from all her Scottish books to date.

Although most of the action takes place in Scotland, there are other, more exotic elements present in this book, which is dedicated to 'Mildred Elizabeth Hills and Gladys Mary Hills, my friends from Samoa—Ma le Alofa'. We know, from Monica Godfrey's research, that the Oxenham/Dunkerley family worked for the London Missionary Society whose main field of action was in the South Seas, and that they had missionaries from Samoa as guests in their home. EJO's interest in, and knowledge of, missionary work reappears in some of her other books, and Jandy Mac makes her home in Samoa when she marries. Many schoolgirls of the 1920s and '30s will have shared this interest, especially those who were 'Pilots' of the LMS. In *Schoolgirls and Scouts*, Elspeth Buchanan and her brother and small sister are orphans who were born 'on a South Sea Island' where their parents are missionaries, and the children are fired with their parents' enthusiasm and plan to go back when they are grown up to carry on their work.

When the book opens, they have been under the care of their mother's brother, a wealthy stockbroker, and his wife, but due to financial problems this uncle has handed over responsibility for them to their father's family, as represented by their cousin Janie Buchanan of Glenleny. The three elder children must now leave their 'good' boarding schools, where they have spent the holidays as well as term-time, and travel north to Scotland.

Although only the first few and the very last chapters of the book are set at school, the importance of school (ie boarding school) is stressed all through. Elspeth's school is a good one, the girls take part in drill, games and swimming and are taken to London for exams 'and sometimes for concerts or museums or picture galleries', so Elspeth has a great deal of 'worldly experience' in comparison with Mysie and Madge Campbell, the rich girls from Glenleny Hall. Again and again in the course of the story Elspeth gives them cause for envy when she meets friends from school and enjoys experiences they would much like to have shared. It is Mysie's greatest wish to go to boarding school, and she cannot hear and read enough about it. But Elspeth presents another side. School is fine, if you have a home to go to in the holidays. For four years she has lived at school, holidays and all, and now she wants 'to have a home. Think how ripping it must be to live in a house without any rules … where you can go anywhere you like just whenever you like, and talk in your bedroom as much as you like … Think of going into the kitchen!'

The Scouts of the title are represented by Elspeth's brother, Jock, and Elspeth when she joins him in his scouting activities. 'Elspeth had never heard of Girl Guides and had no ambition to be one, but she did desire very strongly to be a feminine edition of Jock and had done her best to look like one.' Later on Guides are to figure largely in many of the books, but it seems that at this point EJO did not know very much about them, or about Scouts for that matter.

Schoolgirls and Scouts has two peripheral romances. Mollie Raby and Bill Kerr, who met in *A Princess in Tatters* and, we are told, have spent a fair amount of time together when in Switzerland with their respective charges, finally become engaged—and Eilidh is to live with them. The other romance is bound up with yet another recurrent theme. Janie Buchanan, the cousin with whom Elspeth and her brothers go to live, makes some extra money by designing and executing beautiful embroidery. This is a serious enthusiasm for which she went to college and had training. As she tells Elspeth, she also has a secret hope; she has lost touch with a college friend whose family had 'financial troubles' and cut themselves off from all acquaintances. This friend, Margaret Fraser, had said she would recognise Janie's designs anywhere and Janie hopes that this is what will happen. Elspeth suspects, rightly as it proves, that it is not only *Margaret* Fraser whom Janie hopes to find, and, sure enough, one day Margaret's brother Jack steps off the boat at Glenleny, and he and Janie are reunited.

As well as her embroidery, Janie provides the 'decorative' feminine element; the furnishings of her interesting little house (two towers at the gates of Glenleny Hall) are 'delicate' and 'dainty', and we are continually told of the picture she makes, wearing white and seated at her embroidery with the sun in her hair. Elspeth compares her to the *Lady of Shalott*.

The plot, in so far as there is one, is yet another example of a misunderstanding, which has to be resolved by the participants putting their pride on one side. The misunderstanding in this book, between the elder Buchanan children and Mysie and Madge Campbell, has its roots in an older misunderstanding between their parents. John Buchanan 'from the farm' was a bright boy, determined to study and make his own way. The then master of the big house, Mr Campbell, was interested in him and offered to help with his education, on condition that he became secretary to his own son who was going into politics. However, John Buchanan, a true independent Scot, insisted on making his own way and announced his intention of going into the ministry. This caused a rift between the Campbells and the Buchanans. When the Campbell girls behave in a high-handed and patronising manner, the older Buchanans, or more correctly, Elspeth and Jock, are quick to pick up the feud. (Rob is too adult and sensible to take it seriously and the youngest children in both families, Sybil Buchanan and Ninian Campbell, strike up a friendship and refuse to be influenced by their elders.)

This produces a situation that benefits nobody. The Campbell girls, whose one desire is to go to boarding school, would love to talk to Elspeth about her school and her swimming exploits, while Elspeth and Jock envy them their ponies and their boat. In the end both Elspeth and Mysie, after much heart-searching, allow their sense of fair play to overcome their prejudices. When Elspeth loses her swimming medal, her most precious possession, Mysie finds it and is very tempted not to give it back, although she knows how upset Elspeth will be. However, she does return it, thereby placing Elspeth in a position of having to thank her. This also takes a great deal of courage, but once the ordeal is over the two families become great friends, although the Buchanans do insist on, and obtain respect for, their father's independence.

Some of the boys in this book are old acquaintances—the boy members of the Band, for example, and Lord Larry, who does nothing to make others respect him and only arouses disgust in Jock and Elspeth. He, like Ronald Redworth, is a predecessor of Geoff, the young Earl of Kentisbury. Elspeth's brothers remind us of Robin's brothers in *The Girl Who Wouldn't Make Friends*. Rob, the elder, is serious and sensible and intends to be a doctor, while Jock is not fond of his books but good at practical things and is therefore 'going to learn science and carpentry and all those useful kinds of things'. EJO has, and demonstrates in more than one of her books, a respect and admiration for the genuine 'craftsman' that first shows itself here. This apart, Rob and Jock have the same attitude to girls as the boys in *A Holiday Queen*. Jock's feelings are, perhaps, characteristic, even if they are not very true to life:

> After his years at school, it was very strange to feel that these three belonged to him, Janie, just growing into beautiful womanhood, Elspeth, at the right age to be a comrade and companion in all his plans and Sybil, as dainty a baby sister as he could have wished. It was a new sensation, but a very pleasant one and he had already formed a high opinion of each one of them, though for very different reasons. The Shilfie was sweet, Elspeth was jolly and Janie, he felt instinctively, was beautiful and he was proud of them all.

Among the girls at Elspeth's school, as well as our old friends, are Melany Merrill and her twin sister, Zanne, whose story is hinted at by references to 'running away' and 'Castle Charming'. The 'Princess in Tatters' has grown up but lost none of her warm-hearted impulsiveness. Elspeth is a sunny, friendly girl who reminds us of Rosaly, and the Campbell

Marian Cockshott—a real-life May Queen, 1912
(mother of Sheila Ray)

girls present a pair of sisters, one more quick-tempered and sensitive while the other is even-tempered and happy, usually, to follow where her sister leads. 'If you make friends with Mysie, you'll have no difficulty with Madge,' Janie says.

The social structure of the Scottish village is very well presented. At the head of the hierarchy are the Campbells of Glenleny Hall, currently represented by the grandmother of Mysie, Madge and Ninian, a formidable lady dressed in black widow's weeds, although she does have a sense of humour. Then we have the doctor and the minister, and then the farming and fishing families. The class distinction is again shown in speech—the farmers and fisher folk speak broad Scots, while the Campbells speak standard English.

Janie Buchanan, with her college education, finds herself lonely, in spite of the friendliness of the farmers and their families. There is, nonetheless, a real closeness in the community. The children are welcomed by John Shaw, the ferryman, who knows their names, and remembers their father. Later, when their future education is discussed, Janie tells them that the local doctor, who knew their father, has offered to lend Rob books and to coach him, and the minister, who also remembers their father, has offered to teach Jock. There is a feeling that the children are accepted into the community as belonging. Perhaps one of the greatest appeals of this book is the appearance of familiar characters from other books, rather like meeting old friends among a group of new ones.

In October 1914, *Girls of the Hamlet Club* was published; this not only combined the themes of 'wealthy heiress' and 'queens' but saw the founding of the Hamlet Club and was the forerunner of the famous Abbey sequence. It was the second of EJO's books to be published by Chambers, and it is perhaps significant that Chambers published most of her titles that are in short supply on the secondhand market. Perhaps they published only small editions and did not reprint. They were never major publishers in the field of fiction for young people, although they did of course publish the whole of EBD's Chalet School series with great success.

Girls of the Hamlet Club must be considered a milestone in this study of the books of EJO, although there is nothing to show that she herself considered it as such. Since it was not until six years later that the Hamlet Club made another appearance in one of her books, it would seem that she had no idea, when writing the story of Cicely Hobart, that it was anything more than just another story set in a new background.

The background of this book—the Vale around Wycombe and Risborough—is described in loving and accurate detail. The beauty of the woods in the different seasons and the many little hamlets—Penn, Hampden, Hughenden, Green Hailey and Whiteleaf—are all mentioned. There is also the historical background, with mentions of John Hampden and William Penn and of Edmund Burke's school for French émigré orphans at Penn. The Dunkerleys must have known this area well, since they lived in Ealing, on this side of London, and could easily have gone out to Buckinghamshire for the day.

Unlike most of the later Abbey series, this book does have some reference to contemporary events. Cicely's father is a Peter Pan addict and takes her to Kensington Gardens 'for a first sight of Peter Pan in bronze'. The statue of Peter Pan was erected in 1912. We also hear more about London and the shops, a slightly more frivolous view than Elspeth's, but, of course, the Dunkerley family would know London well. In Cicely's cycling trips around the Vale, she enjoys seeing old buildings, particularly old churches—many of EJO's future girls are to be interested in architecture and 'old things'.

Cicely Hobart, the leading character of this book, is a thorough-going schoolgirl of fourteen, with a direct manner and a distinct talent for leadership. She is also perceptive—she knows when not to insist. Her father, home on leave from Ceylon, brings her to the Vale to show her the countryside of her parents' homes and to tell her the story of her mother, who had died when Cicely was born. Mrs Hobart had been the delicate only daughter of the Broadways of Broadway End. They had been opposed to her marriage and have never wanted to see their granddaughter. Now, however, old Mrs Broadway is ill, and they have decided that they would like to see her. Arrangements have been made for Cicely to board with an old servant of the family in the village of Whiteleaf and to go to Miss Macey's School in Wycombe.

Not surprisingly, Cicely is not enthusiastic about this plan, and, when her father leaves her free to choose, she is very much inclined to refuse to stay. In her wanderings she meets Margia Lane, a young painter, who shows her more of the countryside, including some interesting features of the woods, such as the 'bodgers' making chair legs with a primitive lathe. Margia also has a problem on her mind, and she helps Cicely by explaining her own difficulties and by describing how John Hampden set an example by choosing to stand out against the paying of Ship Money, and finally fought for Parliament so that the less fortunate should not suffer. Once again we find EJO putting the Parliamentarian point of view. Cicely and Margia decide that the question is not what they want to do, but what it is right for them to do, and Cicely knows that what is right for her is to follow her father's wishes and stay at Whiteleaf. Again and again in the Abbey books, and in others, characters are faced with this question of choice, and are required to put their own wishes aside for the sake of some other person, or of a community or school.

Cicely, in the meantime, has met some of her future schoolfellows, Marguerite Verity and Georgie Gilks, and Miriam Honor, who sings folk songs on her way to school. On Cicely's first day she arrives at school in the company of Dorothy Darley, a girl whom the school is ready to ostracise, and becomes immediately involved in school politics. Originally all the pupils of Miss Macey's had come from the same well-off, middle-class family backgrounds, but recently Miss Macey had admitted, on scholarships, intelligent girls from poorer homes, whose parents were struggling to give them a good education and had no money for extras. The school's original pupils were outraged and proceeded to treat these 'Hamlets', as they called the girls from the outlying villages and hamlets, with scorn, cutting them off from all school activities. This snobbish attitude makes Cicely very angry, and although the 'Real School' would be happy to include her she insists on remaining a 'Hamlet'.

It is from this beginning that the Hamlet Club is formed and its motto chosen—'To be or not to be'. On the face of it, this is a clever pun, but for those who know, it means:

> 'The question all have to decide sooner or later, whether they'll just have a good time and please themselves and get all they can and care for nothing else, or whether they'll put more important things first and—and care about other people and try to do great things in the world.'

as Miriam explains it. Once founded, the Hamlet Club needs a raison d'être and Cicely

Cicely's cottage (?), Whiteleaf, 1992

The inn at Whiteleaf, 1992

decides to teach the members folk dancing. Margia Lane, teaching for a time at the school and very much aware of its problems, plays the violin for them and they take to it with enthusiasm, keeping their activities secret from the rest of the school.

During this time, Cicely has gone to live with her grandparents at Broadway End, but she also keeps this fact a secret. The Hamlet Club plans a May-Day Festival to entertain Mr and Mrs Broadway with dancing and a maypole and the extra characters who really belong to the Mummers' Play. At this stage EJO's knowledge of folk tradition was limited; she knew quite a lot about the actual dances, but very little else. About the dances she gives lots of detail, describing steps and figures in Morris, and putting the emphasis on 'hard' dancing like men, and the need for suitable costumes. Cicely disapproves of anything too fancy and has a logical argument ready in favour of her grey 'puritan' dresses.

One of the aspects of the school that Cicely has tried to improve is the lack of 'school spirit' among her fellow-Hamlets, who are not inclined to be interested in the 'honour' of a school that shuts them out. However, when the school play has to be cancelled at the last minute, because of illness in the cast, the Hamlet Club, urged thereto by Cicely, agrees to perform its May Day Ceremony and sacrifice its secret for the good of the school. Cicely's own secret, that she is the granddaughter of the Broadways of Broadway End, also has to come out, and the school as a whole attempts to bridge the gap between the two groups. This is not shown to be easy—there is no 'they lived happily ever after'—and at the end of the book there is still a long way to go.

Apart from the continued enthusiasm for folk songs and the introduction of folk dancing—EJO must by now have joined the EFDS—the other characteristic motifs in this book are the detailed love of the countryside and of old buildings, and the stress on colours and 'suitable' styles of clothes. There is an interesting sidelight on the question of school uniform, later to be considered a levelling and anti-snob influence. When the girls of the 'Real School' plan to have coats, hats and scarves alike, and Cicely thinks this is a good idea, Miriam tactfully points out that the Hamlets, girls from poorer homes, cannot afford special clothes, and Cicely hurriedly changes her mind.

Once more we have a painter. Margia Lane is not the first character to make her living from her pictures and there will be others. Apparently, to use one's artistic ability was considered a 'suitable' career for a young woman.

To read this book, as many of EJO's collector-admirers must have done, after making the acquaintance of the Hamlet Club in later stories is to have filled in, in a most satisfying way, the background to incidents that are regularly remembered in later books: the founding of the Hamlet Club, the story behind the motto and how the Hamlet Club saved the school. Standing alone, it has all the ingredients of a good story, but it is easy to see how EJO came to use the Hamlet Club as a basis for other books and how the Club itself was to live on for another forty years, in fact to the end of her writing life.

Chapter 3

THE YEARS BETWEEN:
FROM ROUNDHEADS TO CASTLE CHARMING

It was to be six years before EJO again took up the story of Cicely and the Hamlet Club and brought them together with the Shirley girls living in the Abbey. In the years between, 1915 to 1919, she published seven books, and then two more in the same year as *The Abbey Girls*. These, of course, were the years of the First World War, and some of the books at least must have been written while EJO was conscious of the terrible and pointless waste of life in Flanders which so stirred her father. However, little of the war intrudes into her books.

The title of *At School with the Roundheads,* published by Chambers in 1915, suggests that EJO is looking back to the historical setting of *Mistress Nanciebel*, but, although there are a couple of links with that book, and the choice of title possibly reflects her Parliamentarian sympathies, this is not the case. *At School with the Roundheads* has a contemporary setting on the Yorkshire coast.

The whole of the story takes place within a school and its immediate neighbourhood, but it is a very unconventional school story. Three girls, Olwen Rees, also known as Polly, and her cousins, Gwenfer (Jenny) and Nesta Davies, are at school in York. Jenny and Nesta are in the habit of spending the Christmas and Easter holidays with their aunt, who is housekeeper at a boys' school in the Yorkshire coastal resort of Redburn, which is clearly based on Saltburn. For this particular Easter holiday, Polly is to join them as there is illness at her home. This basic situation seems unnecessarily improbable. The Davies parents have strained 'slender resources' to send their daughters (there is a third elder sister who is spending this Easter holiday with a friend) to school in York, but cannot afford the fares for them to go home to Wales except for the long summer holiday; the economics of this simply don't add up, but little is made of it.

Little is said of the home in Wales, but a reference to Yr Eifl suggests that it is in the Lleyn Peninsula, the setting for *Mistress Nanciebel*. The other link with the latter book is the constant quotation of folk songs—Jenny has a good voice, and in this she is matched by Trillo, one of the three boys who unexpectedly return to the school when the master who has taken them for a holiday on the moors breaks a leg and is taken to hospital. Trillo (John) and Charlie Bassenthwaite are brothers of fourteen and sixteen, and Oliver Pink (known as Nolly or Pinky) is their orphaned cousin who lives with them.

Jenny, Polly, Trillo and Nolly are thus all about the same age and young enough at about fourteen not to become too emotionally involved, although the boys admire the beauty of the girls and there is much conversation about their hair, which is long and impressive but tucked away neatly for walks and games on the beach, and about Jenny's large eyes. Charlie and Nesta pair off to some extent, the latter being encouraged to take Charlie, who is inclined to swot too hard, away from his books. Nesta is very much the baby, and her precious doll, Desdemona, which she keeps at her aunt's, is quite a feature of the story. When the boys arrive back at school, the girls are sitting on the front doorstep making new doll's clothes; Nesta's treatment of the doll as if were 'real' is made much of, as is the boys' scorn of it. It is the discovery of the doll that leads to the revelation of the presence of the girls after term has begun again for the boys.

The holiday comes to an end with the six young people having become good friends who have benefited from the experience of spending the time together. Inevitably, the girls cannot return to their school because, on the intended day of departure, a telegram arrives to say that the headmistress has gone down with scarlet fever. The second half of the book is about how the girls pretend to be Cavaliers keeping out of the way of the Roundheads. When the girls had arrived at the beginning of the holiday, Miss Davies had suggested the name of 'roundheads' for the boys, saying how tired she was of their 'smooth round heads'. Throughout the book EJO is very preoccupied with the hair of her characters, and there are frequent references to its colour, length and texture.

Jenny and Polly represent the two archetypal heroines of girls' stories. Jenny is pretty, sensitive, domesticated and a singer; Polly is the tomboy, careless of her appearance but good at her books. On an expedition to the moors, she refuses to be outwalked by Nolly and consequently develops a bad blister; although she is energetic and despises the apparently lazy Nolly, he criticises her slatternly behaviour, such as not sewing buttons on. When the boys begin lessons again and the girls are given work by the masters, it transpires that Polly is well ahead of the boys of her own age, and Mr Otway expresses the wish that she could join them in class as it might spur the boys on.

Glenhow School, Saltburn, 1990s

Once their presence is discovered, Polly does join the boys in class and at once impresses them by the promptness with which she answers questions. Although she has not done Latin (EJO doesn't push the girls' educational prowess too far, even with Charlotte Yonge's Ethel May as an example), she can more than hold her own in the subjects that she has done, although the details of the scholarship for which she is trying are left vague. Jenny is eventually persuaded to join the boys in class as well, a different class as she is slightly younger than Polly and not so academically able, although she works hard. However, her presence improves the boys' behaviour; there is more order in class and the boys make a greater effort 'not to give foolish answers'.

On the other hand, the boys' response to the girls, opening doors for them and picking up things they drop, and the way in which the masters cherish them by making sure they are not in a draught, although they also discourage them from using slang and generally unsuitable language, influence the girls. Jenny, after one or two setbacks, becomes more self-confident, while Polly eventually begins to conform to the expected female role, mending her stockings and sewing on her buttons. The girls remain at the boys' school until the end of term although, once Jenny has agreed to stay, we hear little more of events until the end of term concert, in which the girls play a prominent part, including the performance of two Morris dances, although this is the first mention of their skills in that direction. In the final pages we learn that the three boys are going to spend the following summer holiday with the girls in North Wales.

This must have been a quite unusual book for 1915, although the way in which the relationships between the boys and girls are handled has echoes of Charlotte Yonge and Louisa M Alcott. It uses a situation to which EJO was to return in her books about the Torment, but it remains an offbeat school story even by modern standards.

In the same year, 1915, EJO also published *Finding Her Family*, a book that, like *At School with the Roundheads*, is set in North Yorkshire and stands on its own. With its rather melodramatic plot, and the promise of a happy romance for at least two of the female characters, it did not perhaps offer a lot of scope for a sequel, although Monica Howard, destined always, it seems, to be a minor but crucial character, does appear briefly. This was the only EJO book to be published by SPCK, although later on, in the 1930s, some of her books were published by the *Girl's Own Paper* office, originally launched by SPCK, and by the Lutterworth Press, the name later adopted by SPCK. This choice of publisher was perhaps due to the major part played in the story by the Beach Mission; as Monica Godfrey explains, EJO's knowledge of these came from work that her brother Roderic did during his training to become a Congregational Minister.

The plot of *Finding Her Family* is likely to produce two reactions in the adult reader. First, did EJO really have it all planned out before she started or did she change direction because her original idea did not seem adequate to sustain a full-length novel? Secondly, although the plot does undoubtedly creak midway through the book, EJO seems right from the start to prepare for the final working-out. It may be that the creak is due to faulty construction, that EJO had the plot all worked out but could see no other way of telling the story without revealing the final twist at an early stage. In fact, this becomes obvious to the reader around page 81 and is confirmed about ten pages later, and thereafter the suspense lies in how the truth will be revealed to all the people concerned rather than in the truth itself.

Although the heroine who finds her family is Hazel, originally christened Hilda, the strong central character is Audrey Allerby who, when the story opens, is sixteen and living with her stepmother and younger stepsisters, Nancy and Isobel, and stepbrothers, Eric and baby Allan, in Saltburn. Father is yet another sailor, the captain of a trading vessel, and safely away at sea so that letters telling of the latest developments do not reach him. Audrey's older brother, Osmund, has gone straight from school to teach at a boys' school in Scarborough. When Osmund was three and Audrey fourteen months, their mother and elder brother, then aged five, were drowned in a boating accident. It now transpires that there was also a baby of two months, who was adopted by their mother's sister and taken to London; this was Hilda alias Hazel.

The Allerbys are not wealthy, but Audrey goes to the high school in Middlesbrough, and the family appear to enjoy a middle-class lifestyle and standards. Audrey's close friend, Brenda Carew, lives in comfortable circumstances on the moors. The story ranges over a wide area around Saltburn, and the characters cover quite considerable distances by train and governess cart.

Hazel, on the other hand, has been brought up by the Branders in comparative luxury in Ealing. She has a Borzoi dog, named Nicholas Alexander Petrovitch, for the Tsar, and lovely clothes. Mrs Brander has recently died and Mr Brander, who seems never to have been very fond of Hazel, is planning to go to New Zealand for the sake of his health, so Hazel is being sent north to stay with her own family, although she has never heard of them before. The whole story is told to her by her cousin Raymond, a student at Durham University, who happens to be staying with the Branders for a few days.

Audrey welcomes Hazel with open arms, delighted to have a sister so near to her in age. Brenda, when she first hears the news, is inclined to be jealous but takes to Hazel at once, and it soon becomes obvious to the reader that Hazel and Brenda's dead sister, Violet, were

Saltburn Pier, 1996

swapped as babies, a revelation confirmed by Captain Allerby's strange behaviour when he comes home on leave to find Hazel installed in the bosom of his family.

Audrey discovers the truth but cannot reveal it without incriminating her father. She is supported and helped by Mr Dunster, the young man in charge of the Beach Mission, and she finally tells all when her father, having returned to sea, arranges for his family to emigrate to Australia. Audrey decides to remain in England and train as a teacher, helped to do this by the money which the Brander family have settled on Hazel, who no longer wants or needs it. Now that he knows Hazel is not his sister after all, Osmund begins to have a different kind of affection for her, and future romance is hinted at. Raymond Brander and the eldest Carew girl, Margaret, become engaged.

The topography of Ealing and that of the North Yorkshire coast are both described in some detail. As the book was published in 1915, it was probably written before the German bombardment of Scarborough on 16 December 1914, and there is no mention of the war. One wonders if the fact that the North Yorkshire coast was one of the few areas of Britain to experience the First World War at first hand caused EJO to abandon it as a setting for her stories. This part of the country obviously fascinated her, and *Finding Her Family* was the third of her books to use it as a setting, but after this she rarely used it again.

There is much preoccupation with Yorkshire accents, which readers from that part of the world might find rather patronising. All the Allerby children speak with Yorkshire vowels and use 'champion' and other odd words to excess; these speech habits are mocked and laughed at by the people from the south. There is also the usual preoccupation with clothes, hair, the colour of eyes and colour generally. The Allerbys live in Amethyst Street; neighbouring streets are named after other jewels—these jewel streets are still to be found in Saltburn—and much is made of them. Hazel, in mourning for her adopted mother, wears shades of mauve, violet and heliotrope.

The plot is complex, but virtually every incident in this long book contributes to its unfolding. As a background to the story, there is St Hilda's Abbey at Whitby, another source of fascination for the author. In the second chapter, Audrey meets Osmund in the Abbey ruins to tell him the news, and later Brenda, Hazel and Audrey organise a pageant-cum-tableaux, based on the Abbey's story, which they present on the beach at Saltburn to raise money so that children from the nearby mining towns can have a seaside treat. There is interest in the Beach Missions, which are described in detail—in this story the missionary hymns substitute for folk songs—and Mr Dunster, the young, newly-trained minister who leads the Mission, plays a vital part. Apart from this, however, there is little of the religious sentiment which one finds elsewhere in EJO's books.

Theo had taken the fire in hand, and was coaxing it to burn.
(*The Tuck-Shop Girl*)

The last word about *Finding Her Family* should perhaps be reserved for Monica. The reader is not told just how she and Hazel have become friendly; Monica goes to boarding school and Hazel only sees her in the holidays, although she usually spends the summer holidays with cousins in Scotland. However, when Hazel first hears the news that she is to go north to spend some months with the Allerbys, Monica acts as her confidante. Later, she turns up when the girls are presenting the tableaux on the life of St Hilda and Whitby Abbey on the beach at Saltburn. She explains that she's not yet gone to Scotland as her little cousin has measles, a complaint from which Brenda, Hazel and Audrey have just recovered, and that she is staying at Osmotherly. It is Monica who comments to Hazel, 'You're really more like your friend Brenda, I think', thus preparing the way for the final twist. Was Monica one of EJO's ways of writing herself into the earlier stories, bearing in mind the home in Ealing and the Scottish relations?

The Tuck-Shop Girl, Prudence (Prue) Berrill, is the first of many of EJO's young ladies who keep a tea-and-sweet shop to earn their living. The point is carefully made more than once that Prue is a 'lady' and not an ordinary 'shop girl'. Not only does she run the shop with and for her aunt, who makes home-made cakes, but she also continues her studies; we first meet her sitting down with Mérimée's *Colomba* and a dictionary. She always keeps her shop fresh and gay with flowers and, in her spare time, does embroidery to her own designs. She wears embroidered smocks in her shop and designs and makes flags for the Guides. In all these things she is very much an EJO character but, above all, she is the first example of a key figure, the older girl who acts as confidante and giver of advice to a group of other girls, mainly younger than herself. Over and over again girls with a problem, large or small, carry it to Prue for advice and comfort. The girls themselves recognise her value and say so. Prue herself says it is because she looks for the good in people and trusts them.

Prue is the girl of the title, but the central figure of the story is Janet (Jinty) Cameron, another wild Highland lass through whose eyes we first see the school for which Prue keeps the tuck-shop. Jinty arrives in a London suburb, having lived all her life in Scotland, where her companions have been boys and dogs and the local crofters. To come to London, to live on the outskirts of the city, and to join a school for girls where there is also a Guide Company, is for Jinty like going into a foreign country—the language may be the same but the customs of the country are outwith her experience. Add to this Jinty's tendency to act on impulse—'I neffer thought' is her continual cry—and it is not surprising that she makes mistake after mistake until her fellow-pupils coin a new verb, 'to Jinty'.

Jinty begins her voyage of discovery in the company of a cheerful and capable boy called Jock. They are left to their own devices because the aunt with whom they were to stay is seriously ill. Jock does his best to restrain Jinty's wild impulses, but he is not always in the right spot at the right time.

A situation in which children are left on their own, either as orphans or because their parents are abroad or even away for the day, is a familiar one in children's books. It is usually used as a device to allow the children to follow their own particular enthusiasms without the restraining influence of adults—parents or the nannies and governesses who would have been familiar figures in the lives of middle- and upper-middle-class children of this period. The Dunkerley children had first-hand experience of this, as Erica Oxenham describes in the biography of her father, *J.O.*:

When the older members of the family began to reach years of discretion, J.O. and Mother had occasional 'honeymoon holidays' on the Continent and in Scotland together. There was an occasion when they took us and the luggage down to Littlehampton together, left us on the promenade with the luggage while they found lodgings and established us there in the charge of the eldest sister while they went up to Scotland. It was as simple as that in those days!

At first Jinty finds London much too noisy, dirty and crowded, but under Jock's guidance she discovers the excitement of viewing the city from the top of a bus, something that EJO and her brothers and sisters must often have enjoyed doing. In the course of her venture into the great city she discovers Southwark Cathedral, a revelation of a different sort, and shows that there is another side to her character—the tomboy is also susceptible to beauty in the form of ancient architecture.

Before she actually joins the school she watches the girls from a tree in the grounds, and even explores the school buildings when they are empty. This is where her inexperience and her tendency 'never to think' cause one problem after another. The school has no name, but it does have a Guide Company—the first real appearance of the Girl Guide movement in one of EJO's stories. As Jinty, probably like a number of EJO's readers, is completely ignorant of the subject, the activities and aims of the movement are introduced in some detail. Later EJO was to take it for granted that her readers knew all about Guides. These early Guides take themselves very seriously, with regard both to the moral code of the Guide Law and to the many activities for which they can win badges. For a fifteen-year-old with a full programme of school and Guide activities to take on learning shorthand and typing, or a seventeen-year-old with exams in the offing and responsible positions in school and Guides to decide to take the Matron's Badge, 'all about housekeeping and linen and prices and stores and cleaning pans and things', in order to set a good example to her juniors, argues a degree of commitment that you would be unlikely to find in present-day Guides. On the other hand, the shame of having to wear her Guide badge upside-down to show that she has broken a Guide Law affects 'T.V.', as Theodora Violet Carr is known, very deeply (and the more so because she is innocent).

It seems likely that, even at this early stage, EJO was aware that Guiding is not the most rewarding of spare-time activities for all girls, and one of her attractions for girl readers may well be that she never considers all girls to be alike. She continually emphasises the fact that differences in talent, background and training are neither all good nor all bad. Guiding as a character-building activity may well be the best thing for a thoughtless tomboy like Jinty Cameron, but it would not be right for every girl. At Miss Murray's school the alternative to Guides is gardening, yet another activity that is considered very suitable for girls and is later to be presented as a career which girls can take up—Rena Mackay, who appears in *A Go-Ahead Schoolgirl*, is a good example of someone who makes a great success of a career in gardening.

Gardening is not presented as a soft option; it's pointed out that 'you simply must work if you've a garden, or it gets all thick with weeds and everybody can see you've been slacking', and Guides and Gardeners respect and take an interest in each other's activities. Their uniforms are contrasted—the Guides are smart and business-like in their navy blue while the Gardeners wear green smocks, big shady hats and strong gloves in which to work.

Miss Murray does not want her girls to have 'hands like navvies and complexions like cowboys', and they are as particular about following rules laid down for them as the Guides are. The basic difference between the two groups is not spelled out here, as it is in other books, but perhaps, in general terms, the Gardeners are more creative and more imaginative. Helen, for example, is the school's best and keenest photographer and also paints, but she is inclined to concentrate on one thing to the neglect of others.

Not content with their Guiding and their gardens and, one assumes, their ordinary schoolwork, the girls are also encouraged to have hobbies, and to do some kind of craftwork, which can range from crochet to woodcarving. Many of the girls practise unusual crafts, far removed from the humdrum sewing and knitting that were perhaps more usual at this period. This is also to be a recurring theme in EJO's books and it is interesting that some of the crafts that she mentions regained popularity in the 1960s.

Another of EJO's favourite themes, that of a girl who gives up something she cares very much about for the sake of another girl or, as in this case, for the sake of the school occurs here, quite early in the book, when Barbara, the popular Head Gardener, who was once a Guide, lays aside her gardening hat and gloves to take on a Patrol which has lost its leader.

With *A School Camp Fire*, published by Chambers in 1917, we see, for the first time, EJO's great interest in the American movement for girls, the Camp Fire. This, on the whole, seems to have had much more appeal for EJO than the Guides, but at the same time she was realistic enough to realise that many more of her readers were likely to have the chance to be Guides than to be Camp Fire girls. EJO herself was a Camp Fire Guardian, first in Ealing and later in Worthing. Although she later allowed Joy Marchwood to become a Guide Commissioner, very much in keeping with Joy's position in the community, she shows the sensitive and romantic Maidlin as a Camp Fire Guardian, and there is, throughout her work, rather more detail about the Camp Fire activities than about Guide activities.

Leonora stepped into the circle and knelt on one knee.
(*A School Camp Fire*)

The Camp Fire movement had begun in America in 1911, and the idea of running a Camp Fire is introduced in this book by a young woman and her four nieces who, although English, have been living in America; however, this does not happen until the second part of the book, which is divided into four distinct parts. The first of these, ' Buried

Treasure', is the story of Priscilla, aged fifteen, one of the very strong, healthy outdoor girls who stride across the pages of so many of EJO's books. Priscilla's father is a manic-depressive and has apparently hidden all his money, so her mother has been obliged to take a post as housekeeper in an isolation hospital on the Yorkshire moors. Priscilla has left school, although she is keeping up her studies with the help of the matron and of Winifred Mayne, one of the nurses, who, it transpires, has had an excellent education herself. Priscilla is very much a loner, walking miles over the moors.

The exact location of this part of the story is vague. The local big town is Harrogate and the hospital is reached from there by a local train journey. There is mention of a reservoir, and there are several in the area west of Harrogate which would serve the purpose. Rock formations with distinctive names play quite an important part in the story, and these could well have been inspired by Brimham Rocks, but there is also a reference to 'two funny rocks … standing up on the hill like pillars', which is a good description of Yorke's Folly, built by one of the local squires. There is also a visit to Fountains Abbey, in which the fascination that abbeys held for EJO is clearly shown—'That day lived in their memory for months'. For this story EJO needed an isolated setting, well inland from the dangerous (in war time) Yorkshire coast, and the area around and to the west of Harrogate seems to have served her well.

To stay at the hospital come Winifred Mayne's youngest sister, thirteen-year-old Katharine, and the latter's friend, Dorothy Ann Nairn. They make friends with Priscilla and are present when she finds the money (£1700) that her father had buried near one of the strange rock formations. This money enables Priscilla to go to the school that Katharine and Dorothy attend, which is to the west of London, on the borders of Buckinghamshire, and has been identified as at Uxbridge. The money is found around Christmas, and Book II opens at the beginning of the following summer term, when Priscilla has been at the school since the previous half-term. Dorothy Ann has missed much of this previous term, she and her mother having been summoned to Switzerland, where the two old aunts for whom Dorothy is named have been living and where Aunt Dorothy has just died.

Katharine is disappointed that Priscilla has not fitted in better and is still very much a loner, but she is looking forward to Dorothy Ann's imminent return. Dorothy's Aunt Ann has bought a house, Waterside, in the neighbourhood of the school, and the girls are invited to spend Saturdays there although Aunt Ann is painfully shy and does everything she can to avoid meeting them.

A new teacher, Charlotte Tarring, who has previously taught at the school but who had gone to America some twelve years before this, is also expected, together with her four nieces. Charlotte and the four girls have been members of a Camp Fire in America, the youngest girl having been a Bluebird, and at first they meet secretly in the dormitory which they share, merely dropping heavy and mysterious hints to the other girls. This secretive behaviour provides the title of the second part, 'The Secret'.

Not surprisingly, Dorothy Ann is consumed with curiosity, and in the third part, 'The Camp Fire', Dorothy Ann and Katharine spy on a meeting that gives plenty of opportunity for speculation. At this point the plot, as in some of the other books written by EJO at this period, hangs very much on exaggerated interpretations of the schoolgirl code of honour. Katharine and Dorothy Ann, having watched the Camp Fire ceremonial quite shamelessly, are overcome by remorse—at least Katharine is—and they make a great production of confessing to the headmistress.

Once the secret is out, it is decided to form a Camp Fire in the school, although some of the girls think it will be too much 'fag' working for honours. At this stage EJO seems to have had some idea of adapting Camp Fire ceremonial to the English situation, and many of the girls take English rather than Indian names. Miss Tarring tells them: 'In England you must be English, and study the folklore, songs and dances, and history of your own country, and you should use Old English names.' Earlier in the same paragraph EJO, unusually for this period, demonstrates her understanding of, and sympathy for, other cultures: 'The girls [in America] ought to learn about the people of their own country, their history, songs, legends, and customs, and to help them if they can.'

The fourth part is entitled 'Aunt Ann makes trouble'; it is hard to believe that gentle, shy Aunt Ann would 'make' trouble, and 'unwittingly causes' would be a more apt description. One Saturday Miss Tarring and the Fifth and Sixth forms are involved in going to a tennis tournament. The younger girls, including Dorothy Ann and Melda, Leonora and Annabel Tarring, go to Waterside as usual, although Katharine is kept at school with a cold. Before they set off, Miss Chinchin, the headmistress, forbids any of them to enter the house, saying that Miss Nairn is away for a few days. Dorothy Ann wants to borrow a book from her aunt's library but Miss Bingham, in charge of the party, says she should have asked Miss Chinchin's permission and refuses to allow her to go into the house. Melda organises some of the girls into gathering flowers and arranging them in the library, saying that they will confess when they get back to school. As they are leaving, they hear a scream and find that Annabel has also entered the house, to have a closer look at a green cockatoo, which has then knocked over and broken a valuable vase.

Village Green and Round Pound, Rottingdean, 2000

The girls sort things out as best they can, all vowing to confess everything, and prepare to leave, but then they see someone in a pink knitted coat, whom they recognise as Dorothy Ann, slipping into the dining room. Dorothy Ann is kneeling over the broken vase when her Aunt (who has postponed going away until the Monday, but did not want the girls to know) appears and immediately assumes that it is her niece who has broken the vase and forbids her to confess to Miss Chinchin. So, disaster!

Never mind that Dorothy Ann, Melda and her group and Annabel have all disobeyed instructions; Melda and company are now more righteous than the righteous, and because Dorothy Ann does not confess as they do, they send her to Coventry. Dorothy Ann believes that everything will be sorted out quickly; she writes to her aunt at once and thinks that the latter will promptly release her from her promise to keep silent. However, Aunt Ann is taken ill and does not even receive Dorothy Ann's hastily written letter. Only Bernice Tarring, Priscilla and Katharine stick by Dorothy Ann and believe that she has got good reasons for not confessing.

Meanwhile, on the evening of the accident of the broken vase, all the servants at the school are taken ill, and the Camp Fire girls rally round to do the domestic chores, including the cooking. (There is much discussion of cooking in this book—in the first part Katharine and Dorothy Ann could not even boil an egg.) Eventually, of course, all the misunderstandings are sorted out, and at the end of the book the Tarrings, Katharine, Priscilla and Dorothy Ann all spend a holiday on the Yorkshire Moors having, quite literally, buried the hatchet and smoked the pipe of peace in good Indian style.

This book is probably one of EJO's strangest. Not only does it have every appearance of being cobbled together, with some very weak plot motivation and a few loose ends—Priscilla, for instance, never really fits in—it is also very sentimental. When Katharine and Dorothy Ann arrive to stay with Winifred on the moors at the beginning of the book, they are forbidden to kiss because Dorothy Ann is recovering from diphtheria, although she is free from infection and 'there could be no objection to her going away with Katharine, so long as kissing and sleeping together were forbidden'.

The next book, *The School of Ups and Downs*, was published in the following year, 1918, by Chambers and illustrated by H C Earnshaw. It is basically the story of two sisters, Elizabeth and Isobel Mackenzie, known as Libby and Tibby, who have hitherto lived in the north of Scotland. Mr Mackenzie dabbles in literature and clearly has a perfectly adequate private income. When the book opens the whole family have come south on their way to a new home on the Sussex downs as the doctor has recommended a drier climate for Mr Mackenzie, and Mrs Mackenzie wants her daughters to go to her own old school which is nearby.

Libby and Tibby have been very close all their lives and have always done the same things and done them together. It is during their stay in London on their way to Sussex that the difference in their tastes becomes more apparent. Tibby loves the busy shopping streets and the buses while Libby prefers the old buildings and the quiet, secret gardens of the Inns of Court to which her father takes her when he visits his publishers. Here again we see how well EJO knew her London and appreciated it. The difference between the two sisters doesn't bother Tibby in the least; she is more extroverted than Libby and doesn't see the deeper implications. Libby, however, is very much aware of it and it worries her; she cannot envisage a situation where they have different interests and are just as close as ever.

The relationship between sisters is one that EJO clearly found both interesting and important. It is possible that she had just such a close relationship with one of her own sisters, perhaps Maida, with whom she later shared a bungalow. Certainly there are many close pairs of sisters and adopted sisters in her books, Dorothy Ann and Katharine in *The School Camp Fire* being a good example of the latter.

Libby and Tibby embark on their new life even before they've reached Sussex. On the train from London their carriage is invaded by schoolgirls whose conversation intrigues and fascinates them both—as well it might! This school has both a Guide Company and a Camp Fire, and the chatter of the schoolgirls, some of whom belong to one and some to the other, leaves the Mackenzie sisters anxious to learn more. One subject under discussion is the camp, about which the schoolgirls are doubtful because the camping place is in grounds belonging to newcomers to the neighbourhood, and permission to hold it there has not yet been given.

While they are exploring the Downs near their new home, Libby and Tibby meet two boys who are indirectly connected with the school, Ribby and Perks (nicknames seem to be obligatory at this period). The boys have sisters at the school, Rowena, who is in the Camp Fire, and Samantha, a Guide, and they speak of their sisters' activities with scorn, tinged with a little jealousy, particularly in the case of the Camp Fire, which has more secrets. They have a proper male chauvinist attitude to the Guides—girls trying to be like boys—but the Camp Fire fascinates them. Their attitude causes problems for them, and for the girls before the end of the story.

Libby and Tib crept near among the bushes.
(*The School of Ups and Downs*)

The setting of *The School of Ups and Downs* is the area around Rottingdean, a small village to the east of Brighton; it was an area that EJO knew well and she describes it with loving care. It is no surprise to the reader to learn that the school which has already roused the interest of Libby and Tibby is their mother's old school, to which they are eventually to go, and that the place for the camp is in the grounds of their own new home. So, when the Guides and Camp Fire set up their tents, there comes a chance for Libby and Tibby to make friends.

It is now that the difference between the two girls becomes more obvious. Tibby is interested in the Guides and follows them to learn more, while the Camp Fire, with its symbols and romantic side, has a stronger attraction for Libby. Even though they make friends with Rowena and Sammy, who are sisters belonging to different groups who still enjoy a good relationship, Libby goes through periods of heart-searching when she feels she must join the Guides so as not to lose her sister. She is understood, comforted and persuaded by Rowena of the Camp Fire that she can and must follow her own instincts as to what is right for her without losing the close sister relationship, and when Libby and Tibby finally join the school as pupils, they are firmly decided, Tibby joining the Guides and Libby the Camp Fire.

Although the Camp Fire and the Guide Company are both presented with sympathy and enthusiasm, it is clear, in this book, where the author's sympathies lie. EJO was, as has already been mentioned, a Camp Fire Guardian, and the romance and symbolism would have appealed to her as they do to Libby. Another pointer, almost a signpost in this respect, are the pets of the two groups. The Guides have a bulldog called John Bull or Great Britain, who does his duty in guarding the camp and representing the Guides, but the Camp Fire mascot, Grey Edward, a much-pampered cat, shows us EJO's real feelings. There is no doubt that EJO was a 'cat person'; according to Monica Godfrey, Grey Edward was based on a real cat belonging to Elsie and Maida, and 'everything he was shown as doing was based on reality'.

The School of Ups and Downs, published as the First World War came to an end, was written about girls at school during the war, and the effects of the war on these schoolgirls is hinted at a little more than in EJO's other books of this period. There is much talk about rations and exceeding one's rations, and the Beaver (her Camp Fire name) complains about not having enough sugar for her tea. When the Camp Fire members go for walks they take photographs, except where it is not permitted by the War Office.

But the war also comes into the school in a completely romantic way with Captain Jock MacGregor of the Argylls. He is engaged to Miss Helen, the Guardian of the Camp Fire and sister of Miss Robinson, the headmistress. He has been most conveniently wounded and returns to England to convalesce, visit the school and make the acquaintance of the Camp Fire. At first the girls are inclined to hate him for taking away their beloved Miss Helen, but he—and his full Highland dress—soon wins their hearts, and they cluster round him as he tells of 'the charge of the Fifth Argylls in Gallipoli … of the Argylls in the advance posts on the Menin road; and [of] a hundred other incidents in their history'. It is possible that EJO had friends or relatives in the Argylls, perhaps from her mother's family, but the Scottish regiments have always held a romantic fascination for the general public, and accounts of their exploits were certainly published in the newspapers of the time.

Helen Robinson's position in her sister's school is a slightly anomalous one. She is not a teacher but, by virtue of her position as the Guardian of the Camp Fire, she has a certain authority with the girls. She is also the link with the previous book, *A School Camp Fire*, but a link that is difficult to explain. When she marries her Captain at the end of *The*

School of Ups and Downs, among the wedding guests are a group of people who turn out to be Miss Tarring and her four nieces plus Priscilla, Katharine and Dorothy Ann, all the main characters from *A School Camp Fire*. We learn that they are all friends of Helen Robinson from her first Camp Fire and that she is about the same age as the older girls, but, surprisingly, there is no mention of Helen in the pages of the earlier book.

Two possible explanations occur, one being that EJO had another book, either written or planned, that was never published, in which Helen Robinson joined Miss Chinchin's school, became a member of the Camp Fire and later, after she left school, she came to help her sister and started a Camp Fire herself. The other possibility is simpler; it is more than likely that many of her readers wrote to EJO wanting to hear more about their favourite characters, especially during the war years when women began to do more exciting things and to take what they felt to be a definite part in the war effort. If so, perhaps EJO has used Helen Robinson's wedding to give them some account of what happened to the girls of *A School Camp Fire* and in order to do this has made Miss Helen an ex-member of their Camp Fire, without bothering to account for the fact that there is no mention of her in the earlier book.

This book has much more unity than the previous one and follows the story of Libby and Tibby up to their final settling down as part of the school. The title, *The School of Ups and Downs*, is explained as an idea of one of the boys and has two main meanings—either the girls are always 'up in the clouds or down in the dumps', and certainly in this book there are moments when each of these moods occur, or, secondly, the boys see 'up' as standing for the Guides and 'down' as the Camp Fire. For both these reasons, the title, one of EJO's better ones, accurately reflects the content of the book.

With *Expelled from School* (Collins, 1919), we come to the first of EJO's books to be set entirely in her much loved Switzerland. Prior to this, Switzerland had appeared in her books as a place to be visited by her characters. We know from *Schoolgirls and Scouts* that Mollie Raby, Eilidh, Lord Larry and Jack Kerr had all been there, while in *A School Camp Fire* we learn of Dorothy Ann's visit and the fact that her two aunts had lived there. For the British, in the period before the Second World War, Switzerland was 'abroad' par excellence, and those who could afford it went to Switzerland for their health, or to walk, climb or ski. In fact, in *Expelled from School* EJO uses a border area of Switzerland and the action spreads over into the Savoy area of France, another part of Europe that very much appealed to her. All the places and landmarks are easily identifiable on a map of south-western Switzerland and the adjoining area of France.

Since this book must have been written during or very shortly after the First World War, it is perhaps worth noting that there is no mention of the war and that the book was presumably based on memories of a pre-war visit to the area. The dedication, to EJO's parents, is 'in memory and anticipation of happy days in Switzerland'. Although the central characters in the story are English or Scottish, the girls at the Vevey School from which Retta is expelled are French, Italian and German; Linda, one of the 'goodies', is German, while the 'baddies' are French and Italian. So not only is there no mention of war, but the characters are portrayed in a way that shows no influence of contemporary events and national feelings. As the story has a faintly old-fashioned air, it may well have been conceived at a much earlier date, perhaps after a pre-war visit to the area around Lake Geneva and Savoy, since the descriptions appear to be based on first-hand experience.

Vevey was a fashionable resort in the late nineteenth century, visited by Amy March in *Good Wives*, and this image would hold good until at least 1914.

At this point, certainly, there was no question of establishing an English school, run on English lines, with an English headmistress, as EJO was to do a few years later, thus paving the way for Elinor Brent-Dyer and the Chalet School, founded in Austria. It was presumably the early 1920s before it became practicable to conceive of a school of this kind—even Angela Brazil did not use the idea until 1922 when she published *The School in the South*, a story about a boarding school for English-speaking girls whose parents are resident in the Naples area and where the aim is to preserve the girls' Englishness.

EJO's Vevey school is presided over by Madame Dufour, and until Retta and Pamela join it as pupils there is only one English girl there. Although Madame Dufour, sometimes quaintly referred to as 'the madame', is

'Well, my dear, you know what I must do?'
(*Expelled from School*)

somewhat lax in her control of the girls, she has the traditionally British notions of honour and trustworthiness firmly fixed in her mind.

Illness and ill-health play a very important part in this story, accounting for the presence or absence of key characters in the right place at the right time. The heroine, Henrietta (Retta) Garnet, who is fourteen, becoming fifteen in the course of the story, which spans about a year, arrives in the little mountain village of Finhaut with her aunt, who has lung trouble. Retta is in her aunt's charge while her parents are travelling in the East, including Japan, for the sake of her mother's health. Ill-health can have extreme effects in EJO's books—the characters may travel extensively to seek a cure or may barely be able to move from one spot, and both extremes are seen in this particular book.

Soon after the Garnet's arrival, Madame Gay and her daughter Pamela come to visit Miss Garnet and Retta. Miss Garnet and Madame Gay are old school friends, the latter being English and married to a Swiss husband who had died when Pamela was a baby. The Gays live in Argentière, just over the border in France, which had been Monsieur Gay's home. Pamela is eleven and has never been to England as the sister with whom Madame Gay might have stayed suffers from ill-health and would not want children around.

Retta, who is lively and adventurous, welcomes even the quiet and somewhat younger Pamela, and she is invited to stay on at Finhaut for a few days, during which the girls from the Vevey school arrive in the course of a short, early summer tour. Retta and Pamela, who, despite—or perhaps because of—the disparity in age, develop a sister-like relationship, with Pamela looking up to Retta in admiration and Retta protective of and caring towards the younger girl, meet the one English girl in the school, Una. Madame

Dufour canvasses Miss Garnet and, although the Vevey schoolgirls are really rather badly behaved and noisy, Miss Garnett decides to send Retta to the school in the autumn. Consequently, Madame Gay decides that Pamela should go there too, the timid Pamela being reconciled to the idea at the thought of Retta's company.

Meanwhile the two girls have also made the acquaintance of a sixteen-year-old Scottish boy, Malcolm Forsyth, who is staying in Finhaut because pneumonia has left him weak and who is with a nurse, Polly, because his mother cannot leave two much younger delicate daughters who cannot travel—one of them has had rheumatic fever, which has prevented Mrs Forsyth from even coming out on a promised visit. In the trials and tribulations which Retta has to face, Malcolm proves to be an invaluable source of support and advice.

In *Expelled from School* EJO has created one of her really villainous characters, probably the most dramatically so, as befits one of her most melodramatic books. This is the Italian Giulia Tarelli who makes an unfortunate first appearance when she laughs at the bare-legged Pamela (the girls have been out climbing and Pamela has torn her stockings). Una agrees that Giulia is fascinating, 'but', she warns mysteriously, and refuses to say more. Giulia is described gazing out at the storm, singing 'a wild melody' in her rich contralto, and Una confirms that she is in the habit of doing this at the lakeside school at Vevey—'It would be somebody's Storm Music from some opera: Wagner very likely; Giulia's crazy for him. She's a queer girl in lots of ways.'

Giulia, in fact, is treacherous. When Retta and Pamela arrive at the school in September, Retta is taken up by Giulia and made much of, to the chagrin of Yvonne who has been Giulia's friend up to this point. Madame Dufour is in the habit of asking the girls if anyone has broken a rule. Una and Retta always own up, but nobody else seems to think it is necessary to do so. Giulia proceeds to lead Retta astray. On the first occasion, Retta manages to persuade herself that it is a genuine misunderstanding, but on the second decides to have nothing more to do with Giulia. However, an invitation to leave school at night to visit a nearby village festival proves irresistible. When the girls are seen by an English visitor and reported, only Retta and Pamela, who has been ruthlessly involved in the escapade through Giulia's villainy, own up but, of course, refuse to betray the others. As a result of this Retta is expelled and returns to Finhaut shortly before Christmas. It is at this stage that Malcolm proves to be a great comfort. Slightly older and certainly more experienced in the ways of the world, he identifies the problem and suggests that Giulia has been deliberately getting at Retta in order to get her revenge on Una.

June comes round again, and Retta and her aunt go to spend a few days in Argentière with Madame Gay, who has taken advantage of Pamela's absence at school to visit England and has just returned. However they have to cut their visit short as Madame Gay's servant is taken ill, and they arrive back at Finhaut to find that Madame Dufour and her girls are once again installed in the hotel—it had been intended that they should go to the Tyrol but a sudden illness (what else?) in the hotel there has sent them back to Finhaut. Alarm and despondency all round, and fury on the part of both Madame Dufour, who believed that the Garnets had rented a chalet, and Miss Garnet, who thought that Madame and her girls were safely in the Tyrol. But this sets the scene for the final dramatic dénouement when Giulia's treachery is revealed by Yvonne, driven to revelation by her jealousy of a new girl, the French Antoinette, who had usurped her in Giulia's affections.

Retta and Una are revealed as whiter than white, and Retta actually pleads for Giulia not to be expelled. Madame Dufour cannot do enough for Retta and begs her to return to the school—'I would very much like one thing … and that is that you should return with us to school … I would like you to set an example in frank and open behaviour to the rest of the school.' This is the one bit of wish fulfilment in this book—no fortunes or heiresses here, although there is no shortage of money either. The book ends with Malcolm calling to see Retta at school on his way home to Scotland for good, and Retta promises that if they go home, she'll call on him there.

The plot is melodramatic although it comes over as less startling on a second reading. The most striking feature of the book, however, is the description of the Swiss scenery; the timespan of the story gives EJO an opportunity to describe Vevey and Finhaut at different

seasons of the year. When Retta returns to Finhaut after her expulsion, there is snow everywhere; when she goes back to Vevey the 'roses had been a revelation to her'. The mountains, the lake, the valleys and the glaciers, the towns and villages are described with loving care that suggests that EJO's first visit to Switzerland and Savoy had been an influential experience that she was never to forget.

A Go-Ahead Schoolgirl, published by Chambers in the following year, 1919, is also about girls at school; it is wartime and the war has a definite part to play in the plot. We return to EJO's much-loved Yorkshire moors, this time the moors above Sheffield. We know from the Preface to *Ribbie's Book* that EJO stayed with friends near Froggatt Edge, which is in Derbyshire, but the county boundaries run together in this area, and the village where the school is situated has been identified as Bolsterstone, which is just in Yorkshire. While staying with these friends, EJO met the little invalid boy who appears in the book as 'Wriggles' and to whom, with his nurse, the book is dedicated. Again, the scenery is described with care: the moors, the reservoirs, the tiny paths, the shaded valleys and the curious rocky outcrops, like those on Priscilla's moors, with their caves and particularly the mysterious cave which gives away secrets.

Rena Mackay, the go-head schoolgirl of the title, is a very typical EJO heroine, boyish, forthright, cheerful, practical, facing up to problems with courage. She and her great friend, Nancy Morrell, regard themselves as sisters and have a close friendship that is, in some ways, unusual. It is not unusual for there to be one of a pair who is the leader while the other is content to follow—Nancy is often called Rena's 'squaw'—but an important point made in this particular story is that, while Rena makes friends easily with other girls and becomes a popular member of a 'set', Nancy remains quietly on the sidelines and doesn't wish to be part of a noisy crowd but does not resent Rena's popularity. In fact she is rather proud of it.

The story, as we have said, is set during the First World War. Motherless Rena, whose father is a sea captain, and Nancy have come to spend a holiday on the moors with Nancy's mother, who is convalescing from an illness. There is something strange about the fact that

Rena has been allowed to come, just enough to give the reader a hint of what is to happen.

Rena and Nancy take to the moors and in the course of their explorations find a cave which they propose to adopt as a hideout, changing their minds when they discover that someone else, almost certainly another girl, has already done so. The cave has a mystery of its own; strange noises are heard there and the girls cannot discover where they come from. During their walks, they meet two boys, Rufus and Rex, and their sister, Teesa (Theresa). The boys are the usual pair—Rufus the elder and more serious, Rex the younger and more given to mischief and teasing. Teesa is one of EJO's unpleasant girls, bad-tempered, imperious and too proud to apologise when she is in the wrong. She gets off to a bad start with Rena and Nancy, and even though Rena later apologises, Teesa is unable to accept the apology gracefully and dislikes Rena as a result of it.

The cause of the first clash of wills and very much the centre of everyone's attention is Wriggles, the younger brother of Rex, Rufus and Teesa, who has suffered a serious illness and must now lie on his back in an invalid carriage. He is very frail and requires constant care, being looked after by his devoted nurse, Eddy. The patient, suffering invalid child was a popular theme in many books for girls at the beginning of the century but Wriggles was based on a real small boy, with whom EJO corresponded. Very often the fictional invalids were much too good to be true, but, refreshingly, Wriggles has a sense of mischief and enjoys the tricks that his brothers play. EJO was to use Wriggles again and to mention another child in his situation; in fact the long invalid carriage was not such a very unusual sight, even as late as the early 1940s, and the child in it often became a focus for other children as Wriggles does.

Wriggles and his nurse live in a big house on the moors called Rocklands, which belongs to Sheila Thorburn, aunt-by-marriage to the brothers and sister. She is a very young war widow, who has inherited her husband's home and is determined to share it with those less fortunate than herself. This, again, is a favourite theme in EJO's books—the idea must surely have been planted in her youth by the social work done by her mother and later by Erica and EJO herself. Sheila Thorburn is the first of her young women to open her house in this way.

Exploring the cave a second time, Rena and Nancy meet Lisabel Durrant who is the cave's previous occupant. Lisabel's father has been killed in the war and consequently her family is experiencing poverty. Her elder sister, Marion, who was hoping to train as a teacher, has had to take a job as an untrained teacher in a local school, and Lisabel, at thirteen, has left her good school and has since drifted around rather aimlessly. She helps her mother a little and earns some pocket money by doing crochet, but her general attitude is one of resentment—why should this have happened to her? Nancy and Rena are sorry for her, but Rena feels she should pull herself together and take some positive action. Sheila Thorburn has tried to help her, but Lisabel's pride has made her rude and ungracious.

Like Helen Robinson, Sheila Thorburn has an elder sister who is headmistress of a girl's school, and another use that Sheila makes of her inheritance is to give houseroom to the school, which is in nearby Sheffield, during the summer term each year.

It transpires that Rena has been allowed to share Nancy's holiday on the moors because her father has died at sea when his ship was torpedoed, and apart from the tragedy of this loss her financial circumstances have changed. There appears to be no money for her to continue her education; in fact her situation is very much like Lisabel's, and Lisabel is aware of this. However, unlike Lisabel, Rena is not too proud to accept help that will enable her to help herself. She and Nancy have to find a new school as their old one is being moved from London because, according to Rena, their headmistress is afraid of the possibility of air raids. It is now suggested that they should join the school that comes to Rocklands in the summer and that Rena, recommended by Sheila Thorburn, should be entered for a scholarship exam with a view to winning her way through college. Sheila Thorburn also helps Rena, not only in practical ways, but also by talking about the loss of her husband and her reasons for helping others. Rena and Nancy fit happily into the school and make friends; the one fly in the ointment is the presence of Teesa, who retains her dislike of Rena, and is not above making mischief at Rena's expense.

Owing to the war, the boys, Rufus and Rex, cannot return to school when term begins. The son of their headmaster has been seriously wounded in France, his father has gone there to be with him and there is no-one left to hold the school together—in fact they have even had to have women teachers, a theme that EJO was to use in her next book, *The School Torment*. The boys, particularly Rex, resent this enforced stay amongst a crowd of girls, and avoid them whenever possible, but Rex's love of mischief is aroused and he proceeds to inflict a series of tricks on them, including turning a herd of cows loose in the garden (we are not told what the farmer said about this!).

The secret cave originally discovered by Lisabel, and later by Rena and Nancy, has a strange property; as a result of a peculiarity in the rock formation, conversations held in the cave can be heard in the garden at Rocklands, higher up the hillside. One wonders if EJO knew of a cave like this one?

The theme of *A Go-Ahead Schoolgirl* is how Rena meets and faces the change in her situation and prospects, and how, by her influence and example, she leads other people. She shames the boys into behaving better, encourages Lisabel to face up to her own problems and set aside her stubborn pride, and finally induces Teesa to apologise for a piece of malice that has caused her own plans to go astray. Not that this has worried Rena, who makes it clear from the first that she feels she ought to go to college and train as a teacher in order to earn a living but that what she would really like to do is to stay at Rocklands and become assistant to Sheila Thorburn's old gardener, Andrew. When she does finally take up this post, it is clear that she is very happy and satisfied in her new job— yet another example of EJO making the point that it is essential to find a job that is 'right' for the person concerned.

However, EJO also carefully makes another point. Rena could easily lose her qualities of refinement and culture, and Sheila Thorburn insists that she must make Sundays a day when she wears a pretty dress and talks about books and music and pictures. Sheila also calls Rena the 'Garden Maid' or the 'Garden Damosel' rather than the gardener's boy, which is how Rena likes to think of herself. EJO showed great faith in the possibilities of gardening as a career for girls and it is interesting to note that at some time in the early part of the twentieth century, probably before 1919, when this book was published, the Glynde School for Lady Gardeners was established, according to Betty Massingham's biography of Gertrude Jekyll, one of its patrons.

The School Torment, EJO's next book, was published by Chambers in 1920 and illustrated by Harold Earnshaw. It picks up and continues the idea, first used in *At School with the Roundheads*, of a girl in a boys' school, but the reason for this heroine's presence in the school is not only more logical but also reflects the time at which the story is set. Once again we have a pair of sisters; these two are orphans and for this reason very close to each other even though Dorothy, the elder, is ten years older than Tormentil, otherwise known as Tormy or the Torment. Dorothy Grant is the first of the elder sisters whose life is dedicated to a younger one and who feels a very strong responsibility for her. This was another theme of which EJO was very fond, seen later in the characters of Mary-Dorothy Devine and Rachel Ellerton. Since her own Camp Fire name was Wenona, the Eldest Daughter, perhaps she herself had a very strong feeling about this kind of responsibility.

Dorothy is an extremely well-educated young woman with a Maths degree from Cambridge, and very independent. She has made up her mind to be a teacher and to keep Tormy with her as much as possible. She has to face a great deal of family opposition as they have a large number of elderly relatives who are quite prepared to support them both. Dorothy, however, is determined to do her own thing and is also quite sure that Tormy, a lively, active and cheerful schoolgirl, would not be a welcome addition to those calm elderly households. She is determined that she and Tormy must remain a family unit, and that her decisions must be ruled by one question—will it be good for Tormy?

At the beginning of the book Dorothy has been offered a job as Maths teacher in a boys' public school in Wales, where an old college friend is married to the headmaster. Many of the masters have joined up—we are still in the period of the First World War—and, knowing Dorothy's qualifications, the headmaster and his wife are sure that she will be equal to the job. Dorothy is very interested in the post as she wants a country school life for Tormy; she also feels, not so much that 'she would be releasing a man to get on with the war', as the hoardings put it, but that 'in this time of stress she would be helping the next generation, doing her share for the future of the country, taking her part of the general burden'. This is a more enlightened view than that expressed in the stories of many of EJO's contemporaries at this time. It would perhaps be safe to say that when war is mentioned in her books, the emphasis is more on 'the pity of war' than on its glorification.

Tormentil is very enthusiastic about the new plan. It is clear that she will welcome any new adventure, and this, to her, is an adventure. She has very strange ideas about boys, never having had anything to do with them before. This latter fact seems a little odd; did none of the girls at her previous schools have any brothers? If Tormy has strange ideas about boys, the boys, when she meets them, have most peculiar ideas about girls. Tormy's attitude reassures them; she presents herself as prepared to be one of them and anxious to take part in all their activities. Before very long she has made herself thoroughly at home and, in her short skirt and white sweater, with the school badge on her green beret, has become almost indistinguishable from her fellow pupils. Dorothy, too, seems to have no real problems in settling down to her work of teaching the boys. The boys themselves are prepared for her arrival by the inevitable talk from their headmaster and find the situation unusual, but 'are impressed by her grasp of her subject, her quick solution of problems, the ease and clearness of her explanations'. They nickname her 'the Bosser' and soon discover that it is not easy to put one over on her—she always wins in the end.

Dorothy does worry about whether Tormy is becoming half a boy, but her friend Mrs Paterson points out that some of this is a defence mechanism, the only way in which Tormy can hold her own in the very masculine environment. Had it not been for outside elements, Tormy would have had a happy, uneventful school career. However, outside elements do break in, very early in the story. Tormy sees and hears about the local heiress, Antonia Lloyd-Davies. Tygwyn, the Lloyd-Davies estate, is across the lake, not far from the school, and Antonia, the niece of the present owner, is regarded by the boys as the 'super-swank', with some justification, although Antonia herself is not really to blame. The estate has its own private railway halt, which would be much more convenient for the school, but there is no question of the school's being allowed to use it. There is also a public footpath through the grounds of Tygwyn that the boys like to use, especially because they know that the owner would like to be able to stop them. Roger says: 'We're all Socialists when we go round by Tygwyn.' There is a general opinion expressed that all places of natural beauty should be public property—very much a modern idea, but one that was clearly current in the 1920s and 1930s and that also appears in the works of the 'super-snob' Dornford Yates, amongst others.

Tormy is curious about, and anxious to meet, Antonia and takes the first opportunity to speak to her, even though the situation is not the most propitious as an older girl, a seventeen-year-old American, Marsaili, is with Antonia. The acquaintance is furthered when Tormy and the boys appear in time to save Antonia, whose bicycle is running away with her—a precipitous method of making friends that had already been used in *The School of Ups and Downs*. This episode breaks any ice there may have been and gives Tormy an excuse to go over to Tygwyn to enquire how Antonia is.

At Tygwyn Tormy not only meets both girls again but is also introduced to the ceremonies of the Camp Fire movement. The American girl, Marsaili, is staying at Tygwyn with her cousin Beryl, who has been engaged as the family chauffeur. Beryl had originally come over to England to offer her services as a driver for the Army, but her 'boy', who had come over from America with the Army, was killed as soon as he landed in France. 'It didn't make her want to help on the war, for revenge as so many have felt they must do; it made her feel the hideous wickedness of it all and she said she'd have no part in it'. Once again we have the stress laid on the destructive effect of war on the lives of ordinary people.

Marsaili's reasons for being in England are rather mysterious. She tells Tormy and Antonia, also known as Tony, a little of her family's history. Like the Buchanan children in *Schoolgirls and Scouts*, she has been brought up on the South Sea island of Samoa, and could swim as soon as she could walk. Her mother is dead and her father, after making and losing a fortune in America, is now an invalid, crippled with rheumatism and anxious that Marsaili should visit his family in England and lay claim to some of the family money. Marsaili, whose name comes from the Gaelic equivalent of the Samoan pronunciation of

Margery, is very independent, and much prefers the idea of making her own way in the world, so has decided that she will wait and see what her English family is like before she considers making a claim on them.

In America she has been a Camp Fire girl, and the implication is that her Camp Fire activities have helped to make her self-sufficient and able to earn her own living. She has already introduced Tony to the Camp Fire ideals and ceremonies, which also appeal to Tormy, thus bringing out another, more feminine, side to her character. Together the three girls vow to be Camp Fire sisters and to help and support each other.

Tony's guardians, her aunt and uncle, are shadowy figures, whose main role in the story seems first to be seriously ill, and later to die. When her uncle has to go to London for special treatment, Tony and Marsaili move to the school, to live in the Headmaster's house with Tormy and her sister, and to join some of the classes. Tony's attitude to the boys is quite different from Tormy's; she has no intention of becoming one of them and accepts their courtesies and offers of help merely as her due. The boys are charmed by this, and in their eagerness to make a good impression Tormy is frequently left out of things; she cannot understand the new situation, and it does not occur to the boys to explain that they regard her as an equal, a real sport and as good as any boy, and that Tony is just an attractive novelty.

Tormy fights the inevitable battle for control of her feelings. Unlike Christina and Gwyneth in EJO's earlier books, she is not jealous of Tony and doesn't blame her for anything; she just comes to the conclusion that the boys like Tony better and that she must not resent this or show that she is hurt by their neglect. She succeeds so well in hiding her feelings that the boys have no idea of how she really feels and think that she doesn't care.

The next development in Tony's story is the death of both aunt and uncle—a bit wholesale this—and hard upon this news she learns that she is not, after all, the heiress to Tygwyn. There is another, older, uncle in America, who has a daughter, and the estate now belongs to him. Tony's world is shattered by this news, far more so than by the deaths of her aunt and uncle, but the knowledge that she has good friends in her Camp Fire sisters enables her to face up to the situation and begin to consider how she can become independent and earn her own living.

Marsaili's mysterious background is now revealed; she is, of course, the daughter of the older brother, Tony's uncle, in America, and she has been living at Tygwyn in order to get to know her English family and decide whether she will make herself known to them. As soon as she is revealed as the real heiress to Tygwyn, she makes it clear that she has no intention of taking the estate from Tony, whatever the legal authorities may say. This, of course, is a situation which EJO had already used in *Rosaly's New School* and was to use again in the Abbey books; not surprisingly, a happy compromise is reached, and Tony and Marsaili agree to share the estate between them. Things also end happily for Tormentil as Tony becomes aware of the true state of things and spells it out for the boys (or for one of them, at least). To show Tormy how they feel about her and without being in any way sentimental, the boys arrange a dormitory feast in her honour, ostensibly because she has played for the school cricket team in an emergency and has acquitted herself reasonably well.

The main theme of the book is—as indicated by the title—Tormy's career as a schoolgirl in a boys' school. The story of the two heiresses to Tygwyn, despite its fascinating complexities, takes second place to this, serving to develop Tormy's character and pointing out, perhaps, the disadvantages of being too much of a tomboy. The story is set in North Wales, not far from the Lleyn Peninsula, which EJO had already used in her work. To reach the school Dorothy and Tormy travel through a 'smoky Midland town'; both the school and Tygwyn are situated on the shores of a large lake and, although the descriptions of the scenery are more general than in some of EJO's other books, this is clearly Lake Bala in North Wales, although EJO has adapted it to suit her purposes. The lake is about four miles long, quite broad, with the higher mountains at the western end.

This was one of the first EJO sites that we explored, and we discovered that Tygwyn is based on the largest house on the lakeside, once the country home of Sir Watkin Williams Wynn, who owned much of North Wales and who once entertained Queen Victoria there on her only state visit to Wales; it is now used as an activities centre for young people. On the south side of the lake there is a piece of land where the school could have been sited, near which are the remains of the private railway halt. The railway that carries the boys to school is now one of the 'great little trains' of Wales, and, although it no longer connects to the main rail network, it is possible during the summer to take the train journey that EJO may have taken through the area. The landscape must look much the same as it did then, and even today the town of Bala has a somewhat sophisticated air untypical of the inland towns of North Wales.

The second of EJO's three books published in 1920 was *The Twins of Castle Charming*, her only book to be published by the Swarthmore Press and one of the very few to have no illustrations. Almost all of its main characters have appeared in earlier books, and in time it dates from before *Schoolgirls and Scouts*, its plot having also pretty well been given away in the earlier books. The story may just have existed in EJO's mind, but it seems more probable that all or most of it existed in manuscript form as early as 1914.

It is also another story set in Switzerland, and the setting is described with great affection. It begins with a very detailed description of a journey from London by train and boat, across the Channel, pausing at Paris and then continuing to Montreux on Lake Geneva, and up into the mountains to 'Lake Rosenthal', where Castle Charming is situated. Stay-at-home schoolgirls, who had never been abroad and would probably never go, must have followed Melany every inch of the way with fascinated attention. Her reactions to the new sights, her disappointment with the vineyards in the spring and her anxiety lest *café complet* should not provide a sufficiently sustaining breakfast: all of this is almost certainly remembered from EJO's own first-time experience of continental travel. The book is dedicated to 'My travelling-companion in Switzerland, my mother ...'.

The story, first hinted at in *Schoolgirls and Scouts* and here recorded in full, is that of the separated twins Melany and Blanche (Zanne) Merrill. The basic situation is pure romance—the death of a beloved wife at the birth of the twins, the heartbroken husband who cannot bear to see his children and allows them to be separated, sending one to England to his own sister and the other to Italy to his dead wife's parents. Although the girls are permitted to know of each other's existence, they are not allowed to communicate with each other, nor, of course, to meet.

The two girls have been brought up very differently. Melany, living with an aunt who has shown her little affection and left her almost entirely to Jeannette, her Swiss nurse, finds school a happier place than home, while Zanne, the spoilt darling of her Italian grandparents, has been happy and sheltered all her life. Each of them, though, has had a long-felt desire to meet her twin, and feels that they should be together and, if possible, live with their father, however little he may care for them. It is typical of their different upbringings that Zanne should set out, accompanied by her maid Maria and with her grandparents' permission, to go to Castle Charming to face her unknown father, while Melany, travelling with her aunt and Jeannette to Leuk, where her aunt is going to take the waters, should plan to run away in Paris on the same errand, taking Jeannette but sparing no thought for the anxiety she will cause.

Melany is cheered on her way by her schoolfellows, among them Jill Colquhoun and the ubiquitous Monica. On her arrival in Paris she takes an earlier train than the one that her Aunt intends to catch and rushes off with Jeannette towards Montreux and, finally, Castle Charming. She arrives there to find that her father has been called away suddenly but it does not occur to her that this may be because of her own disappearance. She settles down to wait for him and while doing so meets Eilidh Munro, who is touring with Mollie Raby, Lord Larry and Mr Kerr. Zanne also arrives at the gates of Castle Charming, and the two sisters are reunited at last, and with the same aim in view: to persuade their father to allow them to live together, preferably with him.

It is not long before Mr Merrill hears that his daughters are at Castle Charming. He is justifiably annoyed with them and sends on ahead a letter that upsets them considerably; because he feels they can't be trusted, he plans to separate them once again. They are not prepared to accept this so they make plans to run away again, this time to Italy to their Italian grandparents. They plan their escape carefully but are discovered by Lord Larry who, is as usual, making an unpleasant nuisance of himself, and threatens to give them away. He is persuaded not to do so but, having given his word, a promise which Melany rightly does not trust, he follows them, as they change their plans once again, and then returns to his own party and reveals all.

The twins have taken refuge in another wonderful valley in the mountain, and are pausing en route for Italy when Bill Kerr turns up, having offered to search for them, instead of allowing their father to send a policeman. Reluctantly they return to Castle Charming where their father has imported a particularly strict governess to supervise both their lives and their studies. For some weeks they try to conform, full of indignation because their father refuses to see or speak to them, while the governess will concentrate only on German and maths, least favourite subjects for both of them. The only part of their studies they enjoy is music and they prove to have voices that complement each other.

One of the reasons for their father's preoccupation is that he is writing a book, about which Melany has heard something, presumably from her aunt: 'It's about how the different kinds of people in the world are related to each other and that the Red Indians are really Chinese …' One wonders exactly which theory of anthropology EJO had come across to prompt this idea! Melany is interested in his theories and would like to hear more, but Zanne is more concerned about the unhappiness that causes him to wish to have nothing to do with his daughters, whose birth coincided with the death of his wife.

Mr Merrill has also dismissed both the maids, sending Maria back to Italy and Jeannette back to his sister in England. The girls are indignant at being thus deprived of their faithful attendants, although it never seems to occur to them that the maids are likely to be blamed for their own exploits. The strict governess has no real understanding of the girls' problems, the climate at Castle Charming does not agree with them, and finally, in desperation, they are driven to run away once again. Melany plans an escape in the traditional manner, climbing out of a window on a rope made of sheets. Inevitably, the less athletic Zanne slips and falls, and Melany is hurt trying to catch her. Shy Zanne is roused to anger as well as indignation and confronts their father, accusing him of having caused this disaster by his inhuman treatment. He copes efficiently with the crisis but immediately afterwards withdraws into himself again, leaving them to the tender mercies of the governess.

The girls make yet another attempt to get through to their father, this time by letter, but with no success. Under the strict regime imposed by the governess, Zanne falls ill, apparently infected by one of the servants who has a fever, probably typhoid, and this time it is Melany, driven by fear for her sister's life, who confronts the Father/Ogre and asks him to send for a doctor. Something, perhaps the sight of his daughter who, we are told, resembles her dead mother and who is now in tears because of their troubles, changes Mr Merrill's heart and he becomes a caring, loving father, looking after Zanne and making an effort to keep Melany from brooding.

So there is a happy ending, and we know, from other books in which the twins appear as minor characters, that Mr Merrill and his daughters become a happy family group. We also know now why Melany is hoping to have a few words with Lord Larry, who seems destined to continue through life as the spoilt, selfish young aristocrat, an advance blueprint for the young Earl of Kentisbury.

Given the ability to suspend judgment and an affection for romantic plots, this must have been a very readable book for young girls at the time, but it is not surprising that it is one of the rarest of EJO's titles nor that it was not published by one of her usual publishers.

Chapter 4

ALL KINDS OF SCHOOLS, 1920 TO 1924

According to Marcus Crouch, writing in *Treasure Seekers and Borrowers*:

> The twenties were, above all, the age of the school story ... The traditional girls' school story was represented by Angela Brazil ... Christine Chaundler, the Abbey books of Elsie Oxenham ... Elinor Brent-Dyer's 'Chalet' School stories ... and Dorita Fairlie Bruce ... the shallowest of steps towards Elfrida Vipont.

From the 1920s until the outbreak of the Second World War in 1939, the school story seems to have been the most popular type of story amongst girls in their early teens. Until the emergence of Enid Blyton in the 1940s, Angela Brazil, that writer of school stories *par excellence*, was the author who was consistently quoted as the most popular author amongst young girl readers. It is interesting to note, in view of this, that school stories were very poorly regarded by adults in authority. Gillian Freeman in *The Schoolgirl Ethic* describes how, in 1936, the Headmistress of St Paul's Girls' School 'expressed the wish to collect the books of Angela Brazil and burn them', while another headmistress, in an address to a meeting of the Association of Head Mistresses of Boarding Schools in 1938, subsequently reprinted in *The School Library Review*, said that she never allowed her pupils to read school stories.

EJO helped this upward surge in the output of, and interest in, school stories by producing eleven books, most of them school stories, in the period between 1920 and 1923. She sets these in a wide variety of schools, and it is fitting that this chapter should begin with a consideration of *The Abbey Girls*, the first book about her two most significant creations, Joan and Joy Shirley. Although the long series of books that was to follow is sometimes referred to as the Abbey School series, the school is in fact never given a name other than that of its headmistress, Miss Macey.

In *A School Camp Fire* some years earlier, EJO had shown, albeit briefly, that she was attracted by the atmosphere and history of a Cistercian Abbey—in that case, Fountains Abbey in Yorkshire. Some time prior to 1920, on a visit to relations in Somerset, EJO visited Cleeve Abbey, and it is this abbey that she transferred, almost unaltered, to the borders of Buckinghamshire and Oxfordshire to serve as Gracedieu Abbey. It is possible to take *The Abbey Girls* in one hand and use it as a guide to the present-day Cleeve Abbey, so closely did she follow the layout of its ruins in her re-creation.

One reason for transferring the abbey to Buckinghamshire was to bring it within the range of Cicely Hobart and the Hamlet Club. The topography is not described in as much detail in *The Abbey Girls* as it is in the earlier book, but it is possible to find a likely site for Gracedieu Abbey below the western end of the Bledlow Ridge, on the outskirts of the

The Gatehouse at Cleeve, early 20th century

village of Chinnor. Cicely Hobart, fourteen in *Girls of the Hamlet Club,* is now seventeen. The Club has had three Queens because Cicely, having been crowned as the second Queen, had to go away with her father shortly afterwards; Marguerite Verity was chosen to take over and became the Strawberry Queen.

But this is really the story of Joy and Joan Shirley, look-alike cousins of about the same age, Joan being the elder by a month, who have recently come to live in the Abbey with Joan's widowed mother, who has been appointed caretaker. Mrs Shirley is the only parent between them: Joy's mother died many years before, her father disappeared while travelling, Joan's father, his twin brother, has died, and the failure of his business has left his widow and the girls in a state of penury. Cicely and her friends, who visit the Abbey on a Hamlet Club ramble and are shown round it by Joan, can see at once that Mrs Shirley is a 'lady' and that it would not do to offer the bronze-haired Joan money.

Joan and Joy are two of EJO's strongest characters. Margery Fisher, writing in *Who's Who in Children's Literature*, says that they are the 'most strongly drawn personalities in this long cycle of schooldays, representing in their different ways the eager, creative moods and aspirations of adolescence'. Mary Cadogan and Patricia Craig comment in *You're a Brick, Angela!*:

> Joan is the prominent person in this book, but later she fades into the background of the series; she is one of those well-behaved girls whose moral uprightness is

boringly unshakeable … It is in Joy Shirley—at least in the early books—that Elsie Oxenham comes nearest to making at least one of her heroines believable … Joy … is a more complex character than any of the others.

It is perhaps not surprising that in later Abbey books they are absent from the action for long periods. The plot of this first book requires them to be cousins, although their relationship is naturally a sisterly one. Joan is the wise, patient, clear-headed, well-disciplined one of the pair; Joy is impetuous, foolhardy, adventurous and quick-tempered. She has a fine musical gift but cannot settle down to work in the way that Joan can. Joan and her mother are worried about Joy, a wanderer like her father, and also feel a great sense of responsibility towards her because she was entrusted to them by her father; so when Cicely and the Club offer Joan the Hamlet Club scholarship, Joan insists that it is Joy who must be given the chance to go to school. It is an interesting reflection on middle-class attitudes to state education at the time: if the means for private education are not available, the girls stay at home.

Miss Macey's school and the Hamlet Club are in a state of turbulence and indecision when Joy arrives as a new girl, because the rival groups cannot agree on the election of the next Queen. The girls, carrying on the old rivalries that Cicely had sought to heal, have divided themselves into 'Saints' and 'Sinners'. To solve the problem, Joy is elected as the fourth Queen, being neither a 'Saint' nor a 'Sinner', although she had fully intended to throw her lot in with the 'Saints'. She carries out her duties to the best of her ability, and on Joan's advice invites Carry Carter, a 'Sinner', to be her maid of honour; she is succeeding quite well in her unexpected role when she unfortunately mislays the exercise book in which she has foolishly written the good advice that everyone has given her, together with her comments. Inevitably this has been picked up and read by Carry, who then tries to make use of what she has read. Fortunately, the book has been seen by an independent witness, Margia Lane, the violinist who plays for the Club, and she bears witness to the fact that Carry has behaved dishonourably.

Alongside the school saga and the sorting out of the Carry Carter situation is the story of Joan and Joy. It transpires that the reason that the Shirleys are at the Abbey is because the owner, Sir Antony Abinger, is Joy's grandfather. His only daughter, Joyce, had married against his wishes, and he has refused to have anything to do with Joy, although when Mrs Shirley appealed to him for help he went so far as to offer them shelter and a living at the Abbey. His heart is now softened by the sight of Joan and Joy dancing on the cloister garth:

> … the sunny cloister garth, the ruined arches all around, the fierce old man, ill-tempered and lonely peering through the doorway of the tresaunt, and two bronze-haired girls dancing a minuet in the sunshine.

This set piece, first described in terms of Mrs Shirley's vision of the scene when she learns of it from Sir Antony, is described over and over again in later books. A letter written by Edith Cairns, then the Deputy Librarian at the University of Reading, in 1969, says:

> … I remember a rather severe-looking woman I met during a visit to (I think)

Fountains Abbey who said to me 'All I know about cloister garths is that people do country dancing on them!'

and the scene must have made a similar impression on many of EJO's readers. Sir Antony also visits the Abbey and is shown round by Joan, who does not discover his identity until he is leaving; at his invitation, Joan and Joy go, with Margia to play for them, to dance at Abinger Hall. He then has a heart attack and dies, leaving money for both girls to be educated. When it is established that his son has died two years previously in the South Seas, it is revealed that Sir Antony has left the Hall, the estate and most of the money to Joy, but that Joan is to have the Abbey, together with money to maintain it properly. By the time all this comes to pass, another year has gone by. Cicely and Marguerite have spent some of the time abroad but come hurrying home to a May Day ceremony when Joan is crowned as the fifth, Violet, Queen of the Hamlet Club.

Much of the information that, like the set piece of the dancing on the cloister garth, is repeated in later books has its origins in the pages of *The Abbey Girls*. The foundations of a great saga were well and truly laid. In an article in *The Junior Bookshelf*, Lynette Muir has compared the stories to a medieval romance cycle—'A number of permanent characters alternate with individual girls who appear for one book then vanish again, their story complete.' Appropriately, Sheila remembers that she first came across this book when the story was told by one of the girls in her form during her first year at secondary school, 'I think that by this time I must have read some of the later books in the series because I realised at once that here was the great beginning of it all. That afternoon in the early 1940s is as clear in my mind as if it had happened yesterday.'

The Girls of the Abbey School

The Girls of the Abbey School was published in the following year and illustrated by Elsie Anna Woods, who produced the illustrations for the first three Abbey books. Monica Godfrey suggests she was the illustrator whom EJO took to folk dance classes in order to 'capture movement and posture'. This book appeared so hard upon the heels of *The Abbey Girls* that it seems as if EJO had already decided to embark on the Abbey saga and had her head full of ideas for it, ideas not only for the characters but also about the Abbey, which plays an important part in the series right through to the end. *Girls of the Abbey School* begins at the point where *The Abbey Girls* ends, with the crowning of Joan as the Violet Queen of the Hamlet

Club, and immediately introduces the reader to the Club's enthusiasm for folk dancing. It also introduces another character, who is important throughout the whole Abbey story, second only to Joan and Joy, and who eventually takes Joan's place as the contrast to Joy.

Janet Robins, known as Jen or Jenny-Wren, is one of the cornerstones of the chronicles of the Abbey. She is newly arrived at Miss Macey's school, has been looked after by the new Queen, and is introduced to the Hamlet Club through watching the crowning ceremony. She is somewhat younger than Joan and Joy but quickly makes a friend of her own age, Jacqueline (Jack) Wilmot, and is almost immediately parted from her. A case of diphtheria among the boarders—this situation occurs so often in school stories of the period that it must have been a fairly frequent problem in real life—makes it necessary to find other premises for the school for the summer term, and Joy, now established as the mistress of Abinger Hall, offers her house to Miss Macey, who accepts the offer with pleasure.

Jen stays at the Hall in advance of her fellow pupils, and during these first few days her friendship with Joan and Joy is made and established. We are given our first picture of the Hall in Joy's possession: the panelled entrance hall with its family portraits, which is to become so familiar to readers, the grounds and the great trees, and the gate in the wall that leads into the Abbey precincts. Jen is also given a conducted tour of the Abbey by Joan and has her first lessons in folk dancing on the cloister garth.

Jen's love for the Abbey begins on this first visit and continues to develop throughout the book. For this reason she is allowed to share in the various discoveries that are made later in the story. She is also enthralled by her first experience of folk dancing and joins the Hamlet Club, although she has always been keen on cricket and the younger girls are not allowed to do both. Her joy in the music and dances and her interest in the Abbey and its treasures are stressed as indicative of the development of her artistic side, to balance her tomboy characteristics. In some ways, Jen is to be EJO's ideal girl in this respect. Her final acceptance—'She'll do' says Cicely—is when she is invited to make one of the exclusive party who dance at midnight on the cloister garth to fulfil a long felt wish of Joan's.

Trouble appears in the form of a pair of spoilt children, Dick and Della Jessop, whose mother has left them in the charge of Ann Watson, the new caretaker and guide at the Abbey, who used to be their nurse. Ann does not want them, and in fact refuses to have them because Joan, her employer, objects to children (presumably unsupervised children) in the Abbey, but her erstwhile mistress ignores her protests and departs for Scandinavia, leaving the children behind. What Ann Watson should have done was to tell Joan at once— the fact that she doesn't is shown to be a basic weakness in her character and crops up again as a weakness of character to be found in the 'lower classes'. She says nothing and hopes for the best. This weakness is balanced by the irresponsibility for their children shown by some members of the upper middle class, here represented by Lady Jessop.

Dick and Della find the Abbey a magnificent playground, and in the course of their explorations stumble upon a secret passage, unknown to Joan, which leads to the Hall in one direction and out to the hills in the other. Needless to say they explore the passages, although Dick puts them in the way of being discovered by tapping out rhythms on the panelling in the Hall and also—a crime that is to be remembered for years afterwards— beginning to carve his name on the stones of the Abbey. His activities give their secret away, and they are finally captured in the tunnels by Joy, Jen and Jack.

To keep them out of trouble they are taken into the school to be under Miss Macey's charge. Jack and Jen take Della under their wing and undertake to reform her. She is sufficiently grateful to tell them that she and Dick had discovered yet another secret door in the passage to the woods, behind which was a cave whose contents they did not have time to investigate. Joan and Joy do, of course, investigate, in company with Jen, Jack, Mrs Shirley and Miss Macey, and discover the Abbey plate and books and manuscripts hidden away for safety at the time of the dissolution of the monasteries.

This is the first of the discoveries in the Abbey. EJO has several more surprises up her sleeve to be revealed to her characters and to her readers in later books. One can easily imagine how the first readers of her books would look forward to a new Abbey story for this as well as for other reasons. Even in this book there are more secrets in store. Among the ancient manuscripts forming part of the Abbey treasure is the story of the lay-brother Ambrose and his love for the Lady Jehane, and how he hid her jewels in the 'old church'. Ambrose and his story are also part of the fabric of the Abbey and its chronicles, as much so for EJO's readers as are Joan, Joy and Jen.

As might have been expected, Dick does not give up his idea of exploring the passages. Angry with Della for having given him away, he finds himself a new companion, Micky, Ann Watson's nephew from the village, and goes exploring at night. On their first visit they discover the 'old church' but do not realise its importance until Dick hears the story of Jehane's jewels. A few nights later they go again, choosing, unknown to them, the night when Joan and her special friends are having a midnight dance on the cloister garth. While attempting to discover the exact hiding place of the jewels, Dick falls into an old well, and Micky, in a panic, abandons him and runs home, not thinking to go for help. Dick, in his agonised hours of waiting, reflects that someone like himself would certainly have gone for help, but that Micky might not be brave enough to risk trouble for himself—in fact, Micky is presented as being basically as weak as his aunt.

Happily for Dick, Della misses him the next morning, and enquiries quickly lead to Micky who reveals the truth. Joan and Miss Macey go exploring again and Dick, who has spent a very painful and anxious night, is rescued. Miss Macey takes a very active part in this particular story; she emerges from her study, ventures down secret passages and even descends the disused well in order to help Dick, for whom she feels responsible. Further searching finds the jewels and yet another secret of the Abbey is revealed. Had we read this book in its proper sequence as schoolgirls, we are sure that the closing sentences would have left us waiting for the next book:

> 'Has the Abbey any *more* secrets, Joan?' cried Peggy Gilks, when she had recovered her breath.
>
> Joan looked up with a laugh from the jewels she was turning over with her fingers. 'I shouldn't think so. But I'm sure I don't know! But I think we've done fairly well for you in that line!'
>
> 'All the same you never know your luck!' Jen remarked. 'We didn't know when we came here, did we, Joan?'
>
> 'True for you, Jenny-Wren! We did *not*!' the Queen agreed.

For the setting of her next book, *The Two Form-Captains* (1921), EJO returned to

Switzerland. Four years before Elinor Brent-Dyer launched her highly successful Austrian-based Chalet School series, EJO created her own school, or rather two schools, in the Swiss Alps, founded to give an English education to children of many nations, a large number of whom have a parent or relative at a great Sanatorium high up in the mountains. At this time a stay in Switzerland or some other Alpine area was an accepted form of treatment for tuberculosis—for those who could afford it. Monica Godfrey places EJO's sanatorium at Mürren, above Lauterbrunnen, in Switzerland. Although this placing has EJO's own authority behind it, Mabel Esther Allan has suggested that Kandersteg is the only real valley with a tumbling grey river from which the train roars through a tunnel to Italy. In *The Abbey Girls at Home*, Joy refers to the new Lotschberg line that goes through Kandersteg. Whether the sanatorium was at Mürren or Kandersteg, the local language would have been Swiss-German rather than French.

The sanatorium is run by Sir Rennie Brown, the great doctor to whom reference is made in many of EJO's books, and the two schools, St John's for boys and St Mary's for girls,

'I must tell the others!'
(*The Two Form-Captains*)

were founded deliberately with the existence of the sanatorium in mind. Did Elinor Brent-Dyer arrange things the other way round in order to be different? The Chalet School comes first, the sanatorium on the nearby Sonnalpe is founded, apparently by chance, a year or so later.

EJO's schools are the inspiration of Charles Braithwaite, who says to his sister,

'These poor folk must have children and must wish to see them. The journey home is too expensive to be taken often. What about schools for them here … where they could have a thoroughly good education up to the point where they must specialise, and yet be near enough to their people to be able to see them at times and to spend week-ends with them, or be sent for in case of sudden need?'

The Two Form-Captains, published by Chambers, is the first of EJO's books to be set here. In spite of its title, it is not so much a school story as a 'romance' for girls in their teens and, if for no other reason, the existence of the boys' school is therefore necessary. It contains a theme that EJO has used in several other books: a girl (or girls) in a group of boys, the development of relationships between girls and boys, the purely friendly 'chums' and the friendship which is later to develop into 'something deeper'. Thus more of the action of the books takes place in Madame Perronet's boarding-house for boys from St John's, to whose members are added first one girl, then another, from St Mary's, than in St Mary's itself.

To the contented little group of four boys—the two Thistleton brothers, Prickles and the Spud (William and Herbert), Edward Lorimer, known as Dumpy, and the mystery man, the quiet Mr Brown, known as Boney, although his real name is Rennie—is added Anastasia Kingston, known as Tazy or Taisez-vous because she talks a lot. This matter of nick-names, which seems to be essential for a good 'chummy' friendship, is one that appears in almost all of these early books.

The boys are less than enthusiastic at the idea of adding a girl to their select group, but Tazy, like Tormentil Grant in *The School Torment*, knows exactly how to introduce herself and fits in easily, while adding a certain amount of liveliness to the atmosphere. The boys accept her and come to admire her as a girl as well as a 'chum', but are careful not to let her see it. Boney Brown sums up the situation with a clarity and understanding that surprises his companions when he says:

> 'She looked very pretty. She's a pretty kid. But she doesn't let it prey on her mind as some of 'em do. She'd think you were awful asses if she heard you just now. You'd better keep all that stuff to yourselves if you don't want her to turn you down as hopeless lunatics.'

The ease with which Tazy adapts herself to living with the boys pleases her headmistress, Miss Braithwaite, who appears here as a very human person, aware of situations and frankly unofficially enjoying Tazy's account of her rough and tumbles with her fellow-boarders.

One aspect of St Mary's which provides a pivot for this and other stories is the method of choosing form-captains. Each form has two, one chosen by the girls themselves and one by the mistresses. On her first day at school Tazy is plunged into the excitement of the elections of the new form-captains. In her own form, the Fourth, the girl chosen by the mistresses is Karen Wilson, a choice which the girls find hard to understand. Karen is very quiet and reserved and works hard, but appears to have no outstanding qualities. Tazy studies her carefully, anxious to discover what it is about her that has won her this honour. The girls' choice of form-captain is Svea Andersson, with whom Tazy has already made friends. She is one of three sisters who are described as 'obviously placid and easy-going, good company and general favourites'. The two captains are contrasted in Tazy's thoughts,

> '… Svea's all on the outside, or a good lot of her anyway; she may have plenty more inside, of course, but she makes a good show in her shop window … But I'm not so sure of Karen. Whatever she is, it's all inside, in her case. I suppose I'll get to know her in time.'

The plot of the book is woven round the theme of the two captains and the 'silly' relationships between teenage boys and girls. Since EJO seems to base this on an empty-headed boy's desire for feminine admiration and a conceited girl's desire for notoriety and unlimited chocolates, one wonders if she knew anything about such things at all!

Tazy gets to understand and like Karen Wilson, particularly when Karen is added to the select party at Madame Perronet's. She learns that Karen's reserve is due, in part, to the fact that her eyesight is bad; short-sightedness, neglected in her early childhood, means that she must take great care not to strain her eyes, and that she cannot play games. This poor eyesight, together with her long brown hair with its reddish tints, are characteristic of EJO herself, as may also be Karen's knack of seeing further into things than most people. She is a careful observer of people and, from her observations, is able to understand them.

Karen fits quietly into the group at Madame Perronet's and eventually becomes really friendly with Boney, who turns out to be the son of Sir Rennie Brown and whom she had previously met when they were both children. This is the boy and girl relationship that is later to develop into something deeper and the fact is pointed at regular intervals throughout the book,

> There was the beginning of a very real and lasting friendship between them as they climbed the forest path together ... a friendship all the more likely to deepen into something greater because it was so frankly natural and unconscious, on Karen's part at least.

Karen, as Form Captain, eventually finds herself called upon to take drastic action when she discovers that one of the girls in the form is meeting Dumpy secretly and being given boxes of chocolates. Her fellow captain is unwilling to act because she does not want to become unpopular but Karen, braced by Rennie (Boney), persuades her to do so. The unfortunate wrong-doer is later suitably punished — she is meeting Dumpy secretly in the pine-woods during a school picnic and cannot be found in time to reach her mother's death-bed.

In spite of its Swiss setting, English folk music finds a place here, when Karen, attracted by Tazy's whistling of folk-dance tunes, adapts four of them into a prize-winning fantasy performed at the schools' music festival.

Folk music plays a most important part in the next book, *The Abbey Girls Go Back to School,* published by Collins in 1922 and illustrated by Elsie Anna Woods. This is another key book in the Abbey series and one whose main incidents are remembered and talked about in the years to come. It is also, as Monica Godfrey has pointed out, 'the most factual of her books, using real people, incidents and locations'.

It begins, however, at Jen Robins' home on the Yorkshire moors, not far from Rocklands School. Because her father is ill, she has had to leave school at sixteen and stay at home to be 'the daughter of the house'. Cicely and Joan are indignant about this, not because there is any question of Jen taking up a career—at this period it was taken for granted that an upper-middle class girl would not take a job because she would thus deprive another girl who might need the money—but because they are sure she will be bored to tears.

Lively Jen does miss the fun of school and her friends and particularly her folk dancing and when a set of gramophone records of dance tunes arrives, she immediately looks round for some way to use them and starts classes for the children of the village. She has an unexpected surprise at Christmas, when she has been asked to dance during the visit of local 'guisers' or mummers to the house, and a stranger emerges from the crowd with offers of help—and some very direct criticism of Jen's own dancing.

The following summer Jen joins Cicely, Joan and Joy and her first friend, Jacqueline Wilmot, to spend a month at a vacation school. This is the Summer School held at Cheltenham by the then English Folk Dance Society. EJO never refers to the Society by name in any of her books, but its leading members and the ideas behind it are clearly spelled out over and over again. Joan Peck, in a letter to the *EFDSS Magazine*, says, 'the books give a great deal of information about the folk movement and the attitudes and beliefs of Cecil Sharp and can be read for this alone'.

In EJO's account of the Summer School at Cheltenham, she includes what must be nearly all she knew at the time about the traditions of folk dance and song and the techniques of dancing to the high standard required by the Society. To girls whose interest in folk dancing was inspired by her books—and, so far as Sheila can remember, she was one of them—this was almost a textbook. As she says, 'Joining a folk dance group as an adult, I greeted new dances as old friends and discovered that when new steps were taught, I could recall what had been said about them by Madam and successfully followed the instructions.' According to Joan Peck, 'Douglas Kennedy states that over the years he has been struck by the number of people who have told him that they were attracted to the folk movement in this way'.

EJO attended vacation schools and knew or was familiar with many of the leading members of the Society. Those who appear in this and other books do so under nicknames. Among them, The Prophet is Cecil Sharp, founder of the Society, and Madam is Helen Kennedy, sister of

She stood on a chair, encouraging and explaining.
(*The Abbey Girls Go Back to School*)

71

Douglas Kennedy, Cecil Sharp's successor, whom EJO calls Joshua. Helen Kennedy was EJO's own teacher and this book is dedicated to her and to D C Daking, who appears in this and other books as the Pixie. There seems to be no difficulty in identifying any of these characters, although there is no indication that EJO knew them well enough to present them as anything but her own idealised versions. As Cadogan and Craig comment, 'Nearly all the subsidiary characters in this book, in fact, are identifiable members of the Folk Dance and Song Society, who can hardly have taken kindly to Elsie Oxenham's somewhat effusive presentation of them.'

EJO's own enthusiasm and enjoyment of folk dancing dominates the central section of this book and communicates itself to her readers through her characters. To the Abbey group are added three old friends, Tormentil Grant, rather more controlled but in no way subdued, and Tazy and Karen from Switzerland, anxious to learn to dance to the tunes that Karen had learned from her friend. Because of accommodation problems, the Abbey group share their large room, a dormitory in a small school for girls, with the Torment and a 'real' person, disguised under the name of 'Miss Newcastle' and identified by Monica Godfrey as Catherine Ord.

The impact of the vacation school on the Hamlet Club is yet another story that is related over and over again in later books. Suffice it to say that the faults in their dancing are pointed out and corrected, their knowledge of the traditions behind the dances is increased, they learn new dances and new kinds of dances—this is their first introduction to sword-dancing—and, incidentally, Joan and Cicely meet their future husbands.

The account of the vacation school itself, the classes, lectures, demonstrations, buns and milk at break, parties at the end of the week, is lively and attractive because it is 'real'. Indeed EJO wrote at least one article on folk dancing for girls, which was published in *Every Girl's Annual* and reads so like the relevant chapters in the book that one wonders which came first. This must have been one of the reasons why many girls who read the book developed an interest in folk dancing and possibly went ahead and joined the EFDSS.

In amongst classes, dancing and learning, the Abbey party visit neighbouring beauty spots, Joan and Cicely dance and go on excursions with two young men, one an acquaintance of Cicely's from Ceylon, the other a newly returned Army Officer introduced to Joan by the Pixie. Joan's romance proceeds smoothly, Cicely suffers from nervous pride, and the others have to learn to cope with this. Jen also discovers the identity of the mysterious stranger who had criticised her dancing.

Joy, who, in spite of being the same age as Joan, has no romantic inclinations as yet, has recently taken to riding a motor bike with sidecar and has brought this with her to Cheltenham. The two young men also possess this form of transport and with three such vehicles careering madly around, there is bound to be an accident! This is due to Joy's carelessness but the chief victim is Jen and, for an agonised chapter, we do not know if she will ever walk again. This chapter is headed 'When Joy Grew Up', and it illustrates one of EJO's favourite themes, described by Cadogan and Craig as 'the effectiveness of guilt as a means of controlling wilfulness or egotism'. EJO herself describes the situation in this way:

It was while Jen lay suffering that Joy grew up; she was never quite so careless or thoughtless again ... Nothing ... could alter the fact ... that it was her want of care that had brought Jen to this. The knowledge had its result on her whole life.

Cheltenham College, 1991

However, Jen does recover, and the book ends with a meeting of the Hamlet Club, whose dancing has now improved, at which a recovered Jen enjoys the spectacle of Cicely and Joan presenting their future husbands to the Club.

Patience Joan, Outsider was published in the same year by Cassell. We are back with the so-called 'School of Ups and Downs' on the Sussex coast and, as in the previous book about the school, a lot of space is taken up with exploring differences between Camp Fire and Girl Guides. Although this was published four years after *The School of Ups and Downs*, which is still known by the nickname dreamed up by one of the boys, the events in it take place the following year and, probably for this reason, the War is talked about in rather vague terms. In the report about the work of the Camp Fire and the Guides, mention is made of service given at the VAD hospital, entertaining wounded soldiers and sending 'a parcel of knitted comforts to the local men in France'. However, when Miss Helen, now Mrs Macgregor, appears at the end of the book and her husband is described as still being abroad, there is no suggestion that he is in danger.

Patience Joan Ordway is the central character in this book, a typical school-story heroine who arrives at the school as a new girl in the first chapter and gradually finds her place. She is never far from the centre of the story, and this is one EJO book that comes near to being a typical school story of the period. Patience Joan is a new character in EJO's books, and she is an original one at that. She is fourteen, slim, not tall, and, most unusually for the period, her hair is short with 'thin little curls round her head'. On her first appearance, she wears a plain short dress of 'drab dun brown' with a wide white collar and smooth white cuffs. Motherless and with her father in Africa, she has been brought up by

73

Each as she knelt repeated a verse.
(*Patience Joan, Outsider*)

her strict Quaker grandmother, Mrs Pennyfold. Like her grandmother, Patience has very decided views, and announces her disapproval of both Guides and Camp Fire soon after her arrival at the school. When she first meets them, she explains to her horrified fellow pupils that she feels they are being bribed to do things they would not otherwise do by being given 'jam for the powder' as she describes it. She criticises the reward systems of badges and honours, the Camp Fire for its sentimentality and the Guides for their militarism. To some extent the effect of these forthright opinions is softened because each group of girls has been harbouring similar thoughts about the others, but has tactfully kept its views quiet until they are expressed by Patience Joan in no uncertain terms. As time goes on, however, Patience Joan comes to see the good qualities of both organisations and is a strong enough character to be able to admit her change of mind.

Another way in which Patience Joan is an outsider is that she is not allowed to swim in the sea. In the second week of term, Miss Robinson, the headmistress, announces that her sister has decided to give a medal to the best swimmer at the end of term. While they are swimming in the baths Patience Joan's performance is impressive, and she explains that her father is a fine swimmer; but she tells them that she can't go in the sea because she has promised her grandmother that she won't, and that this is because her mother drowned. However, she breaks her promise when it is a case of rescuing a gypsy child who has fallen into the sea. Samanthy comments on her thoroughness:

> 'She isn't half thorough in all she does! When she does break a promise, she smashes it all to smithereens! She doesn't just "go in the sea", like the rest of us, to enjoy herself; she jumps in, with all her clothes on, *off* the rocks, *into* deep water, *with* a rising tide, and saves somebody's life!'

When Samanthy wishes Patience was a Guide so that they would be able to say that one of 'our' Guides had risked her life to save a baby, Patience Joan says that this is 'swank', although Rowena explains it is because Samanthy feels the action would be a credit to the Guides.

When Patience Joan is at last convinced of the value of the organisations, she opts for Camp Fire, and it is her cousin, Mercy Pennyfold, who chooses to join the Guides. For the first half of the book, Mercy is a mystery character. Patience Joan is soon observed to be writing long letters in an untidy pencil scrawl to 'M Pennyfold'. The girls immediately assume that she is writing to a boy, whom they name Matthew-Mark, and Patience refuses to satisfy their curiosity. It is only when M Pennyfold reveals herself about halfway through the book as Mercy, a cousin who also lives with Grandmother but who has no father to intervene on her behalf and insist that she goes to school, that the girls—and the reader—discover the secret.

Mercy's story is woven into that of the gypsies who haunt the downs in the early part of the book, providing the baby to be rescued from the sea by Patience Joan, delaying the camping week because of possible dangers and being suspected of imminent burglary of Grandmother Pennyfold's unprotected house. A plan to give a treat and tea for the gypsy children comes to nothing, but the girls are given a chance to practise their household skills when Grandmother is called to London to nurse a sick daughter-in-law, and the housekeeper is taken ill. This event is also the means of bringing Mercy into the care of the school.

Despite their strict upbringing, neither Patience nor Mercy is above the usual schoolgirl pranks. Patience organises a midnight feast-cum-working party when she and the girls excluded from the camping expedition make gollywogs. (The pre-occupation with gollywogs in this particular book jars on today's reader, conscious of the overtones of racism.) Mercy plans a rag which spoils a Camp Fire meeting and then gets into the classic school-story situation when she disobeys orders and goes to watch the Guides compete in a major competition in the neighbouring town. Patience feels guilty for neglecting Mercy, being too wrapped up in Camp Fire matters, but her problem is solved when Miss Helen persuades Grandmother to allow Mercy to join the Guides.

Throughout her books EJO is fascinated by names. Although so many of her schools seem to lack a name, her schoolgirl characters often have several, and this preoccupation with names seems to peak in this particular book. Uncharacteristically, there is a naming of the dormitories, turning their rather unromantic letters of the alphabet into names like Peculiar (PQR). But there are also the girls—Patience Joan is known as Patty-John or P-J, Mercy as M Pennyfold, Matthew-Mark or Mercy-on-us. Much importance is also attached to the meaning and selection of Camp Fire names, and most of the girls have nicknames as well. Even the gollywogs are named. One of the chief manifestations of the Quaker element in the book is the delight in Quaker names. The girls react when they first hear the names of Patience and Mercy and later at others—'William, Sarah and Rebecca' and 'Fancy going through life as Gulielma Pennyfold! And Sally! They ought to be in a book!'

Gulielma and Sally, in fact, both appear in *The Captain of the Fifth,* which was published the same year. This links back not only to *Patience Joan, Outsider*, in which Patience has explained to her fellow pupils that if Aunt Sarah, the daughter-in-law whom Grandmother has gone to nurse, is seriously ill she will have to go to Switzerland, into the care of Dr Rennie Brown, and Grandmother will have to go with her, but indirectly to *The Abbey Girls Go Back to School,* since we now hear more of Tazy and Karen.

Basically, however, *The Captain of the Fifth* continues the story of St John's and

St Mary's. The captain of the title is Thora Erikssen, the daughter of a Norwegian father and an English mother, who has been absent from St Mary's for a term owing to an accident, but this book is really the story of Sally and Gulielma, who arrive at the school as new girls because their mother has been taken to the sanatorium on the nearby Platz. For the first chapter or so Guly is called Elma—her full name of Gulielma is apparently a female form of William, and so she is sometimes called 'Billy'. Sally is also known as 'princess'. Little is made of the Quaker connection here. Guly and Sally, sixteen and fourteen, are the idealised English schoolgirls of fiction at this period—honest, open, friendly, honourable and attractive, able to settle in and adapt quickly to any new situation.

Although the school is run on English lines, most of the girls are either half-English or not English at all, but few concessions are made to foreignness in the way their speech is represented. The food, the daily routine and so on are essentially English, and EJO made no attempt to reflect the Swiss environment in the way that Brent-Dyer was later to do with the Austrian environment in her early Chalet School books. Although passing mention is made of the mountains and other features of the landscape, there is little that ties the story to Switzerland.

The headgirls of St Mary's are Tazy Kingston and Karen Wilson, who had, of course, attended the folk dance school at Cheltenham the previous summer, and reference is made to this experience although not to their meeting with the Abbey girls, and now, the following summer term, Tazy teaches a mixed group of girls sword dances to perform at the end of term festival, at which they score a great success.

One of the interesting sub-themes in this book is the relationship between Karen Wilson and Rennie Brown, the son of Sir Rennie Brown, the great doctor who rules the Platz. Tazy has made much of this relationship to the Abbey girls. In *The Captain of the Fifth*, at the climax of the story, Karen is spending the weekend with Lady Brown (who is always referred to as Lady Rennie Brown or Lady Rennie, which surely can't be correct—although either does sound better than 'Lady Brown'). She is therefore in a position to be a key figure in the rescue operation which has to be mounted when Astrid sprains her ankle and is unable to get out of a tunnel which leads through the mountain without assistance. The Karen–Rennie relationship seems to be a very idealised one, all the more remarkable because Karen's attraction is evidently an inner rather than an outer one. She is shortsighted, quiet, small and brown-haired, and must have been a great comfort to those of EJO's readers who felt themselves unable to compete with the author's more obviously attractive characters, but easily able to identify with Karen whose virtues and appealing characteristics are all inner ones. However, this relationship is very much part of the background—perhaps wisely—although the ideally romantic relationship between Karen and her future mother-in-law should not be overlooked. It is interesting to note that Tazy's future mother-in-law also makes a brief appearance in the first chapter—'that jolly Mrs Thistleton'.

There are a number of plots in this book, linked together through the characters of Sally and Guly. In the first half of the book Sally is part of the Thora/Pauline/Claude plot while Guly is involved with the Astrid/Louisette/Nils story. Both Claude and Nils are handicapped. Claude, Pauline's elder brother, is a hunchback, and it was while he was driving that Thora and her younger sister, Freda, were involved in the accident (it was not, of course, Claude's fault—he swerved to avoid a small child) which has kept Thora away from school for a term. Now Freda, who is still not fit to return, has made Thora promise not to go in Claude's car again and not to tell the other girls that she, Freda, is afraid. Only the Pennyfold girls know of Thora's promise to her sister, and it is Sally who takes upon herself the task of telling Claude the truth and repairing the rift that has developed between Thora and Pauline.

Nils is either mentally retarded or consumptive, probably both. He is Astrid's twin, and Guly discovers that he and Astrid correspond by sending notes along a line stretched over the river that flows between the two schools. Louisette, the villain of the book, tries to blackmail Astrid into letting her use the line to get notes to Dumpy Lorimer, who appears to be the St John's equivalent of Louisette: the all-purpose villain. Just what Louisette and Dumpy get up to, or try to get up to, is never made quite clear, but in view of the silliness of some of the things that Guly and her friends do with the boys, and which are

She strode across, her eyes on the plank.
(*The Captain of the Fifth*)

apparently regarded as quite acceptable, one can only fear the worst. Louisette is moved out of the bungalow annexe because she cannot be trusted, and thus the first two plots come to an end about halfway through the book. As a climax to this part, Thora, already regarded as a heroine because of her behaviour after the car accident—when she held her little sister safe on a steep slope until rescue came—manages to increase her heroine rating by rescuing Nils from the raging river.

The letter-line is now used by Guly to develop her friendship with 'Peter', a mystery character whose identity is claimed by six boys. The resulting correspondence and the jokes played by the boys are regarded as great fun by all who become aware of them, but when Thora points out to Guly the error of her ways, she agrees that the secret notes sent across by letter-line are perhaps not very honourable. This does not, however, prevent her from joining in an even madder escapade a few days later. Sven, who proves to be *the* Peter, owns a gramophone, and he and the boys invite some of the girls over for a 'concert' when most of their seniors have gone to a real one. Pauline, left in charge of the younger girls, insists on going with them, but when two girls are caught climbing back in through their windows and the others all confess, Pauline lacks the courage to do the same.

Meanwhile Nils has not recovered from his fall into the river, but Astrid has heard of an old woman who brews herb potions up in the mountains and is convinced that one of these will save her brother. One afternoon she and Guly manage to excuse themselves from a dance practice and set off up into the mountains with old Jacques, who is also somewhat mentally retarded, although he and his twin, Jules, teach the boys carpentry and the girls woodcarving. Inevitably, there is an accident and Guly has to fetch help; it is while she is doing this that she finds Karen and Lady Rennie enjoying the quiet and idyllic picnic already mentioned.

This book is very much a book of the early 1920s, with, for example, the almost hysterical excitement about Sven's gramophone (also referred to as an 'old bus') and the slang used by the boys. The Swiss background is not particularly important to the story, apart from the slightly romantic air it provides. There is a preoccupation not only with sisters (Sally and Guly, Thora and Freda) but also with brothers (Pauline and Claude, Astrid and Nils), and with the relationships between boys and girls, indicating the different kinds of friendship that can exist in EJO's eyes. There is the serious friendship between Karen and Rennie, the light-hearted one of Sally and Sven, and the implicitly bad one between Louisette and Dumpy Lorimer. It is interesting, in passing, to note that Lorimer is exactly the kind of name that was invariably given to the villain in boys' school stories

of the period.

With her next book, *The Junior Captain*, published in the same year (1923), EJO was back once more on the Sussex coast but in a different, unnamed town, and with a new set of characters. This, like *Finding her Family*, is properly a book about girls who live at the seaside, for whom the sea and especially the beach are part of their everyday life, as opposed to the girls at the school of Ups and Downs, for whom the sea is something they visit. The Junior Captain of the title is Hildegard Svenssen, known as Gard. Her mother is dead, and her Swedish father is another sea captain, so she and her three brothers, Svante (Aunty), Torkel (Turkey) and Gregor, live with their maternal grandmother, Mrs Unwin, in a small house only minutes away from the sea. No one, so far as we know, has speculated on EJO's interest in things Scandinavian.

Lunch time at the groyne
(*The Junior Captain*)

Norwegian girls turn up in her Swiss school, and girls from Sweden or of Swedish blood appear in the retrospective Abbey books. In *The Junior Captain* the Svenssen children are all typically English girls and boys, and it is only their names and perhaps their looks that mark them out as different.

Gard is the Junior Captain at a small school called The Haven. In this nameless seaside town, based on Bognor Regis, there are two girls' schools and, unusually for EJO, they both have names. The Haven is small and is slowly running down because its headmistress is getting old and lacks capital, while the other, The Castle, is pretentious and snobbish. The Castle charges high fees and only accepts pupils 'after enquiries as to their parents' social standing have been satisfactorily answered'. Fees at The Haven are low, and any girl whose parents can afford them is accepted. On the face of it The Castle appears to be the better school, but The Haven, despite its lack of facilities, competes on equal terms in both the sports and academic fields. It is the old Hamlet Club situation again. The Castle girls are snobs and look down on the Haven girls because they play games on the sands and have picnic lunches there; they compare them to 'tripper-kids' (the ultimate insult). In return the Haven juniors give as good as they get. Neither school has many seniors, as most of the girls leave at fourteen to go to the High School in a neighbouring town. Gard's position as Junior Captain is therefore quite an important one.

Until the book opens, the differences between the two schools have not affected Gard personally, though she has taken part in the exchange of compliments, but it suddenly becomes very important when her cousin Ven (Vendela) Morris arrives to stay for three months because her mother had been ill and her father, yet another sea captain, is taking his wife for a long voyage. Gard is not exactly enthusiastic at the idea of an unknown cousin, whose arrival is sprung on her with very little warning. This is something EJO considers important—girls do not like to have their little ways upset; they have an affection for the *status quo*. But worse is to come—Ven is to go to the Castle!

It is clear that there are going to be problems, but when Ven does arrive the problems turn out to be of an unexpected kind, for Ven is one of EJO's do-ers. She is intelligent and straightforward, friendly and determined, and in this case she is determined that the rivalry between the two schools shall not prevent her from living happily with Gard and having friends at both schools. This attitude, and a few strongly spoken criticisms of both sides of the quarrel, begin to break down the barrier between the two schools. Other factors contribute. The cousin of a Castle girl goes to the Haven and is hotly defended by Gard. Then Gard rescues a Castle girl who has been cut off by the tide, and both schools unite to make a cricket match between them into a really sporting affair. Finally the book ends with the news that both schools are to close and a new school is to be opened to which all the girls will go and where, it is assumed, they will have to work and play together, forgetting old differences.

Sister and brother relationships are again considered here. Svante, Gard's eldest brother, is a thoughtful boy and understands his sister much better than their guardian grandmother does. Gard respects him and values his good opinion—he points her in the right direction and she follows his advice but only after thinking it through for herself.

Gard and Ven, cousins like Joan and Joy, seem at first sight to be a corresponding pair, but there is a difference. In their case it is the younger of the two who is the more understanding and who has had to make the sacrifice. It had been accepted that when Gard was fourteen she would go from the Haven to the High School in Eldingham. However, Ven's mother turned out to be seriously ill, and her husband, who had been extravagant, wishing his wife and daughter to have the best, cannot afford the necessary operation. Gard's father, his brother-in-law, finances the operation but this means that Gard will not be able to go on to the High School after all. Gard's sacrifice is not made voluntarily, but her acceptance of the need and, after a struggle with depression, her decision to face it bravely and not tell Ven what it has meant to her are as courageous as any of the sacrifices made by characters in other books by EJO. Ven, of course, does find out eventually, and her gratitude to Gard continues throughout her story, which is told in later books.

We have here the necessary ingredients for an average schoolgirl story—feuding schools and their reconciliation are not unknown in the genre. *The Junior Captain*, however, has a big injection of Camp Fire and folk dancing, which are introduced through a new character, Barbara Holt. Barbara appears in later books, and her character is unusually complex for a relatively minor figure. She is the younger of two sisters who live in a bungalow made up of former railway carriages on the shingle bank near the sea on the outskirts of the town. Converted buses, trams and railway carriages were a familiar sight at the seaside in the 1920s and '30s, although it is doubtful if they were generally as luxurious inside as that of the Holts seems to be. The settlement that was the real-life inspiration for this particular 'village' was still in existence when we visited it in 1997 and were lucky enough to be shown round one of the railway-carriage homes.

Barbara is as introvert as Ven is extrovert, very musical and artistic. Her sister, Audrey, attempting to explain her character, says:

'Barbara is a queer shy girl and doesn't always get on with others. She has certain ideas and certain things that mean a great deal to her and if she thinks anyone will laugh at them, she shuts up inside herself and you can't get anything out.'

Barbara has discovered Camp Fire through a story book, and her account of this is interesting. She wrote to the author and 'asked her if she could spare a moment to tell me how I could find out all about the Camp Fire'. In her reply the author said she 'was very busy with a new story and had hardly a minute, but if I'd write to an address she gave me I'd get the Manual and it would answer all my questions; and if I could find a Guardian and five other girls, there was no reason why we shouldn't have a camp'. The tone of this exchange is so much like EJO's own letters and articles that it could well be quoted from real letters received and sent.

Barbara has had a personal private Camp Fire for some time, and is also a keen folk dancer who has been to classes in London and has very high standards, but when it comes to sharing her enthusiasms and becoming part of a real Camp Fire she hesitates before agreeing. Gard and her friends have seen Barbara in her gown and playing her pipe, and have been fascinated and curious. Ven, deciding to go and look for herself, recognises the Camp Fire costume and actions and, encouraged by the fact that Barbara's elder sister is the new music mistress at the Castle, bravely writes to Barbara asking about Camp Fire. She is invited to tea, and as a result of this Barbara is asked to start a real Camp Fire; she herself is too young to be a Guardian, but Audrey is persuaded by the younger girls to take on the job. Barbara has moments of generous friendship and moments of withdrawal: not an easy character but an interesting one, and EJO clearly had plans for her as early as this.

The New Abbey Girls, also published in 1923, is yet another key book in the Abbey saga. It was only the fourth Abbey story (and the fifth about the Hamlet Club) to be published and now, eighty years later, after all the retrospective books have been published, it is difficult to see this book as the girls reading it at the time it first appeared must have seen it. Even if they had read all the earlier books, they would have a relatively limited knowledge of the 'old' Abbey girls, although the characters of both Joy and Jen were well established.

Basically there is little plot, and it is a book that is concerned with ideas rather than action, but it does lay firm foundations for the rest of the series, introducing two new characters who are to play major roles in the future, and initiating the idea of girls coming to the Abbey and becoming part of the family. EJO had by this time created an imaginatively romantic environment for the Abbey, set picturesquely in the Chilterns, and had established the pattern of the May Day festival with the crowning of a Queen. However, if the story was to continue she needed to introduce some new adolescent characters with whom her young girl readers could identify.

The previous Abbey book, *The Abbey Girls Go Back to School*, ended with Joan and Cicely introducing their future husbands to the Hamlet Club at a party held early in the New Year. *The New Abbey Girls* opens the day after

'Isn't it nice to see you here.'
(*The New Abbey Girls*)

Joan's wedding in March of the same year. It is surprising that EJO gives so little attention to actual wedding ceremonies in view of the loving care with which she describes the coronations. Cicely gives only one week's notice of her wedding, Joan can have had little time for preparation, yet these girls were from a social class where a reasonable period of engagement and a lavish wedding would have been the order of the day. Why did EJO, with her love of colour and ceremony, not make more of her opportunities where weddings were concerned? In *The World of Elsie Jeanette Oxenham* Monica Godfrey tells us that Doris Acland had explained to her EJO's feeling that weddings and funerals were purely private occasions, and that when she did include details about weddings it was to satisfy some of her younger readers.

With Joan married, it was obvious that some new element was required if the series was to continue. Jen and Joy fooling about was not enough to sustain it, and the secret/treasure themes probably seemed to have been played out by this stage. Two important things do concern Joy in this book: she has acquired a car which gives her more scope for movement away from the Abbey, and the man whom she eventually marries makes a brief appearance. However, if the Abbey were to be the central factor holding the series together, new characters had to be brought into its orbit. It was no longer a series of stories about schoolgirls. With a school as the central feature, there is every excuse for introducing new characters in each new title in the series; with a ruined abbey it is more difficult, and EJO needed schoolgirls with a reason for living there. This is the point at which the concept of the Abbey as a place of sanctuary becomes important, and the 'new' Abbey girls who find sanctuary there serve the purpose very well. Rosamund Kane is fifteen, Madalena di Ravarati a year younger, and they both turn up, metaphorically speaking, on the Abbey doorstep just when Joy and Jen seem to have time on their hands after the excitement of Joan's wedding.

Maidlin, as Madalena is known, is one of EJO's heiresses, the product of a romantic marriage between the maid in a large house and a visiting Italian. Her mother had died many years before and, although her father has maintained an interest in her upbringing, she has been brought up by one of her mother's sisters in Cumberland. She is now staying, temporarily, with another aunt, Ann Watson, the caretaker of the Abbey, when it is learned that, owing to an accident of will-making, she is due to inherit the estates of her rich Italian grandfather. It is clear to her aunt that Maidlin needs a different kind of upbringing to fit her for her new responsibilities and Joy is asked to provide it. Maidlin's pride at first makes her resentful of the situation, but she settles down to the new regime fairly quickly, with only a slight setback when she is jealous of Rosamund, an even newer arrival in the Abbey household.

Rosamund is a complete contrast to Maidlin both in looks—she is fair, whereas Maidlin is dark—and temperament, but, most importantly, and unlike many of EJO's characters, she achieves success through natural ability and determination. She epitomises 'the great American dream', the heroine who achieves through her own ability, and as such she is an entirely suitable heroine for the early 1920s. Miss Macey asks Joy to have her to live at the Hall because the town air does not suit her, but there is little that is unhealthy about Rosamund. Although she looks a little pale when Joy first sees her, her eyes are bright, her face is eager and she is not at all shy. She has many of Jen's characteristics, but is more independent. Like Jen, she is a thinking and thoughtful person, easy-going and well adjusted, and she is immediately on good terms with Jen and Joy, much to Maidlin's chagrin, although she can appreciate Maidlin's feelings. Her election as Queen of the Hamlet Club is unsurprising and makes an appropriate climax to this book. Rosamund's parents are abroad and little is said about them, although they are later to emerge as some of the most important parents in EJO's books in the way in which they serve as catalysts for plots. Motherless Maidlin's father dies bravely at the end of *The New Abbey Girls*, and Joy adopts both girls as 'twin daughters'.

However, this is primarily a book of ideas, the dominating theme being that one must share one's good fortune with those less fortunate than oneself and try to improve their quality of life. To give money is not enough, one must also give one's time and effort. In her approach to storytelling, EJO adopts something of the traditional fairy-tale approach, concentrating on the rich and the poor, with very little said about the mass of people in between, the class to which most of her readers must have belonged. Even teachers are portrayed as 'working too hard; dancing all through their holidays—and the school holidays are short enough when you've fifty infants in your class all the year round—because they could get a better position if they had their certificates … going back tired with the hard work in the holidays'. The poverty and drabness of London's East End, brightened, it seems, only by folk dancing, are in sharp contrast to the richness and colour of life at the Abbey.

As a result of her experiences at Cheltenham the previous summer, Joy has decided that she must use her inheritance wisely, and Jen becomes her enthusiastic supporter in all this. This book is dedicated to Cecil Sharp, who once again appears in its pages as The Prophet, and EJO herself appears as 'the Writing Person' on two occasions when Joy and Jen go to classes and a party in London. After the first occasion, Joy buys one of EJO's books for Maidlin, evidently *The School of Ups and Downs* since there is subsequently a conversation about Grey Edward, the cat, and Camp Fire. All this reinforces the view that this is one of EJO's more significant books. Because it is a book of ideas, it lent itself to what might be described as 'Children's Press treatment', and a very much abridged edition, with much of the discussion removed, appeared in the 1960s.

EJO's second and last published historical novel, *The Girls of Gwynfa,* was published by Warne in 1924. True to her ideas, she again writes from the Puritan point of view, but the events of this novel predate those described in *Mistress Nanciebel,* and take place at the very beginning of the Civil War, beginning just after the Battle of Edgehill in 1642.

Although most of the action takes place in Wales, on the Lleyn peninsula, the original home of the Dane family is in Buckinghamshire, where 'Mr John Hampden was a near neighbour and talked much with father as they walked and talked together'. EJO's hero is the hero of her main characters. The argument, carefully and clearly put, is that of the early Puritan party who had no idea of disloyalty to the King himself but considered that 'there were things even a King must not do and rights which even he must respect'. There is no fanatical Puritanism in this book, and emphasis is always laid on regret for what civil war is doing to the country and the people. The way that civil war can divide families is illustrated by the two brothers, Geoffrey and Edmund, who have taken different sides in the conflict and, after heated words on both sides, have become estranged because of a letter that has gone astray, a not unusual occurrence in war-time.

'You do not understand. I am Owen Madoc—'
(*The Girls of Gwynfa*)

The story of the girls of Gwynfa is narrated by Maisry Dane, the eldest girl of the family. EJO wrote only three books in the first person, and in each case the narrator is an older girl who has some responsibility for the younger children; this is the 'elder sister' theme which she seems to like. Maisry has a great deal of responsibility. She, her younger sisters, Betty and Moll, and a younger brother, Jack, have been sent for safety into Wales, where their mother has inherited her family's house in the Lleyn. Mrs Dane has taken the children there but, having established them in her old home, she has returned to England to be with her husband who is fighting for Parliament. This reflects a middle-class convention that EJO takes for granted in her modern books—a wife's place is with her husband, and she will always leave her children, except for very young babies, to be with him. Less well-off mothers, of course, could not afford boarding schools and did not have friends or relatives with large nurseries and well-trained staff.

So Maisry, aged seventeen, has the responsibility for the house and servants, her own sister and brother, old Nurse who is feeble and ill, and to these are added two cousins, Lady Margaret and Lady Penelope, known as Lady Peg and Lady Pen, who also come from England for refuge. Lady Peg is a little younger than Maisry but she is a child-bride, married to a husband whom she has not seen since their marriage. Their branch of the family are Royalist supporters, but the girls do not allow this to make any differences between them and, in fact, in their later dangerous situation, the two Royalist girls join willingly in the Sunday Bible reading and study in which Maisry leads her little family.

However, the position of the English girls in Wales is not as secure as their parents had hoped it would be. Surrounded by Welsh-speaking peasants whom they cannot understand, and by Welsh gentry who are wholeheartedly Royalist, they are very vulnerable. The greatest threat is posed by Madoc of Plas Madoc, a local landowner, who also considers that he has some title to the Gwynfa estate. Having first lured away their servants, he or his followers set fire to the house, and it is only because their suspicions have already been aroused that the children escape. They live in hiding, first in the cellar-kitchen of the house, which escaped the fire, and later in a cave out in the bay. Maisry, as the responsible one, takes careful thought for the others, and they are also helped by Owen and Deiza, the son and daughter of Madoc, who do not support their father's treatment of defenceless children. Deiza is openly rebellious but Owen, out of loyalty to his father, refuses to admit his father's responsibility.

The younger children react very naturally to their situation, alternately afraid and excited, frightened of the cave in the dark but paddling happily in the sea and playing on the beach in front of the cave. This is particularly true of Betty, in her way the most interesting character and certainly the one with whom most of EJO's schoolgirl readers would identify. Betty is a tomboy, brave, impulsive and loyal, and she shares the narration of the story with her elder sister. She also has the habit of interpreting for the family pets as Marjorie, the Beaver, does for Grey Edward in *The School of Ups and Downs*.

The other interesting child is Lady Penelope, a shy silent little girl who communicates very little with other people but has a gift for dealing with animals. This type of girl is later to occur in the modern books as Elspeth of the Rose and Squirrel in *The Abbey Girls on Trial*, but is a curiosity rather than a character that can be developed. Elspeth becomes an ordinary young woman while Lady Pen comes out of her shell when she acquires a niece.

The story has its fair share of excitements. Betty and Deiza rescue a man from the sea

Llanengan Church, which the girls of Gwynfa sometimes attended, 1990

after a shipwreck. He proves to be Lord Edmund, the Puritan brother-in-law of Lady Peg, who has in fact come in search of them all, rumours of their dangerous situation having reached England. Their danger increases when Madoc returns, realises that the children are still alive and searches for them. Owen is caught and beaten but refuses to betray them; Deiza—she is only a girl, of course—proves to be less brave and reveals their hiding place.

The end of the story is dramatic. Madoc attempts to reach the cave but is thwarted by the weather. On his second attempt his boat is dashed against the rocks, and he and his men are killed. Meanwhile Lord Geoffrey arrives to rescue his wife, and a concluding chapter marries off the eligible characters, Maisry and Edmund, and Betty and Owen, and provides Lady Peg with a baby.

One other feature that *The Girls of Gwynfa* has in common with *Mistress Nanciebel* is the use of star-lore. Maisry tells the other children stories about the constellations to distract them from their fears and the younger ones accept the idea enthusiastically. It is interesting to speculate why EJO seems to have associated star-lore with this part of Wales in particular—it features little elsewhere in her work. Perhaps the Dunkerleys tended to stargaze when they were in this part of the world. If so there is a connection with the present, as it was stated in 2003 that parts of Wales are now some of the few places in the British Isles where one has a clear view of the night sky, views elsewhere having been affected by pollution.

The historical background gives *The Girls of Gwynfa* a good sense of period, but the basic elements are much the same as in many of EJO's modern books. Her two published historical novels are, however, worthy of a special comment here. They are both set during the English Civil War and its aftermath, and in the great heyday of girls' annuals and bumper books, between the two wars, a 'Civil War' story was an almost obligatory feature of such volumes, while Angela Brazil more than once included such a story, either told as a legend or acted out by modern schoolgirls as a play, within her full-length stories. Usually, however, the viewpoint is that of brave Royalist girls who help the King directly or indirectly, and EJO's sympathy with the Puritan view is rarely found in the work of other authors of the period. It does, however, feature in Captain Marryat's *The Children of the New Forest* (1847), and some of the incidents in both EJO's Civil War books have overtones of the nineteenth century boys' adventure stories with their Crusoe theme of landing in a strange country and fending for oneself. This perhaps accounts for the choice of the Lleyn as the setting for both books—*Mistress Nanciebel* in the area along the north coast, *The Girls of Gwynfa* on the southernmost tip, near the great bay of Porth Neigl. The historical context combined with this location made it possible to write a convincing and realistic Crusoe adventure story for girls, with girls as the central characters, fighting for survival.

To schoolgirl readers in 1924, accustomed to 'St Monica's' or 'The Gables', the title of *The School Without a Name* must have been intriguing, although the Nina K Brisley illustrations and the characteristic Chambers production are typical of the period. In fact, as has already been suggested, the naming of her fictional schools was not one of EJO's strong points, and the rather brilliant idea behind the naming of Gregory's is most unusual, so it is not surprising that attention is drawn to this feature in the title. The headmistress of the school is Miss Angel, and Berry suggests that girls are sent to Miss Angel's school to lose their angles—'Not Angles but Angels', as Pope Gregory said. It is typical of EJO not to use the original Latin version.

The School Without a Name is the second book about Gard Svenssen to be published, and quite a lot of *The Junior Captain*, in which she was the heroine, can be deduced from it. One of EJO's recurring problems is demonstrated—her inability to settle on her heroine. It seems almost as if her mind was such a teeming mass of characters interlinking with each other that she was unable to build a complete story around just one of them. To a very large extent this book is the story of Beryl Blaydon (Berry or Blackberry), although she is missing from the climax of the story—the expedition to the Downs when a girl is injured—and soon after the beginning Gard Svenssen emerges as a major figure.

The Castle and the Haven schools, rivals in *The Junior Captain*, have both closed down, and Miss Angel has established a new school, taking pupils from both. Quite a lot of detail is given about the problems of setting up a school of this kind; Miss Angel is using an inheritance to fulfil her lifelong ambition of establishing a school in her home town. She comes over as a very real person, someone who realises the problems of the situation, who knows her girls and talks to them with sympathy and understanding. In contrast with the precision of detail about the finances of the new school, some of the domestic arrangements seem a little vague. As there is yet no boarding house, the girls who do not live locally in the seaside town are boarded out in private houses. This was not an unusual situation in the 1920s when 'school buses' were unknown and public transport timetables did not meet everyone's requirements, but the fact that Elizabeth, a Scottish girl, has spent only one night with two old ladies before she has to be found new accommodation because a third sister wants to come and live with them seems like a blatant piece of plot manipulation.

However, it enables five girls—Berry, Elizabeth, Monica, Rita and Molly—to establish themselves firmly as a gang on the first day, before the situation is made more complex by the discovery that not only is Elizabeth now to board at Gard's home, but that this is next to the house where Berry and Monica board with Suzanne Thorne and her mother. Seventeen-year-old Suzanne and her friend Marjory Angus, who is eighteen, represent the fourth strand in the new school, the girls who have previously gone to the high school in the cathedral city of Eldingham (in reality Chichester) seven miles away. Seventeen and eighteen may seem to be rather old to be transferring to a new school, but EJO accounts for this by explaining that the High School was much too full and had a waiting list, so it seemed only fair that those girls who could should go to school in their own town. Examinations did not loom so large in the early 1920s, and it is a convenient way of providing experienced senior girls for the new school.

'Oh!' squealed Monica. 'It's coming back again!'
(*The School Without a Name*)

One of the things that EJO seems to have had in mind for this book was to explore the effect of environment on five girls of roughly the same age—thirteen. Berry has five brothers and a small sister of six months and has been sent to school 'to get used to girls'. Monica is an only child and is used to being consulted by, and discussing things with, her parents. Molly is the eldest of seven girls, Rita the middle girl of three, while Elizabeth is the youngest in the family, and all her brothers and sisters are grown up. There is much discussion about families and their effect on the girls, but the action does not really arise from any characteristics the girls may have developed as a result. EJO perhaps recognised the limitations of this theme at an early stage, having raised the matter as a result of her own experiences in a large family of children.

Be that as it may, Chapter 4 is named for Gard, 'Hildegard of the Haven'. The more Berry hears about Gard, who has been painted in an unfavourable light by Molly and Rita, who were previously at the Castle School, the more she is attracted to her, partly because she is apparently one of a family of boys; and she is wildly jealous (in a perfectly nice way, of course) when she hears that Elizabeth is to board with the Svenssens. Rita and Molly are alarmed when they observe this growing attraction, and Rita reminds Berry that 'we said we'd try to keep together'.

When they get back to the Thorne house on their first evening, Berry and Monica do not yet know that Gard lives next door, and nor does the reader. In fact the reader has been deliberately misled, because she has been told that Gard and Elizabeth can go home via the beach but at this stage no mention is made of the fact that such a route is possible for Berry and Monica as well. While the latter are getting ready for tea, a butterfly net is pushed across the gap between the two houses, from one upper room to the other, and three toys are sent across, obviously chosen and labelled by someone who knows something about the girls at the Thorne house, and purporting to be from Aunty, Turkey and Greg, which names subsequently transpire to be the nicknames of Gard's three brothers, Svante, Torkel and Gregor. In fact, the joke has been perpetrated by Gard and Elizabeth, and it is not until the following morning that Berry and Monica learn of the relationship between the three boys and Gard.

The Svenssens are, of course, of Viking stock, and it seems that Viking stock had a special appeal for EJO, it appears so frequently in her books— although it is mainly a case of names and looks, and seems to be tied in with EJO's frequent choice of the sea as a career for adult male characters—the Svenssens' father is yet another sailor. Despite their names and their Swedish father, the Svenssen boys protest that they are English.

Berry soon has to decide what to do about the Haven/Castle rivalry. Gard says that if they're to be friends at home, they must also be friends at school. Rita realises that Berry is too strong a character to be diverted from her liking for Gard and, although she and Molly make it clear that they don't approve of Berry's taste, they have to accept defeat on this point. The discussion of snobbery and the gradual breaking down of snobbish attitudes is, as already pointed out in discussion of *The Junior Captain*, reminiscent of *Girls of the Hamlet Club*.

When Berry learns that Gard is a member of the Camp Fire movement, she reveals that she has always wanted to join, and she has to make another decision. She could be fitted into the Shingle Beach Camp but many of the other girls want to join and there is not enough room for them all. Berry is a great one for going to the top to get results—she has already approached Miss Angel successfully on the matter of playing cricket on the new playing field—and she now goes to Miss Angel to ask her to find a Guardian for them. Berry is the kind of girl who can establish a good relationship with adults quite easily, and throughout the book she is developing her diplomatic skills, facing a succession of very real problems, unconscious of her powers of leadership until she is asked by Miss Angel to become the Junior Captain.

Miss Angel identifies Marjory Angus as a suitable Guardian. Marjory is very much a reflection of the period; her father, she tells Miss Angel, feels very strongly 'about it being wrong for girls who can afford to live at home to take jobs from girls who need them … there are too many teachers for the jobs already, everyone says. I mustn't take one of the places …'

The new Camp Fire is launched, the two Camps decide to combine to produce an ambitious pageant, and it is this that brings about the final reconciliation of the two groups. By this time Berry has been appointed Lower School Captain while Christine Haynes, formerly Captain at the Haven, has become Captain of the Upper School. The two Captains have been given silver girdles, which Miss Angel has fortuitously brought back from Rome, the city of Gregory.

On the day of the Pageant, Rita and Molly go up to the Downs to get some special flowers for Rita's wreath. Gard, Freda and Berry have planned a long walk in the same area but Berry, summoned by Miss Angel, has had to withdraw from the plan. Inevitably someone is going to have an accident or miss a bus! And, of course, the inevitable happens. Gard and Freda are returning in good order when they see Rita calling for help—Molly has fallen and cut her leg badly. One girl can catch the bus and get home in time for the pageant, the other two must help Molly. Although Freda hadn't particularly wanted to be in it, both Gard and Rita are very much looking forward to it, but it is Rita who has the vital part so Gard decides to stay and help Molly, while Rita catches the bus and arrives home in time to take her place in the pageant.

Gard's selfless behaviour finally convinces Rita of her worth, and Rita, full of gratitude, apologises to Gard and wants to be friends. The scene of reconciliation culminates in the dancing of Sellenger's Round with Gard and Rita in the middle of the

Nobody seemed to be thinking of her at all.
(*The Abbey Girls Again*)

circle and then, horrified, escaping. At the very end, after Berry has suggested Gregory's as the name of the new school and the idea has been accepted by Miss Angel, Berry takes Gard to see GREGORY'S painted on the gate pillars, and one of the few EJO schools to have a real name has a very distinctive one indeed.

Also published in 1924, *The Abbey Girls Again* is, like *The New Abbey Girls*, a book of ideas rather than happenings, and this too received the Children's Press treatment, appearing in an abridged edition in 1959. Although Joy's romance reaches a further stage, there is little in the way of plot. The book does, however, develop themes that have already been introduced in earlier books: the need to share with the less fortunate and the adoption of new characters into the Abbey family. Both of these contribute to the rescue and rehabilitation of someone who is to become another key figure in the Abbey series, Mary-Dorothy Devine.

Mary is thirty, works in an office in London and spends her evening darning and daydreaming. With her lives her younger sister, Bridget (Biddy), aged fifteen, who went to a good school and is now studying at a commercial college. The sisters are orphans, like the Grant sisters in *The School Torment*, and, like Dorothy Grant, Mary has accepted responsibility for her much younger sister but feels that she has failed in it. Biddy finds life with Mary dull, as what fifteen-year-old would not, so spends her evenings at the pictures with unsuitable friends, who encourage her to use make-up and wear grown-up clothes. Mary argues ineffectually and, when she fails to influence Biddy, resigns herself to her daydreaming.

All this changes with the advent of Jen Robins, who first meets Mary in the office where she has gone on business for her father. Jen sweeps into the office, her hands full of violets, which she gives to the quiet typist who looks at them with longing. This is yet another famous occasion that is to be quoted many times in subsequent books. Mary is attracted by Jen's happy personality, but Jen has also noticed Mary and makes an excuse to visit her again. Helped by Joy, she introduces her to folk dancing at the London classes of the English Folk Dance Society, at a children's party in Plaistow run by the Pixie and finally in a class of her own. Biddy is drawn into these activities and the sisters now share an enthusiasm that improves their life together.

The new interests also revive Mary's desire to write. Her father had been a journalist, but when as a young girl she had tried to write, and had shown him her work, his criticisms had been so discouraging that she had given up. This blow to her ambition is such an important part of Mary's story that EJO describes it in some detail:

> It had happened so simply. She had a vivid imagination inherited from her father. She had tried to write down her dreams, but he had told her plainly that she was on the wrong lines and was producing nothing that could be published. To change all her way of thought and become practical in her imagining had been too difficult and troublesome. She had kept the dreams, but had kept them for herself alone. Whenever the outer world was dull, or when problems were too hard, Mary lapsed into her dream-world and was happy.

It seems likely that EJO had known, or known of, girls who took refuge from the real world in daydreaming. She was very much aware of the dangers of this habit—apart from making them very dull people to know, there is a real danger of mental deterioration—because the topic occurs elsewhere in her books, with Mary always as the prime example. It is, of course, not unusual for adolescent girls to live in a fantasy world and one wonders if some of her readers recognised their own symptoms.

A visit to the Abbey also contributes to Mary's awakening. This takes place the week after Rosamund's coronation, thus placing the action of this book as being during and after the events of *The New Abbey Girls*. It is during this stay that Mary confesses her failures and daydreaming to Joy and Jen. Anxious to help and aware of their inexperience, they once again consult the Pixie. Mary also gets help and encouragement from the Writing Person (EJO herself), who encourages her to take up folk dancing although Mary feels she is too old: 'It's a tremendous help to one's work, too, you know … If you do any work that needs imagination, all this helps intensely.' Through Jen, she also gets advice on how to take up her writing again.

The system does not quite succeed with Biddy, although she becomes great friends with Rosamund and Maidlin; she still makes remarks that are not in the best of 'Abbey' taste, although they are quite natural for a girl of her age in her situation. This flaw in Biddy's character is to be developed in later books. During the visit to the Abbey, the three younger girls are involved in an escapade that brings Andrew Marchwood back into the picture. The girls trespass in the Manor grounds and Maidlin is nearly drowned in the lake. Andrew saves her life and Joy is heard to say 'He's a dear!'. This book, therefore, marks yet another stage in the Abbey saga. Ideas are developed, new members are added to the Abbey circle and Joy's romance moves a step further on. Most importantly, the Abbey provides a sanctuary for Mary and brings about a major change in her life.

Throughout the 1920s EJO contributed short stories and, in one year, a serial to the *British Girl's Annual*. This annual, published by Cassell and edited by Eric Wood, included the work of many of the leading girls' writers of the time—Ethel Talbot, Dorita Fairlie Bruce, Bessie Marchant and May Wynne, for example, all contributed to the 1921/22 volume. Volumes seem to have appeared at the end of the year but were dated for the following year, and the publishers obviously visualised that they would be given as Christmas presents. EJO used all kinds of schools as backgrounds to the stories that she contributed; most of them are linked to each other or to full-length books that were subsequently published.

Dancing Honour (1921) and *Honour Your Partner* (1923) are stories set in the same school and about the same characters, although the events in the second apparently take place before those in the first to be published. This fact, taken together with the evidence of other stories that are known to have been recycled, suggests that they may have been part of a longer, full-length book that was never published. As the titles suggest, both stories are about folk dancing, reflecting EJO's very active interest in all its aspects at this period.

In *Honour Your Partner*, Hilary Branson is a visiting teacher for folk dancing and gym at a nameless boarding school. She and her class plan for them to perform a sword dance at a big schools' competition, but she is taken ill and Janice, a girl new to the school that term but who has had the advantage of having been to a Cheltenham school, takes over and teaches the dance to the class. Needless to state, they win the competition and, more importantly, Janice has contrived to heal a rift in the friendship of two other girls, Ruth and Margaret.

In *Dancing Honour* Margaret has a crush on Hilary Branson. There is to be a display on which the latter's future depends—if the girls she has taught manage to impress the 'great authority on folk-dancing' who is to witness the display, Hilary will be more likely to get an important London post for which she has applied. Margaret is upset to hear of the likely departure of her beloved teacher. She is a good dancer and knows that the success of the display depends to a large extent on her; shall she break—or pretend to break—an ankle? Her better nature triumphs, but she is then given a cast-iron excuse for absenting herself when she is summoned to her sister's wedding. However, she decides to sacrifice this and dance in the display, which is, of course, a great success. Hilary Branson gets the new job and Margaret is offered a scholarship to study at the same college in due course. These two stories do not really stand up to close examination, either in the circumstantial detail or in their relationship to each other.

In between these two short stories, the 1922 volume contained a 'long complete school story', a regular feature of the annual, by EJO. This was *Tickles and the Talking Cave*, which was published as a full-length book by Partridge in 1924, with the title, *"Tickles", or The School that was Different.* (Partridge published only one other book by EJO, *Peggy Makes Good*, which also had links with the *British Girl's Annual.*) The text of the story about Tickles as it appeared in the annual differs little from the text of the book, although the book is somewhat shorter than the other books that EJO was producing at this period; a cursory check revealed one paragraph, the last paragraph of Chapter 6, which appears in the book but not in the annual. Its title makes it a particularly appropriate book on which to finish this chapter.

Tickles is set at Rocklands School, which had first appeared in *A Go-Ahead Schoolgirl* in 1919. Tickles, short for Tekla, is the young cousin of Philippa Morgan, a fairly minor character in the earlier book who has now left school. Tickles is very much the central character, all the events being seen from her point of view. She is a typical EJO junior schoolgirl, only twelve, but full of bouncy cheerfulness, good-natured, independent and strictly honourable.

Tickles arrives at Rocklands by a rather circuitous route, and one feels that EJO perhaps started writing this story without much idea of how it was going to work out. It should, of course, be noted that strictly speaking it is not Rocklands School—Miss Maitland's school is based in Sheffield, and the reason that it is different is that every summer term it moves to Rocklands, the lovely house on the moors owned by Miss Maitland's young widowed sister, Sheila Thorburn. Tekla's home is in the south of England, and she has been sent north to spend the summer with her aunt because her mother is going home to Sweden—another Scandinavian link here—on a long visit; there is no mention of a father. Country bred, she hates the idea of spending the summer in Sheffield, a smoky, dreary town, which she regards as the last place on earth. Her aunt has offered to take her in and send her to 'a very good school', but in fact puts very little effort into the enterprise, for no sooner has Tekla arrived than she is packed off to school for the last few days of term because the aunt and Philippa are off on a trip to Europe and suddenly speed up their departure, leaving Tickles at her new school, with the prospect of spending the Easter holidays there in the company of the headmistress.

It is perhaps just as well that Tickles is so very resilient, because no sooner has she adjusted to this idea, and decided that Miss Maitland will be a pleasant companion, than Miss Maitland announces that she is off to the seaside and that Tickles is to spend Easter at a cottage near Rocklands—in fact the Morrell cottage—in the care of Mrs Thynne. At last Tickles is settled. During the holidays she meets Rena and Lisabel and is introduced to the mysterious cave which, because of the lie of the surrounding rocks, gives away any secrets spoken within it. This discovery proves useful in her efforts to improve the tone of the school, a task with which she has been entrusted by Philippa.

With Chris McLean, Philippa, Rena, Nancy and Elsa all having left the school, the 'top' First form now includes Teesa Courtney and Betty McLean. Teesa, of course, is one of EJO's villains, well established as thoroughly unpleasant in the first book, but for the past term Head of the school. Fortunately in this school the position of Head is rotated, and Betty McLean takes over for the summer term, a position naturally not made easier for her by the fact that Teesa, having tasted the delights of power, is still in the school. The other juniors class all the seniors together as useless and it is only Tekla, alerted by her cousin, who recognises Betty's worth. She is very reluctant to join the other juniors in the SSS, Squashing Seniors Society, and they, led by Margot and Babbles, are torn between admiration for her independent spirit and resentment at its results.

Teesa tricks the juniors, who are unaware of the properties of the talking cave, into using it for discussing secrets—Tickles has been sworn to secrecy by Rena and Lisabel—and Margot and the other juniors think that Tickles has given them away. When Tickles sees Teesa, Vera and Fanny creeping out to a midnight feast, she guesses that they are going to the cave, and although schoolgirl honour prevents her from sneaking when she sees Betty following them, it allows her to show Betty where they are.

This incident, coupled with good advice from Rena, leads Betty to appeal to both juniors and seniors to pull together for the sake of the school and to forget past events. Teesa is persuaded to agree for the sake of her small invalid brother, Wriggles, who doesn't like things to go wrong in the school. (He is away in the south and doesn't appear in person in this book.) So all ends well.

In this chapter, therefore, we have seen through EJO's eyes all kinds of schools—Miss Macey's, which moves to the Abbey for a term; St John's and St Mary's schools in Switzerland; the folk-dancing vacation school in Cheltenham; the School of Ups and Downs; the Castle and the Haven schools in Sussex, which then combine to become Gregory's; the school that was different because it moved to Rocklands each summer; and the nameless school that features in the two short stories. Although the reader is never told how many girls there are at any of the schools (and some of them must be very small), EJO manages to create a convincingly real impression of them—juniors, seniors and staff are all created as real people, and already we can see the linking of books and series which is such a major feature of her work and possibly accounts for a large part of its appeal.

Chapter 5

ALL KINDS OF PROBLEMS, 1925 TO 1928

By the beginning of 1925, EJO was forty-four, well established as one of the leading writers in one of the most popular genres, school stories for girls, she had published thirty books and was regularly invited to contribute to annuals and collections. She was a Camp Fire Guardian, had a good working knowledge of the much more popular Girl Guide movement, and was active in the doings of the English Folk Dance Society. Although the income from her books was unlikely to have been great if, as Mary Dorothy Devine does, she sold the copyright in them outright, it must have provided her with money to travel abroad and visit the places that she describes in loving detail in her books. She had also developed an almost late twentieth/early twenty-first century concern with folk arts, being a great admirer of hand-made pottery and hand-woven materials, and it is interesting to speculate just how much influence she has had in the field—on, for example, the middle-aged and elderly ladies who support these active craft workers at the present time!

EJO's wider knowledge, however, seems to have been somewhat limited. For example, when she moves into the realms of ballet and music her descriptions lack the detail that is an essential part of her descriptions of folk dancing and places. By this time, her interest was already moving towards the portrayal of characters with problems, and the title of *Patience and Her Problems* (1927) provides a useful indication of the concerns that seem to have been predominant in her mind during the next period, 1925 to 1928. Through the EFDS she had come to know D C Daking, who is portrayed as the Pixie in her books and who seems to have had a gift for, and interest in, solving the problems of her friends and acquaintances. The Abbey girls all have a very high regard for the Pixie's skills in this respect, and this may well reflect EJO's own admiration.

Published in 1925, *The Abbey Girls in Town* is dedicated to Margaret Bayne Todd, who is presumably the Margaret who appears in the story, accompanying the Writing Person, her Camp Fire Guardian, to the vacation dancing school in Chelsea during the Christmas holidays. Thus EJO herself, as the Writing Person, again appears in fiction, although it seems likely that Mary-Dorothy, having been given the good advice that starts her on a successful writing career, is about to take over the role of an idealised and romanticised portrait of EJO. Margaret Bayne Todd, incidentally, was destined to become Lady Simey, and during the early 1980s frequently featured in the media as Chairman of the Liverpool Police Authority. Television appearances suggested that she had become exactly the kind of person one might have expected from her fictional persona half a century earlier; she tended not to use her title. When she died in 2004, the obituaries paid tribute to her role in public life.

Two characters, Mary and Joy, have problems in *The Abbey Girls in Town*. Their problems are cleverly linked together by the introduction of a new and entirely credible character, Ruth, Mary's cousin. She is eighteen, the daughter of an uncle who had emigrated years before to South Africa or Rhodesia (the details are rather vague) for the sake of his health and who has now become rich as the result of a diamond find on his farm. The British girl brought up in the colonies was a popular figure in girls' fiction at this time, but there is nothing of the wild colonial about Ruth. She is old for her eighteen years, with the mature confidence that might well come from having travelled from South Africa without her family. The arrival of Ruth, who can observe and comment, enables EJO to examine the problems that arise from the characters of Joy and Mary, which affect both their relationship to each other and that of Joy to Andrew Marchwood.

Joy is perhaps the only EJO character who has real problems during her courtship. In every other case the girl fights (or seems to fight) off her suitor until she suddenly decides to give in, and thereafter treats her fiancé/husband as a chum, bag-carrier or father of her children as the need arises. Most of the husbands are nice, uncomplicated young men of very little character, who fall in love at first sight and refuse to take 'no' for an answer, who have incomes that can keep their wives in the state to which they are accustomed—or would like to be accustomed—and who are quite happy for their wives to do exactly as they like with regard to visiting friends of long standing and entertaining them, bringing up the family, pursuing careers and so on. Perhaps this is one of EJO's appeals—an attractive picture far removed from most women's experience. In return the women provide good and plentiful home comforts, judging by the number of children produced. Not so with Joy.

Jen walked round and round the cloisters.
(*The Abbey Girls in Town*)

Joy alone falls in love with men who have very definite characters and careers of their own. Both Sir Andrew and Sir Ivor, her second husband, are 'famous', the first as an explorer, the second as a conductor. They do share one special advantage: neither of them threatens to take Joy away from her beloved Hall—this advantage, in fact, is one reason why Joy hesitates to accept Andrew's initial proposal. As Jen explains to Ruth, 'If she married Sir Andrew … she'd keep her home for ever, and add all the Manor grounds to it.' The romance of Joy and Sir Andrew is much more akin to the typical romantic-novel romance—it has nothing of the schoolboy/schoolgirl relationship that is characteristic of most of EJO's romances. Sir Andrew (and one always wants to call him 'Sir Andrew') has seen Joy in various apparently unfavourable circumstances. On the first occasion she is

Entrance to the pottery works, Farnham, 1998

wearing her tunic in the Abbey when she has to be rescued by him, on another occasion she is seen by him dancing 'Bacca Pipes' on the open road to entertain her party of handicapped children. He is portrayed very much as a father figure, comparable with Jane Eyre's Mr Rochester or the nameless heroine's Maxim de Winter in *Rebecca*. It is almost as if Joy has got so much else that she must struggle for her men. As the Pixie explains to Ruth: 'She's had everything she wanted all her life. She's exactly what you would expect when you remember the happy sheltered time she has had, with every luxury and every gift you can think of.'

In contrast there is Mary, who has had to struggle. The comparative poverty in which she and Biddy still live is emphasised—the cramped flat at the top of bare stone steps, the shabby furnishings, the need to choose between beautiful pottery and a new sports coat, and the difficulty of affording the fees for the vacation school. The pride that prevents Mary from accepting things from those who have so much more is portrayed as a very natural feeling.

However, some of Mary's problems have already been solved by the time Ruth arrives in London at the beginning of *The Abbey Girls in Town*. She is a happier and healthier person as a result of her meeting with Jen and Joy, a meeting which has introduced her to not only the beauty of country dancing but also the importance of beauty in one's life. As she says: 'Jen gave me a fearful rowing about the duty, as well as the joy, of wearing and surrounding ourselves with beautiful things and colours. It's almost a religion with her ...'

As a result of these influences Biddy has settled down, and she and Mary have become good companions for each other despite the difference in their ages. Mary has started to write and has had some stories and articles accepted. Naturally she worships Jen and Joy—to an extent that horrifies Ruth—and her double problem in *The Abbey Girls in Town* is that she must get used to managing without weekly doses of Jen, who decides to return to school for at least a term, and to accept that Joy is not perfect.

Joy's major imperfection in this book arises from the inner turmoil caused by her romantic involvement with Sir Andrew. At his mother's request, she asks Mary to arrange for her children's class to put on a folk-dancing display and is anxious for it to be a success. Mary is only too delighted to do this and, with Biddy's help, slaves over the planning and the practices, oblivious of the fact that Joy, quite unthinkingly, appears to be taking the credit for it. Ruth notices but is too mature to say anything, although her noticing enables the reader to appreciate the situation. The outspoken Biddy, however, has no such inhibitions and embarrasses Joy by voicing a protest in front of the Marchwood party. Joy is furious, and it seems as if the relationship between her and Mary is in danger. Mary is most hurt by Joy's complete lack of understanding of the situation and of how she feels, but she comes to accept Joy's imperfection. This enables her, with Ruth's support, to go to see Andrew Marchwood at the Manor and persuade him to ask Joy again to marry him before he goes away. It is typical of Joy's relationship with Andrew that she now presents him to her friends as a father figure who will help her to be more thinking in the future. He is to be her support, whereas in most similar situations in EJO's books it is the girl who is seen as the support.

This book has a particularly joyful ending, with Mary's first book virtually sold to a publisher, Joy's engagement, and Jen's coronation as Queen Brownie imminent. Like the two previous Abbey books, it shows EJO's preoccupation with the EFDS at this period of her life, but the most important event perhaps is the one that is least emphasised—the arrival during the Christmas period of Janice Raymond, the first of the next generation of Abbey girls.

A topic that links *The Abbey Girls in Town* and the previous Abbey book, *The Abbey Girls Again*, is the interest in crafts, specifically weaving and pottery. In the earlier book, Pixie describes how she is working in a little shop in London's West End, making up handwoven material into dresses, 'designing them to suit people'. Both Joy and Jen go to see her at work and admire the piles of beautiful handwoven materials.

When Ruth first arrives at Mary and Ruth's flat, she admires the blue pottery in Biddy's room and the same pottery in a deep rich brown in Mary's room. Biddy explains that it comes from Farnham, a village in Surrey, and that Joy, driving from the Hall to Sussex to visit Joan, had come across the 'factory where these lovely things were being made by hand'. Ruth later visits the pottery with Joy and orders a complete set of tableware in green, as a St Valentine's Day present for her cousins. She has already ordered a dress in the handwoven material, and Mary orders one when she receives her first significant cheque as an author.

This interest in crafts becomes an integral part of the Abbey story—we are later told that Joy has already set up a weaving school in the village and will establish a school to teach pottery as soon as she can find a teacher. It is true that we hear much more about the music school that is also the result of Joy's wish to share her good fortune with other people, but Rosamund carries on the idea of handweaving in later Abbey books.

Ven at Gregory's, also published in 1925, continues the story of Gard and the now firmly established Gregory's. Mrs Thorne, Suzanne's mother, has been ill and has to take things easily, but the school is so successful that Miss Angel has asked Gard's grandmother, Mrs Unwin, to take the vacant house next door and run this and her own house as a boarding house for the school. Mrs Unwin lives in one house with the boys, while the girls live in the other with the maid. Meals are taken all together in the big dining room of one house, while the sitting room of the other is set aside for evening prep.

Both Gard and her cousin Ven Morris are off stage when the story begins, and the first chapter is concerned with three new girls whose problems are to form an important part of the story. Frances and Phillida Merton are twins of seventeen, while Lucinda Searle is thirteen. The twins are quickly established as 'pretty, dainty and very well dressed' girls who will never have to think about earning their own living. They are representative of the upper-middle-class girls who, in the early 1920s, were expected to stay at home, helping their mothers and enjoying a pleasant round of dances and tennis parties until they married. They live at home. Lucinda, on the other hand, joins Berry, Elizabeth, Monica and Gard at Mrs Unwin's boarding house—she has a face 'almost medieval in its saintliness', a fact that is quickly exploited by the other girls.

The reader learns that Ven, who had spent a term at the Castle School the previous year and whose father, like Gard's, is a sailor, has been away on a voyage with her invalid mother. When Ven's imminent return is announced, it is assumed by Gard that she will be returning to the new school as a pupil. In fact Ven, as she explains in a letter to the headmistress, Miss Angel, is determined to earn enough money to be able to make some contribution to her keep. The story of her indebtedness to Gard's family is told, and Miss Angel, very sympathetic, finds the ideal solution.

Gard cannot believe Ven's decision, pointing out that she's 'had no decent school life since [she] was fifteen!'. Gard is even more hurt and unbelieving when Ven insists that she wants to pay for her board and lodging. But Suzanne presents the commonsense practical approach. While admiring Ven's determination, she suggests that it would be wise for her to be properly trained, a view reinforced by Barbara Holt, Ven's Camp Fire Guardian. The importance of a girl having proper qualifications so that she can have a career rather than a job is emphasised several times in this particular book.

The ideal solution found by Miss Angel is that Ven shall work for part of the day with Miss Barclay, the school secretary, but, for at least two hours a day, she will join her peers and work at relevant subjects, such as languages, and also go to evening classes. This might seem to be a pretty full programme, but it does not prevent Ven from being involved in yet another problem that is explored in this book. When Miss Angel receives an appeal for some of her older girls to become involved in the town's Guide companies, Ven leads the way in sacrificing her own preference for Camp Fire in the interests of the greater good of the community.

The story of the Merton twins is also an important part of the plot. The differences between them are

'Who goes there? Wohelo?'
(*Ven at Gregory's*)

emphasised. Phillida is very conscious of her social standing, pleased with her affluent home in The Crescent, with its exclusive private beach, and critical of her twin who is keen to make friends with Suzanne, who seems to her to be less socially worthy. She prefers Suzanne's friend, Marjory, who lives in 'a huge house with lovely gardens', and dismisses Suzanne as somebody who will probably 'go and be a teacher in an elementary school'. Frances admires Marjory but is determined to get to know more about the 'girls who mean to be teachers and working people'. She seeks Suzanne out very early in the book, and this is a convenient way of explaining the background to the present situation as revealed in earlier books. Snobbery is apparently disapproved of in this book, but that EJO subscribed to some of the snobbish attitudes of the middle class in the early 1920s is shown by a revealing comment towards the end of the book. When Fran and Ven go off one Sunday (in fact to a Guide Service), Elizabeth advances the theory that they may have gone out to meet boys. The others fall about at this idea and Gard says scornfully: 'Girls do, of course; shop girls and nursemaids and servants! But not girls like Ven. She's got too much to think about.'

Fran decides to join the school Camp Fire and begins to think she might be interested in going to college. Phillida works hard at her music but otherwise is determined to enjoy the social whirl. Fran, like Ven, answers the appeal to help with Guide activities in the town, agreeing to become a Tawny Owl. EJO's own preference for Camp Fire comes through very clearly in this book—anyone who gives up Camp Fire activities for those of the Girl Guides is seen to be making a great sacrifice.

Miss Angel makes a direct, unsuccessful appeal to Phillida, talking to her about the importance of widening her experiences in order to develop the sympathy and understanding which in turn will enrich her musical skills. Phillida rejects this idea totally, but one Saturday, after she has spent the afternoon with her music teacher (female, of course), she misses the bus home and, as there isn't another for an hour, sets off to walk. She hears crying and finds a small girl, Molly, with two younger children, locked in their 'hovel' while mother has gone to fetch father home from the Gun and Rabbit. Phillida stays and comforts them, and is gradually made aware of things that have not impinged on her life so far. Molly tells her that she is a Brownie, and Phil realises that 'even in villages and hamlets there were girls who gave up their time to helping small children to be brave and cheerful in emergencies'. The importance of helping those younger as well as less fortunate is made clear. Mrs Merton, who emerges as a strong adult character quite untypical of EJO's work, puts forward the view that the organised movements for girls are a force for good in society, as the girls who join them will want something better for themselves and their children when they grow up.

More problems are explored through the character of Lucinda. Called Sindy at home, she is quickly nicknamed Cinders and soon merits the alternative name of Cinderella. She is temporarily in danger of being ostracised when she tries to put the blame on Gard for something that she has done. Only Elizabeth, amongst the younger girls, and Frances, amongst the older ones, give immediate support to Sindy, but they manage to bring the others round to their way of thinking, and Frances tells more of Sindy's story—she's never had a mother, her father is 'old and queer' and there is only a housekeeper at home—and persuades Berry and Gard that they must help Sindy to become a worthwhile person. Sindy's father subsequently dies, and Berry, told the news in advance by Miss Angel, tells

Phil the whole story. The latter, now very sympathetic, takes upon herself the task of breaking the news to Sindy and then suggests to her mother that they adopt her.

In fact, when the fact that Sindy is now an orphan becomes known, Miss Angel receives three visitations, each with a proposal for adopting Sindy—from Phil, from Barbara and Audrey Holt, and from Berry and the other girls at Mrs Unwin's. Thus all the various threads come together, and the book ends with a specially arranged meeting of the two camps at which Phillida becomes a Camp Fire member and the three girls who have sacrificed their Camp Fire activities for the sake of the Guides—Ven, Fran and Barbara—are present.

With the Abbey saga well established and the Sussex books as a lively second string, one wonders why EJO should at this stage have revived Tormentil Grant and have written two books in successive years with Tormy as their central character. True, she had appeared as another inhabitant of the dormitory at Cheltenham in *The Abbey Girls Go Back to School*, which shows that EJO had not forgotten her. The action of these books—*The Testing of the Torment*, published in the 'New Girls Library' by Cassell in 1925, and *The Camp Fire Torment*, published by Chambers in 1926—takes place before Tormy's visit to Cheltenham. These books are significantly shorter than *The School Torment*, the first book about Tormy, and it is possible that they were written as one volume especially for the Cassell series and judged to be too long to fit into the series format. EJO then made the first half into a free-standing story for Cassell, and re-jigged the second half into a separate book, which was then accepted by Chambers.

Be that as it may, the events in the second book follow on immediately from those in the first—in fact the first chapter of *The Camp Fire Torment* describes the same events as the last chapter of *The Testing of the Torment*—and in both books the Camp Fire movement plays an important part. The copy of *The Testing of the Torment* that we used has a coloured picture of Camp Fire girls on the cover, the coloured frontispiece also features the Camp Fire, and throughout both stories it is the Camp Fire spirit of sisterhood that influences the characters to do what they know to be the right thing, and to conquer their personal prejudices.

When *The Testing of the Torment* opens, Marsaili has just reached her eighteenth birthday and is now old enough to be a Camp Fire Guardian. Tormy and Tony are both very keen to turn their private Camp Fire into a 'real' one and to become part of the Camp Fire movement. The snag is that to establish a Camp Fire you must have six girls and a Guardian, and it seems very difficult to find six 'suitable' girls. In this situation, class barriers are very apparent. When Tony tentatively suggests asking girls from the local farms, Marsaili dissuades her:

> 'How could Welsh village girls come into a group with you and be your Camp Fire sisters? They'd never feel at ease; and you would be uncomfortable because they were. You'd never get the feeling of comradeship that way. This isn't America and the division between them and you is too deep.'

Marsaili's words are a direct and regretful comment on the state of things in British society at the time. There are some 'possible' girls, the twins at the Vicarage, who are only twelve and could easily be influenced, and 'the girl at the Red House', against whom 'the Torment' has a quite unreasonable prejudice. Tony is happy to share their Camp Fire and invite other girls, but Tormy does not want to share either her friends or the Camp Fire, and Tony is unwilling to do anything to upset her. To do the Torment justice, she is fully aware of the fact that she has the wrong attitude and freely admits it. What she cannot admit is the possibility that her attitude will change. She is very soon faced with another situation of the same kind. As the only girl in a boys' school, she has made and kept her place with the boys, and both she and they are content. Now they are asked to accept another girl, the stepdaughter of a former master who has come back to the school to teach. Tormy does not want to share her unique place and the friendship of the boys, while the boys themselves, who well remember the misunderstanding when Tony spent some time in the school, are not at all disposed to welcome Penelope, known as Pen.

Pen flung back the bed-clothes bravely, and disclosed an enormous spider.
(*The Testing of the Torment*)

Pen's story is a romance in itself, but this rapidly fades into the background. The central problem of the book is the need for Tormy to conquer her personal prejudice and accept Pen; if she does, so will the boys. Pen is made aware of Tormy's feelings when she accidentally overhears her telling Tony and Marsaili about Pen's impending arrival at the school. She is very unhappy, but she is also proud and determines to brave it out. Her arrival at the school is delayed by an outbreak of measles, and, looking round for something to do in the meantime, she constitutes herself the play-leader of the younger local boys, forming them into a group called Pen's Pack or Pen's Penguins.

When Pen finally joins the school, she meets Tormy's strained politeness with the same, and easily holds her own against the boys' teasing, which makes Tormy angry. Pen would very much like to be friends with Tormy and join the unofficial Camp Fire, but she conceals her feelings and appears to be self-sufficient. Tormy, on the other hand, cannot bring herself to change her attitude to Pen, even though at heart she is ashamed of her lack of Camp Fire spirit—a lack on which Marsaili frequently comments. She refuses to consider qualifying as a Fire-Maker because she doesn't consider herself fit for it.

The situation gets no easier, particularly when Tormy and the boys tease Pen about her 'Pack'. However, Pen continues to conceal her feelings so well that Tormy believes that she does not care at all about her exclusion, and it is only when Marsaili suggests that Pen may be deliberately concealing her unhappiness that Tormy's Camp Fire spirit finally conquers. Of course, the two girls make friends in the end; there is added excitement when Pen's Penguins are accused of burglary, and there is a suggestion of romance between Pen's stepfather and Tormy's sister (readers of *The Abbey Girls Go Back to School* will have anticipated this). The unofficial Camp Fire now has three members and a much less exclusive outlook, thus preparing the way for the publication of the second 'Torment' book the following year.

The Camp Fire Torment was illustrated by Enid W Browne, whose spare line-drawings invited the young reader to provide her own colours—in the edition we used one of the four plates had been neatly coloured in! The opening chapter, describing Penelope's first visit to Tygwyn and her introduction to the Camp Fire, overlaps with the ending of *The Testing of the Torment*. With the addition of Pen, it will be possible to establish a real Camp Fire if they also invite the 'stodgy' Vicarage twins and the girl from the Red House—Tormy is persuaded to overcome her prejudice against the latter—and another possible recruit has appeared in the person of a 'real' Camp Fire girl from America who is living in the town.

The Vicarage twins, Petronel and Claribel, known as Nel and Bel (were these names later combined for Nell Bell who appears in the Abbey books?), are willing to join the Camp Fire, but the Red House girl, Veronica Davey, is a Lone Guide, attached to the 1st Llanfair Company—she cannot attend parades as the journey to Llanfair involves a hour's trip by train—and as a loyal Guide she does not feel she can join the Camp Fire as well, although if she'd been asked earlier she would have been happy to do so. Here again, the class barriers of the period are seen. Nobody could object to 'receiving a call from the joint-heiresses of Tygwyn', and when Veronica is asked about her education—'We didn't know there was any decent school in that tiny wee town'—she explains that she goes for lessons to one of her mother's friends, who is a BA, and that Sadie Sandell, the American Camp Fire girl, is going to join her.

Sadie Sandell also appears in *The Bungalow Baby*, a short story published in the 1926 volume of the *British Girl's Annual*, which, with another short story, was to be expanded into a complete book, *Peggy Makes Good* (1927). She, her widowed sister and baby Robin have come with Captain Nicholls to help his daughter run the boat business on the lake. Sadie very soon makes her influence felt in the new Camp Fire. Her Camp Fire name is Chekesu, pronounced Tschekayzu but quickly turned into 'Cheeky Sue' by Tormy, and although she is only twelve her previous Camp Fire experience and her natural force of character provide her elders, Pen, Tony and Tormy, with serious problems. Sadie easily influences the placid twins and persuades them to vote with her, thus splitting the Camp Fire neatly into half over matters such as should the girls who have been 'playing' at Camp Fire keep the honours they have already won, should they pay for their beads, and should they do action songs? All this provides a very real problem for Marsaili.

There is the statutory exciting incident. The Captain, Miranda, Sadie and the baby are out for an evening sail when, driven by an unexpected squall, they run ashore on a shoal from which they are rescued by Marsaili in the Tygwyn boat and taken safely to land. However, the story is more concerned with the relationships between the girls. The friction between Tormy and Sadie comes to a head when Tormy calls Sadie 'Cheeky Sue' to her face. Sadie feels that her Camp Fire name is spoiled and rushes away from the meeting, very unhappy.

Once again, Marsaili's influence triumphs. She points out to Tormy that Sadie is four years younger than she is, that Tormy has spoiled her pretty name, which must mean a lot to her, and driven a Camp Fire sister from the circle by her unkindness. Tormy is sorry for what she has done and goes with Marsaili to apologise and try to make amends. Sadie is pacified and chooses a new name, but Marsaili, feeling that the wrong was not all on Tormy's side, also talks seriously to Sadie, pointing out that her behaviour has been less than perfect and asking: 'What do you think these British girls will think of American girls and American Camp Fires?' Sadie admits she's been silly and promises to do better in future.

Finally, Veronica joins the Camp Fire, arriving in response to a telegram from Marsaili, who has written to her Guide Captain and explained the situation. Ronny is encouraged to join the Camp Fire but also to continue to be a Lone Guide. It is noticeable that, in these two Torment stories, the boys gradually fade into the background now that Tormy has another girl in the school with her. The boys are no less part of Tormy's day-to-day life, but these stories are more concerned with her out-of-school activities. Another interesting development is that the telephone begins to play a more important part in the stories—possibly EJO was becoming more accustomed to its use.

The only date available for another of EJO's short stories, *Muffins and Crumpets*, is 1926 when, according to Monica Godfrey, it appeared in the *Bumper Book for Girls*. However, it also appeared in at least two other collections, and it may have been written and published earlier as, despite a number of features characteristic of EJO's other work, it is really a throwback to the 'street Arab' stories that were very popular in the 1870s and flourished into the early twentieth century, finally disappearing, apart from one or two famous stories that remained in print, in the 1930s. *Muffins and Crumpets* lacks the religious, evangelical fervour of the stories by Hesba Stretton, 'Brenda' and Mrs O Walton, who were the most famous and long-lasting authors in this field, but it certainly has overtones of their work.

Crumpets (Muffins is her dog) is a young crippled girl in Dick Fraser's sister's Sunday School class; Dick takes her to watch a drill class, led by Ruth Polmont, whom he obviously admires. Crumpets is fifteen and a half but looks about nine, and lives with a bed-ridden and paralysed grandmother and a drunken father in a large room at the top of 'a gloomy house in the poorest part of the town'. Ruth gives up a hockey practice the following Sunday afternoon to visit Crumpets there and teach her those parts of the drill that she can manage. At one point, while Crumpets is exercising her dog, the grandmother tells Ruth that Crumpets does not want to grow up—while she is a child people accept her small stature, but as an adult she will be stared and laughed at.

Ruth's absence from the hockey practice leads to a momentary coolness on Dick's part, but Crumpets senses this and explains the situation to him, and all is well again. The weeks go by, and Crumpets begins to realise that all the drilling in the world is not going to make

MUFFINS AND CRUMPETS

BY ELSIE JEANETTE OXENHAM

her normal. Then, one day, she meets Ruth and Dick in town—something is wrong with Muffins and she has come to seek their help. Dick goes to fetch a vet, but when Ruth and Crumpets arrive outside the house they find there is a fire on the top floor; grandmother has been carried out but Muffins is missing. Ruth races up the stairs and finds Muffins, but faints near the door on her way out. Crumpets rescues Ruth, dragging her onto the landing in time for Dick to carry her down, but when she goes back to fetch Muffins she falls to her death, surviving just long enough to assure Ruth she's glad she won't have to grow up and that she knows Ruth will look after Muffins.

Crumpets is a heroine typical of this kind of story, making a brave effort despite overwhelming odds. The Sunday School class, which would have been her salvation, is there, but more important in her life are the girls' club and the drill which EJO substituted for her customary folk dancing, no doubt because drill exercises could be more realistically adapted to meet Crumpets' needs. The pathos of the final solution has all the tear-jerking qualities of *Froggy's Little Brother* or *A Peep behind the Scenes*.

Also published in 1926, *Queen of the Abbey Girls* follows on from the events of *The Abbey Girls in Town*. It is early May; Ruth has gone to join her parents in France, but Mary and Biddy are still at the Abbey for the Easter holidays, Easter being late that year. Jen, Rosamund and Maidlin have not yet gone back to school, nor Biddy to college. The book opens with the reappearance of Dick and Della Jessop, now very grown-up and sophisticated. With their younger sister, Sheila, they are on their way to revisit the Abbey. The car breaks down, and while Dick is repairing it Della and Sheila continue their journey by train and meet Kenneth Marchwood, Sir Andrew's younger brother, just returned from Africa where he runs a coffee plantation—thus reflecting the experience of EJO's brother Hugo, who went out to be a coffee planter in Kenya in 1920.

At the Abbey ruins, Della and Sheila find Jen with Mary and Biddy, Rosamund and Maidlin; they are welcomed and invited to stay for lunch. Della must be told of all that has happened since she was last there, and this helps to put new readers in the picture—in several other Abbey books the return of a character who had appeared in an earlier title provides the same good excuse for recapitulation.

It is very early made clear that Ken Marchwood has been introduced as a prospective husband for Jen. Della puts her foot in it by suggesting this as a possibility, and damages her own situation by doing so. Dick also makes a bad impression by pretending to carve his name on the Abbey wall and is thoroughly shaken by Jen before she realises who he is. Dick and Della, therefore, are not encouraged to stay, though everyone is kind to Sheila, who is to go to Miss Macey's school. Dick is presented as another possible husband for Jen, but his chances are clearly nil from the start; he remains a nuisance who keeps cropping up. The problem for Jen is not which of the two young men she will marry, but whether she wants to 'grow up' and get married at all. First Joy and then Mary introduce the idea, but Jen refuses to take it seriously.

Ken Marchwood has come home from Africa, anxious to meet his brother's future wife and to be adopted into the Abbey family. When he first sees Jen, she is 'framed in the old Abbey gate, the afternoon sun lighting up her waving curls', and only a few pages further on he feels jealous when Dick Jessop is mentioned. Ken's arrival in the Abbey is very quickly followed by Joy coming to suggest a good job in France for Biddy. Biddy herself, characterised as having a keen eye on the main chance, is anxious to go, especially as it will help her to prepare for her future job as Maidlin's secretary, but she is reluctant to leave Mary.

However, this is a careful piece of plotting; removing Biddy will make it possible to establish Mary at the Hall, where she is to remain for the rest of the series as everyone's guide, philosopher and friend—and dogsbody. Joy's plan for Mary is that she should live at the Hall to be a secretary for Joy and a substitute companion for Mrs Shirley. Joy then produces her bombshell—she is to be married in a month in order to go to Africa with Andrew. The spirit that gave her the nicknames of Traveller's Joy and Wild Cat is attracted by the adventure, and the prospect of travelling with Andrew means that she is no longer reluctant to leave her beloved Hall.

Joy's impending departure affects both Rosamund and Maidlin. The latter, still very young for her age and devoted to Joy, is desperately unhappy, and it requires the united efforts of all the others to induce her to do something practical in the way of making a present and helping Joy. Rosamund, on the other hand, is hurt because Joy does not understand her depth of feeling for her and cannot appreciate that she too is unhappy. But, even at this early stage, Rosamund applies her intelligence to solving her own problems and sees that the most helpful thing she can do now is to understand Joy's feelings and to help Maidlin in her misery.

In the midst of the wedding preparations, Jen has her official school crowning as Queen of the Hamlet Club. She has chosen to have a train of beech brown, decorated with yellow leaves and flowers, a choice that leads to her being given the long-lasting nickname of 'Queen Brownie'. Once again, there is no detailed description of the wedding; on the morning of the wedding Jen and Rosamund go out early to gather flowers to scatter outside Joy's door, and two pages later Chapter Ten begins: 'Joy's wedding-party broke up quickly.'

What seems to EJO to be of more importance is Mary's introduction to the rooms that Joy has prepared for her—the rooms of her dreams. The green sitting room and the brown bedroom are described in very great detail, with special emphasis on the flowers and the pottery. Mary's brown room, although a bedroom, echoes the Brown Study in the Holt sisters' bungalow in *The Junior Captain* and, according to Monica Godfrey, the room in which EJO herself used to write in 'Inverkip', the house she shared with her sister Maida. For the Abbey people it becomes a place of confidences, sympathy and the discussion of serious subjects.

On Mary's first evening here, she and Jen discuss a problem arising out of her duties as Joy's deputy. Nell Bell, one of the girls at the hostel in the village, has stayed on because she has been ill but does not seem to be improving. Prompted by Jen, Mary wonders if this is a case like her own and, advised by the Pixie, talks to Nell and finds this is indeed so. Nell lost her fiancé before they could marry and now lives in a world of daydreams about the home and family they might have had. Mary solves this problem by persuading Nell to help at the Children's Home, which is another of Joy's projects in the village, and also, naturally, persuades her to join the village folk-dance class. Folk dancing is also part of the cure for another of Mary's problems. Amy Prittle, a girl from her old office, who used to hang around her, now turns up in Wycombe, where she has taken a job so that she can be near Mary. Mary is impatient with Amy but feels she must give help if it is needed—so she introduces Amy to folk dancing and to Nell Bell, to whom Amy confesses that Mary's influence has saved her from 'unsuitable' company.

Jen's reign as Queen is beset with difficulties, among which are the attentions of both Dick and Kenneth. After a Hamlet Club party at which they are both present and at which Rosamund teases her about the need to choose between them, she runs off early one morning to visit the Pixie in her caravan and ask for advice. The descriptions of the Pixie's van, its surroundings and her housekeeping are very compelling, and we have always felt that EJO must have had friends with a caravan like this. Now, thanks to research carried out by the late Olga Lock-Kendell and others, and published in *The Abbey Chronicle*, we know they were based on reality.

Ken comes to fetch Jen, bringing a letter from her mother calling her home to Yorkshire because her father is dying, and then drives her and Mary north, and Mary stays for a while. In the course of this and later visits, she and Jen talk seriously about death and what it means. This probably reflects EJO's own preoccupation with the subject at this period, as her mother had died in 1925. This period of sadness brings a new maturity to Jen, and she becomes engaged to Kenneth Marchwood.

After her father's death, Jen returns to the Abbey to find that Mary's first book has been published, that Nell Bell is happily busy in the Children's Home and that Amy Prittle has gone to work with Biddy in France. But there is a new problem, unperceived by Mary—Maidlin, waiting only for the time when Joy will come home, has slipped into a dream world as Mary had once done, and it is affecting her health, not to mention her school work. Jen and Mary together attempt to solve this problem by arranging for Maidlin to have singing lessons and thus work at something practical to please Joy on her return. To reassure themselves that they have taken the right course, Jen and Mary go up to London to consult the Pixie, who encourages their efforts and, in the final words of the book, provides what is, perhaps, a key to EJO's books of this period when she says: 'You'll have problems of course; but those are what makes life so exciting.'

In 1934 part of *Queen of the Abbey Girls* was published as *The Call of the Abbey School*, a romantic title which no doubt lent credence to the idea of an 'Abbey School', but which was probably chosen by the publishers rather than by EJO herself. It consists of the first nine chapters of *Queen of the Abbey Girls* and ends on the eve of Joy's wedding. These chapters are not abridged but the last half of the last sentence of Chapter 9 is omitted, so the book ends rather poetically, '… and they crept upstairs together to strew Joy's corridor with white flowers', leaving out the decidedly unromantic reference to foraging in the larder. The text does not appear to have been reset, and although the smaller margins in the shortened version give the impression that a smaller typeface has been used, this is not the case. *The Call of the Abbey School* hangs together quite well as a book in itself, and it would be interesting to know just how it came into being.

In the same year that *Queen of the Abbey Girls* was published by Collins, Chambers published *The Troubles of Tazy*. Ven Morris and Fran and Phil Merton, last seen in *Ven of Gregory's*, arrive, a year or two older, at the Dorf in Switzerland, the home of St Mary's and St John's schools. Ven has come to be a secretary at St Mary's because her invalid mother has come for treatment at the Platz, while Phil has come to study the violin with M Chardelot, whose daughter is also at the Platz. They are met by Tazy Kingston to be taken on the last stage of their journey to the Dorf, and this meeting gives EJO the opportunity to bring the new reader up to date on both the series from which characters are brought together in this book. Ven tells Tazy all

Tazy lit a candle and led the way into the cave.
(*The Troubles of Tazy*)

about Gregory's, while Tazy fills her and the Mertons in on the background to St Mary's and the Platz.

The obligation that the well-off have to look after the needs of their less fortunate brethren is mentioned at once. Ven explains to Tazy that the Merton parents have gone off to visit various missions in Africa and the East: 'It's an awfully decent thing of wealthy people to do, and bucks up the missionaries no end.' Sindy, who had been adopted by the Mertons, has been boarded out with Gard.

Tazy's troubles arise from the fact that she really hasn't enough to do; her mother does voluntary social work at the Platz, while she and Karen have left school and are living in a hostel near St Mary's. Karen is working at her violin but, as Tazy says, she herself has no special talent, and, as she tells Phil about Fran, '… she couldn't take a teacher's job when she can afford to live without earning her living. It's a horribly wrong thing to do.' Tazy's energy and intelligence, with no outlet, have turned her into a careless and forgetful person. She causes the new arrivals to miss the last train up to the Dorf, and the next day she almost forgets an appointment with her mother and dashes off, leaving the three girls to arrive at the Dorf on their own and to make their own introductions.

But Tazy is not the only character with problems. There is also Eve Prideaux, the daughter of the woman who runs the hostel with the help of another daughter, Nela. Eve is like Nell Bell, Maidlin and Mary—she is a dreamer who sits around doing beautiful embroidery and taking refuge in her cat, Toni. She needs to be needed, but up to this point has been overwhelmed by her super-efficient mother and sister. Guly Pennyfold, now head of St Mary's, also has a problem: Astrid, the other head girl, chosen by the staff, who is also her great friend, is jealous of Guly's friendship with Sven Pankridge, the head boy of St John's. (This problem is not explored here to any great extent; later, in 1932, EJO published *The Camp Mystery*, the events of which pre-date those of *The Troubles of Tazy*, where it is more fully discussed.) Phil Merton also has problems, coming back from her first meeting with Professor Chardelot bitterly disappointed because he hasn't enthused about her playing. Karen Wilson has a different kind of problem: Rennie Brown has asked her to marry him, and she wonders whether it is wise to do so since her mother died of TB and his is only kept alive with great care.

Fran and Phil are told of Guly and Astrid's adventures in the mountain caves and passages three years earlier, and are also told of rumours that there is an underground lake so far undiscovered. Tazy, challenged to do something worthwhile by Sally Pennyfold, persuades Phil, sore from her meeting with the Professor, to go off on an expedition to look for the lake. Inevitably they run into trouble. When they are in the network of passages, having found the underground lake, Tazy belatedly remembers a snatch of conversation she has heard in the village—today is the day when the workmen are to try and blast a way through to the lake. While she is trying to get Phil out without Phil suspecting that anything is wrong, there is an explosion and the girls are trapped. Tazy is persuaded by Phil to pray for help, her prayer is quickly answered and the girls are rescued, although they are both injured, Phil to such an extent that she will never again be able to play her violin at the standard she had achieved.

The tower of strength in all this drama is Fran Merton, who points up, by her difference from Tazy, the latter's faults. Like Tazy, Fran has no obvious talents but, unlike Tazy, she is thoughtful and caring. She provides support for her disappointed twin, and after the accident encourages her to find another outlet for her musical gift. She very successfully helps Eve by asking Eve to help her. Karen finds in her a sympathetic ear, and she responds to Sally Pennyfold's ideas for organising a play-hour for the children of the herdsmen. Finally, she tells Tazy, '… it seems to me you ought to be mixed up in jolly movements, working with keen people who do things because they believe in them. You can organise and run things.' As we learn much later, in *An Abbey Champion* (1946), Tazy follows this good advice to great effect! In the final chapter Tazy becomes engaged to Bill Thistleton and thus takes another step towards her reappearance in the Abbey books some years later.

There is one other engagement in this book—Thora makes a brief appearance to become engaged to Pauline's brother, hunchbacked Claude, a match which is met with less than enthusiasm by everyone except Pauline, who explains to Fran (who else?): '… if a man gives a girl a great love for many years, she forgets all things for the sake of love.'

EJO may have been irritated by the way in which Elinor Brent-Dyer used her idea of attaching a school, organised on English lines, to a sanatorium, but she herself makes little use of the Swiss setting. The English girls immediately move into the centre of life at the hostel, and the 'Frenchies' and the Germans are regarded as very minor characters—a person only counts if at least one parent is English. The hostel for business girls, which has been opened partly as the result of Miss Braithwaite's influence, is only one example of the attempt to transfer an essentially English life-style to the Dorf. Sally's idea about Tazy's organising a play-hour for the children of the herdsmen, who are said to have nothing to do in the long light summer evenings—'They'll think about it all the time in between'—is a suggestion that has all the overtones of Jen doing good in Tin Town, the Pixie in the East End of London and Pen in the Welsh village.

Jen of the Abbey School, published by Collins in the following year, 1927, presents a bibliographical problem of some magnitude. It goes back in time to fill in the gaps in Jen's story. The fact that Jen's home is in Yorkshire was already well established, and the link with Rocklands was an obvious one. *Jen of the Abbey School* keys into *Tickles* as well as into *The Abbey Girls Go back to School*, as the story opens during the term when Tickles arrives at Rocklands as a new girl, before the vacation school in Cheltenham. When Rhoda tactfully tells Jen that her interpretation of the folk dances is not quite right, Jen refers to the incident of the blue-eyed stranger which takes place early in *The Abbey Girls Go Back to School*.

Why did EJO go back to fill in Jen's story at this stage? Perhaps she decided to expand it after Jen became engaged in *Queen of the Abbey Girls*, or perhaps she thought ahead to introducing Betty McLean into the Abbey story and therefore needed to provide an excuse for Betty to turn up at the Abbey. However, the following explanation seems the most likely:

The content of *Jen of the Abbey School* was later published in three short books: *The Girls of Rocklands School*, *The Second Term at Rocklands*, both published in 1930, and *The Third Term at Rocklands*, which appeared in 1931. The first of these consists of the first five chapters and part of Chapter 6 of *Jen*, up to the point when Jen arrives back after her accident in Cheltenham and tells the girls that Rhoda was right in her opinion of Jen's dancing, and Betty nods happily. Although, on the face of it, *The Girls of Rocklands School* seems an odd little book, it does make a coherent story with a satisfactory ending.

'Even fairies get tired!' she answered him seriously.
(*Jen of the Abbey School*)

The Second Term at Rocklands begins with the new Mademoiselle asking: 'Who is this Miss Jen?', which provides an excuse for a recapitulation of the plot in the middle of *Jen*, and finishes at the end of Chapter 18 of *Jen*. This part seems to have been abridged in the most amazing way, with a whole page of *Jen* apparently hacked out here and there. For example, page 98 of *Jen* is completely omitted, so that the story goes straight from Jen saying, 'Oh, I'm tired!' to 'Rena laughed, and rose.'. It is surprising that it works as well as it does, especially as it consists of two separate plots—the story of the jumper and the pipe given to Jen as 'welcome back' presents, and the story of the Carrs and the Basque pipe.

Chapters 19 to 27 of *Jen*, beginning with Betty and Rhoda asking the Pixie's advice about the folk-dance competition at Stonecliffe, make up *The Third Term at Rocklands*, which is concerned entirely with the competition. The title is a misnomer since the events in both the *Second* and *Third* terms actually take place in the same autumn term.

We know from the publication dates that the three short Rocklands books came after their inclusion in *Jen*, but they may in fact have existed as separate stories at an earlier date and been published in a variety of annuals and collections. We know, from Monica Godfrey's bibliography, that *The Girls of Rocklands School* appeared in at least four different collections, one undated, two in 1924 and another in 1925. This story describes Jen's meeting with the Rocklands girls, the dancing lessons she provides for the children of

Tin Town, and Rhoda's arrival at the school. Rhoda knows enough about folk dancing to know that Jen is not doing it correctly, and is exactly the kind of character that EJO was fond of using in her short stories such as *Dancing Honour* and *Honour Your Partner*.

Jen's Presents is known to have appeared in five collections, four of them undated. It appears as the first half of *The Second Term* and as Chapters 6–12 of *Jen*. One chapter title is changed—'The Hideous Present' becomes 'The Accident'. *Treasure from the Snow*, which appeared in four collections, two of them undated, makes up the rest of *The Second Term* and appears as Chapters 13–18 of *Jen*. This tells the story of the Carrs and the Basque pipe. The opening of Chapter 13 is exactly right for the beginning of an exciting short story, and Chapter 18 is actually called 'The End of the Story' although there are still nine chapters to go in the complete book. These, also published as *The Third Term*, may have appeared as a short story in some yet undiscovered collection, but it seems more likely that they were written to make *Jen* up to the required length. A consideration of the timescale suggests that the events described—the heavy snow in *Treasure from the Snow* and the time required for rehearsal for the competition—must in fact have overlapped.

The evidence seems to suggest that EJO wrote part of Jen's story as a series of long short stories somewhat before 1927, then brought them together and added nine chapters to make *Jen of the Abbey School*. *Tickles* had first appeared in 1921, with *The Abbey Girls Go Back to School* being published the following year, so the framework for the events recorded in *Jen* was there at least five years before it was published. There is also the matter of the title. Joan makes a brief appearance but the Abbey is never mentioned, and the title must have puzzled girls who happened to read this particular book as their introduction to the Abbey saga. It also suggests the existence of the Abbey School, which, as has already been mentioned, is incorrect. As further proof of this theory, Mabel Esther Allan found an advertisement printed at the back of Katherine Oldmeadow's book *The Pimpernel Patrol* for *The School on the Hills*. From the brief description there it is clearly the book that was actually published as *Jen of the Abbey School*, and it seems likely that Collins had first intended to make it part of the Rocklands story, and then changed the title to tie it in with the more famous—and more popular—Abbey story. A good example of commercial enterprise in the children's book world!

Finally, the Seagull edition of *Jen* shows how EJO's books were updated to remove references to the First World War—and perhaps partly explains why she avoided any detailed mention of the Second World War in her later books. Betty, telling Rena's story, says 'her father's ship was lost—he was Captain of an Atlantic liner …' and there is no mention of it having been torpedoed as there is in *A Go-Ahead Schoolgirl*. EJO became increasingly reluctant to include anything that dated her books too precisely, an understandable reluctance when one considers how she was interlinking her characters and series by 1927.

EJO continued this interlinking in her next book, *Patience and Her Problems*, published late in 1927. Here the focal point is the Dorf in the Marienthal, and the events follow on almost directly from those in *The Troubles of Tazy*. Tazy had troubles, Patience has problems—her own and other people's—and the two major problems are hinted at in the opening chapter when Patience and her cousin Mercy meet Barbara Holt on the lake steamer that is the penultimate stage of the journey up to the Dorf. Patience and Mercy have come out to spend a holiday with Guly (who is more often called Billy in this book), while Barbara is on her way to visit Ven Morris and the Merton twins. Patience and Mercy are joining Guly at St Mary's, staying in the bungalow that saw most of the action in *The Captain of the Fifth*, while Barbara is sharing Ven's room in the hostel. EJO conveniently uses the introduction of the two groups of friends to tell the reader about previous happenings that are relevant to this story.

Patience Joan's personal problem is presented at an early stage and runs through the book as a unifying thread. As far back as her early Camp Fire days she has felt the need to do something really worthwhile, and it was a story of missionary work among the Red Indians that inspired her Camp Fire name, Noonatomen. Later a visit to Africa with her doctor father, who has since died, developed the idea, and her aim now is to qualify as a doctor and go out, preferably to Africa, as a medical missionary. She has been living in London with her grandmother while studying, and already has her Inter BSc. However, old Mrs Pennyfold has now had a serious illness, and there is a definite possibility that she will become a permanent invalid and have to retire to the country, so Patience feels that she must give up her ambition and devote her life to her grandmother. It is not a question of money, but a certainty that her duty is a family one. She says:

> 'I think it's awful when old people have nobody of their own to take care of them; and perhaps their daughters, or nieces or grandchildren are all busy having careers or doing things they think are wonderfully important. Their own people ought to come first.'

It is interesting that this is a statement of a problem that must often have arisen in the 1920s when women first began to think of a career as a possibility. Before this, the daughter at home automatically took upon herself the care of aged parents; if she was unmarried, there was not much else for her to do anyway, as long as there was no real shortage of money. Now, with the possibility of a career that might not combine with domestic responsibilities, she was faced with a difficult choice.

Patience has no problem of choice; she knows what she has to do but cannot, at first, reconcile what has happened with her strong conviction that she has been 'called' to be a missionary. In her own deliberate way, she thinks the matter out; at first she feels lost and abandoned as if her original idea of a 'pattern' of life must be completely wrong, but later, helped by words of Ven's, she feels there must be some reason for the setback, although she herself cannot yet understand it. She faces up to the rather tedious life that looms ahead with courage and determination. In the meantime, her clear thinking and understanding are called upon to help with other people's problems.

Astrid also comes to the Dorf to join Patience, Mercy and Guly in the bungalow, and with Astrid comes the problem of her jealousy of anyone who is friendly with Guly. Karen Wilson, who is at the hostel, although Tazy has gone to England to visit her future in-laws, gives Patience a hint about the situation, and while all four girls are together Patience manages to keep the atmosphere fair and friendly, apart from an odd fit of the sullens on Astrid's part.

Later, however, Patience goes to spend a night at the hostel when Fran and Phil have gone to Annecy to stay with an aunt. In her absence, the 'threesome' situation provokes Astrid, who storms off into the woods; when she has not returned by evening, the other two set off to find her. When they, in turn, do not return, a maid telephones Patience at the hostel, and the three older girls set out in search of the missing girls. It transpires that some days of heavy rain have led to the mountain river being in flood, so when Astrid is found she is marooned on a rock in the midst of a raging torrent and in danger of being swept away. Then the girls see that there is a further danger in the shape of great tree-trunks being swept down by the river and making straight for Astrid. Patience, at risk of her own life, plunges in and, with the help of Ven and Barbara, manages to save Astrid.

Not surprisingly, during the night that follows, Astrid wakes with nightmares. Patience goes to comfort her, and in the course of their conversation Astrid admits that her jealousy is unreasonable; Patience underlines this by saying: '... you don't trust her. The splendid thing about Billy is the way she sticks to her friends; and yet you, her friend, thought she'd let you down.' From then onwards, Astrid makes even greater efforts to overcome her jealous feelings and causes no more difficult situations.

They carried lighted tapers and thrust them among the leaves.
(*Patience and Her Problems*)

Earlier books have prepared us for the way in which Barbara Holt has developed. Her solitary life at Shingle Beach had accustomed her to being alone, and Audrey had warned Gard that she was a little strange. She had also been the one most reluctant to leave the Camp Fire for Guides. Now Ven and the others call her 'The Hermit', and Ven says she has grown slack over the Guides, apart from the folk-dancing element. Barbara herself says she doesn't like people and prefers to be alone to appreciate the beauty in music and in nature. Her self-centred attitude provokes Patience to expostulate and to argue that just to appreciate nature in all its forms is not enough. Patience herself always feels the need to 'do something in return' and not to waste the creative feeling thus evoked, but Barbara is not immediately influenced. This would seem to be a further development of an idea already established as a favourite by EJO, and it is more than likely that she herself subscribed to it.

However, the presence of Patience, and listening to her ideas, do gradually have some effect on Barbara. At first they merely give rise to a general dissatisfaction with herself that drives her, unconscious of what she is doing, to take on the largest share in an entertainment that the girls are planning for the patients at the Platz, picking up on an idea of Tazy's in an earlier book. The younger girls are quick to feel that Barbara is hogging the limelight, and, in spite of Patience's attempts to keep the peace, matters finally come to a head. Mercy accuses Barbara of wanting to monopolise the affair and Barbara storms out, but not before she has heard Mercy referring to her as 'just like Astrid'.

Barbara goes for a long walk to fight her battle alone. Having decided to pack up and go home—to run away, in fact—she returns to the hostel and finds Patience with supper all ready. Nothing is said about the situation, but that night Barbara comes to Patience, who is in bed, and apologises. With Patience's help the matter is smoothed out; the concert goes ahead, and Barbara has still more to think about.

At this point Patience is urgently recalled to England, and Barbara travels with her and Mercy, taking the latter back to Shingle Beach until term begins again. Patience's ideas have continued to influence Barbara and she begins to put her talents to some use, first of all going, as Jen had done, to dance for an invalid child. She then goes to London to visit the aunt and uncle who had brought her up, and while there becomes involved in teaching folk dancing and running a Guide company in an East End settlement, echoing this time the activities of the Pixie. She visits Patience, who is living with her grandmother at Woodlands, and on one occasion is caught in fog on the Downs, an incident that leads to a confrontation between Patience and her grandmother when Patience insists on going to look for her. Barbara is no longer welcome at Woodlands, but Patience visits her in London occasionally, and is delighted by the changes in her—'… a new alertness and keen interest in life seemed to have awakened in her and to blaze in her black eyes, and presently it became obvious in her talk also.'

That Christmas Barbara fills her bungalow with children from the East End, again reminding us of Joy's activities and EJO's articles about her own work in an East End mission. Finally Patience is reprieved. The mother of Sally and Billy, who has been an invalid for many years, dies at the Platz, and Sally is therefore able to take Patience's place with their grandmother. Patience plans to work with Barbara in the East End before returning to college, and, inspired by her enthusiasm, Barbara considers joining her in her missionary work, 'to teach little Africans country-dancing'. This is the only EJO book to be illustrated by Molly Benatar and it has six illustrations, including the frontispiece. The pictures appear to be black-and-white reproductions of watercolours, and the girls in them are very stylised in their attitudes, especially Barbara, who always seems to strike the same pose.

EJO had written *The Junior Captain*, her first book about Gard Svenssen and her cousin Ven, in 1923, and during the following two years two short stories had appeared in the *British Girl's Annual*, which were set around Barbara's bungalow on the shingle beach. Barbara is given her original name, but the Svenssen family have no surname and are given English names. Svante becomes Andrew, Torkel is Billy, Gard is Nancy, and Ven is now Meg. Perhaps EJO or the publishers felt that the Scandinavian names would require more explanation than could reasonably be included in an annual story, while readers of her books would recognise familiar characters anyway. The first story, *Peggy Plays a Part*, appeared in 1925, the second, *The Bungalow Baby*, in 1926. The latter introduces Sadie Sandell and her widowed sister, Miranda, who had already appeared, at a later stage in their fictional lives, in *The Camp Fire Torment*.

A year later, in 1927, came a complete book, *Peggy Makes Good*, which includes the substance of these stories and another, *Christmas Quarantine*, that had appeared earlier in *Schoolfriend*, and which restores their Scandinavian names to the Svenssens. This is a

THE BUNGALOW BABY
By
Elsie Jeanette Oxenham

retrospective book, since EJO had already chronicled later episodes in the lives of Gard, Ven and Sadie, but, in view of the fact that short stories are difficult to date, it seems very likely that they had existed in some form long before they were published, and may well have been written around the same time as *The Junior Captain* (1923). Monica Godfrey gives 1922 as the date of the *Schoolfriend* in which *Christmas Quarantine* appeared, so EJO must certainly have written this soon after *The Junior Captain*—being a magazine story, it would appear before the book.

The timescale is rather vague, but, since Gard and Ven are still at different schools, *Peggy Makes Good* must be set at the Christmas following the events of *The Junior Captain*. Probably, as with *Jen of the Abbey School*, it was a matter of using short stories to produce a book about earlier events in the lives of characters whose stories had already been taken further. Like *Jen*, it also differs from most of EJO's books at this period in having very little discussion of serious matters; in fact, it is a series of 'jolly' adventures of the type suitable for inclusion in an annual.

The first part of the book introduces the Svenssens and Ven Morris. It looks as if their Christmas holidays will be spoilt because Gregor has scarlet fever, and not only will the quarantine affect their Christmas fun but it will also run on into the new term, thus making things difficult for Svante who has exams ahead. Barbara Holt comes to the rescue with the offer of her bungalow on the beach, Pro Tem, as a holiday home for the four of them— Gard, Svante, Torkel and Ven. She and Audrey are going to London, but their housekeeper will be there to keep an eye on the party.

The Svenssens have a riotous Christmas, their fun increased by the arrival of Barbara, who comes back from London to join them on Christmas Day. During the evening they hear mysterious noises that lead them, the next day, to investigate the empty bungalow next door. To their surprise they discover a collection of silver cups that have been stolen from a local jeweller. The police are notified and they and the Svenssen boys lie in wait the following evening. Their vigil results in the capture of a small girl, the Peggy of the title, who comes from a village family—her father is the blacksmith—and who has been sent out to see if the loot is safe by her uncle, who is the thief. The Svenssens and Barbara take care of Peggy, and Barbara employs her to help Mrs Batching, the housekeeper, with the work of the bungalow. Peggy is very happy, and soon becomes devotedly grateful to Barbara and the others.

The short story *Peggy Plays a Part* appears as Chapters 9 and 10 in the book. The Svenssens make friends with Captain Bob Nicholls, a retired sea captain, who was the original builder of the bungalows and who has come back to the village to visit his married daughter. Because his daughter's house is really too full to take him in, he joins their party, sharing the hitherto empty bungalow next door with the boys, who have taken to sleeping there. He enjoys the lively young company and they like to hear his stories. A 'treasure' arrives in the shape of all the Camp Fire things that Audrey has ordered for the new camp, including silver rings and bracelets and beads of all colours. Peggy unwittingly causes another break-in at the bungalow when she tells her family about the 'Indian jewels' she has seen. This time the burglar's accomplice is the brother of Captain Bob's son-in-law, who had been misled by Peggy's chatter, and when he is chased he throws the Camp Fire things away in disgust. All is recovered and the would-be thieves are warned off—nobody wants to make too much fuss owing to the connection with Captain Bob. These two chapters, with an explanatory opening paragraph, make up an exciting short story with a good ending. It is agreed that everything is to be kept secret, but Ven adds: 'If you ever say "Twelfth Night Party" we'll all know what you mean!'

The next two chapters, 11 and 12, with the addition of a couple of introductory paragraphs and a neatened ending, are textually the same as the short story *The Bungalow Baby*. The differences are the restoration of the Svenssens' real names and the substitution of 'vurry' for 'very' in the speech of the American girl, Sadie Sandell. Two Americans, Sadie and her older widowed sister, Miranda, with Miranda's baby, Robin, have settled into yet another bungalow further along the beach from Pro Tem. Their arrival interests the Svenssens, and their friends, and they plan to call on their new neighbours. Before they can do so, however, there is a bad storm and very high tides, and the Americans' bungalow is in danger. The boys and Captain Nicholls go to the rescue and carry off Sadie, Miranda and the baby to Pro Tem. There are two surprising revelations—the American girls are Camp Fire members, and Miranda is the young widow of Captain Bob's son, unknown to the Captain because he had disliked the idea of his son marrying an American and had refused to communicate with them. Now, of course, he is overjoyed to welcome his grandson, and he takes Miranda, her sister and the baby back home to his wife, thus preparing the way for their presence in Wales in *The Camp Fire Torment*. This link, of course, also supports the theory that *The Bungalow Baby* was in existence before 1926.

The Svenssens' stay at the bungalow is not yet over and neither are the excitements. Peggy, the little girl from the forge, has yet another part to play. Her devotion to Barbara and her friends evokes a desire to do something for them to show her gratitude, and her lack of material resources drives her to the idea of gaining good luck for them in the form of a blessing from the local 'witch', old Mrs Hay. She is an interesting character, a foreign refugee from either France or Belgium, who had come to the south coast of England some fifty years before to escape from the Germans. Refugees from the First World War are a familiar idea to the children, but it is Svante who places Mrs Hay as a refugee from the Franco-Prussian war of 1870. She lives alone with two black cats and a parrot, and is thought odd by the villagers—quite enough to make her into a witch with uncanny powers.

Peggy first tries to pluck up courage to go and ask the witch to invoke good luck for her benefactors, but she is frightened by the old woman and runs away. She then kidnaps the two black cats, Mrs Hay's only friends, maroons them on a small island just off the coast and, after two days of hue and cry, persuades Barbara and the Svenssens to go and search the island. Both Barbara and Svante have their suspicions of Peggy, but the island is visited, the cats are found and their rescuers find themselves marooned—Svante had not tied the boat up properly. After a cold and hungry night on the island they are rescued, and the cats are restored to their anxious mistress. She asks their rescuers to go back to the island and dig up a box containing her valuables that had been buried there by her husband. From its contents, which include some valuable old lace, she rewards the saviours of her cats and, since she has no need of more money, asks them to sell the rest and use it to help 'those who are in need'. With Peggy in mind, Barbara and Svante plan to set up a Trust Fund to administer the money in the best way possible.

During the night on the island Peggy, who had accompanied the rescue party, is stricken with remorse and confesses her part in the disappearance of the cats to Barbara, who lectures her gently on the errors of her ways but is sympathetic to her idea of wanting to help. This is the longest piece of speech we hear from Peggy, and it illustrates EJO's not very successful attempts to reproduce the speech patterns of the 'lower classes'—unless they are Welsh or Scottish, when she manages the Celtic cadences quite well. Peggy, a blacksmith's daughter from Sussex, uses a mixture of bad grammar and false Cockney. EJO is not much more successful with the old lady's French-accented English, but this was always one of her weaknesses.

In 1928 an omnibus volume, *The Abbey School*, was published; this contained the first three 'Abbey' stories, *The Abbey Girls*, *Girls of the Abbey School* and *The Abbey Girls Go Back to School*, and the title, perhaps chosen by the publisher rather than EJO herself as likely to have popular appeal, helped to reinforce the idea of an 'Abbey School'. Although three-in-one volumes were not unknown at this period, the fact that Collins felt it worthwhile to publish this reflects the popularity of the Abbey books in the late 1920s.

The Abbey Girls Win Through, published in the same year, follows on from *Queen of the Abbey Girls* and is very much the same kind of story, exploring philosophical ideas in a way that may possibly have been helpful to adolescent girls of the period. *Queen of the Abbey Girls* ended in November with Jen's return to the Abbey after the death of her father, and now it is the following spring. Joy is

still away in Africa but is expected home soon and eagerly awaited by Mary, Jen, Maidlin and Rosamund. The new character introduced in this book to act as a catalyst and a reason for recounting some of the essential past history is Ann Rowney, who comes with two other girls to stay in the hostel in the village which Joy has opened to cater for working girls. Ann is in her late twenties, a journalist who happens to have been working in Mary's old office in order to get an insight into the life of working girls, and who has been able to take advantage of the invitation to join the other two, only one of whom actually worked in the office anyway, for this unexpected holiday. The idea of providing rural holidays for town-dwellers seems to have loomed large in EJO's mind at this time as, later in the same book, Jen is planning to use her old home on the Yorkshire moors for the same purpose.

Ann has frankly come in search of 'copy', but her conscience soon begins to prick her when she becomes involved with the lives of the Abbey girls, and she confesses to Mary and the others. When told of this, Joy graciously gives her permission to write about the village, although she expresses a wish to see anything she writes before it is sent off for publication. Joy's hope that Ann can give publicity to the craft workers, and the emphasis on the value and pleasures of rural life, have an interesting contemporary ring and might well have been written at the beginning of the twenty-first century.

Ann introduces herself to the people at the Hall by coming in search of Mary because her younger sister is a fan of Mary's books. They recognise her as one of themselves, and she sees them through a series of problems and tragedies, helping to strengthen their religious faith at this time of crisis. To a very large extent, she takes over the role of the Pixie; one can only surmise that EJO herself underwent some religious crisis at this point in her own life, experienced some deepening of her faith—this would also tie in with Patience's ambitions described in *Patience and Her Problems* the previous year—and wished to pass this on to her readers to replace or reinforce the simple, practical and cheerful commonsense philosophy preached by the Pixie.

Jen, having lost her father in *Queen of the Abbey Girls*, now suddenly loses her mother as well, and it is Ann who comforts her, pointing out that her mother has gone to join her father and that it is all for the best. It also releases Jen to become a permanent part of the Abbey household, but that is by the way. Mary has to look on helplessly, hurt that Jen so readily turns to Ann for comfort, but she learns from this experience and as a result begins to develop her own beliefs. The reader learns that Mary's escape from the world of dreams has not been as easy or as complete as has previously seemed to be the case, but now, in talking to Ann and thinking more deeply, she begins to develop into the tower of strength which she remains throughout the rest of the series. When Joy returns there is no question of Mary leaving the Abbey, although Jen offers an alternative, working with Ann as joint matron of the Yorkshire home.

Rosamund also has problems; she is virtually reigning as queen for a second year as Jen is not at the school. Although she is normally clear thinking and responsible, she plans some mischief with three other girls, one of whom is Pat Mercer. It seems a fairly harmless piece of mischief—she plans to let the others into the Abbey and secret passages early one morning to tease Jen, who is in charge—but when Jen suddenly receives the news of her mother's death, Rosamund realises that the prank would be inappropriate and goes to meet the girls to tell them that the plan must be abandoned.

The three girls refuse to take any notice of her pleas, and Rosamund, feeling that Pat in particular takes advantage of the situation, is furious and resolves not to speak to Pat again. Mary seeks strength to help her, and finally Rosamund overcomes her feelings to help Pat in a time of trouble. Soon after they return to school for the summer term, and just after the crowning ceremony, Pat's father is taken ill abroad. and Rosamund offers practical comfort, including an invitation to the Hall and the Abbey. Although it is not discussed here, this puts the Abbey firmly in position as a place of sanctuary for all who need it.

The Pat–Rosamund situation also provides a solution to Maidlin's problem. Maidlin has been invited to be Queen but is terrified at the idea; if she does not accept, Pat is the next choice. When this situation arises the feud is not yet over so, to help Rosamund 'out of a hole', Maidlin accepts the invitation and, having made the decision, she develops 'a shy, quiet dignity which added a couple of years to her age and made her fit her sixteen years, instead of seeming still a child'.

The greatest tragedy, however, is that of Joy, who becomes a mother and a widow almost simultaneously. She comes home ahead of Andrew to have her baby, and a telegram bringing news of Andrew's rumoured disappearance on safari is such a shock that, in 'a terrible night' when the other girls fear for her life and Ann competently boils up the traditional kettles of water, she gives birth to twins, who are named Elizabeth Joy, for Andrew's mother and herself, and Margaret Joan, for her aunt and cousin. The choice of Elizabeth and Margaret is interesting, since the book was published in 1928, exactly midway between the birth of Princess Elizabeth in 1926 and that of Princess Margaret, also of course a Rose, in 1930. To Sheila, as a child, the names seemed an obvious choice for twins, but bearing in mind the fact that the Marchwood twins, if they really had been born in 1928, would have been of the same generation as Queen Elizabeth II and the first British woman prime minister, Margaret Thatcher, their naming probably reflects the popularity of these names at that period.

Their new religious faith enables the girls to help each other in this latest crisis. The twins are seen as a special gift, the extra one replacing Andrew, whose death is confirmed shortly afterwards. The tragedy precipitates Jen and Ken's wedding, which is planned at less than a week's notice although Joy, with great presence of mind, stage-manages a good crowd of Hamlet Club girls at the church and gets Jen into her own wedding veil.

The impending arrival of Joy's baby is treated with great delicacy. Although various hints are dropped, and most of the girls, apart from Maidlin to whom the whole thing appears to come as a complete surprise, are aware of the fact, nothing is actually said about Joy's pregnancy until there is 'a sudden new sound in the quiet house'. Even the sex of the twins is seen as a blessing. As they are both girls, Joy can bring them up in her own old home, while Ken inherits the Marchwood title and he and Jen can move in next door. Although he has to go off to East Africa almost immediately to sort out his own and his brother's affairs, Jen can stay at home, and he will return as soon as possible, at which point they will settle in at Marchwood Manor together.

Ann proves to be a tower of practical, as well as moral, strength. She has great cooking ability, and steps in and takes over when the cook is called away to her mother who has been taken ill suddenly. Although it is obvious that the Hall must be well staffed with domestics—no male butler, though, only male chauffeurs—little is said about them until there is a crisis, and this may be because EJO was aware of her own lack of ability to handle the speech of the lower classes. Joy shakes her head over the idea of Ann being the cook, and it is obvious that she is not going to be allowed to take over the job permanently. Being matron of a hostel or children's home was an acceptable occupation for a middle-class girl; being in domestic service was not.

EJO's second book to be published in 1928 was *The Crisis in Camp Keema*, illustrated by Percy Tarrant, who didn't know a one-pound jam-jar when he saw one. In previous books we have seen the Girl Guide and Camp Fire movements compared and contrasted, and it has always been clear where EJO's own sympathies lay. She was, herself, a Camp Fire Guardian, and to give up Camp Fire for Guides is always presented as a great sacrifice.

After 'problems' and 'troubles' a 'crisis' would seem to reach a high point, but in fact the problems in Camp Keema are very much extensions of situations that have already appeared in earlier books of this period. Camp Keema is a thriving Camp Fire run by Miss Moore, the gym mistress at yet another nameless school on the Sussex coast. Just as the School of Ups and Downs was sited in real-life Rottingdean and Gregory's in Bognor Regis, the Camp Keema School is located in Worthing, which EJO knew best of all.

Camp Keema is led by its Torch-Bearer, Maribel Ritchie, and her friends in the Sixth Form, among them Phyllis Grainger, the Story Teller. In what seemed to be becoming a pattern at this time, EJO sees the events of this book through the eyes of an intelligent and mature observer, in this case Rosalind Firth, aged 18 and really past her schooldays, although she has come back for a while since she has to spend the winter on the south coast with her younger brother and sister, John and Gina, who are twelve-year-old twins. Like Astrid's brother, John is delicate, although there is no indication that his intellect is impaired, and he joins in all the activities of boys of his age, except when struck down by bronchitis. However, it is his health that has brought the three Firths south.

Rosalind and Gina are very quickly put in touch with school affairs and most particularly those of the Camp Fire, which Gina joins at once and to which Rosalind would like to belong if there were a place for her. Camp Keema, however, has a problem. Miss Moore is leaving the school and the Camp Fire has been pinning its hopes on the new gym mistress, Miss Curtis, as a possible new Guardian. From her more adult, uninvolved viewpoint, Rosalind can see how unlikely this will be—only a committed Camp Fire person would be likely to agree to take on such a position.

When Miss Curtis arrives, the problem becomes a crisis. Far from being a possible Guardian, she is a Guider and, with the support of the headmistress, Miss Ransome, decides to start a Guide Company in the school. She appeals to the members of the Camp Fire to join the Guides and help to promote a strong Guide spirit in the school, but she is very understanding and does not for one moment underestimate their loyalty to the Camp Fire—her appeal to them is to make a sacrifice for the good of the school.

It should, at this point, be emphasised that EJO presents Miss Curtis's view with sympathy. She has already shown in earlier books that she feels it is part of the Camp Fire spirit to give up Camp Fire for some other, more important, duty, and more than once this sacrifice has involved joining Guides. Miss Moore herself, perhaps acting as EJO's mouthpiece here, at her last meeting with Camp Keema, had warned the girls against becoming self-centred and had urged them to put the school first and support her successor in every way. It could be postulated that this book was written at a moment when EJO began to realise that Guiding, not Camp Fire, was becoming the obvious out-of-school activity for her average reader. She did not give up her interest in Camp Fire, but it ceases to play a large part in her books, with the exception of *Peggy and the Brotherhood*, published in 1936—the events of that book had already appeared as short stories in the 1927–31 period. And, of course, Maidlin later takes up Camp Fire.

The choice of whether or not to give up Camp Fire and join the Guides for the sake of the school is the root cause of all the other difficulties that arise in this book, and all of these have to be faced by Maribel Ritchie—Kataga, the Stormy Waves—Torch Bearer of Camp Keema. Up to this time Maribel's special friend in Camp Fire has been Phyllis Grainger, although their ideas of what makes a friendship have always been different. Maribel has shared friends and friendship while Phyllis, like Astrid with Billy, has always tried to be exclusive. As she says to Rosalind: 'My idea is to be the one to do everything for Bel and let her know that nobody cares for her as much as I do.' Rosalind finds this strange, and her comment is much like that made by Patience to Astrid in the earlier book: 'You don't trust Maribel much, although she's your pal.' Rosalind herself is keen to be friends with Maribel, but is careful not to intrude and upset Phyllis.

The moment of truth comes at a meeting of Camp Keema when the decision to join the Guides or not has to be made. Maribel, a thoughtful and responsible head girl, does not feel that there is any choice. Like Patience, she knows what she ought to do, although she is very reluctant to do it. Phyllis, leading the other Camp Fire seniors, is quite unable to understand. She sees Maribel as a traitor to the Camp Fire and, during the discussion, attacks Maribel with hard and bitter words. Her attitude causes the majority of Camp Fire members to agree to join the Guides, not so much because they feel it right but, out of their admiration for Maribel and lack of respect for Phyllis. The majority of the Camp Fire members now become Guides, including Rosalind, who was not really a Camp Fire member anyway and who is able to give Maribel help and support. The Camp Fire is left with just six members—Phyllis and two other seniors, Jane and Ruth, and three juniors who include the younger sisters of Jane and Ruth.

This break-up is as painful to Maribel as it is to Phyllis, but she is much more self-controlled although, having coped with the inevitable scene among the Camp Fire girls, she does break down later when she is telling the story to Miss Curtis. Maribel is more than willing to remain friends with Phyllis and to show a warm and friendly interest in the Camp Fire, but Phyllis makes it quite clear that she cannot be friends with someone she doesn't understand—and she doesn't understand Maribel. Each is badly hurt by the attitude of the other, but Maribel at least can see Phyl's point of view while Phyllis does not even try to understand Maribel's.

Things are made easier for Maribel because she has Rosalind's advice and support, and their friendship develops during this time, especially because there is no longer a need to consider Phyllis's feelings. Phyllis has no such support as Ruth and Jane are not strong characters. Ruth tends to be spiteful and Jane to be weepy, and Phyllis now has only three juniors in Camp Keema; nevertheless, she tries very hard to keep the Camp together, and to keep the members interested and happy.

Maribel and Rosalind, watching from a distance, hear what goes on because the school juniors, who are not so seriously affected by the feud, talk among themselves and Gina talks to Rosalind. Phyllis, who is not a leader, gets into difficulties very quickly, and Maribel helps her by indirect means. More directly, she persuades Jane not to leave the

Chanctonbury Ring, 1997

Camp Fire. Throughout the autumn term, Camp Keema's solidarity is due mainly to Maribel's influence behind the scenes. Phyllis remains inflexible, although she would really like to talk about the Camp Fire to Maribel and especially to show her their private Lodge, decorated and arranged by themselves in the loft above her father's garage. (She does not know that the original idea came from Maribel and Rosalind.)

Maribel makes one final effort at reconciliation. While in London for Christmas, she buys a gift for the Camp Fire, beautifully lettered and framed copies of the Law and Credo. She offers them, through Phyllis, to the Camp Fire, but, although the members are keen to take them and to end the feud, Phyllis, while she gives way to their wishes, is still bitter and unresponsive. Rosalind finally loses patience and, making an excuse to see Phyllis alone, tells her plainly about all that Maribel has done for the Camp Fire. This could have been disastrous but in fact it succeeds, and does at last bring the feud to an end and establish a measure of friendship between Phyllis and Maribel, and between the Camp Fire and the Guides. As at the end of *Girls of the Hamlet Club*, we are not led to expect that all's well that ends well.

One short story, *Freda Joins the Guides*, which appeared in the *Girls' All-Round Book* in 1931 and the undated *Nelson's Budget for Girls*, ties in with the problems of Camp Keema. In the book we are told that Freda and her sister Audrey are Camp Fire members who follow Maribel's example and leave the Camp Fire because they have no respect for Phyllis. Unfortunately for them, their father doesn't approve of Guides, and since they refuse to go back to the Camp Fire they are left out of both. The events of the short story appear to take place in the Christmas holidays following the crisis, and therefore fall within the period covered by the book, and are concerned with a Guide treasure hunt on the Downs. The topography is quite detailed and confirms that the school is located in Worthing, 'The Ring' that features in the story later being identified by EJO as Chanctonbury Ring.

In the story Freda, accompanying the Guides on a treasure hunt organised by Rosalind, inadvertently finds the important prize, which means that the success cannot count for their patrol. Anxious to help, she suggests they should conceal the fact that she was the person who discovered it and claim the prize. The indignation expressed by the Guides at the very idea of doing such a thing is overheard by Freda's father, who is sheltering behind a nearby tree. He now changes his mind and allows Freda to become a Guide because he believes she needs the discipline—'I can't have a girl of mine left behind in the matter of honour.'

The Camp Keema characters are the only new group to be introduced in EJO's writings of this period, where her books have been mainly concerned with making decisions, solving problems, and the giving and receiving of advice and help along the way. It is significant that the help that is asked for and obtained comes not only from friends and sympathisers; spiritual help is also requested consciously or unconsciously in prayer. There is a parallel here with Elinor Brent-Dyer, and it seems likely that the reaction of EJO's readers was the same as that reported by Helen McClelland in her book *Behind the Chalet School*—they either ignored the 'religious' bits or found them of help. One young modern reader, persuaded to try the books her mother was collecting with so much enthusiasm, reported that they were 'too moral'.

Chapter 6

HOME, SCHOOL AND AWAY, 1929 TO 1932

During the next four years, EJO's output was comparatively small but represented an interesting range of work. Four more Abbey titles appeared, and there were traditional school stories based on misunderstandings and schoolgirl pranks. There was also the uncharacteristically exciting *The Camp Mystery*, set in France on the shores of Lake Annecy. *Biddy's Secret*, the fourth of the Abbey books, also saw Maidlin chasing Biddy across France to the shores of Lake Annecy, and it seems likely that EJO had recently visited this area. In addition, the three books about Rocklands School that make up *Jen of the Abbey School*, and were discussed in the last chapter, and *The Girls of Squirrel House*, part of *The Abbey Girls on Trial*, were also published at this time. This was the last period in which non-Abbey stories were to be as well represented as Abbey tales, and even here *The Camp Mystery* serves to provide the background to *The Abbey Girls Play Up*.

The Abbey Girls at Home was published in 1929 and continues the story from the point at which *The Abbey Girls Win Through* finishes. When it opens, the twins are only three weeks old. The character who is introduced to the Abbey here and who acts as a catalyst for the events in this book is Betty McLean of Rocklands. Since we last met her in *Jen of the Abbey School*, she has lost her twin sister, Meg, who has died at the sanatorium in the Marienthal, one of the victims of TB whom Sir Rennie Brown could not save. Betty is now twenty, keenly interested in music (a fact that, like the existence of Meg, has never been emphasised in earlier books about her), but 'lost' without her twin. She is staying near London with her married elder sister, Chris, and, inspired by Tickles, she decides to look Jen up. Betty's visit to the Hall enables Jen to bring her—and the reader—up to date on recent events—Joy's widowhood, the arrival of the twins and her own marriage.

Betty's visit is prolonged because, as she is leaving the Hall, her chauffeur-driven car swerves to avoid Maidlin and Rosamund who, in avoiding a hen, have fallen off their bicycles, and crashes into a hedge. Betty is badly injured—worse than at first appears—and she stays at the Hall throughout the book, gradually recovering and learning to come to terms with the death of her twin. Although they have always been known as Betty and Meg, their names are, of course, the same as those of the Marchwood twins. By the end of the book, she is looking forward to taking charge of the music school that Joy plans to establish for girls who need but cannot afford specialist training.

This book is a consolidation of the enchanted Abbey circle. Joy has to come to terms with her widowhood and struggle back to everyday life and some kind of routine. Jen, now married into the Abbey family, is like a whirlwind, dividing her time between the Hall and the Manor, sorting people out and finally giving birth to Andrew, named for Joy's husband

and described as the first of a 'Morris six'. Maidlin grows up, forced into some degree of independence by Joy's need of her and by Rosamund's departure for Switzerland when her mother returns ill from Ceylon and goes straight to the sanatorium at the Marienthal. At the end of the book Joan returns from Malta, and it is announced that Jack Raymond is leaving the army and that the Raymonds will now settle down at Jack's old home about thirty miles from the Abbey.

The Abbey Girls at Home also reinforces the hitherto rather tenuous link between the Abbey saga and the Swiss books. When Mary returns from having escorted Rosamund to the Marienthal, she explains that they were met there by Karen Wilson and that Karen is looking after Rosamund. She says that Karen and young Rennie are not yet engaged, and describes her meeting with Sally and Tazy. Karen has told Mary that she knows of the Abbey and of Joy, Joan and Jen through meeting them at Cheltenham.

Both Mrs Shirley and Lady Marchwood die in the course of this book, although Mrs Shirley at least cannot be much more than fifty. They are both continually described as frail and fragile so the reader is prepared for their demise: '… Mrs Shirley … died in her sleep one night … old Lady Marchwood was seriously ill, and very soon she too passed on …' Rosamund's mother also dies—the Abbey girls have just come to terms with the fact that Rosamund has left the enchanted circle when they receive a telegram from her: 'Mother gone. Coming home. Rosamund.' This means that all the Abbey girls are now orphans, apart from Rosamund, who still has a father—at this stage safely out of the way overseas.

Although the titles of the Abbey books published around this time seem rather haphazard and merely to reflect the kind of titles that girls' stories tended to have at this period, houses, schools or heroines being 'on trial', 'winning through' or 'playing up', the title of this particular book does reflect the emphasis that is given to the importance of 'home' to the various girls who form the enchanted circle at the Abbey around this time. Joy has come back to bring up her twin daughters in her own beloved home; Jen regards the Hall and the Manor as home, as indeed the latter now is; Joan has come home; and both Maidlin and Rosamund look upon the Hall as their home, a fact that pleases Joy, who asks wistfully: 'Did you mean it when you spoke of us as "home"? Is that how you feel about us, Ros?', and Rosamund flashes back at her: 'It's the only home I've ever had, that I can remember … Of course this is home …' For Mary, too, the Hall is home, with 'her green study and the loved brown bedroom in the setting of the gardens and the Abbey

and the woods'. Joy, Joan, Jen, Maidlin, Rosamund and Mary have all found sanctuary in the setting of the Abbey and its nearby houses, and, whatever trials and tribulations are to come, their fortunes are forever interwoven around this quiet, beautiful and romantic setting.

The younger generation is, of course, growing up. 'Rosamund Grows Up' is the title of the chapter in which she prepares to leave the Hall for the Marienthal to see her mother, while 'Goodbye to "Poor Little Maidie"' is a later chapter in which Maidie is shown how she can now help Joy. Leaving Jen to Joy for a time, she talks to Betty, vowing to work at her French. One mystifying fact is the emphasis on the importance of French for Maidlin and her potential secretaries—first Biddy and then Rachel go to France to improve their French—when the estates that she is going to inherit are in Italy. EJO seems to have had something of an obsession about her characters learning French, although none of them ever seems to manage to master the language, or come anywhere near it, even when they spend some time in the French-speaking parts of Switzerland. The only exception up to this point seems to be Betty, who is pushed into service as someone on whom Maidlin can practise her French conversation. Perhaps, in the late 1920s, the idea of anyone learning Italian seemed completely far-fetched!

Maidlin's major triumph, however, is coping with the Princess who visits the school to see the activities of the Hamlet Club, of which Maidlin is currently Queen. It is not only Maidlin and Rosamund who are growing up. Jen and Mary begin to wonder whether they are growing out of dancing. When Mary says she has preferred to watch, Jen comments '... I've been wondering lately if I were caring for it less than I used to do', and Mary suggests that country dancing will no longer be the most important thing in their lives. Joy, in her widowhood, is not dancing, and the pregnant Jen is taking things carefully (from now on not dancing or dancing little becomes the standard indication of impending motherhood in the Abbey books).

There are probably both internal and external reasons for this change in attitude towards folk dancing. Maidlin, the youngest of the present Abbey girls, is Queen, and although she says that the Hamlet Club members are already talking about twin queens and planning what colours they will choose, it is obvious that this lies well into the future— even further away than the ten years suggested by Joy. The close involvement of the Abbey girls with the Hamlet Club is therefore coming to an end, at least for the time being. The external reason may have been that the English Folk Dance Society scene was changing and perhaps no longer appealed to EJO as much as it had done in the past. This book would have been written in 1927 or 1928; Cecil Sharp, the 'Prophet' of her books, had died in 1924, Cecil Sharp House was to open in 1930 and must have been in the planning stages for some years, and joining up with the Folk Song Society was shortly to follow in 1932. The whole movement was becoming more established and perhaps lacked the pioneering excitement that had appealed to EJO. The EFDSS *Leaflet 12*, published in 1974, states: 'By the end of the 1920s ... there was a feeling of change and also a realisation that the great period of collecting might be over.' EJO must have been aware, possibly subconsciously, of these changes and this found its way into her books. Both these reasons help to account for the retrospective books, although this solution also lay some years into the future.

The Abbey girls are developing in other ways. Joy is still struggling to get the better of her thoughtlessness—Rosamund reproaches her for her hurtful attitude towards Maidlin, and later she fails to understand Jen's feeling and anxiety about Betty. She feels guilty, and reminds herself that this is not 'what Andrew would have wanted me to be like … He'd have hated to see me as I've been these last few days.' But EJO appreciates that although people develop, they do not basically change. Although Joan has been brought back to England, she is kept at a safe distance from the Abbey—those very characteristics that made her such an attractive and worthy model schoolgirl make her a rather boring, although useful, adult.

In this book the affluence of life in the Abbey circle seems to be particularly emphasised. When Rosamund has to go to Switzerland, not only does Mary go with her but Joy also arranges for a lady courier to accompany them. Mary asks: 'Won't it be terribly expensive?', but Joy reassures her: 'My dear, the money's there to make things easy for you.' When Mary returns two days later, she is met in London by the chauffeur-driven car—and a note from Jen, asking her to delay her return to the Hall until Maidlin is back from school; so Mary goes into her old office, 'laden with roses from a florist', and then to Liberty's where she buys silk scarves for everyone. This spending spree was followed by the 'luxury of that quiet, swift run through the suburbs and the country'. It sounds a very attractive way of life, and must have seemed like heaven to girls who were living through the difficult period of economic recession and unemployment between the two world wars.

The Abbey circle are entering into a period of enchantment, the period of romance for

which, as Lynette Muir wrote in her article in *The Junior Bookshelf*, 'the idealised setting of wealth and comfort and fine weather' was essential. This means that Joy is free to do whatever she wishes as long as money can do it, and she now decides to establish her music school—'The old vicarage is empty, and would do splendidly.' This, of course, provides the answer to Betty's problems, and brings her permanently within the enchanted and romantic circle. The period of problems is over; henceforth everything can apparently be solved or minimised with the help of Joy's money, as far as the Abbey girls are concerned.

The first of the three school stories of this period was *Deb at School*, published in 1929 and illustrated by Nina K Brisley. EJO wrote three books about Deborah Lely, but only two were published in her lifetime; these had the same basic theme, the danger of blind devotion to an older girl who does not merit the idolatry. It is a theme that EJO used on other occasions, her aim being to encourage a balanced and considered attitude to relationships with other people.

Deborah lives with her aunt at Lely Court in an atmosphere of stuffy formality. There is never, at any time, an explanation for these arrangements and we are never told what has happened to Deb's parents—presumably they are dead or she would have had a means of appealing against her aunt's decisions. Her only escape from a life that she finds very confining is in the company of Derrick Langley, the eighteen-year-old son of a neighbour, of whom her aunt does not approve. He has helped and encouraged Deb and tried to teach her to be 'a good sport'. An escapade with him—a ride on the pillion of his motorbike—finally causes Lady Lely to decide to send Deb to school. This prospect, of which Deb has dreamed for years, throws her into a sudden panic, in spite of Derrick's words of encouragement. His college, Waring, is not far from St Margaret's, but he refuses to attempt any secret meetings, and offers her a word of warning. He knows she is liable to develop enthusiasms for people, and warns her against choosing an unworthy object for her admiration.

Arrived at school, Deb soon finds someone to admire—Chloe Marlowe, the head of her dormitory. Chloe is clever, pretty and proud—the adjectives used to describe her are 'beautiful' and 'queenly'—but she is not worthy of Deb's admiration and loyalty. Chloe likes to be admired and she makes a play for the admiration of her juniors, handing out forbidden chocolates at night. On the very first day she sends Deb on an errand for her which involves the latter in breaking school rules. Knowing that she's in the wrong, Deb nevertheless goes because she is loyal to Chloe. She's caught by a teacher, Miss Willis, known as Bill, who is wise in understanding and is very well aware that someone else has sent Deb, and who that someone is.

Deb refuses to give Chloe away but naturally expects Chloe to come forward to support her, and is a little uncertain when Chloe doesn't do so. Chloe, using specious arguments, manages to persuade her that what she has done is the 'sporting' thing and also, with a few carefully chosen words, puts doubts in Deb's mind about Miss Willis, although Deb has been impressed by a few well-chosen words from the mistress on the subject of friends, 'Don't give your admiration and loyalty to anyone who is unworthy. Be sporting and demand true sportsmanship in anyone you try to copy.'

Nevertheless, spurred on by a strong sense of loyalty and blinded by her own admiration, Deb follows Chloe's lead and finds herself taking the blame for more than one incident of which Chloe is the instigator, but by which Chloe herself remains untouched. Her contemporaries in her own dormitory, some of the Sixth formers who know Chloe and appreciate the situation, and Miss Willis, who sees it very clearly, all try to dissuade Deb from her blind devotion, but in spite of a feeling in her own heart that Chloe has let her down, Deb's loyalty cannot be broken.

A central incident involves Deb's friend Derrick. Discovering that Deb knows a boy at Waring College, Chloe persuades her to find a way to write to him, enclosing a letter from Chloe to an acquaintance of her own in the school, ostensibly asking for chocolates—there is an echo here of the situation and the ensuing problems with which Karen Wilson has had to deal in *The Two Form-Captains*. Deb knows exactly what Derrick will think of this, but she goes along with it to please Chloe, and the letter to Derrick reaches him via one of the maids at Lely Hall, who had been a playmate of Deb's. Derrick's reply, a forthright condemnation of the act, also reveals that the letter was not just about chocolates—Chloe was making arrangements for a clandestine meeting in the holidays. This is the point at which Deb's faith in Chloe begins to lessen, and when the affair is partially revealed, with Deb at the centre of it, and Chloe makes no move to confess her share in it, Deb loses faith in her altogether.

St Margaret's School has no Camp Fire, and its Guide company is only briefly mentioned in this book, but the organisation of the school itself reflects EJO's enthusiasm for colours and themes. St Margaret's is in Sussex, standing in a valley near the sea, the Downs and the woods. The school has three houses—Sea, Hills, and Woods—and while the outdoor uniform is a conventional navy and white, in school the girls wear dresses of their house colours, blue and green for Sea, brown and green for Woods, and amethyst and green for Hills. The idea of the colours appeals to Deb immediately; on her first day she has an idea for a school pageant, based on the three houses, which is received with enthusiasm, and preparations begin. Chloe has a leading part in Sea's contribution, with Deb as her attendant.

After the affair of the letter and the chocolates, during which Deb is injured and has to miss nearly a whole term of school, and because she will not admit that anyone else was involved in the affair, Deb is excluded from the pageant. On her return to school, by now completely disillusioned, she makes one attempt to persuade Chloe to own up, and then refuses to have anything more to do with her. There is a neat little incident when Chloe, who does not realise just how completely she has lost Deb's admiration, drops a chocolate on her pillow as a sign of favour, and Deb throws it back at her—'She hurled the chocolate with careful aim, and it struck Chloe's shoulder.' Miss Willis, who has completely understood the situation, offers Deb sympathy and warns her yet again to be careful when choosing an object for admiration.

The pageant is described in detail and includes old singing games, folk dances and songs, sea shanties and modern and classical dances, combining all EJO's enthusiasms. Derrick, who, with his mother, is in the audience, now knows the truth about the letter and is full of indignation about the girl who refuses to confess, but is also very anxious to meet the girl who 'danced so rippingly'—this is, of course, Chloe. Finding herself in a difficult situation, to say the least, Deb introduces them and then disappears, leaving Chloe to hear of Derrick's scorn for the unknown girl. His opinion makes an impression on her, and this is backed up by a talk with Deb and by the attitude of the younger girls in her dormitory when they discover that she has a secret peephole in her cubicle wall, through which she has caught them out in various misdeeds. At this point, she realises just how badly she has behaved. Meanwhile Derrick has learned the identity of the girl he so despises, and feels that he must attempt to clear Deb with the headmistress. Perhaps fortunately for Chloe, he arrives too late to be needed. Chloe has finally broken down and confessed, at first in private to Miss Willis and later, in public, to the whole school.

The school breaks up for Christmas with Deb and Chloe friends again—now that Chloe has confessed, Deb's strong sense of loyalty leads her to help and support Chloe, and they are to spend their Christmas holidays together—but the wholehearted admiration that she once felt has completely disappeared. Derrick, who plays quite a large part in the book, also forgives Chloe and joins Deb in her support. He is, in fact, the only active male character in the book, which lacks adult males to an amazing degree. Lady Lely is a widow, Derrick's father does not appear to be alive, while the staff of St Margaret's seem to wage their battle against the boys of Waring College without any co-operation from their male counterparts at the boys' school.

Deb at School originally appeared as a serial under the title of *St Margaret's*, in *Schooldays* just prior to its appearance as a book, but this does not seem to have caused the bibliographical problems posed by EJO's next published book, *Dorothy's Dilemma*, which came from Chambers in 1930, with illustrations by Nina K Brisley. As a book this appears to be very strangely constructed, and it seems to be composed of a number of shorter stories that had appeared in the various girls' annuals to which EJO contributed regularly in the 1920s.

The White House School, known as 'Old Whitey', is yet another Sussex school, situated by the sea with the downs rising behind the town. The building that EJO chose for the school still exists in Worthing, quite easily identifiable, although the town is never named. When the story begins, there are two Dorothys; the Dorothy of the title is Dorothy Bayne, also known as Dorry, Dorothy B or DB, and the other is Dorothy Cheyne, known as DC. They are close friends, both in the Fifth Form.

Living near the school is a wealthy American lady, Mrs Warner, with a fifteen-year-old daughter, Evangeline. She offers a prize for a set of three essays, all on travel topics, to be produced under examination conditions by a girl of fifteen or sixteen. To the reader of the meanest intelligence, it is obvious that the prize will be to accompany Mrs Warner and Evangeline on their travels, but this is concealed from the contestants, who assume that the prize will, as usual, consist of books. Six girls, including the two Dorothys, compete. DC is known to be the best essay writer but lacks ideas. The competition is held on the last day of term, and DC later reveals to DB in a letter that she has used three ideas that really belonged to DB, having described a beautiful church that DB had shown her, a holiday adventure that had actually happened to DB, and DB's holiday in Buckinghamshire the previous summer.

DB's reaction is that 'If DC takes the prize, she'll have won it on my ideas', and she immediately feels inhibited about writing an account of the holiday that she is currently enjoying. She is even more dismayed when she returns to school and finds that DC has already departed on the six-month trip to Europe that is the prize. She is hurt, not because she has lost the prize but by what DC has done. DC's conscience is eventually stirred by a letter she receives from another girl, Merle, while she is in Switzerland, and she confesses what she has done to Evangeline and Mrs Warner. Arrangements are made for her to return to England and to see DB, and the two girls make their peace at a dewpond on the downs, and learn that Mrs Warner has now invited both girls to join the tour. DB, however, is unable to accept the invitation as her mother is ill and has to undergo a serious operation, so DC alone rejoins the Warners.

Another Dorothy, Dorothy Denton, known as DD or Dot, has joined the school at the beginning of this term. She is younger than DB and DC, and when another girl of her age, Blodwen Hall, arrives at the beginning of the following term, the latter is immediately nicknamed 'Blot' to go with 'Dot'!

Two of the staff, Miss Dickinson and Miss Thame, suggest to Miss Willcox, the headmistress, that a Guide company should be formed in the school. This is an instant success, and DB, who becomes a patrol leader in the Ranger Company, is very enthusiastic about it, writing long letters to DC who shows so little interest that DB eventually begins writing to Evangeline instead. DB is now in the Sixth form, and is very thrilled with the two original pictures by a local artist which Mrs Warner has given to her as a consolation prize.

The treat of the Easter term is to be an evening visit to the theatre to see *The Merchant of Venice*. The reader now learns for the first time that DB has ambitions of becoming an actress; little is made of this, and the idea seems to have been introduced merely to emphasise how important the theatre visit is to her. On the day of the performance DB is quite uncharacteristically rude to Miss Dickinson, although the reader is never told the exact nature of this rudeness, and cannot bring herself to apologise. However, the sympathetic Dicky does not report her, Dorothy is thrilled with the visit to the theatre, and later she does apologise and is forgiven. This episode has all the air of a short story, of which more later.

At the beginning of the summer term DB is made a prefect, and DC, joined by Evangeline and expecting everything to have stood still in her absence, although she has been away for two terms, arrives back at school. There is a new girl in the Sixth Form, Marjorie Rogers, who is one of EJO's 'observers': an able, mature and curious girl who comments on the situation as she sees it and thus points the reader in the right direction. DC's return is fairly disastrous in many ways. DC resents DB's being both a patrol leader and a prefect, thus leaving her behind, and makes things as difficult as possible for her. The situation is not helped when the fact that DB and Evangeline have been writing to each other now emerges.

To try and improve things for DC, DB persuades the headgirl and the other prefects to make DC editor of the school magazine, a job that DC takes on with great enthusiasm—after all, she can write good essays, even if she lacks ideas. DB has written a story called *June's Decision*, which Marjorie thinks is 'ripping'; she urges DB to submit it to the new editor, which she does in a rather embarrassed way. DC, one of EJO's thoughtless girls, doesn't say anything about it, and Marjorie, angry at this lack of appreciation, does her best to persuade DC to comment.

The next incident is yet another example of the weak plotting in this book. There is a school picnic when DC and Evangeline get into trouble because they try to walk home after this has been specifically forbidden for everyone except prefects. Needless to say, their exploit is made worse when a mist suddenly comes down. Since DC is to blame, she is condemned to be excluded from a school outing to Evangeline's home. Since she's just spent six months with the Warners, one might have supposed that she would at some point already have visited their home, but this is apparently not so. She plots with Evangeline to go early one morning before the official visit just so that she can say she's seen it before the other girls. Evangeline doesn't really like the idea, but goes with DC and is then hurt when DC shows little interest in looking round, and is obviously anxious to get back to school before their absence is discovered. Unfortunately their escapade is revealed by a bus-conductor later in the day, although DC believes she's been betrayed by Evangeline. Inevitably, she loses her editorship, but this incident does lead to her final reformation. She decides to join the Guides, and she, DB, Evangeline and Marjorie form a 'four square friendship'.

Miss Dickinson (Dicky) plays a key role in the first half of the book. She is the understanding form mistress who listens sympathetically to DB when the latter feels she has been betrayed by DC, and it is she who escorts DC, on her sudden return to England, to the downs to meet DB. She is involved in the launching of the Guide company and is a central figure in the theatre-visit episode. However, she disappears from the scene at the end of the Easter term, after a brief reference to her coming departure, for which no reason is given. During the following term DB mentions her to Marjorie, who has of course never known Dicky, and later tells her that she wants to hand on 'to Vangie and DC what Miss Dickinson did for me. She showed me that what I really wanted was to find the real DC again.' Dicky is therefore a key figure in helping DB to come to terms with DC's weaknesses. Why does she disappear so suddenly in the middle of the book?

One of the answers may be that she'd already been used in another school, for she is surely the same Miss Dickinson who appears in *Dicky's Dilemma*, published in the *British Girl's Annual* in 1927. The Dicky of this story has the same qualities of sympathy and understanding, but the events take place in a quite different, day school where Dicky has introduced the girls to the delights of country dancing. Eleanor has a crush on Dicky, and must not know of the present that Madge, who has been a Camp Fire member, has made for Dicky. Kathy plans to trick Eleanor by sending her a note purporting to be from Dicky, inviting her out to tea. Sylvia reveals this trick to Dicky, who in fact meets Eleanor for tea, shows her Madge's present and persuades her to share her own pleasure in it. Eleanor grows up a little and learns to 'share' Dicky.

The existence of this story alerted us to the fact that *Dorothy's Dilemma* was evidently cobbled together from stories that had previously appeared in annuals. This would help to account for the weaknesses of plot and characterisation, and much of our speculation was subsequently confirmed by Monica Godfrey in correspondence.

The first part of the book, the story of the essay competition, ends with DC's return and her reconciliation with DB: 'Dorothy Cheyne caught [DB's hand] eagerly, and the two went off together through the autumn woods.' With the exception of a slightly altered opening sentence, Chapters 1–8 constitute *The Silence of Dorothy Cheyne* as it appeared in *Little Folks* in 1928.

Chapter 9 deals with the fact that DB cannot take up the Warners' invitation to join the European trip and with Mrs Bayne's operation, which seems very contrived on the spur of the moment. Chapter 10, 'Guides at "Old Whitey"', reads as if it could be the beginning of a new story, introducing a new interest, Guides. This, together with Chapters 11 and 12, could stand alone as a story in which Dot and Blot play an important role as catalysts for

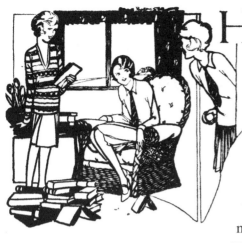

HELEN WINS

the plot. In fact, *Dicky's Way*, which appeared as a short story in the *British Girl's Annual* in 1928, consists of most of Chapter 12, so presumably the rest of this section was written to bridge the gap and account for the fact that DB did not join the Warners on their trip.

Chapter 13 marks the beginning of the summer term when DC and Evangeline arrive back at school, and in which Marjorie arrives as a new girl. This and the rest of the book, with a few cuts and modifications, constitute *The Return of Dorothy Cheyne*, which was serialised in *Schooldays* in 1929.

There is one other short story that ties into this sequence, *Helen Wins*, which appeared in the *Bumper Book for Girls* (1934) and which deals, yet again, with the problem of passionate attachments between girls. Judging by the names that are mentioned briefly in the first paragraph, it seems to be set in the same school as *Dicky's Dilemma*, although the headmistress is Miss Wilcox, the same as the head in *Dorothy's Dilemma*. It may well be that EJO was in a hurry, didn't pay her usual attention to naming her characters and merely used names she'd recently used elsewhere. One could, of course, invent a scenario in which the reason for Miss Dickinson's sudden departure was that Miss Wilcox of the White House School learned that her sister, the head of a day school (which the school in *Dicky's Dilemma* definitely is), had staffing difficulties, and generously despatched one of her best members of staff to help out! (We made this up.)

Helen Wins, to complicate matters further, appears to be set in a boarding school. In this story Sybil had, in the Third Form, seen that it is no use 'attaching' oneself to seniors or members of staff, and made friends with Clare who was in the same form. Together they have moved up the school to the Sixth, at which point they are entitled to a study. Miss Wilcox doesn't approve of 'couples', so she puts them into one of the larger studies and moves a new girl, Helen, in with them. The rest of the Sixth watch with interest. Helen is one of EJO's breezy girls and does her best to be friends with both Sybil and Clare, trying not to come between them. In the end she decides that she cannot cope with this uncomfortable situation any longer, and she goes to Miss Wilcox and asks to be moved. Miss Wilcox explains that she'd hoped Helen's presence in the study would encourage Clare and Sybil to widen their friendship, but agrees that Helen can no longer be sacrificed to this end. Inevitably, while Helen is actually in the process of moving out, Sybil realises that she doesn't want her to go after all, and the three apparently settle down as a successful trio. It is a very slight story, bulked out and made readable largely by the fact that it is told by one of the girls, who observes the situation with interest. It is unusual for EJO to write a story in the first person, which perhaps gives the story its air of freshness.

It is as well not to worry too much about the relationship of these apparently connected books and stories. They were written at a time when EJO's work was much in demand, and reflect the popularity of school stories, short and long, at this period; this undoubtedly led to the best authors making mistakes and to low standards in editing, so the mistakes were not picked up as they should have been by an experienced editor at the publishing house.

The Abbey Girls Play Up, published in 1930, follows on quite quickly from *The Abbey Girls at Home*. The setting of quiet unostentatious comfort and luxury, added to the 'woods and ruins and dancers' mentioned in this book, which must have attracted many of EJO's readers of the period, is now fully established, ready to open its arms and take in new arrivals. Two of the important new arrivals are already known to EJO readers—Maribel Ritchie and Rosalind Firth were central characters in *The Crisis in Camp Keema*. The reason for their introduction into the Abbey circle is a young girl of fifteen, Cecily Brown, whose story is told early in the book by Rosalind in conversation with Joan Raymond and Jen Marchwood. Briefly, Rosalind and her younger brother and sister had joined a camp on the shores of Lake Annecy, run for the students of St John's and St Mary's schools in the Marienthal. Maribel and her Guides were staying nearby, and both groups had become involved with an international gang of crooks, who had used a small girl as a spy in the camp. This girl, Cecily Brown, unhappy with the task she'd been given, had been so overwhelmed by the kindness and friendliness of the campers and Guides that she'd 'made a clean breast of the whole thing and begged us to protect her from the gang'. As a result of this she had been adopted by the Guides, and Maribel and Rosalind had taken on the responsibility for her.

Two years later, EJO published *The Camp Mystery*, in which the whole story of the camp and the gangsters is told; the many references to that story in the Abbey book, not only to Cecily's past but also to Rosalind's possible future engagement to Alan Kennedy,

The Silent Pool, Abinger Hammer, 1997

relate to the serial *The Watchers on the Lake* and the long short story, *The Missing Link*, published in 1927 and 1929 respectively, which together subsequently formed the first half of *The Camp Mystery* (see pages 145–8 and 165–7).

The introduction to the Abbey circle in *The Abbey Girls Play Up* comes via Joan, who is now established in her home at Rayley Park with a small son, John, as well as her daughter Jansy, who is now five. Joan, who had never achieved her early ambition to be a gym mistress, is nevertheless sparing time to teach folk dancing in the villages near her home, and it is an incident in one of her classes that brings Maribel, Rosalind and Cecily to visit her and to be drawn into the charmed circle of life at the Abbey.

Cecily has been boarded with an old servant of Maribel's family and goes to school in the nearby town where Maribel lives, her guardians feeling that she needs a quiet, well-ordered life after her earlier excitements. Having joined the Women's Institute folk-dancing classes taught by Joan, Cecily has discovered an enthusiasm for music and obviously has some inborn talent. Another of Cecily's discoveries is Mrs Alexander, known as 'Sandy', a young widow who plays the violin, has pupils in the surrounding area and lives in a delightful bungalow near to the downs and also to the Silent Pool, a small tree-bordered lake, a place of peace to which Cecily brings her irritations and bad tempers to be charmed away. Sandy Alexander is an interesting person, and one wonders if she was based on a real acquaintance—it has always seemed a shame that she does not appear in any later books.

Maribel, in her own car—active and efficient young women are now beginning to have cars of their own, often referred to as 'the old bus', which are usually good-tempered and don't object to being driven on rough tracks or over bad ground—drives Rosalind and Cecily to see Mrs Raymond at her home, where they also meet Lady Marchwood (Jen), who is visiting. References to folk dancing break the ice, a friendly rapport is very quickly established, and the problem of Cecily and what to do about her new enthusiasm for music is discussed. For Joan and Jen there is no problem—here is another pupil for Joy's music school, which has now been in existence for two years. All this, in turn, allows for explanations about the Abbey circle and the relationships of those who are part of it, not to speak of the Hamlet Club. Naturally, an invitation is given to Rosalind, Maribel and Cecily to visit the Abbey.

On their arrival there they are greeted by Joy and yet another set piece is established— her likeness to Joan strikes new visitors all of a heap, and they are also amazed that a widow should be so young. This has always seemed very strange, especially in view of Cecily's friendship with Mrs Alexander. They are also introduced to the children, another must for new arrivals, and with them they meet Maidlin, who asks for their help as Guiders. Discussion with Maidlin brings in Mary Devine who would also be glad of advice. In fact, once arrived at the Abbey, Cecily is largely relegated to a minor role. She stays to play with the children or goes off to the Music School to meet her fellow pupils, and we hear of her only in brief episodes while her Guider guardians become involved in friendship with the Abbey crowd—in fact, more than friendship, as almost everyone at the Abbey has some difficult choice to be made and Maribel and Rosalind are in a position to offer help or advice.

Maidlin and Mary are both being urged, by their consciences and their sense of responsibility to those less privileged, to cope with a group of teenage girls for whom none of the village activities is completely suitable. The Guide company is full and can take no more girls until a new Guider can be found, the folk-dance classes are for younger or older age groups, and the girls have just lost their Sunday School teacher. Mary feels she should take on the Sunday School class but is conscious of her own unfitness for such a task, while Maidlin views with horror the idea that she ought to be a Guide Lieutenant. Her problem is solved by Rosalind's suggestion that she should start a Camp Fire, and Mary is strengthened by Maribel's admission that she has similar feelings over the same type of problem.

Some observations made by Rosalind persuade Jen to speak to Joy and urge her to take an active part in life once more—to give of herself as well as her money. This is a dangerous topic, especially with somebody of Joy's character, but Rosalind's argument, put forward by Jen, that the twins are going to wonder why their mother 'doesn't do things' persuades her to dance again and also to consider becoming a Ranger Captain so that she will be able to do things with her daughters. A very modern idea, when one comes to think of it!

A chapter headed 'That Little Bit Extra' puts forward an idea that, as Stella recalls, was part of her own upbringing. This is that we have our job or our tasks laid down for us, but that there is a duty, especially for those with leisure time to spare, to give something extra, to find a way of helping others in which we also gain some satisfaction. This idea is put forward by Mary, and it is later seen by Maribel as part of the atmosphere of the Abbey.

Joy continues to mature and in this book shows a new understanding of other people's feelings. Having braced herself to take up Guiding, motivated by thought for her twins, she finds sympathy for Cecily when the latter, terrified but determined, approaches her on behalf of Sandy, suggesting her for the vacant place in the Music School. Joy visits Sandy and briefly a real rapport is established between these two young women, both widowed after a short, happy marriage. Such a shame that this friendship was never developed!

In the meantime Maribel is becoming more closely attached to the Abbey circle through the attentions of Ken Marchwood's cousin, Mike. Mike Marchwood has not appeared in any previous book and does not appear in later ones, but this relationship puts Maribel in

The Abbey Girls Play Up

a good position to start Maidlin's Camp Fire, and she later becomes a useful fiddler for dancing and the producer of yet another Abbey 'grandchild'.

Rosamund is in Switzerland, 'visiting friends', and does not appear until nearly the end of the book, but she has been mentioned frequently. When she does arrive, it is as the bearer of startling news—Cecily's mother has been found in the hospital at the Platz, recognised by Rosamund from her likeness to Cecily in a photograph of Maidlin's Camp Fire. There is an anxious rush to the Abbey, a dramatic moment when Cecily is told the news, and the book ends with a grateful Cecily walking on the Platz with Rosamund. However, during her short stay in England, Rosamund, talking to Maribel, reveals a certain dissatisfaction with her own life, a sense of only half-belonging to the Abbey circle, of not having a real place where she is needed. Being Rosamund, she thinks practically and looks forward, certain that at the right time her work will appear, although she also knows that she will have to face opposition to her urge to go out and do it.

In *The Abbey Girls Play Up*, there seems to be a deliberate attempt to put into words the 'spirit' of the Abbey, which is so often an important theme in the later and retrospective books. Although EJO was probably not aware of it, to modern readers there is an element of snobbishness here—the atmosphere of friendly comradeship, offered on equal terms to newcomers like Maribel, Rosalind and Cecily, is not extended to the lower classes—Cecily does not find it in the village where she lives, although the WI welcomed her to its folk-dance class. Even Jen, when asked to dance by a small girl who was brave enough to send her a formal note, dismisses the child as 'only village'. Cecily finds herself at home at Rayley Park and the Abbey, and in Rosamund she finds an embodiment of the Abbey spirit.

In spite of, or perhaps as a result of, their very ordinariness, and the fact that they occur so often in the girls' school stories of the time, it is possible that EJO chose her titles with care. Certainly in *The Abbey Girls Play Up* several of the characters are required to make an effort to live up to the ideals they have set themselves, and in the next book, *The Abbey Girls on Trial*, published by Collins in 1931, some of them, notably Joy, Maidlin and Rosamund, go through a difficult period in their relationships with each other, those same relationships being tested to the utmost, and only come through with the help and understanding of the better-balanced or more experienced Jen and Mary.

Not only new people but a new location is established in the early part of the book, and, again, the introduction comes through Joan, who calls for coffee at the Squirrel Tea House. This is run by two sisters, Audrey and Elspeth Abbott—there is a middle sister, Eleanor, who is currently away in Ceylon with friends and who, when she is at home, is hardly a good companion for either of her sisters. In fact, it becomes clear that Eleanor is a real little go-getter with no obvious redeeming features. No one, least of all EJO, can find any virtue in Eleanor.

Joan arranges to meet Rosamund and Maidlin at the Squirrel to hear all the news of the Abbey because her children have measles and she must not take infection to the Hall and the Manor, where Jen has a new baby. That same day Audrey and Elspeth have received a letter from Eleanor, telling them that she has married a Mr Kane, a middle-aged man whom she has met in Ceylon. Not wanting to come home and work with her sisters, she has taken the first opportunity offered and married a man old enough to be her father. Her sisters are disgusted and Audrey, at first, is completely disheartened; Eleanor was not a lot of help but her outlook at least was more adult than Elspeth's. Elspeth is a dreamer, who forgets about the washing-up to go and watch squirrels in the woods. However, there is backbone in Elspeth, and when she understands Audrey's feelings she quickly pulls herself together and promises to give all the support that is needed.

Their discussion of the crisis is interrupted by the arrival of Joan, Rosamund and Maidlin. Audrey, like a good hostess, shows an interest in their conversation, and Rosamund's open friendliness responds to it. When Maidlin, quieter and dreamy, upsets Elspeth by a chance remark, Rosamund rushes to make things right, so by the time the visit is over the Abbey and its people have been properly introduced—but not individually by surname, the only family name having been mentioned being Marchwood. Consequently, even when Audrey and Elspeth hear that their new brother-in-law has a daughter the same age as Eleanor, they do not connect her with Joan Raymond's friends. They do, however, feel that this unknown girl may be as unhappy about the marriage as they are.

A visit from Maidlin, come to apologise to Elspeth on her own account, continues to bring the reader and the Abbott girls up to date on the Abbey story and establishes Maidlin's character—artistic with a tendency to dream and to rely on others, especially Rosamund, but aware, all the same, of the dangers. At the end of her visit she puts into words the new Abbey spirit when she says: 'We're always adopting somebody … Joy and Jenny-Wren will do it; it's their way.'

At the Abbey, the news of the Kane/Abbott marriage is greeted with even stronger reactions. Rosamund receives the news in a letter from her father and is, quite naturally, disgusted; it brings to the fore her feeling that she must branch out on her own, make a life for herself and not remain in the protective luxury of the Abbey. Her friends react predictably; Jen and Mary sympathise and understand, Joy considers the whole idea absurd and Maidlin is terrified of losing her friend and protector.

Rose Cottage inWashington, the Sussex village identified as the location of the
Rose and Squirrel (see p151), 1980s

Letters from Ceylon to the Abbotts and from the Abbotts to their new 'niece' quickly establish the fact that it is Eleanor Abbott who has become Rosamund's stepmother. When Rosamund learns that she is related to the 'Squirrel girls', who are now her step-aunts, she is delighted and prepared to forgive her father. Joy, however, with her usual lack of understanding, flares out at Rosamund and accuses her of selfishness, saying that if she leaves the Abbey, it will make Maid and Jen as well as Joy herself very unhappy and 'We're three to your one'. Joy cannot appreciate that Rosamund wants to make her own way and find a future that will satisfy her wish to be really needed. Mary, who has become a much stronger character, warns Joy of the danger she is running, telling her: 'You'll lose her if you keep her here. Let her go, and she'll love you for ever.' Joy calls Mary 'an old bully' but goes and makes her peace with Rosamund, who has sought sanctuary in the Abbey. Happier once she has got Joy's support, Rosamund arranges to meet her new aunts, and a car is sent to bring them to the Abbey where there is a happy reunion.

The story thus far was published by Collins in 1932 as *The Girls of the Squirrel House*, just as they had also published the shorter books that make up *Jen of the Abbey School*. There is no evidence, however, that these twelve chapters had appeared earlier in any form, and, apart from the title of Chapter 12, which becomes 'The Abbey' instead of 'A Day at the Abbey', the texts are identical. A smaller size of paper was used, so this book is in a smaller format. One hopes that the publishers did not set out deliberately to make readers believe that here was a brand-new title by EJO, but there may have been a few disappointed girls in 1932. Again, its appearance reflects the popularity of girls' stories—and certain authors—at this time, and the pressure on publishers and authors to meet the demand. There are hints of problems to come in *The Girls of the Squirrel House*, but not enough is said about these to leave the young reader unsatisfied. A letter from EJO to Regina Glick shows that this shorter version was in fact published without EJO's consent: '… atrocious *Squirrel House* … I knew nothing about it.'

Once the Squirrel girls have recovered from the shock of learning the identity of their new niece, they realise that their original idea of inviting her to join them in their teashop is unlikely to be needed, but Rosamund has her own ideas. A childhood dream of having a shop so that she can keep things in cardboard boxes has developed in the telling until it has become an idea, curiously up-to-date, for a craft shop which would be an outlet for people who produce good work but have no idea how to sell it, and to whom the money would be useful. Conveniently the cottage next door to Squirrel House is empty, and plans for a joint venture are enthusiastically laid.

Rosamund's father nearly puts paid to all this when he writes to explain that he can no longer afford to pay her an allowance now that he has a young wife to support, but he offers to pay for her to be trained for some career. As a gesture from father to daughter this probably seems worse to modern readers than it would have done, perhaps, at the time when the book was written, but it certainly makes sure that nobody will regret the death of Rosamund's father when it occurs later in the book.

The news of this unexpected blow gives Joy the opportunity for a further attempt to persuade Rosamund to change her mind and return to the protected luxury of the Hall, accusing her of wasting her education and personality in a little teashop. Rosamund's reply is typical of her and the sort of girl that EJO admired: 'The first thing for a girl of my personality and education—if they really exist—to do, is to show that she can keep herself and pay her way.' She insists on going ahead, in a much less ambitious way, with her project, and is soon in the thick of it, working hard, missing her freedom, but sticking to the job she has chosen. There is not too much poverty about it—her cottage is cleaned, repaired and furnished by her friends, after being vetted by Ken Marchwood, who comes down heavily with practical male advice—and insists on 'giving Rosamund a bath'.

This is where the strain placed on the tie between Joy and her 'first' twins becomes more apparent. Joy does not really understand Rosamund's desire to be independent and can only see it as a sign of lightness of character, an enthusiasm for new friends and a new life that leads to the neglect of old ones. Unwisely, she passes on her thoughts to Maidlin, who is feeling bereft anyway, although she can really manage without Rosamund and has done so before. In an attempt to win back a friend she has not actually lost, Maidlin, in conversation and in letters, asks Rosamund's advice about Camp Fire problems, but Rosamund's lack of age and experience let her down. She's been told for so long that Maidlin must be allowed to stand on her own feet that she ignores all the requests and talks only of her own affairs. Joy takes Maidlin's part, and the friendship between Maidlin and Rosamund is in very real danger.

It is Jen, as usual, who puts things right by explaining Maidlin to Rosamund and giving her a piece of advice that is very much a favourite of EJO's: 'The question is—and it's a very hard question to answer—has anyone the right to refuse help to someone who has asked it?' In Jen's eyes—and again it is EJO speaking—the whole situation has arisen because of the lack of trust between the three of them—Rosamund, Maidlin and Joy. The final chapter brings news that is to be of great importance in Rosamund's life. Her father has died and her stepmother has just had a baby boy, Roderic Geoffrey Kane, whose existence is to lead to a very important future for his half-sister.

DEB
OF
SEA
HOUSE

ELSIE J.
OXENHAM

CHAMBERS

EJO's third school story of this period was a second book about Deb Lely, *Deb of Sea House*, published by Chambers in late 1931 and illustrated by Nina K Brisley. In this EJO continues to warn her readers against giving devotion where it is not deserved, and picks up the story of Deb and Chloe almost exactly where it finished in *Deb at School*. They are introduced to new readers through the eyes of a new younger girl at St Margaret's, Hilda Rutherford. Hilda first meets Deb and Chloe at a party during the Christmas holidays and finds reason to admire them both: 'Hilda's loyalty wavered between the beautiful Chloe and the understanding and comradely Deb.'

From their conversation she quickly perceives that there is some problem or mystery attached to Chloe and, being a bright child, determines to find out what it is. She is even more intrigued by conversations in the train on the way to school, during which time she also makes friends with another new girl, Diana, who is to be in Woods House while Hilda is destined for Hills. Inevitably, and because, owing to the Houses being redecorated, they have to sleep at first in Deb's dormitory in Sea House, they hear the story of Deb and Chloe, which arouses their admiration for Deb, an admiration that is increased by Deb's staunch support for, and championship of, Chloe in front of the whole school.

Deb herself is in a very difficult position. Having learned by experience the effect of misguided admiration, she does not want to be the recipient of it. Nor can she see the difference between her own previous sentiment for Chloe and the respect given to the new dormitory head, Selina Linton, who is also Head Girl of the school, by her own friends. Selina, who has been away from school for a year on a trip around the world with her parents, is definitely worthy of respect, a good leader and a very understanding person. Unfortunately, Deb starts out determined to support Chloe, to shake off her own admirers and to mistrust Selina, who would very much like to be friends.

Miss Willis, as wise as ever, explains Deb to Selina,

> '… She likes you and she's afraid of being disloyal to Chloe. She'll probably be difficult at first; that will mean she is fighting against her feeling for you. She'd like to let herself go as the others will do; but Chloe has hurt her badly and has made her shy of showing her feelings. You'll need patience and perhaps gentleness with Deb. But if she's awkward and seems to resist you, I'm sure it will be because her liking for you is clashing with her loyalty to Chloe.'

In a defiant mood Deb takes Hilda with her on a late-evening trip to explore the newly decorated upper floors of Hills House, which are out of bounds, and is punished, not only for the escapade, but also because she has led Hilda astray. Hilda's admiration for Deb, however, loses nothing of its strength and is shared by Diana—at quite an early stage in the story the two younger girls have become known as Hild and Di.

Their devotion worries Deb who, although she does not admit it, is afraid of the responsibility, and her antagonism towards Selina increases because Selina understands. The two well-meaning juniors bring the matter to a head. Miss Cameron, the science mistress and head of Hills House, is known to be writing a botany textbook which she is illustrating with her own drawings and paintings. The book is kept in a drawer in her room and everyone would like to see it. By accident Hild happens to know where it is kept, and, in an attempt to cheer her up, the children take it from its hiding place to show it to Deb.

Their plan goes awry because Deb is deliberately avoiding them and before they have time to return the book its loss is discovered, and Miss Cameron has a clue to the thief, having found a tunic-button in her study. The button proves to be Hild's, and Deb learns the whole story when she finds Di in tears because Hild is being punished. Deb accepts some responsibility for the behaviour of the younger girls and goes to confess to Miss Cameron, but all she will say is that Hild did it for her, thus giving the impression that it had been done under her instructions. Not unnaturally the authorities take a very serious view of this, although Miss Delius, the headmistress, is not entirely blind to the characters of her pupils. She does send Deb to isolation in the school sanatorium for a day, but although Deb thinks this is a punishment it is really an attempt to help her to get her thoughts in order. During Deb's banishment, the real truth comes out when Hild confesses the reason for taking the book.

However, before the matter is finally settled, Deb and Selina have an adventure in the snow. An unexpectedly heavy fall of snow, unusual so far south, causes Miss Delius to give the school a holiday for snowball fights and long walks. Selina, a privileged person, gets leave to take Deb out with her for a long walk and lunch at a cottage, and during the walk she helps her to understand her problems, to see where she was wrong in her treatment of the two juniors and in her attitude to Selina. By now good friends, Deb and Selina set off to return to school but get lost in snow fog. Two small Indian boys, sons of a Maharajah and pupils at Waring, are also lost in the snow, and they literally fall at the girls' feet. Deb goes for help while Selina looks after the boys, and the two girls are acclaimed as heroines by both schools.

Indian princes, a new theme for EJO, were nevertheless a popular ingredient in boys' stories of the time. The somewhat patronising attitude towards them shown by the other boys would nowadays be condemned as politically incorrect, and EJO's representation of them is, in any case, scarcely logical. Their father, the Maharajah, speaks English perfectly 'with a slight Oxford accent', so it seems unlikely that the boys would have been sent to an English school with the small command of English that they appear to have—and would they speak Tamil? This Indian element seems to have been introduced to add romance and excitement, and EJO seems to have been out of her depth in dealing with it. The pageant which had been Deb's brainchild is performed again, with a prologue written for Selina, Deb, Hild and Di to perform, and the two older girls are rewarded by the Maharajah with jewelled pendants.

EJO signals the third book about Deb in Selina's words, when she says to Deb: 'In another year, you ought to be head of South Dorm, in two years Captain of Sea and, perhaps, some day, head of Margaret's.' *Deb Leads the Dormitory* was apparently written and submitted to the publishers, but EJO was told that '… there is no longer a great demand for school stories'. This was patently untrue, and its rejection may also be a reflection of the weakness of the Deb books compared with EJO's other work. The unpublished manuscript was discovered in the 1990s and published in 1992.

Although she doesn't actually become head, *Deb Leads the Dormitory* does indeed end with Deb leading the South Dorm, but not before she has experienced more trials and tribulations. The Deb–Chloe situation is put at risk by the arrival at St Margaret's of Chloe's young cousin, Claudia, which coincides with the sudden departure of Selina, who has had to go home to help her mother care for a sick grandmother. This unfortunately leaves Deb bereft of a good and supportive friend, just when she is going to need one.

The main theme of this book is the attempt to keep from Claudia the story of how Chloe let Deb down over the matter of letters, chocolates and the boys of Waring College. Claudia admires her older cousin, and Chloe is afraid that if she knew the truth she would no longer respect her. Deb—and most other people—feel that the best thing would be to tell Claudia the whole story. Claudia's mother and Miss Delius rather agree with Deb, but are prepared to leave the final decision to Chloe. Claudia is a lively and inquisitive thirteen-year-old, who settles easily into her place in Sea House and her bed in South Dormitory. Selina's departure means that a new Head of Dormitory must be appointed, and Miss Delius chooses Pamela as the oldest of the seniors, though Pamela herself thinks it should be Deb. However, supported by Deb's undoubted qualities of leadership and by Barbara, another reliable supporter, she does her best.

Through all the usual school activities, the attempt to hide from Claudia the truth about her much admired cousin makes for difficulties and misunderstandings. Claudia, nicknamed Santa Claus, makes herself unpopular, even with her contemporaries—so much so that, on a picnic to the downs, they take her for a walk, tie her to a gate and abandon her. The situation is not really dangerous as she can free herself and could have rejoined the school party if she hadn't tried to be too clever, fallen down and had to be rescued by Derrick and a group of Waring boys.

One of Deb's problems is that Claudia admires her and insists on praising her for things that are not true, and pestering her for answers to questions. In the end Chloe is persuaded to tell Claudia the truth in order to get her off Deb's back. Then, of course, Claudia turns against Chloe, and Deb has to explain and comfort her and try to change her mind. Claudia becomes another of Deb's admirers along with Di and Hild. So this, like its two predecessors, is a book about feelings rather than actions, with Deb as the central character.

Biddy's Secret, published in 1932, was the first book about the Abbey girls that did not have 'Abbey' in the title and was published by Chambers. Collins, who had published all the previous Abbey books, did not publish another until EJO began to write what have become known as the retrospective books at the end of the 1930s. The changes in publisher and in title style may be due to the changing nature of the Abbey books written during the next few years, which are romances likely to appeal to older girls.

The events of *Biddy's Secret* follow on directly from those of *The Abbey Girls on Trial*, at the end of which Rosamund and her step-aunts had departed to Malta to bring home her stepmother and the new baby half-brother. Rosamund appears only briefly at the end of *Biddy's Secret*, which is essentially a book about Maidlin. Maidlin has already made various firm efforts to grow up when crises have arisen. She met the visiting princess when Rosamund was called away to her dying mother and she took on the job of Camp Fire Guardian to help in the village, but she feels that she has never been allowed to stand on her own two feet, particularly by Joy. How is the final process of growing up to be achieved in her case? She has plenty of money, and her full inheritance will come to her when she is twenty-five. She therefore lacks the stimulus to go out and find a job as Rosamund had done. Her proposal to run away and find a job seems artificial, particularly in view of EJO's oft-stated insistence that jobs must be left for those girls who need to earn a living.

Biddy Devine, Mary's younger sister, has always been EJO's 'bad' girl, never a fully reformed character despite the influence of the Abbey girls, and eventually despatched to a secretarial job in France as a preparation for being Maidlin's secretary because EJO could find no other role for her when Mary moved to be Joy's secretary and personal assistant at the Hall. Biddy's secretive behaviour seems perfectly in keeping with all we already know about her character, though her failure to announce her marriage to her old friends does on the face of it seem a shade unlikely. Surely the reactions of the Verdier family would have become clear before the wedding? Why, if Biddy thought marriage into the Verdiers was a good thing, would she even have thought of keeping the whole operation secret?

The catalysts in this plot are Ruth Devine, who returns to England for another visit after a gap of six years, and the inevitable illness, when several people are thrown into quarantine and cannot do the things they had planned to do. Ruth's return also provides the excuse for bringing the new reader up to date on events and people, and making the established Abbey reader aware of the current situation. When the book opens, Ruth is staying near Liverpool with some friends she has met on the boat from South Africa. The descriptions suggest that she is at Crosby or Blundellsands, areas that EJO knew well and to which she felt she belonged; as she wrote to Andrea Polden in 1951: 'I have stayed at Waterloo, so I know all about Crosby and Blundellsands. They are lovely sands to play on—if you keep away from the black patches of quicksand ... I was born at Southport, so I really belong along there.'

Ruth is now twenty-five and is the object of attentions from two young men, one of them the young man of the Fisher household where she is currently staying. It is the prospect of his imminent arrival that sends her off to London, where she is met by Maidlin and taken to the Abbey. Mary is away in Yorkshire for the weekend so Ruth is entertained at the Hall by Joy and her twins and Maidlin. Joy is wearing a green dress, the first time she has worn colours since Andrew's death. This small company makes it possible for Ruth to observe and size up Maidlin's problem, her wish for more independence and her difficulties in the face of Joy's treatment.

Jansy Raymond has developed mumps, which puts Mary, Jen and Jen's children in quarantine, and, with no Mary available at the Hall, Joy cannot accompany Maidlin on her annual visit to her Italian estates. Ruth had intended to visit Paris to meet some Americans whom she had also met on the voyage to England—it is the young man of this family, Ralph Norman, who has gained her affection and to whom, later in this book, she becomes engaged—so she offers to travel with Maidlin as far as Paris and see her safely on the Italian express. Maidlin then decides to meet Biddy on the journey from Paris to Turin.

Just the day before she and Ruth set off, Maidlin puts her ideas to Joy,

'I think I ought to do something useful ... I don't know anything about how other people live ... it's been too easy ... I want to know ... what it feels like to work and earn ... I believe if I had a job and worked at it for a year, and lived on what I earned ...'

Joy dismisses the whole idea as absurd, and Ruth's arguments in favour of such a scheme are dismissed as equally absurd. However, on the way to Paris, Maidlin tells Ruth of her plan to consult Biddy and ask her to help her find a job. Ruth is horrified and threatens to tell Joy, but in the end they reach a compromise, and Ruth promises to listen to any plans made with Biddy and, if she approves of them, to 'think out what's the best thing to do about Joy'.

Biddy has sent a telegram arranging to meet Maidlin at Aix-les-Bains, but when Maidlin arrives there she is met by a stranger, a young woman who talks about 'Madame Bidet'. (The irony of this rather unfortunate choice of surname was presumably completely lost on EJO, and her contemporary young readers were probably too unknowing or too innocent to notice.) The stranger takes Maidlin to Annecy, where Biddy is found with a week-old baby daughter. Almost the first thing she says to Maidlin is 'I'm married.', to which Maidlin's reaction is 'Of course.'. Later on there is some speculation as to whether the marriage is valid, but Biddy is not the kind of person who would be caught out in a matter like this. The story of her secret marriage to her boss's nephew, Claude Verdier, is told. It transpires that Claude has always been the black sheep of the family, and, the novelty of his marriage to Biddy evaporated, he has gone off to South America. The situation has been made more complex by Biddy's discovery, too late, that the Verdier son, Etienne, really loves her. (She does eventually find happiness with him and disappears, apart from the occasional mention, from the Abbey saga.)

The experience necessary to Maidlin's growing-up process is thus provided for her. She has to look after Biddy and persuade her that the right thing to do is to return to the Abbey and tell all; it's not so much the actual marriage that is the problem, but the deception that Biddy has practised for nearly a year. Maidlin, with a deepened and more adult understanding of Joy, realises they must go in person to tell the story—writing would merely cause more problems. Before they can reach the Abbey, however, much of the story has been revealed, and perspicacious Jen has even guessed there is a baby. On the morning when they are to leave Annecy, a telegram from Ruth arrives asking 'Is Biddy married?', and when they arrive in Paris she tells them that an announcement has appeared in *The Times*:

> Verdier-Devine. If Biddy Devine, who married Claude Verdier at Lyons on April 30th last, will communicate with Messrs. Verdier et Cie, Lyons, she will hear news of the greatest importance. Urgent.

Rosamund too has seen the advertisement and sent Ruth a telegram, which arrives while Maidlin and Biddy are still in Paris. This development heightens the tension—have Mary, Joy and Jen also seen the notice in *The Times*? Jen *has* spotted it and taken it over to the Hall for Mary and Joy to see. This gives them all time to adjust to the situation and, more importantly, to begin to realise the magnificent job that Maidlin has done in coping with the situation. Jen also realises that they are coming to confess and suggests that this is not spoiled, saying: 'I'm certain Maid has been having a fight with Biddy about it, and Maid has won. She's insisted that Mary must know. It will fall horribly flat if Mary meets them and they find we know already.'

The characters of Joy, Jen and, to a lesser extent, Mary are all developed in this book to respond to Biddy's misfortunes in ways that seem appropriate. Maidlin has finally grown up and, what is more, has managed to convince Joy that she has done so. Biddy learns that Claude has been killed in an accident in South America and there is a hint of the romance with Etienne Verdier that leads to Maidlin's words that close the book: 'I don't think you'll ever be my secretary, Biddy dear.'

By this time EJO had visited Annecy and had clearly developed an attachment to this attractive area of France, for it is also the scene of her next published book, *The Camp Mystery* (1932). As has already been said (see page 134), the events in this adventure story precede the ones described in *The Abbey Girls on Trial*, and those in the first half of the book had originally been mentioned in *The Watchers on the Lake*, serialised in *Toby* magazine in 1927, and *The Missing Link*, a 'long short' story in *Little Folks* annual for 1929. We do not know if the second half of the book had also appeared earlier. The events in *The Camp Mystery* take place two years after those of *The Captain of the Fifth* (1922) but before those of *The Troubles of Tazy* (1926). It has a very complex plot and enough material to make up several stories, and it brings together characters from a number of series in a quite incredible way.

'Look who are following us.'
(*The Camp Mystery*)

When the story opens, Rosalind Firth, who is nineteen, and her brother and sister, John and Gina, fourteen-year-old twins, have been travelling with their parents in Switzerland, and have just reached Lake Annecy nearly at the end of their tour. These three are well-established characters, having already appeared in *The Crisis in Camp Keema* (1928) and in *Peggy-Perfect goes to School*, a serial story that had appeared the previous year, 1931, in *Little Folks*. John, as the informed reader knows, is not very strong, and the Firths receive a letter from a doctor they have visited in Geneva to say that John has lung trouble but will outgrow this if he can live in the mountains.

As it happens, St John's and St Mary's schools from the Marienthal are camping on the shores of Lake Annecy with Mr and Miss Kennedy. Astrid and Guly, the latter now generally known as Billy, are head girls for the coming term, Astrid being the choice of the staff and Billy the choice of the girls. The latter is good friends with Sven (Peter) Pankridge, the American boy who is head of St John's. Astrid is very jealous of this friendship, which developed, as she explains later to Rosalind, while she was in England for a year after the death of her twin brother, Nils. The Firths' curiosity leads to a visit to the camp, and Rosalind suggests that she and the twins join the camp while the possibility of the twins going to the schools is investigated. The arrangements for this are made, and Gina attaches herself to Astrid, while John becomes friendly with Peter.

The friendship between Peter and John means that Peter can give John, and thereby the reader, the information that is vital to an understanding of the 'mystery' of the title. He explains that an important invention has just come the way of his father, Mr Pankridge, and that some mysterious Americans, who appear to be watching the camp, want to find out about it. At this point Mr Pankridge himself arrives and apparently leaves some important papers with his son. Billy, aware of the meeting between Peter and his father, tells John to say nothing about this as it's none of his business. Unfortunately, Astrid, who is portrayed throughout as incredibly strong-headed and foolish, qualities that are increased by her fondness for Billy and her jealousy of Peter, has also overheard the transaction between Peter and Mr Pankridge. In her wish to do something special for Billy, she persuades John and Gina, when the rest of the campers have gone off for a walk, to row across the lake with her to ask permission for the whole party to visit an interesting and mysterious castle which Billy has expressed a wish to see. As they are returning they get into difficulties with the boat, and are rescued by one of the Americans to whom, despite Gina's commonsense discouragement, Astrid tells all she knows about Peter and the papers. Although Astrid is confined to camp for a week for taking the boat out, Gina realises that she cannot report her for talking so openly to the American.

Peter and John now disappear, kidnapped by the mysterious Americans. Astrid's stupidity is revealed and she repents the rashness brought about by her wish to harm Peter. However, John and Peter turn up unharmed within twenty-four hours, dumped by the men when they find nothing in Peter's envelope of papers. It has all been a trick (somewhat irresponsible, one might think) to mislead the rival gang.

There are new arrivals at the lake: a Guide company, on a three-week trip to France, are staying for a fortnight at the Hotel des Cyclamens on Lake Annecy, with a week in Paris to follow. The company includes Maribel Ritchie, Rosalind's close friend—despite their closeness, the two girls are utterly surprised to find each other here, but Rosalind especially is delighted as she is feeling rather out of things.

Gina finds a notebook, full of mysterious figures and signs, near the hut where Peter and John were trapped after they were kidnapped, and there seems to be a connection between this and the strange Americans. A young girl, called Cécile or Cecily, is also staying at the hotel with a 'Madame' who passes her off as French. Cecily hangs around the camp, gets hold of the notebook and throws it, fortunately now safely enclosed in a box, into the lake. The girls discover that she is really Cecily Brown, an English girl originally brought up in England, who was taken to a convent in Paris. From there she has been brought for the purpose of infiltrating the camp—it is hoped that by appearing to be French but understanding English perfectly she will learn something useful by accident. At this point Mr Kennedy is kidnapped—one feels inclined to ask 'Why?'—but turns up again almost immediately.

There is yet another new arrival, Phyllis Grainger, who is now friendly with both Maribel and Rosalind, but still hates the Guides for taking Maribel away from her. She knew that Maribel was in the area and has come to look for her. The first person she meets is Astrid, and the two soon develop sympathetic feelings for each other, Phyllis through her attachment to Maribel, Astrid as a result of her similarly jealous friendship with Billy. It is interesting that their cases are seen as similar although in one case the third party is female—Rosalind—in the other male—Peter. Phyllis sprains her ankle and has to stay at the camp for a few days to recover.

A telegram arrives, somewhat belatedly, to tell Peter to take great care of the notebook as it is of great value. Fortunately, it isn't at the bottom of the lake, although the box in which it was contained is. The notebook fell out before the box reached the water and by some fluke landed in a passing boat, where it was found by a local village boy who gives it to Rosalind. Maribel suggests that it will be safer if the Guides take it back to the hotel and look after it. Although most people believe it is in Maribel's suitcase, it has in fact been put into the pocket of Miss Curtis, the Guide Captain. (Surely, even in the 1920s, there must have been hotel safes!)

Rosalind alone suspects that an old man who now turns up at the camp, having been rescued by Mr Kennedy and Peter after his boat has been run down by a speed boat during the night, is a spy, cleverly planted in the camp. Naturally Astrid, although this time by accident, reveals that the Guides have got the notebook, and the old man promptly disappears. It is Rosalind, too, who takes Cecily and Gina for a picnic when the Guides go off for a long walk, giving Cecily the opportunity to tell her and Gina of her three great wishes—to do something 'magnificent' for Rosalind and Maribel, who are to be her Guardians when she is adopted by the Guides, the plans for which are already in hand; to go a place where she cannot be found by the dreaded 'Monsieur', who had brought her from the convent and put her into the care of Madame; and to know the truth about her own mother and father.

Astrid offers to look after the notebook but, not surprisingly, Maribel refuses the offer. Nevertheless, when Miss Curtis decides to take the Guides, plus Rosalind and Billy, on a two-day expedition to climb Tournette, Astrid persuades Gina and Cecily to go with her to spend the night in the hotel to look after the book. Gina points out the foolishness of this enterprise but in vain. Monsieur arrives at the hotel, lures Cecily outside and promises to tell her about her father if she will tell him the number of the room where the book is hidden. She refuses, and Monsieur pretends to throw the papers that supposedly reveal the truth about her father into the lake, and then disappears. Cecily is very upset, but Miss Kennedy points out to her that he was undoubtedly deceiving her in the hope of obtaining the information he wanted. Fortunately, Mr Pankridge arrives to collect the notebook, and then returns a week later for the celebration party that brings the story to an end. Although she has not yet found out about her parents, Cecily is happily looking forward to going to live with Maribel's old nurse on the Sussex Downs, and the way is open for her future involvement with the Abbey girls.

This is not one of EJO's best books and could very possibly be described as her worst. The plot is unnecessarily complex, and the link between the two sets of villains—the mysterious Americans on the one hand and the combination of Madame and Monsieur on the other—is somewhat vague. They are evidently part of the same 'international gang' with François, the boy who does the cooking at the camp, providing the link, since he is seen on one occasion talking to the Americans and on another in conversation with Madame. The notebook was apparently stolen in Rome, and Cecily hears Monsieur talking to some Italians.

The mixture of plot and problems also helps to make this book somewhat indigestible. EJO was evidently reluctant to leave her examination of problems, particularly of the damage that jealousy can do to friendships, sufficiently alone to concentrate on a plot that was quite uncharacteristic of her anyway. This fascination with the way in which jealousy affects friendship is the only thing that can account for the arrival of Phyllis Grainger, who is such a good example of a girl who doesn't like to share her friends and who can be deliberately malicious. One can also ask why, if Rosamund can later identify Cecily as the daughter of little Mrs Perowne on the basis of a group photograph sent from England, the St Mary's girls don't see the likeness as soon as Mrs Perowne arrives at the Marienthal? *The Camp Mystery* has all the characteristics of a book which has been cobbled together from a variety of short stories, including the use of familiar characters from full-length books, and additional chapters to try to make it all hang together. (See also pages 165–7.)

By now the Abbey saga was very much at the centre of EJO's writing life, and during her next period EJO turned with vigour to the task of continuing the story of the Abbey girls and, in particular, allowed her interest in the character of Rosamund Kane to develop.

Chapter 7

ROSAMUND: EJO'S FAVOURITE CHARACTER? 1933 TO 1938

'Rosamund and Roderic seem to me more than a novelette. They're a fairy-tale', says Maidlin on the final page of *Rosamund's Victory*, to which Jen replies prophetically: 'Rosamund's a fairy-tale heroine of romance. We shall see her reigning over that castle yet.'

As we have seen in Chapter 4, EJO introduced Rosamund and Maidlin in *The New Abbey Girls* to provide younger central characters with whom younger readers could identify and whom they could emulate, and her belief in the importance of setting standards for the young is nowhere more clearly seen than in *Rosamund's Victory*, published in 1933. Not only do Rosamund and Maidlin, and others on their behalf, pay tribute to the important and valuable influence of the older Abbey girls, but the need to bring Roderic up properly is at the very centre of the book.

From her first appearance in *The New Abbey Girls*, Rosamund is a golden girl. She is tall, attractive, fair, an English rose, the epitome of all that is admired in English girlhood. Even before she has the advantages of living in the environment of the Hall and the influence of Joy and Jen, she can get on easily with people; Maidlin envies the ease with which she enters into a relationship with the older girls, and the way in which she can joke with them and give as good as she gets. Rosamund is an attractive character from the moment of her first appearance, and it is no surprise when she is chosen Queen of the Hamlet Club at the end of the first book in which she appears.

However, despite her basic advantages of appearance and personality, Rosamund does not have everything her own way. When she is standing in for Queen Jen she

Through the window was pushed a board on which were printed big white letters.
(*Rosamund's Victory*)

has the problem of coping with Pat Mercer, although her natural generosity enables her to overcome her worst feelings. She loses her mother. She is the first major EJO character to come up against the problem of too little money when her father remarries and cuts off her allowance, and the money she has inherited from her mother is not sufficient for her to carry out the plans she has made. Being Rosamund, however, she does not sit down and bemoan her misfortune. Instead she takes advantage of her father's offer to pay for her training for a career, and takes a cookery course that will enable her to play her part in the enterprise at the Rose and Squirrel.

Thus Rosamund, like Cinderella, is a character who deserves her good fortune. She is determined to make her own way, and is achieving modest success by the time the reader begins to get an inkling of the splendid good fortune that lies ahead for her. Rosamund, unlike many other EJO heroines, works for this. Her determination to get legal control of her half-brother for his own good, and her willingness to take responsibility for him both morally and financially, are indicative of the fact that she has put herself into a situation where good fortune is possible. She has not inherited money or a comfortable lifestyle, as Joy, Maidlin, Jen, Lexa, Eilidh and other EJO heroines have done, or gained access to them through someone else's generosity, as Mary Devine and others have done; instead she has earned them through making the most of her natural gifts.

The beginning of *Rosamund's Victory*, which was published by Harrap, overlaps the end of *Biddy's Secret*. This time the device used to put the reader in the picture is that of introducing old friends, Rena Mackay and Lisabel Durrant, who are still employed at Rocklands by Sheila Thorburn. The latter has just inherited an old house near the Rose and Squirrel, and they have come to tidy up the grounds before it is sold. Subsequently, their acquaintance with Jen is revealed and there is a grand reunion; in the meantime they provide an audience to whom Rosamund can tell the story of the Rose and Squirrel, explain her relationship to Audrey, Elspeth and Eleanor, and account for the existence of Roderic, who is both Eleanor's new baby son and Rosamund's half-brother. This book also sees romance for Rena and Lisabel, since Rupert (Rufus) and Rex come to propose to them, and there is good fortune for Rena at the end of the story. Rufus is to take over Rocklands as Sheila is marrying a wealthy American and going to live in the United States; by now he is a qualified doctor and plans to use Rocklands as a place to care for children who suffer from the same disease as Wriggles, the small invalid brother who is now dead. As a result of the time lapse between the publication of *A Go-Ahead Schoolgirl* and *Rosamund's Victory*, we are told that Rena's father died when his ship went down in the Atlantic—the war is not mentioned, and the circumstances of the sinking are left unspecified.

Rosamund's Victory, however, is primarily Rosamund's story. Eleanor, her young stepmother, wants to return to India with some friends, and there is a general feeling that she will remarry. Nobody, not even her sisters, thinks she is fit, sensible or mature enough to look after Roderic, and Rosamund, who is delighted to have someone of her own at last, is only too pleased to take on the task. Being Rosamund, she is determined to do things properly—she's not going to care for Roderic while Eleanor goes off to have a good time and perhaps come back to claim him in a few years' time. Her decision is given point by the new revelation that Roderic is a possible heir to the earldom of Kentisbury. The first hint that Rosamund is so well connected comes when she reminds Jen: 'It hasn't occurred to you to ask why I'm so determined to take Roderic out of Eleanor's hands ... You've forgotten ... I was only a girl and there were too many between. But it's different with a boy ... He's going to have a good start ...'

The situation as described by Rosamund to Jen at this point is fairly straightforward. The Earl of Kentisbury, now aged 86, is dying; his eldest son has been killed in a flying accident and *his* son, Geoffrey, Viscount Verriton, is a minor; a second son is said to have died unmarried the previous year, and the third son, another Geoffrey, is a middle-aged invalid. Rosamund's grandfather was a brother of the dying Earl, and her father would have been next in line if the young Viscount Verriton failed to produce a male heir, so now Roderic, a small baby, takes his place. Later, of course, more branches are added to the family tree (see page 223).

Kentisbury Castle, the seat of the family, is based on Arundel Castle, but at this stage EJO seems to have been rather vague about its exact location. The journey when Rosamund takes Roderic to see their cousin, the invalid Geoffrey Kane, is described as 'a long one'. In fact the village in which the Rose and Squirrel is to be found has been identified as Washington, which is not far from Arundel, especially by EJO's standards, in view of the way the Abbey folk pop over to the Rose and Squirrel for tea and cars are sent to fetch Rosamund from there to the Hall.

Kentisbury manifests itself as a fairy-tale castle, filling the landscape with its 'towers and battlements', but it is to Verriton House that Rosamund goes. Cousin Geoffrey tells Rosamund of the family tradition of naming boys 'Geoffrey' and giving girls 'Rose' names. Despite the fact that he is a middle-aged invalid, his interest in Rosamund is immediately

Arundel Castle, 1980s

apparent: 'It was the most interesting afternoon the invalid had spent for months ... the sick man's eyes followed her tall figure wistfully, and he sighed and wished she need not go.'

Rosamund's deserved good fortune, which comes to her so unexpectedly, contrasts markedly with the way in which go-getting Biddy got into difficulties. Prudently and uncharacteristically, EJO does not hint at the possibility of a future romance for Roderic and Biddy's Madelon-Marie, although the fact that they are the same age is mentioned. Biddy, in fact, draws a parallel between her own behaviour and that of Eleanor, commenting that she is 'nearly as bad as Mrs Kane', and that had it not been for Maidlin she might have left Madelon-Marie in Annecy to be looked after by someone else and merely visited her now and then.

The small Marchwood children, Andrew, Tony and the twins, bounce through the story, providing humour (the twins) or acting as catalysts to plot development (Andrew and Tony fighting, which results in concussion). Rena and Lisabel discuss with Rosamund the attractions or disadvantages of marriage, but eventually the overwhelming factor is seen to be the 'right' man. Provided that it is to the right man, marriage is seen as vastly preferable to a career, however absorbing. Rosamund, however, is to continue with her career for the present, and Cousin Geoffrey admires her as 'a good business woman'. Jen's vision of Rosamund 'reigning over that castle' still lies in the future.

What is the wild, mad object playing at?
(*The Reformation of Jinty*)

In 1933 Chambers published *The Reformation of Jinty*, illustrated by Rene Cloke, and this was quickly followed by a third book about Jinty Cameron, *Jinty's Patrol*, in 1934. This repeats the pattern of the Torment books, where the first book is fairly complex while the two shorter books that follow are comparatively lightweight. Since girl readers seemed to enjoy stories about tomboys who were always getting into scrapes, and since EJO seems to have been very sympathetic towards letters from her young readers, it is quite possible that both the Torment and Jinty were revived 'on request'. The Jinty stories about the tomboy from the Highlands who 'neffer thinks' seem to have been designed for younger readers rather than the older girls who might be anxiously awaiting the next stage in Rosamund's adventures.

Much of *The Reformation of Jinty* was in existence before the publication of the book, having been published as three short stories in *Hulton Girls' Stories*. Although it was seventeen years since the first book about Jinty, *The Tuck-Shop Girl*, had appeared, little time has passed in Jinty's life, and the events of the second book take place in the following term. Despite the title, Jinty was very much the central character in *The Tuck-Shop Girl*, and in *The Reformation of Jinty* virtually everything is seen through her eyes and her name appears in eight of the twenty-one chapter titles. Her adventures are linked to two themes, the first of which is her friendship with the Poet, who, like The Writing Person, is never given a name. He lives next door to the school and hates publicity. Jinty meets him when she trespasses in his garden to try to take a photograph of him to please T.V., who is now known as Theo, a name more closely related to her given one of Theodora Violet. This escapade, however, is not the disaster it seems. The Poet lectures Jinty on behaviour unbecoming in a Guide, but when he realises that her one idea was to give pleasure to a friend, he is more sympathetic.

Since Jinty became a Guide she has tried harder to improve and to think before she acts, but now the problem girl is to be confronted with a problem of her own. The second theme of the book is the arrival of Jinty's two young cousins who are, if Jinty is to be believed, much worse than she ever was, and for whom she is expected to be a good example.

An important character in this story is a small black-and-white dog called Roger who belongs to an old woman who sells lavender in the street and has a son who is a petty criminal. Roger first comes to board at the school while his mistress goes away to some sort of rest home in the country, and he enjoys his visit so much that he keeps on coming back. He is, soon afterwards, used as a pretext to lure Jinty away from the Hobby House so that petty thieves can break in.

An unselfish act on Jinty's part brings the Poet back into the picture, and he invites Jinty to have tea with him and talk about the Guides. During this visit, she hears the story of his granddaughter Molly, who was a keen Guide and who died trying to save another Guide from drowning. During her lifetime, he had shown no real interest in her Guide activities, in fact he'd laughed at them, but since her death he has regretted his former attitude and come to appreciate the good they do. The story of Molly affects Jinty deeply and she tells it to her fellow Guides with a sincerity that impresses them. It has affected Jinty herself, calling out the more serious side of her that is rarely seen in these early tomboy days, and making her regret even more the thoughtlessness that means she dare not allow the Poet to tell her a secret because she has no confidence in her ability to keep it.

Jinty and Roger's affection for the Poet provide the opportunity for another good deed when Jinty and the Guides are helping to protect the Poet's treasures on a day when his house is open to the public. Thanks to Jock, Jinty and Roger, a burglary is foiled, although the gang, one of whom is the son of Roger's owner, manages to get away. Roger becomes Jinty's property and goes to live in Pets' Corner. That the wireless, to which EJO clearly listened with great interest, was now becoming more widespread is clear from this and other books of the period. The Poet, who is a very keen wireless fan, introduces Jinty to broadcasts from all over the world, and her amazed interest must be very typical of people's reaction at the time.

Jinty's young cousins arrive, introduce themselves with a bang and proceed to create havoc in the school, not, as Jinty did, through thoughtlessness, but by sheer defiance of discipline and by doing just what they want to do despite rules and regulations. The reader must surely agree with Theo's suggestion that as punishment: '... a good whipping and bread and water for the rest of the term, and a week in bed in separate rooms, and double prep for months, and no pocket-money all this year, would be about right'.

A few words of caution from Jinty send them off in the opposite direction, and the results of this serve to make Jinty more and more conscious of her own need to set them a good example and behave in a more responsible way. The others note that Jinty 'has improved; she's thinking about the consequences; she's thinking for Morag and Sheila; she's willing to take the blame'. Her elders and particularly the Poet are much impressed by the way she thinks out her problems and sets herself to face them. The Poet, more confident now, reveals his secret: when he dies, his house is to be left as a rest-house and conference centre for Guides, and when Jinty grows up she is to be on the Committee running it. As Theo comments: 'Topping! ... By the time you're twenty-one, perhaps you'll be a reformed character, Jinty Cameron.' From which remark we may justifiably infer that Jinty's reformation is by no means complete at the end of this story.

Monica Godfrey in *The World of Elsie J Oxenham and Her Books* lists four short stories about Jinty, all published in *Hulton Girls' Stories. Jinty of the Girl Guides* (n.d.) and *The Honour of the Guides* (1933) are the same story with different titles, telling of Jinty's meeting with the Poet when she trespasses in his garden to take his photograph for Theo. *The Guides and Roger* (1926) brings together the chapters about Roger, the small black-and-white dog, describing how he first came to board at the school, then is used by thieves to lure Jinty away from the Hobby House, and finally, after helping to foil a burglary of the Poet's treasures, becomes Jinty's pet. *One Good Turn* (1928) is about Jinty's unselfish act in helping another Guide Company at a Rally, which impresses the Poet and gives him more confidence in her. It seems likely that the story of Jinty's cousins, which provides the second theme, was added to make the full-length book.

Jinty's Patrol, published in 1934 by Newnes, was the only EJO book to be published by this firm. Like its immediate predecessor, it is a very slight book, a fact to some extent disguised by the production which is typical of the period—thick, featherweight paper, large print, generous margins and plenty of blank space at the beginning and end of each chapter. It was published in Newnes Bluebird Library, and the blue cover has on it a black seaplane which presumably was the colophon of the series; this was typical of the period, too, when it was not uncommon for girls of little more than school age to fly their own aircraft, at least in books, and when Amy Johnson was the nation's darling.

The third book about Jinty, and the last to be published in EJO's lifetime, *Jinty's Patrol* is made up of two interlinked stories. First Jinty's patrol takes upon itself the task of going out in the middle of the night to correct the spelling and punctuation of the sign put up by the man who has set up a café in a wooden shack just outside the gates of the school. Because they dislike his establishment, seeing it as a rival to Prudence's tuck-shop, they manage to convince themselves that they are being extremely noble and doing a good deed appropriate to them as Girl Guides. This conviction crumbles fairly swiftly when they are caught by the headmistress as they return home in the early hours of the morning. The second part of the book is taken up with Shallow Brown, who not only manages to overcome the fear of tents that she acquired at the age of four, when a tent blew down on top of her, but also to rescue Jinty when a similar thing happens during the Whitsuntide camp which is held in the grounds of the Poet's house next door to the school.

The story opens at the beginning of the summer term. Betty, the leader of the Thistle Patrol, is not returning, and a new Patrol Leader must be chosen. Surprisingly, the choice falls on Jinty, though it is really very much a case of Hobson's choice. Although the Thistle Patrol now includes Kirsteen and Drusilla, who have forsaken gardening (and whose garden overalls come in useful for the midnight painting spree), they are latecomers to Guides and are therefore not eligible to become patrol leaders; they do, however, provide some ballast in the patrol to counteract the impulsiveness of Jinty and Sheila, who is her Second.

Salome Brown is a new girl. Tall, mature, keen to become a Girl Guide, she reveals that her father, who used to sing sea shanties to her and consequently gave her the nickname of 'Shallow', is dead. It soon becomes clear that there is some mystery about her, and this proves to be that when she was four her parents took her camping and during a storm a tree fell on their tent. Her father was badly injured, never stood or walked again, and eventually died three years before Shallow came to the school. The whole story is told only to Kirsteen, who sees that Salome is upset at the idea of going to camp when the Whitsuntide camp is announced. Jinty is desperately keen to have all the members of her patrol at the camp, so Salome resolves to overcome her fears after Prue of the tuck-shop, at Kirsteen's suggestion, has been consulted and offered some helpful advice.

As a punishment for the painting escapade, the Thistles have been condemned to miss the first night in camp and to pay a fine of ten shillings to the old man who runs the café. In fact the other girls and even the staff are so pleased that the corrections have been made—this episode has some of the most appalling overtones of condescension and snobbery to be found in EJO—that various people rally round with contributions, and one can't help feeling that Miss Murray is an unusually tolerant headmistress not to ban the Thistles from attending the camp altogether; one feels that, even in these more permissive times, such a ready-to-hand punishment would not have been unreasonable. The girls also have to apologise to the café-owner, although this ordeal is lessened when the man is found to be a Scot from Glasgow, and several pages are filled with Jinty and Kirsteen conversing with him in their thickest Scottish accents. In the end the Thistles have to sacrifice very little for their misdeeds. The Poet kindly organises his affairs so that he can delay his welcome to the whole camp until the Thistles have arrived there. The Thistles also get credit from the rest of the school by sportingly turning out to see the rest of the Company setting off to camp.

The Thistles join the camp on the second day. On their second night in camp there is a great storm and a branch comes down on top of the tent in which Jinty, Shallow and two other Thistles are sleeping. They escape, but Jinty goes back to rescue Roger, the dog, whose presence in the tent is quite illegal anyway, and is only saved from injury by a second falling branch by Shallow, who goes back to rescue her. The full extent of Shallow's bravery is now revealed, first by Kirsteen to Miss Kingdom, the Guide Captain, and then to the rest of the Guides. The next day the storm blows out, and the Guides are allowed to have a final night in camp so that Salome can prove that she has finally conquered her fear of tents.

One interesting side issue is raised early in the book when Drusilla and Shallow compare notes about their reactions to the fact that their widowed mothers have both remarried, indicating that concern about unusual or exceptional family circumstances is by no means a new thing in books for young people. On the eve of the camp, Drusilla is summoned home to see the new baby in her family, although she returns in time to go to camp with the others, the importance of all the Thistles going to camp together being the reason for Salome's attempt to overcome her fears.

The book falls neatly into two halves and, like its predecessor, may have originated as two short stories although there is no evidence of their ever having been published. The midnight painting spree in the first half and the second half in which Shallow's story is told both rely on coincidences—the existence of two rival cafés close to the school, and Shallow sleeping in a tent hit by a tree during the only two camps she has ever attended—which seem more appropriate to short stories than to a properly planned full-length novel.

EJO wrote a fourth novel about Jinty, *A Divided Patrol*, but this was not published until 1992, when the manuscript was found by EJO's niece and published for the interest of the members of the EJO Appreciation Society. In this Jinty, now sixteen, is still Leader of the Thistles. Catriona, a Scottish girl from Edinburgh, arrives as a new girl, saying that she has come 'instead of Irene', one of the Thistles who has gone travelling with her parents 'to broaden her mind'. Prudence has gone to the south of France with her invalid aunts, so the school is without its tuck-shop and, which is perhaps more of a tragedy, Jinty and her friends are deprived of their guide and counsellor.

The title reflects the main theme of the book. The Thistle Patrol is split into two factions, in part due to the arrival of the new girl and the departure of Irene, which upsets the balance of the patrol. Catriona is only thirteen and therefore goes with the younger Guides, Sheila, Morag and Anne, who are in fact highly qualified Guides. The older group, Kirsteen, Drusilla and Shallow, are all sixteen like Jinty but less experienced as Guides. This has not seemed obvious to the Guides themselves until Catriona points it out, and the younger girls begin to talk about 'you' and 'us'. This upsets Jinty, who bursts out suddenly and makes things worse. However, the division is finally mended, there are interesting accounts of fund-raising, and the book comes to an end with a romance and happy ending for Prue. In fact there is more depth in *A Divided Patrol* than in its predecessor.

Published by Chambers and illustrated by Rene Cloke, whose pictures have a real feel of the period and emphasise the youth of Rachel and Damaris Ellerton as compared with Maidlin, *Maidlin to the Rescue* also appeared in 1934. In Abbey time it follows on the events of *Biddy's Secret*, in which Maidlin proved that she was not the helpless babe people thought her, and overlaps the events described in *Rosamund's Victory*. It says something for

EJO's skill that she could handle this kind of complication and maintain the balance between making each book satisfying both for the new reader and for the reader who was already familiar with the characters and situations. It is possible that, in this book, she was attempting to balance the interest between Rosamund and Maidlin, so while Rosamund is making an independent life for herself, and acquiring a baby half-brother for whom she is happy to accept responsibility, Maidlin goes out on a different rescue operation, to save her two young cousins, Rachel and Damaris, for whom she will now make herself responsible.

In the Ellerton sisters, EJO was introducing two new characters, one of whom, Rachel, was to become a key figure in the Abbey circle, while Damaris was to have a life away from the Abbey and, in her career as a dancer, to introduce ballet into the Abbey saga at a time when ballet was becoming a popular interest, especially amongst the girls for whom

'You sneak!' cried Damaris. 'Oh, you rotter!'
(*Maidlin to the Rescue*)

EJO was writing. It must be noted, however, that in this book there is no mention of Damaris's early ballet training or her enthusiasm for dancing.

The first half of the book introduces Rachel and Damaris. Their widowed father is in America where they were born, but on their mother's death he had sent the girls to live with his sister, also called Rachel, who lives with her husband on the family farm, Crossrigs, in the Lake District. He had two other sisters, Damaris, who had married an Italian and died, leaving a daughter, Maidlin, and Ann Watson, who is caretaker of a ruined Abbey 'somewhere in the south'. Readers of the Abbey books would have immediately recognised the connection, while for new readers it provides an interesting mystery.

When the book opens, Aunt Rachel, now a widow, has just died; the girls' father has not been heard of for some time, nor has he sent any money for their upkeep, and Aunt Rachel has used all her savings to pay for their education at St Dorothea's, a 'good' school near Liverpool. Rachel is sixteen and has passed her Matric, and Damaris is a year younger. Mr Ward, the family lawyer, considers that the only possible solution is to apply to their cousin Maidlin who, having inherited her father's Italian estates, could now be expected to provide for them.

The girls are violently opposed to this. Nobody at the farm has seen or heard anything of Maidlin since she became rich and went south, and they consider her a snob who is too 'swanky' to want to know them. In view of the way Rachel and Damaris develop in later books, it is interesting that at this stage Rachel is the one with less control and more temperament, while Damaris is the more reasonable and is inclined to think before she acts; the reader is told: 'Rachel's prejudices and enthusiasms were alike uncontrolled, Marry, though younger by a year, was often troubled vaguely and was moved to remonstrate.'

Rachel, however, is the leader in the plan the girls make to go off and be independent and prove that they don't need help from their rich cousin. The opportunity to do so presents itself in the person of Miss Baldry, who is about to start a teahouse two-thirds of the way up 'a famous pass' and has said that she would need some help. To forestall pursuit, they write to the lawyer and to Maidlin, in each case saying that they need no help, have found a job and 'would prefer a business life to school'. The only concession they are willing to make is to ask that Maidlin should buy or rent the family farm that 'has belonged to our people for centuries'. The letter to Maidlin is very bitter and hurtful, accusing her of being too snobbish to want to know her poor relations.

Life with Miss Baldry is not quite what they had hoped. Keeping a teahouse is one of EJO's suitable occupations for young ladies, and Rachel dreams of an 'artistic tea-house with dainty china, coloured cloths and curtains to match—strawberry pink, perhaps, or pale mauve, or daffodil or deep green—and carefully arranged flowers on every table'. Miss Baldry's place is not at all like the Rose and Squirrel, but primitive and stark with no conveniences and not even beds for the girls to sleep on. Rachel and Damaris do improve matters in so far as this is possible. A chance remark from Damaris names the spot 'Hikers' Halt' and Miss Baldry is quick to catch on. Rachel's sense of what is proper is offended by Miss Baldry's insistence that they should wait at table in the shorts they wear for the fells— Miss Baldry, in fact, is more up-to-date than Rachel. She is also shrewd enough to realise that there is something odd about the girls' arrival to help her and, having asked a few searching questions, shamelessly exploits their desire for secrecy.

The first half of the book tells of this exploit, including their first customers at the café, a brother and sister who are to reappear in later books, and the solution to the mystery of their suitcases, which had disappeared from the place where they had hidden them on their escape from the farm. These had been moved by a schoolfriend, Philippa (Pip) Russell, who had watched them being hidden and wanted to play a joke on Rachel and Damaris. The girls grow more and more unhappy with Miss Baldry, and Miss Baldry, with a keen eye on what will do her most good in the long run, has searched their belongings, found Maidlin's address and written to say that the girls are with her

It should be noted that although the book about St Dorothea's, *Damaris at Dorothy's*, was not published until 1937, it must certainly have existed, either in manuscript or in the author's mind, for the school is well established with descriptions of its colourful uniform and significant ties and girdles, and Pip is a well-rounded character, even though her appearance is a brief one.

Halfway through the book, the reader is transported from the cold and misty Lakeland fells to the Abbey, where it is bluebell time. Maidlin is back at home, helping Joy with the twins but with a new maturity marked by a change of colour scheme—she has a blue dress that is a new colour for her. Biddy is living in the Abbey with her baby, and there is anxiety about Ann Watson, who is ill. With Maidlin's singing and Joy's composing, classical music is coming to the fore at the Hall, no doubt to prepare the way for Sir Ivor Quellyn. Maidlin and Joy are anxious to listen to a Beethoven concert from Vienna, in contrast to the 'philistines' at the Manor, where Ken is described as singing away to a concert of student songs from London. In this book folk dancing is very much left to the children.

Out of the blue come messages to Maidlin about Rachel and Damaris, first a telegram from the lawyer to say they are missing, then his letter explaining their situation and finally the letter from the girls themselves. All this comes as a shock to Maidlin, who had not previously known of their existence because her Aunt Ann had tried to cut her off from her humble origins when she inherited her Italian fortune. At first she is bewildered and seems helpless in the face of the news, but she has truly matured since her adventure in France and, with advice from Joy, Jen and Mary, she determines to go and meet her cousins and make friends with them. Miss Baldry's letter tells her where they are, and she and Jen drive north to find them.

It seems probable that EJO had just come to know the Lake District; certainly she presents it through the eager eyes of Jen Marchwood as a new and exciting discovery. She also knew about fell walkers or hikers and their exploits. Jen and Maidlin make friends with the girls without revealing their real identity, and very quickly sum up the situation and Miss Baldry. Jen is recalled south because Rosemary has croup and Ken is panicking—as Jen says: 'He's all right for lions in Africa, perhaps, but he's just an infant where Rosemary and the boys are concerned.'

Maidlin, now on her own, goes back to Hikers' Halt and walks in on a row between Miss Baldry and the girls. In her urgent desire to help she tells them who she is; both the girls are indignant and Maidlin's temper makes her flare out, but she convinces them of her previous ignorance of their existence and of her genuine desire to help. When Rachel and Damaris learn that Miss Baldry has betrayed them, they willingly leave with her.

The men in this book do have their little parts to play. As well as Ken requiring Jen's presence in a crisis, Henderson, the chauffeur from the Manor, who has driven Jen and Maidlin to the Lakes, is anxious to get home because his wife has just had a baby, and Maidlin uses this as a means of persuading the girls to agree to a long day's drive in order to be home for the twins' sixth birthday. Henderson also falls in love with the Lake District and his enthusiasm is remembered in later books. Both Henderson and Frost, Joy's chauffeur, are portrayed as father—or perhaps grandfather—figures.

The new mature Maidlin, having dealt very firmly with Miss Baldry, also handles the girls' desire to be independent with great understanding. She tells them of their father's death and plans jobs for them, for Rachel to take Biddy's intended place as her secretary and for Damaris to keep hens and bees on the family farm. There is also the problem of Ann Watson, for whom nobody seems to feel much sympathy. However, Maidlin manages to make her cousins accept and appreciate that Ann, without their advantages of education and a broader outlook, could not look at things as they would. A typical bit of EJO snobbery! Altogether this book presents us with a more mature Maidlin, who is graduating in the understanding and sympathy that the Abbey requires of its supporters, and ends on a suitable Abbey note with all the Hamlet Club children dancing Sellenger's Round for the twins' birthday.

EJO's preoccupation with both Rosamund and Maidlin at this period can be clearly seen in *Joy's New Adventure*, which was published by Chambers in the following year and, again, illustrated by Rene Cloke. Although the central thread of this book is Joy's romantic relationship with Sir Ivor Quellyn, both Rosamund and Maidlin are having new adventures too. Subtitled 'a romance of the Abbey girls' and surely one of the most romantic of all the books, it is dedicated to 'Margaret Linn who has always maintained that Joy's story was not finished'.

The events of *Joy's New Adventure* take place a year after those described in *Maidlin to the Rescue*. Joy has now been widowed for seven years and her friends are ready for her to find new happiness. Her friendship with Sir Ivor Quellyn has developed because he has sought her advice about his ward, seventeen-year-old Abigail Ann Alwyn. Gail is the central character of this story, which begins with her arrival at the station before Princes Risborough, when Rosamund springs into her compartment on the train, having been looking for her since Paddington. Joy, already half in love with Sir Ivor and anxious to be helpful, has suggested that Gail, the granddaughter of a now-dead distinguished 'modern' composer whose music she is destined to play as a concert pianist (although she hates the idea), should join her music school, and Gail is on her way there. As well as being the cause of bringing Joy and Sir Ivor closer together, Gail is the new character, the observer of the Abbey scene, who can ask questions and be given the facts that the reader requires. She also assumes the role of consultant and confidante, and is conveniently present at most of the main action of the story.

Gail and Rosamund are met at Princes Risborough by Betty McLean and seen into the local train to Whiteways. The beginning of this book provides some of the most detailed information available about the precise whereabouts of the fictional Abbey. Combined with the revelation in *Maidlin to the Rescue* that it is in Oxfordshire (not Buckinghamshire as we had previously been led to suppose), it makes sense of EJO's statement that it was near Chinnor. A map of the period shows the branch line which ran from Princes Risborough to Watlington, with a station at Chinnor on the way. When we visited the area in 1997, it was still possible to match EJO's description of Whiteways to the real-life Chinnor of today, and there was undeveloped ground just outside the village which could have accommodated the Abbey and the Hall.

Betty tells Rosamund, who has apparently come on the spur of the moment to see her old friends, of Joy's friendship with Sir Ivor and suggests that Joy may be planning to marry him. Betty

Princes Risborough Station, 1992

has to go off almost at once to a Guiders' meeting, so Rosamund takes Gail to look at the Abbey and then to meet Jen, who has a new baby, Michael, at the Manor. Jen tells Rosamund that she's been expecting her to come. Rosamund is surprised at this until she learns from Jen that the young Earl of Kentisbury has been killed, that Geoffrey is the new earl and Roderic the heir. Rosamund, unaware of all this since she hasn't seen the morning's papers, has in fact come to talk to Jen about Geoffrey, who wants to marry her. Jen thinks little of this idea, believing that Rosamund will be wasted on an old invalid, even if he is nice—and an earl.

Their talk is interrupted by a potential disaster. The twins, playing at Camp Fire with Andrew and Tony in imitation of their 'Aunty Maid', have managed to set fire to a garden hut. Gail saves Elizabeth, who had been left behind in the hut, and gets badly burnt in the process. Her brave action of course puts the Abbey people under a special obligation to her, while the damage to her hand means that she cannot become a concert pianist, thus providing her with a perfect escape from the career she did not want.

Sir Ivor eventually appears in Chapter 15 when he is brought to the Hall to meet the twins. By this time the reader knows that his father was a cousin of Robert Quellyn the painter, who had left the family property to an English girl, thus linking back some twenty-six years to *The Girl Who Wouldn't Make Friends*, and there is talk of the famous Welsh pictures in the Quellyn collection. Joy also explains that Ivor's title has been bestowed on him for his services to music and that his mother is a 'Mrs' who lives in a nice little house in Shropshire. Thus EJO, with some foresight possibly, solved the problem that might have arisen for Joy; she can bring the twins up in her own old home and provide a convenient home for Sir Ivor who, though titled, has no magnificent estate to which Joy will be required to move.

Maidlin, who has just arrived back from a trip to France and Italy and has been brought up to date on events by Gail, immediately guesses that Ivor wants to marry Joy. Sir Ivor, though, is impressed by the way in which Maidlin's voice has developed and insists on her singing for him after dinner each evening. Joy is uneasy about this—is Ivor in love with Maidlin rather than herself? Even Maidlin sees his interest as embarrassing.

At this point we have what is probably the most erotic scene in the whole of EJO's work. Maidlin has been out to a meeting of her Camp Fire one evening and returns to the Hall wearing a long cloak over her Camp Fire robes. Passing through the room where Joy and Ivor are sitting, she bends over to pick something up and the cloak falls away, revealing her in all her beauty, enhanced by her long hair hanging loose and her romantic costume. Joy cannot contain her resentment, cries 'Maidlin! You did it on purpose! Go to bed at once!' and rushes into the garden.

Gail, a witness to this incident, sends Ivor after Joy and goes to comfort Maidlin. Joy does not come to apologise to Maidlin within a reasonable space of time—having been to consult Jen, who has advised her to take the happiness that is offered, she has met Ivor on the way back and subsequently decided that it is too late to disturb Maidlin that night. Maidlin, feeling badly hurt by Joy, decides to run away and Gail goes with her, first to seek refuge with Rosamund, to whom Gail can explain the situation. Rosamund tells Maidlin that she is going to marry Geoffrey, and Gail now serves as a useful sounding board for Maidlin's views on this. Rosamund also says that if she is asked directly by Joy whether Maidlin is with her, she can't lie to her.

In view of Rosamund's refusal to conceal Maidlin's whereabouts, Gail and Maidlin take Biddy's advice and go to St Valéry near Boulogne in France—it seems likely from the detailed description that we are given of St Valéry that EJO had recently enjoyed a visit there herself. At last an apologetic letter from Joy arrives, and Maidlin's return to England is hastened by the news that Margaret has had an accident and a wire from Rosamund saying 'Joy needs you'.

When Gail and Maidlin arrive back at the Hall, Sir Ivor is waiting on the terrace, due to leave for Manchester where he is engaged to conduct a concert in the Free Trade Hall. Maidlin urges him to go, and says that Joy will understand, but Rosamund, standing in the background, takes a shrewd look at Ivor's face and thinks: 'He isn't sure of that. He's realised already that understanding isn't Joy's strong point though he's very much in love.' Joy later tells Maidlin that Ivor had first seen her and been interested in her eight years previously, just after her engagement to Andrew Marchwood, and has been waiting in the wings ever since, so to speak. In Sir Ivor, EJO created one of her most powerful and interesting male characters and it is not surprising that his role is played out mostly off-stage in subsequent books; he, unlike Jack Raymond and Ken Marchwood, would have upset the peaceful femaleness of the Abbey circle.

Joy's New Adventure is very much a core book. Although Gail's story, which is completed by her appointment to run the tuck-shop which is being opened by the Rose and Squirrel for the benefit of the new school starting up in the nearby big house, is one central thread, and Joy's romance with Sir Ivor another, the stories of Maidlin and Rosamund are woven round these. In the last chapter Rosamund arrives to announce her engagement to Geoffrey, Earl of Kentisbury—despite the misgivings of her friends, she is going to fulfil her destiny. Maidlin, having been a stumbling block to Joy's happiness, if only in the latter's mind, has moved closer to her career as a concert singer, which is to be an important factor in later Abbey books and which is to lead to her own romance.

In this book Jen plays only a minor part, mainly as the maker of fairly brisk remarks. She makes no secret of her feelings about Rosamund's relationship with Geoffrey. With Ken's support, she makes some acid comments about the way in which Andrew went off hunting big game when he had a young and pregnant wife. She also says to Joy: 'I don't mind telling you, now, that you were rather a trial to us all, till you were safely engaged to Andrew.' The twins bounce through the story as usual, acting as catalysts to the action by setting the shed on fire, Margaret having the accident which brings Maidlin speeding home, and giving their approval to Sir Ivor. It is a vintage Abbey book, and it is very sad that it is in such short supply. It was, incidentally, the last of EJO's books to be published by Chambers.

The open-ended tone of the last chapter of *The Crisis in Camp Keema* left the way open for further chronicles of the Camp Fire/Guides situation, but it was several years before EJO was to write an immediate follow-up. In *The Camp Mystery* (see pages 165–7) she jumped ahead to the summer holidays, while *The Abbey Girls Play Up* took Rosalind and Maribel even further into the future. However, a short story, *Camp Keema Finds a Guardian*, was published in the *Girls' All-Round Book* for 1929 and later, in 1931, a longer story called *Peggy-Perfect Goes to School* appeared as a serial in the magazine *Little Folks*. These two stories, plus four additional chapters, were published by the office of the *Girl's Own Paper* in 1936 as *Peggy and the Brotherhood*.

BIDDY'S SECRET

A ROMANCE OF THE ABBEY GIRLS

ELSIE J. OXENHAM

DEB at SCHOOL

ELSIE J. OXENHAM

JOY'S NEW ADVENTURE

A Romance of the Abbey Girls

ELSIE J. OXENHAM

MAIDLIN TO THE RESCUE

A Story of the Abbey Girls

Elsie J. Oxenham

THE CRISIS
IN CAMP KEEMA

ELSIE J OXENHAM

P J

THE
REFORMATION
of JINTY

Elsie J. Oxenham

At School with
the Roundheads

By ELSIE OXENHAM
Author of "Rosaly's New School"

The SCHOOL WITHOUT
a NAME

ELSIE J.
OXENHAM

The Two Form-Captains

Elsie J Oxenham

THE CAPTAIN OF THE FIFTH

BY ELSIE J OXENHAM

P. Tarrant

THE JUNIOR CAPTAIN

ELSIE J OXENHAM

VEN at GREGORY'S

Elsie Jeanette Oxenham

PATIENCE AND HER PROBLEMS

BY
ELSIE·J·OXENHAM

THE TWINS OF CASTLE CHARMING

ELSIE J·OXENHAM

A GO-AHEAD SCHOOL-GIRL

ELSIE·J·OXENHAM

The Troubles of Tazy

ELSIE J OXENHAM

Camp Keema Finds a Guardian, which forms Chapter 1 of the book, stands on its own as an interesting short story which would introduce Camp Fire to girls who had not heard of it. Camp Keema is seen through the eyes of Peggy Mason and her older sister, Marian, aged twenty-four, who meet the depleted Camp Fire members on the Downs where they have been holding an open-air meeting that, unfortunately, has been spoiled by boys who have stolen their food. The Masons, newly arrived in the district, are interested and helpful. The story of the crisis is told and the Camp Fire girls are quick to claim Marian as a possible Guardian. Mrs Mason, one of EJO's supportive mothers, considers it would be good for Marian and for them, especially as Peggy is to go to Miss Ransome's school. Marian promises to think about it but lays down, as a condition of her acceptance, that the unfriendly feeling of the Camp Fire towards the Guides must come to an end.

The serialised *Peggy-Perfect Goes to School* forms Chapters 2–16 of the book, and the story is again seen through the eyes of Marian, now established as the Camp Fire Guardian, and Peggy, a new junior in the school, and also those of a third new arrival, Miss Ransome's niece, Charlotte (Sharly), who has come to join the Sixth Form of her aunt's school. Marian is the well-balanced and sensible older girl trying to do her job of leading the girls who have asked her to be their Guardian. She learns to know them and their different needs very quickly, and she works especially hard towards achieving a better feeling between the Camp Fire and the Guides and helping Phyllis, the Story-Teller, to overcome her bitterness towards both Maribel and the Guides. By the end of the book, Phyllis has learnt to put her bitter feelings behind her and is rewarded by being made a Torch Bearer.

Sharley Ransome and Peggy Mason illustrate one of EJO's favourite themes, that of finding the job or activity that is right for a particular person. Sharley begins by wanting to be a Guide, attracted by Maribel as a person, and Peggy automatically goes into Camp Keema. It takes them a great deal of shared heart-searching before each girl admits she was wrong and settles happily into the place that is most suited to her.

The 'Brotherhood' of the title is an interesting and unusual new move on EJO's part. Founded by Gina Firth for her delicate brother John, who has had to give up all his other activities, it includes Freda, whose father won't allow her to join the Guides, Freda's brother, who can't be a Scout for the same reason, and Tom, Phyllis's brother, who is indignant because Phyllis keeps the Camp secret. Unusually, there is some discrepancy here because there is another short story, *Freda Joins the Guides*, which was discussed earlier (see page 122), the events of which could only have taken place during the previous Christmas holidays. The full title of the Brotherhood is The Outcast Brotherhood and the Riotous Redskins. Sensible activities like doing crosswords and puzzles are combined with a ritual that is a subtle mimicry of the Camp Fire. This aspect is the brainchild of John Firth, who has evolved, amongst other things, a parody of the Abbots Bromley Horn Dance. It is to EJO's credit—and perhaps some of us would not have expected it of her—that, while not basically approving of their Camp Fire imitations, Marian and the intelligent Camp Fire members regard this as a cause for amusement, not indignation. This is the point at which the serial story ends. The four remaining chapters that round off the book show Sharley in Camp Fire, Peggy in the Guides, and the two groups working together for the school bazaar. Miss Ransome expresses her pleasure in the changes that have taken place and, speaking from the platform, comments on 'the pleasant spirit of

The Riotous Redskins
(*Peggy and the Brotherhood*)

co-operation that has been shown'. We also see the result of Marian's work as Guardian of Camp Keema, particularly when the Riotous Redskins, in desperate mood because they are to be split up, raid Camp Keema's lodge, and Phyllis, influenced by her Guardian, is able to understand and forgive, actions which lead to her promotion to the rank of Torch Bearer.

Yet another short story, *The Last Night in Camp*, featuring Maribel and Rosalind, the Guides and the Camp Fire with Marian as the Guardian, was published in *Hulton's Girls' Stories* in 1929. All the internal evidence shows that this story takes place in April, the month following Marian and Peggy's introduction to Camp Keema and therefore during the Easter holidays between Chapters 17 and 18 of *Peggy and the Brotherhood*.

It is a real annual-type story. The two groups, Guides and Camp Fire, are camping together, and are referred to as being good friends although they run independent camps. For one night there is no adult supervision and Rosalind and Maribel are in charge. The inevitable excitements follow a discussion about a new elocution mistress who has been appointed at the school to replace a much loved one who is retiring. The girls are prepared to disapprove of the new teacher who is young and inexperienced. Then the Camp Fire has three mysterious visitors. The first is an old gypsy woman, the second, who comes while Camp Keema is holding a meeting, an Indian stranger wearing a Camp Fire gown but the wrong headdress, who charms them with a recitation of Emerson's poem 'Each and All', and delivers a message from their Guardian, and a third, an old sailor.

In the midst of the sailor's visit, there is more excitement. Horses have got out from a neighbouring field—because the Indian stranger had left a gate open, and stampede through the Camp Fire tents, and, to add to all this, one of the tents catches fire. The Guides and the Camp Fire, plus the old sailor, put the fire out and set all to rights. Phyllis confesses that she had a candle lit in her tent. The old sailor then reveals himself to be a young woman who was also the gypsy and the mysterious Indian and is, of course, Miss Cecily Allen, the new elocution mistress, who is now going to be a great success in the school. This is an odd little story; it looks rather as though EJO, at a stage when she was concerned with Camp Keema and its connections, was asked for an annual story and quickly wrote one about the characters who were in her mind at the time. There is no mention in *Peggy and the Brotherhood* of camping in the Easter holidays or of a new elocution mistress at the school in the summer term.

As *Peggy and the Brotherhood* is the last published book to deal with the Camp Keema

The Last Night in Camp

characters, apart from brief appearances by Maribel after her marriage to Michael Marchwood, this is perhaps a good point at which to make a final comment on that puzzling book *The Camp Mystery* (1932), which has already been discussed in some depth (see pages 145–48). It seems as if, between 1926 and 1930, the Camp Keema characters were very much in EJO's mind. Although the first book about them, *The Crisis in Camp Keema*, was published in 1928, it has recently been discovered that some of the characters had already appeared in a story, *The Watchers on the Lake*, which was serialised in *Toby* magazine in 1927 and which, in a slightly abridged form, later became the first twelve chapters of *The Camp Mystery*. This is discussed in more detail below.

After she had written *Crisis*, which was obviously conceived as a whole, it would appear that EJO decided to use the Camp Keema characters as the basis for a series of long and short annual stories, some of which were subsequently put together to make full-length books. In 1926 EJO would have been 46; it was a peak period in her production, she was well established as a writer and her work was probably in demand by editors of annuals and collections. The fact that she had to work quickly to keep up with this demand helps to account for the discrepancies that have already been mentioned, which make it difficult to work out a chronology for these stories that are quite uncharacteristic of EJO's work generally. As has already been suggested, EJO evidently realised at this time that the Camp Fire movement was not going to establish itself to any great extent in this country, and that the Girl Guides were to be the main leisure-time activity of this type. Perhaps she wanted to make the most of her interest in the Camp Fire before it had to be abandoned completely, apart from Maidlin's involvement.

The Crisis in Camp Keema, which introduced Maribel and Rosalind, was published in 1928; they appeared as adults, old enough to be responsible for Cecily Perowne, in *The*

Abbey Girls Play Up (1930). We know that *Camp Keema finds a Guardian* and *The Last Night in Camp* both appeared in annuals for 1929, published in 1928, while *Freda Joins the Guides* and *Peggy-Perfect goes to School* were both published in 1931. Another story using Camp Keema characters, published in 1929, was *The Missing Link*, a Guide story which, slightly abridged, became Chapters 13–20 of *The Camp Mystery*.

When all this is borne in mind, what appears to be the very odd three-part structure of *The Camp Mystery* becomes much clearer. The first part, Chapters 1–12, is basically the story of *The Watchers on the Lake*, with some descriptions and conversations slightly abridged, and the second part, Chapters 13–20, differs from *The Missing Link* only in omitting some of the explanatory material which readers of the 'long-short' story needed if they hadn't read *Watchers*. Once one knows this, it makes sense that Chapter 12 includes such remarks as 'the danger's over' and 'All's well that ends well', and ends with the reconciliation between Astrid and Billy.

The beginning of Chapter 13, 'The Guides Arrive', which reads so much like the beginning of a new story:

> The Guide Company marched along the road by the side of the lake, brisk and neat and wildly excited. No one would have believed they had been in the train all night.

is in fact exactly that! The viewpoint has shifted completely, and events are now seen from Maribel's point of view. This also makes it clear why so much repetitive detail from the first twelve chapters is included in Rosalind's explanations to Maribel—it was all part of the background for those who hadn't read *Watchers*. Furthermore, this chapter sees the first appearance of Cecily/Cécile, who plays such a major part in the rest of the book. The main difference between *Link* and the second part of *Mystery* is that the former ends with a very brief discussion of Cecily's future while Chapter 20 of the latter ends with Rosalind's remark to Maribel: 'I'm sure we'll have to take her on. So you can be thinking it out.' This paves the way for the final third of the book, which continues the story of the notebook and neatly ties it in with Cecily's past and future.

There is no indication that Chapters 21–32 of *Mystery* ever appeared in any other form than this, and it seems extremely likely that EJO had planned this expansion of Cecily's story to explain the end of it as it appeared in *The Abbey Girls Play Up*; it is also possible that either EJO or her publishers felt that the book would be too short if it were merely composed of

'Will you please get off the counter?' she said, polite but definite.
(*Rosamund's Tuck-Shop*)

the two stories. Once all these factors are considered, *The Camp Mystery*, although one of EJO's less successful books—she was never at her best when trying to write a thriller-mystery—does make more sense than on a first examination. For those who wish to explore this further, there is a detailed Publishing History in the GGBP edition of The Camp *Mystery*.

Three of the books of this period have Rosamund's name in the title, and the first of these, *Rosamund's Victory*, provides the keynote for all three. In each of them, Rosamund's innate generosity and strength of character win over some person or solve a problem. In *Rosamund's Victory* she finally succeeds in adopting her young half-brother; in the second, *Rosamund's Tuck-Shop*, which was published in 1937 by the Girl's Own Paper Office, she conquers the prejudices of the other Kanes of Kentisbury on her approaching marriage to the Earl. This and the third book, *Rosamund's Castle*, are rather lighter in tone than *Rosamund's Victory*, and both of them are concerned with the newest of EJO's schools, Wood End. It was perhaps an attempt to meet requests or suggestions from the publishers, who no doubted wanted stories that would appeal to schoolgirls rather than romances for older girls. Wood End, however, is very different from the conventional girls' boarding or day school of the period, and much more modern in concept than Jinty's school or any of the earlier EJO foundations. Wood End has been set up for girls who 'aren't going in for professions and don't need to go to college and don't want to pass exams, but who do need special training for the sort of life they're likely to have'.

These girls are from upper-middle-class families and their parents are likely to have large houses and estates. They are clearly expected to marry into their own class and need to understand the running of an estate, to learn about gardening and farming and how to take the lead in village affairs, to drive and to understand their own cars. The WI comes in for a mention—EJO clearly knew a lot about that—and country dancing is part of their programme. There is a slight link with Jinty's school in the working uniform of the Wood End girls, who wear breeches and boots and smocks (or 'round frocks') and big slouch hats, rather like the 'gardeners' in the earlier story.

The school and its pupils are new to EJO readers, but into the new setting are drawn threads from the Abbey circle and from other books—old-established readers must have enjoyed recognising old friends as they appeared. Wood End School is established in the old house whose gardens Rena and Lisabel were setting in order in *Rosamund's Victory* The grounds, therefore, back onto the wood behind the Rose and Squirrel, where Elspeth is running the teahouse with the help of Gail Alwyn, by now recovered from her dramatic rescue of the twins in *Joy's New Adventure*. Gail, in fact, runs a tuck-shop for the school and plays the dulcitone for their country-dancing classes. Lisabel Durrant is the gardening teacher for the first term, although she expects to be married soon, and among the pupils are Robin Brent and Gwyneth Morgan from Quellyn in North Wales. Rosamund, now formally engaged to the new Earl of Kentisbury, spends part of her time at Verriton House, where her young half-brother is looked after by nurses, and the rest at the Rose and Squirrel.

Rosamund has offered to take on the teaching of country dancing in the first term, with a particular object in view. She wants to make friends with Rhoda Kane, the sister of the young Earl whose death had led to Geoffrey inheriting the title, and Rhoda is one of the pupils at Wood End, along with her cousin Rosalie, whose brother, Geoffrey-Bill, had been the next in line for the title until the birth of Rosamund's half-brother.

Rhoda is very unhappy; naturally she's sad as a result of the death of her brother, but she's also bitter and angry at the idea of Rosamund's marriage to her Uncle Geoffrey. She accuses Rosamund of marrying an older man and an invalid to get the title and turn them all out of Kentisbury, but her real feeling, when she is pressed by her friends, is jealousy because Rosamund will take her mother's place as chatelaine of Kentisbury. Neither Rosalie nor Rhoda's own friends, Tamzine Trenow and Sonia Raymond, the niece of Joan Raymond, share her strong feelings—and all this is before any of them have met Rosamund herself.

Rosamund decides to conceal her true identity when she begins to teach country dancing to the girls. This works for a while until a slip of the tongue on Lisabel's part gives the secret away, after which Rhoda refuses to have any more to do with Rosamund. She gets no support from her friends or sympathy from the headmistress. The other Wood End girls like Rosamund and feel that Rhoda is being unreasonable. They try to make her see Rosamund in a more sensible light, but when she can't, or won't, they do stand by her. It takes time, an accident—when Rhoda in a rage causes ink to be spilled over a length of very special silk that Rosamund has woven for a dress for Maidlin—and a moment of danger for Rhoda and Rosamund to break down Rhoda's bitterness and bring the two cousins to a friendship that gives the book its happy ending.

She scrambled on board.
(*Sylvia of Sarn*)

In this book readers are being prepared for Rosamund, the Countess of Kentisbury. The Wood End girls are all attracted by her charm and friendship but are also aware of a certain dignity. The reader can also see this touch of dignity that someone describes as a 'sort of Lady-of-the-Manor air'. Rosamund's temper flares up once or twice, particularly when dealing with Rhoda, but she is quick to apologise, and the book ends on a happy note when Rhoda asks if she can be a bridesmaid for Rosamund, and Rosamund can feel that, when she becomes Countess of Kentisbury, she will have all the Kanes behind her.

For *Sylvia of Sarn*, published by Warne in 1937, EJO returned to an earlier favourite setting, the Lleyn Peninsula—perhaps another visit there had also reminded her of Robin Brent, who had reappeared in *Rosamund's Tuck-Shop*—although it is not named as such and EJO is rather vague about its precise location, not naming the railway station to which people travel from

London. However, the descriptions of the views over the Atlantic and over the bay towards Cader Idris, and the facts that Sylvia goes to school in Barmouth and Liverpool is the town to which they travel for lawyers and other such conveniences pin the story firmly to the north-west coast of Wales, and the rocky headlands and beaches suggest the landscape of Lleyn. EJO may have refrained from naming it precisely because she wanted to invent some geological features, such as Sylvia's hideout, Gwynfa, for the sake of the plot. *Sylvia of Sarn* is a pleasantly romantic title and Sarn is a placename, meaning 'causeway' in English, that is to be found all over Wales.

The story is a romantic mystery, different from the general run of EJO's books but not untypical of girls' stories at this period—a kind of female version of the Buchan-type adventure stories that were being produced for older boys. It begins with seventeen-year-old Megan Lewis, the motherless daughter of a sea captain, at school in London, where she has spent most of her time in recent years, including holidays; she is told that she is to spend the summer at Sarn. Her father suggests, somewhat mysteriously, that there is a job she can do for him, and she also receives an anonymous and even more mysterious note telling her to 'look after Sylvia'.

Megan travels north to Wales, and arrives at Sarn to find Mair Sylvia Thomas living at Plasgwyn with her uncle and aunt and their three-year-old son, Tommy, who is the apple of their eye. Uncle John and his wife (we don't think she is ever given a name) are strange and unfriendly characters, and Sylvia, yet another of EJO's redheads, is left very much to her own devices. When we first meet her, before Megan's arrival, she is accidentally cut off by the tide and then rescued by an unknown boy who introduces himself as Hugh Lewis. Hugh says that, although he has been brought up and sent to school by Captain Lewis, he is no relation to the Captain as far as he knows.

Sylvia appears to be in some sort of danger, and she and Megan assume that this is because she and her brother Tom, who is expected home from South Africa in time for his eighteenth birthday, are due to inherit the land and money which belonged to their grandfather. Tom gets as far as the local station but then fails to arrive at his destination, and the girls, out looking for him early in the morning, come across the car lying on its side, and Hugh lying nearby on the road. In the unexplained absence of Tom, Hugh takes his place—nobody except Sylvia knows him, although both Sian, the faithful old servant, and the aunt evidently observe a resemblance to someone they know. Uncle John disappears at the same time so his possible reactions to Hugh's masquerade don't have to be faced.

The young people learn that Uncle John and Tom have both gone on a voyage to South America with Captain Lewis. Megan is disturbed by her father's role in all this—he seems to be in league with Uncle John, both in the business of smuggling and in aiding and abetting him in his plot against Sylvia and Tom. Megan, Sylvia and Hugh survive one crisis after another—the arrival of some friends from South Africa who have to be told the truth, an attempt at blackmail and the aunt's illness. In Uncle John's absence, Hugh sets to work to run the farm very efficiently, helped only by a labourer, William, who is generally dismissed as not much good. In doing this, Hugh discovers his love of the land and his desire to take up farming rather than a life at sea.

The story behind this strange situation is gradually revealed. Richard Thomas, who owned Plasgwyn and made the money, had three sons. The eldest, Dick, quarrelled with his father and ran away never to return. The second son, who was the father of Sylvia and

Tom, went out to South Africa. John was the youngest. The grandfather left Plasgwyn to any grandchildren who might be alive when he died, and the farm to John, who had apparently always been regarded as slightly untrustworthy, but who had been asked to look after Plasgwyn until his elder brother could return from Rhodesia (EJO still did not seem too clear about the difference between South Africa and Rhodesia). John, resentful that his own son would not share the inheritance of Plasgwyn, had used the Thomas money to try and make his own fortune and had run into difficulties. The second brother had never returned as he had died three years previously, at which point Sylvia had been sent home to Wales.

Megan is mystified about her father's role in all this, as well she might be. He has obviously connived in the kidnapping of Tom and has evidently been involved in some shady deals with John but, on the other hand, he has paid for Hugh's upbringing without, apparently, revealing the fact to his daughter. The job of sea captain is yet again seen as a fairly affluent one—EJO seems to have had an inflated idea of both the status and the wealth of sea captains.

In the end, of course, Captain Lewis is revealed as a goody, as we always knew he must be. Hugh turns out to be the son of the eldest Thomas boy, Dick, who was married to Captain Lewis's sister Polly; she had died when Hugh was born, her husband Dick having been drowned a month before. Hugh, therefore, is also a grandson of old Richard Thomas and shares the inheritance of Plasgwyn. It is clear that Hugh will marry Sylvia and that Tom, who has acquired a taste for seafaring, will marry Megan, so all ends happily. The aunt produces a baby—again, a total surprise to one and all since there has been no hint of her pregnancy—and she and Uncle John will presumably settle down on the farm with their two small children.

This book seems to hark back to EJO's earliest period as a writer, with its elements of romance and mystery, but it is very much a book of the mid-1930s with its use of telephones (although Sylvia has no idea how to use a call box), and there is even a suggestion of ringing up the BBC to try to get Tom speedily returned. The women's fashions, too, belong to the 1930s. When she first appears Sylvia is described as wearing 'neat brown shorts and a brown suede hiking-blouse, with a gilt zip-fastener ...', and although it is still regarded as somewhat progressive dress for a sixteen-year-old schoolgirl, it does not give rise to quite the same

She saw Pip and threw herself down beside her.
(*Damaris at Dorothy's*)

amount of reaction and comment as the Abbey girls wearing tunics had done a few years previously, or even as much comment as there was in *Maidlin to the Rescue* about the shorts worn by Rachel and Damaris.

Sylvia of Sarn is very much an odd book out, having no connections with any other book. EJO may well have been making an effort to produce something different, but it is not one of her most successful books. Megan, Sylvia and Hugh are attractive and convincing characters, and the landscape against which their story is played out is painted with EJO's usual skill, but complex mysteries are not her strong point, and, although the setting and central characters carry the story along on a first reading, the plot does not stand up to too close a scrutiny.

Damaris at Dorothy's, published by the Sheldon Press in 1937, is a book that seems to have been in existence, either in manuscript or as a well-thought-out idea in the author's mind, for some years before it was published. Whatever the truth of the situation is, we now have the story of Rachel and Damaris Ellerton before the happenings described in *Maidlin to the Rescue*. From it we glean a few more facts about the Ellertons of Crossrigs. Their father, Ralph, was the youngest of the four Ellertons—his three sisters were Rachel, to whom he sent the girls when his wife died, Ann, the sister who went south and became the caretaker of an Abbey, and Mary Damaris, Maidlin's mother, to whom he was particularly devoted. There is a reference to Maidlin as the rich cousin: 'She's been adopted by some swish people who have taught her how to swank. She hasn't any use for the farm where she was born.' There is also a hint of the trouble to come when Rachel, in conversation with the head girl, is not sure whether she will be able to go on into the Sixth Form—her father may think that she should leave school and train for a job. All this paves the way for *Maidlin to the Rescue*.

The background to this story is another school for EJO's collection—St Dorothea's near Liverpool. From the careful descriptions it is clear that the school stands in an area that EJO knew well. We are told that New Brighton and Wallasey can be seen on the other side of the Mersey, and that there are dangerous black patches of quicksand on the beach. In letters to Andrea Polden, written early in 1951 when Andrea was living in Crosby, EJO said 'My *Damaris at Dorothy's* is all about that coast' and states categorically that 'Dorothy's was at Waterloo, of course'. The school has its colour theme in the ties and girdles of the school uniform—different colours for each form, and the choice of blue or green dresses. This distinctive outfit is the method by which St Dorothea's girls recognise each other in later years when they are wearing out their dresses.

We see St Dorothea's, known as Dorothy's, the Ellerton girls and the main theme of the story through the eyes of a new girl, Philippa Russell (Pip), whom we have already met in *Maidlin to the Rescue* as the perpetrator of a practical joke. Pip is arriving late in the term, excited but a bit apprehensive and determined not to be bossed or patronised, especially by the Ellertons, whom she has never met but who, she has been told, will look after her because they live in Grasmere and her home is in nearby Windermere. She has very little trouble fitting in to the school, partly because she is taken in charge, on her arrival, by Damaris, substituting for Rachel, whose job it really is. Pip is quickly attracted by Damaris's friendly and downright manner and she later comes to have a deep admiration for Rachel.

As in *Maidlin to the Rescue* the Ellerton sisters are contrasted—Damaris the cool, sensible, balanced one, and Rachel the one who feels more deeply and has difficulty in keeping her feelings under control. In fact it is Rachel's feelings that provide the main theme of this book—a favourite of EJO's—the mistake of giving devotion to an unworthy object. In Rachel's case the unworthy object is a contemporary of her own, a girl called Margery, who has now left the school and whose departure has left Rachel lonely and bereft. As a result, she has become dreamy and introverted, forgets things and has lost interest in her work and in sport—in fact she is generally regarded as being 'not much good'.

The arrival of Pip is the beginning of Rachel's awakening. From Pip's conversation she learns what the other girls think of her—that she is silly and sentimental. She has enough pride to want to pull herself together, and with help from Roberta (Robin), the sensible Head Girl, and from Damaris, she begins to wake up and take part in things again. Her courage in facing up to what, to her, is a deeply felt sorrow impresses Pip, who, because she sleeps in Rachel's room, is often a witness to Rachel's unhappiness.

We are warned, from the conversation of other, older girls in the school, that Margery was a shallow, selfish girl who did not share Rachel's feelings, so we are prepared for the body-blow, a letter from Margery to another girl, Vida, asking her to tell Rachel 'not to be an idiot'. It is a thoughtless letter, although it does include a postscript suggesting that Rachel should not be told this bluntly if it would hurt her. Vida, the games captain, who has no intuitive understanding of other people's feelings, barges straight in and lets Rachel read the letter. The result is that Rachel's sorrow is turned to anger, but it hurts deeply.

The solution to Rachel's problem, seen by Pip, Robin and Damaris herself, is that while Margery seemed the most important person in her life, her loss is a very small thing compared with what would happen if she lost the love and loyalty of her sister:

> So long as she had Damaris, the loss of Margery could be borne. Without Damaris the world would be emptier than it was now, though Margery had gone, Damaris mattered more.

It is already clear, in this book, that Damaris cares deeply for her sister, an indication of the close bond between them that continues through their story and another example of EJO's close relationships between sisters or girls who are like sisters. Rachel and Damaris are perhaps the ultimate example of this. The book ends with them taking Pip for a hike from Grasmere up the side of Seat Sandal to Grizedale Tarn and, finally, with Rachel's successful exam results which mean a move into the Sixth Form and becoming a prefect.

On another level, this is a good, lively school story with junior pranks, an important cricket match, a thoughtful and helpful head girl and a wise and understanding headmistress—a good read for a lover of school stories at the time it was written. But there is one vital omission—no mention is made at all of Damaris's dancing—there are no performances in the dormitory at nights or new pairs of ballet shoes—at this moment, ballet is not part of the EJO saga.

By 1937 the readers of the Abbey books had become part of a magic circle. The books of the Rosamund period are so closely interlinked that it seems almost as if EJO were losing sight of her potential audience, and this may explain why she moved from publisher to publisher at this time, even for the Abbey books, with Harrap publishing one, Chambers two and the Girl's Own Paper Office, a successor to the Religious Tract Society, the remaining three of the mainstream Abbey books published in this period.

Maidlin Bears the Torch, published by the Girl's Own Paper Office in 1937, follows a pattern very similar to that of *Joy's New Adventure*. A new character with musical connections—in this case a brother who aspires to be a composer—falls in with the Abbey girls via Maidlin, pays her admission fee by rescuing one of the twins at the cost of her own safety—here it is Margaret who gets into difficulties when the twins have gone out to spend a night in the Abbey—and thereafter becomes a recurring character in the series. It is interesting to note that *Maid of the Abbey*, which was not published until six years later, follows the same pattern, and it seems that it may have been written immediately after *Rosamund's Castle*, failed to find a publisher, been rewritten to take account of later books and then placed successfully with Collins.

The central theme in *Maidlin Bears the Torch*, the events of which take place in the spring following those in *Rosamund's Tuck-Shop*, is the idea that when everyone else has left the Abbey, Maidlin will carry on its

'Gail, tell me! Didn't you save Elizabeth from a fire?'
(*Maidlin Bears the Torch*)

traditions, although this idea is only expressed in the final chapter when Rosamund describes her friend as a Torch Bearer for the family. The 'torch' is seen as 'a spirit of welcome … and helpfulness … and kindness', belonging to the Abbey with its 'right of sanctuary' and 'bringing back the old rights and the old spirits'. In her *Junior Bookshelf* article, Lynette Muir comments on this spirit, and describes how characters are 'drawn to the Abbey … as knights in the old romances were drawn to the Court of King Arthur and the Fellowship of the Round Table'.

Although Maidlin gives the title to the book, Rosamund is a key character, for it is in this book that she at last marries her earl and becomes Countess of Kentisbury. The forthcoming marriage is mentioned early in the book, and the preparations are in full swing when the new character, Benedicta Bennett, arrives at the Abbey. The wedding day sees a series of major events and crises and the final conversation between Maidlin and Rosamund about carrying the torch comes when the latter returns from her honeymoon with the news that Geoffrey is stronger and better than the specialist ever believed he could be. Once again EJO avoids a description of the actual wedding service, an occasion which, typically, is dogged with ill fortune. This time Jen and Joan miss the wedding because Jen's Rosemary is in danger through appendicitis and Joan is keeping her company. The seriousness of Rosemary's condition has to be kept from Rosamund until the service is over, but all this gives the new character a chance to render service by bearing the latest news to Rosamund as she leaves the church after the ceremony.

When the book begins, lint-haired Benedicta Bennett is leaving her unnamed London school at the end of the Easter term to go to Wood End. Just before the end of term, she and her mother go to a concert at which Maidlin is making her debut. Benedicta (Benney) and her mother recognise Maidlin as the girl they met briefly in a café at Annecy some years previously—Benney is the small girl of *Biddy's Secret*. The Bennetts, as well as enjoying the concert, are also fascinated by Lady Quellyn and the Marchwood twins, who are in a box, and they notice a tall and pretty girl 'with yellow hair' who is the about-to-be-married Rosamund, later identified by Jim, Benney's brother. Jim is persuaded to find out more about Maidlin; he brings the information that she lives with the Quellyns in Oxfordshire and that in the grounds of the house there is a ruined Abbey that is open to the public. Jim harbours a grudge against Sir Ivor Quellyn, who has discouraged his romance with Gail Alwyn, but he has no idea that Gail is part of the Abbey circle.

Mrs Bennett, Benney and Jim decide to visit the Abbey and, on a perfect spring day, the Bennetts are shown round by Maidlin, who, when she discovers that Benney is a Camp Fire girl, invites her to stay for a Camp Fire meeting that evening. Unfortunately, Mrs Bennett is badly hurt in a car crash as she and Jim are returning to London; although Benney is naturally distressed, this is a means of extending her stay at the Abbey. There is a slight sub-plot involving a blossoming romance between Maidlin and Jim, but it is clear right from the start that nothing will come of this—apart from Jim's love for Gail, Maidlin is older than Jim not only in years but also in experience, and she regards him as a mere boy. This romance is handled very lightly—it is all part of EJO's romantic concept that all young men fall in love with her heroines at first sight, while young women protest that marriage has never entered their minds. (Surely the opposite is much nearer the truth.)

In *Maidlin Bears the Torch*, there is quite a lot of discussion about marriage. First of all, Benney's headmistress pronounces ruthlessly on Jim's being 'terribly keen' on Gail, saying: 'It will be time enough for your brother to think about her seriously if he meets her again in five years' time.' Despite Jim's temporary infatuation with Maidlin, which brings him regularly to the Abbey on the pretext of visiting Benney, the latter believes that his real love is Gail, telling Maidlin: 'But Gail came first, and he's really fond of her.' Gail and Jim's story has a happy ending when they are reunited at Rosamund's wedding. To Gail:

> … it was wonderful that a man should look at her in that eager way … In the last few months she had seen married happiness in the case of Joy and Jen, and joyous anticipation of marriage in Rosamund. She was much more ready … to admit that there might be 'something in it', where marriage was concerned.

In this book, too, Joy, owing to her recent marriage, faces one of the crises of her life. On the evening of Rosamund's wedding day, Ivor comes to consult Maidlin; he has been offered the chance of a lifetime, to go to New York for three years, to reorganise the David Orchestra. If he accepts, it may break Joy's heart. Much to everyone's relief—and surprise in some cases—Joy decides to go with him. As Jen tells Maidlin: 'Joy's never really come up against what it means to be married, until now. With Andrew, her married life was all honeymoon', and goes on to point out the necessity of giving in sometimes. Is there a discreet hint here that Joy is expecting a baby at the end of the year when she tells Maidlin:

'If all goes well, I shall be at home during November and December.'?

Jen and Ken's happy marriage supports them through a crisis, too, in Rosemary's illness that prevents their being at Rosamund's wedding. When Maidlin is talking to Ivor about the New York invitation, she says: 'You ought to see it through together—like Jen and Kenneth, over Rosemary's illness; they helped one another.' Thus Rosamund's wedding day provides a background for these other looks at marriage, and Rosamund's own marriage provides the example that Maidlin needs, when Benney suggests that marriage is 'more fun for the men than the girl'. Maidlin agrees that the 'girl has to give up a lot. Look at Rosamund; she gives up her cottage and the life she has chosen, and starts out on a new big job, all to please Geoffrey. Of course, she loves Geoffrey; you must remember that makes a difference.'

Nevertheless, towards the end of the book Maidlin is saying, in answer to Rosamund's suggestion that she should marry, 'I don't think I shall ever marry', which gives Rosamund an opportunity to expound on the importance of finding 'the right man'. The test is to be that she must like him better than Joy or Jen or Rosamund herself but Maidlin 'can't imagine such a person existing'. If these views really do represent EJO's ideas about marriage, it suggests that there must have been a tremendous conflict in her mind between a very feminist ideal and a wish to support the more orthodox view generally held at that period.

Despite their happy marriages, the Abbey girls are still very dependent upon each other, and their husbands seem to give wholehearted support to this dependence—using it, if necessary, as Ivor tries to use Maidlin to explore Joy's possible reactions to his American invitation. Jen, Joy and Rosamund all invite Maidlin to join their households without consultation with their respective husbands, although, admittedly, they were none of them inviting her to live with them in a semi-detached house. Rosamund also happily proposes to abandon her new husband on the day after her wedding and return to give support at the Abbey when Joy and Maid are laid low with shock as a result of the twins' night-time escapade in the Abbey.

EJO had clearly reached a crucial point in her saga. There was one more book in it to cover Rosamund's marriage, but what then? If Maidlin is married off as well, who is to take over the job of maintaining the Abbey traditions? Did she at this time see a possible role for Jansy? Is this why Joan makes something of a comeback in this particular book, playing more of a part than she has played for some time?

Rosamund's Castle, published by the Girl's Own Paper Office in 1938, does bring this phase in the Abbey story to a close. When the book opens it is the November of the year of *Maidlin Bears the Torch*, and Rosamund is now established as the Countess of Kentisbury, living at the Castle. We are provided with a more detailed description of the Castle, with its great quadrangle and towers, the Park with the Dower House at the edge, and the various entry gates. We are told of the lake, the beechwood, the many paths and the wildlife, which includes water birds and peacocks and, important to this story, the deer who roam the park with the stags that are dangerous in the autumn, the season in which this story is set.

Rosamund, reigning in the Castle, has been an instant success with everyone except one young girl—Tanis (Tansy) Lillico, niece of the housekeeper at the Castle and her sister who manages the Dower House. Tansy had been the friend and playmate of Geoff, the young earl, and his sister, Rhoda, and their cousins, Bill and Rosalie. She had shared in their games and projects, especially their private playroom in the Castle, but after the tragedy they have forgotten her. Rhoda and Rosalie have gone off on a world cruise, and not even sent her a postcard. Tansy is very hurt by their behaviour and as a result has developed a feeling of violent hostility towards the new Countess, whom she blames for their neglect of her. Her feelings are further exacerbated by a set of chessmen in ebony and silver that the young earl had given her because she could beat him at the game. The set is still in the Castle, and her Aunts will not allow her to have it because there is no real proof that it is hers. Tansy's hostile attitude to the new Countess, from whom her existence has been kept secret, has resulted in her being banished to the Dower House when she is at home from school. The Dower House is now all prepared for Rhoda and her mother and awaits their return from travelling—all very conveniently, as it turns out.

Rosamund has not lost touch with Wood End School, which now has a new pupil in Benedicta Bennett, finally arriving, somewhat belatedly, to become Daffodil's friend and take Rosalie's place in the 'Robin' room with Robin Brent and Gwyneth Morgan. Benney, with her previous acquaintance with the Abbey circle, provides a further link between Rosamund and Wood End. On her first night at the school there is a fire, and enough of the building is damaged to make it impossible for the girls to sleep there until repairs have been carried out. Rosamund comes to the rescue and arranges for the schoolgirls to live at the Dower House and commute to the school each day for lessons. Kentisbury has moved a little nearer to the village of the Rose and Squirrel! The Wood End girls have not lost their admiration for their 'special Countess' and are agreed that 'being a Countess suits her'—they would probably have agreed even more had they witnessed her gentle but firm handling of the Misses Lillico when Tansy's existence at last has to be revealed to her.

All this means that Tansy is in a good position to get to know the Wood End girls, and to get some news of Rosalie and Rhoda. She picks out Benney and Daffodil as being the youngest and most approachable and they are very willing to be friends, while disapproving strongly of her attitude to Rosamund. In fact, they try hard to convince her that Rosamund would understand and agree that the chessmen should be hers, but although she is quite friendly, and develops a strong admiration for Benney, her prejudice is too strong for her and she continues to wage her own private war.

There is a very brief mention of Camp Fire here, used, once again, as a setting of standards. Tansy has 'played' at Camp Fire and Benedicta, a Camp Fire girl, points out that some of her actions are not 'straight' but both deceitful and disloyal. Tansy is 'perceptive enough to see the baseness of the act she was considering … But she had not quite the grit to put her idea aside … '

The Marchwood twins have a bigger part to play in this story. They are now growing up and are nearly ready to step into leading roles. Just now they and Maidlin are staying at the Castle because Joy has returned to the Hall to have her new baby, her first Quellyn child, named David after Ivor's orchestra in New York—this, of course, is the baby whose arrival was hinted at in *Maidlin Bears the Torch*. By now Ivor refers to the twins as Joy's 'adventurous and enterprising daughters', and as such they make the most of the freedom of such an exciting place as Kentisbury Castle. They find the playroom full of books and toys that had belonged to the young earl, his sister and cousins, and are anxious to play with all the fascinating treasures. They show their discovery to Benney, who feels that Tansy should be told and persuades them to wait a little.

Tansy is furious and worried about her treasured chessmen. She enters the Castle secretly at night, removes the chessmen and hides them in another secret place, a cave that she and the Castle children sometimes used when they were together, but the cave is also discovered by the twins and Tansy sees only one way out—to frighten them off so that they will go home.

During their stay at the Castle, the twins are not being as closely supervised as usual. Maidlin's career is developing, moving towards recital and oratorio singing under the guidance of Dr Robertson, who seems to know what will suit her best. We learn that he is younger than Ivor Quellyn, although Rosamund warns Benedicta not to 'start making up a romance for her'. This from EJO means a lot, and it would seem even more likely from this that *Maid of the Abbey*, if not already written, was at least conceived by this time, but for some reason put aside. Rosamund is not as active as usual because she is pregnant. This is one pregnancy that is subtly prepared for all through the book. There are hints among the Castle staff, Rosamund is twice described as wearing 'a loose blue gown', and the fact of her pregnancy is crucial to the most exciting moment in the story,

Tansy, in a bid to frighten the twins away from the Castle, offers to take them into the Park and leads them to where they will be near the roaring stags, but her plan gets out of hand when they come face to face with the largest and fiercest animal, known as Alexander the Great. Tansy, scared but brave, sends the twins to hide and faces the stag alone. She is seen by Rosamund and Maidlin as they drive through the Park, and Rosamund, sending Maidlin to run for help, scrambles down to support Tansy. There is a dramatic moment when Rosamund falls and Tansy, her prejudice forgotten, throws herself on top of her in an attempt to protect her. They are saved by the arrival of Maidlin and the men, and Tansy is left amazed by her own reactions.

Rosamund is not physically hurt but badly shocked by her experience, and there are anxious moments for the Earl and Maidlin. However, after Rosamund and Tansy, now completely won over, meet and talk, all is well, and the book ends with the birth of an heir for Kentisbury. The arrival of this baby is clearly a high point, establishing EJO's favourite heroine in the Castle to which she has come by virtue of her own efforts and personality. Jen's picture of Rosamund reigning in the Castle is presented in a properly feudal atmosphere of curtseying tenantry and devoted family retainers. From now on Rosamund, when she appears in the later books, is always Rosamund the Countess.

Chapter 8

BACKWARDS, FORWARDS AND SIDEWAYS, 1938 TO 1946

The first three books of this next period show how EJO resolved the problem that seems to have faced her at the end of *Rosamund's Castle*. All her important heroines are now established married women, apart from Maidlin, who would have been if *Maid of the Abbey* had been published at this point, and although she could almost certainly have written about their lives and their babies, she was a writer of books for girls and her readers wanted to hear about girls as, no doubt, did her publishers.

She had a new generation coming up—Jansy Raymond and the Marchwood twins—but they were still a little too young. She needed some older girls to lead the way, and they had to be girls connected with the Abbey. Also the Abbey itself had for some time been only the spirit of the place in the background and yet, as far back as *The Girls of the Abbey School*, there had been a hint of more discoveries to be made.

EJO now began to write what have come to be known as the 'retrospective' Abbey books, returning to the time when Joan, Joy and Jen were still at school. The Abbey has a very key role in these books, partly as new discoveries are made, but also as embodying the spirit of welcome and sanctuary that was expressed in *Maidlin Bears the Torch*. The third reason for these books is the introduction, at this early stage of the storyline, of a new character whose early marriage produces a daughter, older than Jansy Raymond and ready to lead the new generation when EJO picks up her original storyline again. One must admire the way in which the stitching together of the original and the retrospective books was done so seamlessly and brilliantly that most adult collectors are unaware of the stitching until it is pointed out to them or they notice the dates when the books were first published.

The vital new character appears in

The four girls stared at the stones.
(*Schooldays at the Abbey*)

Schooldays at the Abbey, first published by Collins in 1938, which opens at a key point in the Abbey story—the crowning of Joan Shirley as the fourth May Queen of the Hamlet Club and the moment when Jen Robins joins Miss Macey's school. We now learn that also present at that Coronation was a visitor from Australia, an eighteen-year-old girl called Janice Macdonald, shortened to Jandy Mac, who, on her first visit to England, has deliberately come to Wycombe in search of the Abbey. She has been told about the Abbey by her Uncle Tony, a courtesy uncle who had wanted to marry her widowed mother. Mrs Macdonald had, unfortunately, died before this was possible, but Uncle Tony had played an important part in Jandy's youth, and on his death at sea she had been his heir—it is this inheritance that has made her journey to England possible. Uncle Tony's interest in the Abbey is explained when we learn that he was Antony Abinger, the son of old Sir Antony who left the Hall to Joy and the Abbey to Joan. He had predeceased his father, otherwise Jandy would have inherited both.

Jandy arrives in Wycombe in time to hear about the Crowning at the big school at the end of the town; she persuades Miss Macey to allow her and her aunt, who is travelling with her, to attend the ceremony and in this way learns about the Hamlet Club and the Abbey girls and, incidentally, meets and talks to Jen. She also visits the Abbey and makes the acquaintance of Joan and Joy.

She goes off to Scotland to visit relations, and during her absence the school, as we know, takes up residence at the Hall. The episode of Dick and Della described in *The Girls of the Abbey School* now takes place, and when it is over Jandy reappears. Her aunt has gone to Canada, and Jandy has persuaded Miss Macey to allow her to come back and join the school while her aunt is away. She and the reader are brought up to date on the story of Dick and Della and the new discoveries in the Abbey. She learns folk dancing with the Hamlet Club and also plays cricket for the school, starting a tradition of 'demon bowling' which she teaches to Jen and which is later inherited by her own daughter and Jen's.

EJO is careful to draw her threads together. Janice's Scottish relations live at Vairy, the site of the Kentisbury Scottish residence. She tells them that 'my grandpa Fraser is old now, but he was the factor for the Earl of Kentisbury', and that during her visit she saw Viscount Verriton and his family—Geoff and Rhoda as babies. In Scotland she also meets a cousin, Alec Fraser, and this meeting leads to a serious talk with Joan about 'falling in love'. Once again it is the man who is sure and the girl who is not yet ready to think about marriage.

Jandy Mac is a true EJO heroine. She does not tell Joan and Joy the whole truth about her Uncle Tony, who was of course Joy's real uncle, for fear they should think that she covets their inheritance. She refers to him merely as someone who had known the Abbey well and had been a great friend. This makes things difficult at first; following an idea of Uncle Tony's, the girls discover the Monk's Path leading from the Abbey up on to the hills to a cave, probably an ancient hermit's cave, where they make a more modern discovery—Tony Abinger's diary. Joy is delighted to learn more about her uncle and to find mentions of her mother, but Jandy has to hide her own interest.

There is also the matter of a ring with seven sapphires. Joy has a modern copy, and Jen, reading the old manuscript book found in the Abbey, has discovered that there was an old one, made by Ambrose for the Lady Jehane. The girls speculate on the whereabouts of this ring, but Jandy knows that her Uncle Tony had it. To make matters worse comes the possibility that the date of Tony Abinger's death was later than that of his father, which would make Jandy the owner of the Abbey and the Hall. The idea appals her, but she tells only Miss Macey of her worries, although it preys on her mind, and people wonder what is wrong, while she waits anxiously for the matter to be sorted out.

At the end of term, when the schoolgirls leave the Hall, both Jandy and Jen stay on, Jen because her father is ill again—a preparation for later events—and Janice owing to the illness of her aunt. In this way just the four most important characters are present when Janice receives the welcome news that Tony Abinger did indeed die before his father. In her relief she pours out the story incoherently, and her listeners react as we would expect. Joan is full of admiration and gratitude for Jandy's consideration, but Joy, in the first moment of shock, bursts out violently against Jandy.

When all is resolved and, incidentally, the old sapphire ring comes home to the Abbey, Jandy decides that she will marry Alec Fraser and go and live on a South Sea island. Her only regret is that she is not really related to the Abbey girls, but Joy enthusiastically adopts her as a cousin and Jen comments: 'Of course, it's really the Abbey that has made Joy adopt Jandy, isn't it?'

This, the first of the retrospective books, is full of important points: there is a new discovery in the Abbey; the Abbey is seen as a place of welcome and sanctuary; the interest in the Hamlet Club and its procession of Queens is revived; and, possibly the most important, the vital new character of Jandy Mac has been introduced, and she has committed herself to marriage through her engagement to Alec Fraser, well ahead of Joan and Joy. In a light-hearted conversation she says: 'I shall come back to see you when we're all middle-aged ladies and I'll bring my family to see the Abbey. I shall call the girls Joan and Joy and Janet.', and Joy tells Joan, '... you can call your first daughter Janice'.

Having created Jandy Mac and once again brought the Abbey into the foreground, EJO made use of it in short stories. One story that stands on its own, *Adventure in the Abbey*,

Two small figures darted out and the girls pounced.
(*Adventure in the Abbey*)

appeared in the *Collins Girls' Annual* of 1955, and in two other, undated, collections, the *Girls' Own Story Book* and the *Girls' Own Book*, while *Mistakes in the Abbey* followed in the *Collins Girls' Annual* of 1956, and also appeared in two undated collections, another *Girls' Own Book* and the *Girls Story Omnibus*. As they both take place at a time when Jandy was at the Abbey, it is convenient to deal with them here, although they may not have been written until some years later.

Among the illustrations for *Adventure in the Abbey* is a coloured plate of Joan, Joy and Jen, by Frank Varty, which is said to be a picture that pleased EJO as being the nearest to her own idea of the characters. It shows the three girls framed in an archway, with the Abbey ruins behind them. Jen has fair plaits but they are short, and Joan and Joy have fairly adult, 1930s-ish hair styles. The critical eye misses Joan's coronal of plaits, and remembers that Joy did not have her hair cut until just before she married Sir Ivor Quellyn. Nor does the likeness between Joan and Joy appear very strong. The modern reader will find it difficult to appreciate the author's enthusiasm.

The story is very slight. Young Micky Watson, the same who was Dick Jessop's accomplice in earlier exploits, takes advantage of the fact that Ann Watson is at his grandparents' cottage and steals her key to the Abbey. Taking his 'simple' cousin Frankie with him, he then goes to look for the jewels of which he has heard. Joan, having given up her bed to Jandy, is sleeping in the Abbey, and Jen worries about her because she is alone. Inevitably, Jen, Jandy and Joy foregather in the Abbey with Joan and catch the culprits.

Not content with this slight adventure, or perhaps in answer to a sudden call for an 'annual' story about the Abbey, yet another night of alarms and excursions in the Abbey is described in *Mistakes in the Abbey*. These events take place three nights after those recounted in *Adventure in the Abbey* and, once again, are sparked off by young Micky Watson. On his previous visit Micky had dropped his 'special' knife in the Abbey crypt and, in a note to Jen, he begs her to let him in at night and help him find it. Jen enlists Joy's help, knowing that Joan would not co-operate, but it is not until Joy remarks that she has had to 'pinch' Joan's key that Jen realises that Joan would not merely disapprove, but would be angry and upset at being deceived. She almost turns back, but is persuaded by Joy to carry on.

The excitements in this story are all because Micky has brought his dog, Rosie, with him, and in the crypt Rosie meets the Abbey cats, who take exception to her presence; in the resulting confusion Joy trips and overbalances on the brink of the famous well. Jen and Micky are able to prevent her falling in but cannot pull her to safety. Needless to say, Joan and Jandy appear in the nick of time and all is finally well—Micky even gets his knife back.

The title here has a double significance. It was a mistake to take a dog into the Abbey, but the bigger mistake was made by Jen in not realising at first that she was deceiving Joan. This is the young, enthusiastic Jen, who does not always control her wilder impulses but is desperately anxious to gain Joan's approval.

Schooldays at the Abbey and the two short stories also gave EJO a golden opportunity to clear up a point that may have puzzled some of her readers. Mrs Clarke, Micky's grandmother, is also the mother of Ann Watson, and therefore the grandmother of Maidlin, Rachel and Damaris. Joan explains to Jandy that Mrs Clarke married again, 'a man living in our village; she comes from the north', and this second marriage, to which reference is made only in the retrospective books, thus accounts for the fact that Ann

Joy tripped and lost her balance.
(*Mistakes in the Abbey*)

Watson's mother is called Clarke rather than Ellerton. Conveniently, Mrs Clarke has died and Micky and Frankie have left before Maidlin comes to the Abbey, otherwise they would have provided inconvenient relations. The fact that her mother came from the north accounts for Ann Watson's presence in the Abbey.

Looking back to *The Girls of the Abbey School*, published seventeen years previously, it seems surprising that EJO did not at some earlier stage choose to write about secret passages and lost treasures; there was undoubtedly a rich seam waiting to be mined, and the elements of mystery and adventure, and the attractive character of Jandy Mac, who was to provide a way of continuing the Abbey saga beyond Maidlin's marriage, came together splendidly in *Schooldays at the Abbey*. Having produced an Abbey adventure rather than an Abbey romance, EJO immediately went on to write two more similar stories. The first of these is *Secrets of the Abbey*, which was published in 1939 and dedicated to Dorita Fairlie Bruce, a contemporary writer of girls' school stories, acknowledging the pleasure EJO had received from 'Dimsie, Prim and Nancy'.

Bearing in mind the year of publication, another of the attractions of moving backwards in time may have been the excuse it provided for ignoring the Second World

War. Unlike Dorita Fairlie Bruce, who allowed Dimsie, Primula and Nancy all to get caught up in the war effort and to capture German spies, EJO was never to mention the Second World War, except in the very vaguest terms, in any of her books. Sheila recalls being conscious of this when she read the Abbey books as a schoolgirl—most of the other writers of school stories, including Elinor Brent-Dyer and Angela Brazil, were only too pleased to make use of the possibilities of a war-time setting.

Secrets of the Abbey, which is made up of two interlinked plots, takes place in the summer term, a year after the events of *Schooldays at the Abbey*. As Lynette Muir comments, ' … it is never winter in the Abbey!', and although this is perhaps an oversimplification, EJO and her readers may have shared with Jen the vision of a 'sunny evening and a perfect lawn, and long shadows on the grass, and a cool wind after a hot day … and Miss Lane's fiddle sounding through the trees … '. This is an attractive vision for an about to be war-torn world.

In this book Jandy Mac comes on a second visit from Australia, a final one before her marriage to Alec Fraser, with maps which apparently show more hidden passages leading from the Abbey, and Jen faces a time of decision, her 'to be or not to be' of the Hamlet Club motto. EJO has not forgotten the new reader, and the beginning of Chapter 2 provides the vital information about Joan and Joy, the Abbey and the Hall, and about Jen and Jandy Mac's special relationship with them. Joan's maid, Muriel Bayne, has been chosen as Queen so Jen is invited to become Joan's maid in her place.

This makes Jen's decision to give up the Hamlet Club and dancing for the summer term in order to play cricket for the sake of the school all the more of a sacrifice— younger girls are not allowed to do both. Earlier examples of Hamlet Club members making sacrifices are quoted, although Cicely's is said to be having to uproot herself from her school and friends in London to move to Buckinghamshire rather than the more frequently cited one of her having to reveal the secret of the Club for the sake of the school.

The Junior Cricket Team of which Jack, Jen's best peer-group friend, is Captain, is short of bowlers, and Jen, used to playing cricket with her brothers, has been coached by Jandy and encouraged by them, so her bowling skills would be a real asset to the team. In her first match her performance is disappointing, but in the vital match against St Anne's College all is well, and she takes seven wickets, thus justifying her

Jen hung over her shoulder.
(*Secrets of the Abbey*)

decision. The idea that the mantle of Elijah (Jandy Mac) has fallen on Elisha (Jen) is mooted by one of the defeated rivals, an idea that appeals to Jack.

Thus the first part of the book is taken up with Jen's first appearance in the Coronation procession and her prowess at cricket. Then Jandy arrives with her 'two pieces of crumpled paper' that she has found in Tony Abinger's belongings, given to him by 'John Miles, of King's Bottom Farm, who had it from his grandfather, whose father had given it to him when he was dying'. These take the girls into a passage that leads from the old underground church to the Abbey gatehouse. En route, they discover a hoard of guineas—loot apparently mislaid by a highwayman—Ambrose's grave, and a book telling more of his story, which has been buried with him by his adopted son, Peregrine Abinger. Jen is injured but fortunately this means that, when the other three girls are trapped in the gatehouse passage, she is able to get help from some young men who are visiting the Abbey.

In the midst of the excitement, Jandy is called to Scotland to see her sick grandmother. There seems to be no particular reason for this illness except that it enables EJO to move on quickly to the party three weeks later, when Jen's ankle has recovered, and Jandy returns for the setpiece of a Hamlet Club party, at which Cicely tells the members about the Club motto and uses Jen as the text of her sermon.

This book gives EJO an opportunity to reinforce the more obvious characteristics of her four main characters—Joy's quick thoughtless reactions and Jen's excited shrieks contrasting with the quiet and thinking responsibility shown by Joan and Jandy. It becomes clear in this book that the introduction of Jandy helped to strengthen Joan as a character in the Abbey series—the latter's goodness and sensible maturity no longer stand out in such stark contrast to the more credible failings of Jen and Joy. Jen's future closeness to Joy is also hinted at when she says to Jandy: 'I always thought I liked Joan heaps better than Joy, and I do, of course; but sometimes Joy is just terribly nice and kind, you know, Jandy.' More hints are given of future developments. Jandy's future, of course, is assured—she is going to marry her cousin Alec and live in the South Seas—once again Samoa appears in EJO's books.

When it is suggested that a local magistrate should be consulted about the ownership of the highwayman's hoard, Joan mentions Sir Keith Marchwood, the local Lord of the Manor, who lives next door; he is an invalid and has no children, so the Manor will eventually belong to his much younger stepbrother, Andrew Marchwood, the explorer. Jen imagines that the monogram on the purse and locket they have found in the highwayman's hoard, KM, stands for Kate or Kitty Marchwood, and later suggests that she will marry the explorer's son and bring Ambrose's ring back to the Abbey. It is Jandy who suggests that the explorer may have younger brothers.

On a more serious note Joy, commenting on the love affair of Ambrose and Jehane, says: 'It's a marvellous way to feel about anybody who has died … I've sometimes thought I'd go out of my mind if I lost anybody I cared about very much. It's so final … I'm afraid I couldn't be as brave as that.' Jandy says bluntly—more truly than she knows: 'You might have to be.' Finally, the spirit of the Abbey is stressed when Ambrose, living in the old gatehouse after the dissolution of the Abbey, is seen as 'carrying on the old tradition of welcome and kindness'.

The third of these Abbey adventure stories was *Stowaways in the Abbey*, published by Collins in 1940. The events follow on after *Secrets*; Jen's ankle is now better and she is able to play cricket and dance, and despite its title this book is about her. Its main ingredients are more discoveries in the Abbey and the development of Jen's character. Her enthusiasm, which she never loses, is at this stage a trifle overwhelming, but she eventually learns to control it. She already has her quality of understanding, but that too has to develop and extend as she grows up.

In many ways this book is typical of children's stories of the period. It concerns the adventures of two younger girls, in this case Jen and Jack, who are left to their own devices owing to illness in the family. Joan and Joy have measles, and Jen, who is staying at the Abbey, and Jack, who has been invited to keep her company, are kept away from school in quarantine. Given the run of the Abbey and the exciting discoveries made in the previous book, Jen's curiosity leads her on to find out more, specifically about the possible 'Kitty Marchwood', the owner of the locket she found in *Secrets of the Abbey*.

A young man was coming from the car.
(*Stowaways in the Abbey*)

With Jack's somewhat reluctant support, she engages in a little breaking and entering of Marchwood Manor next door to the Hall, to see if the family portraits give any clue. They find their clue, and more than that, paintings of the old Abbey church that was destroyed. But they are caught trespassing and have to confront Sir Keith Marchwood, the owner of the Manor, another crusty, elderly man with arthritis, who is won over by Jen's enthusiasm and honesty, and by the end of the book has become, like Sir Antony Abinger, a looker-on at the Hamlet Club as it dances in the Abbey. His restoration of the paintings of the Church to be hung in the Abbey marks the beginning of friendly relations between the Hall and the Manor. Sir Keith is also able to add more details to the Abbey story. The original owner of the locket was indeed a Katharine Marchwood, born in 1585, who later married Peregrine Abinger (Joy's ancestor) and, with him, was the protector of Ambrose, the old lay-brother who returned to the Abbey after the dissolution. Jen is allowed to keep the locket on condition that she promises to call her first daughter Katharine. Another foundation stone for the future!

The stowaways of the title are Timothy Spindle and his sister Susan, who are orphans. Susan is a little maid at the Hall and Timothy is the bootboy at Sir Keith's London house. Accused of a serious theft of which he is not guilty, he has run away to Susan, who hides him in the Abbey, where they are discovered by Jen. This is when Jen's romantic ideas take a hard knock. She is thrilled by the idea that Timothy has taken sanctuary in the Abbey, and it has to be carefully explained to her that the rights of sanctuary no longer apply in these modern times. However, Joan's advice and a letter from Jen to Sir Keith make things right for Timothy and earn her Susan's gratitude.

Susan's adoration of Jen does not, unfortunately, prevent her from unwittingly giving away a secret of Jen's that she wanted to tell Joan herself, the existence of the pictures of the old Abbey church. Jen is furious and confronts Susan, thus upsetting Susan so much that she takes refuge in the Abbey in floods of tears. Jen has to be made to understand Susan's trouble, and it is Joan who, once again, talks to her carefully, presenting Susan as another seeker of sanctuary in the Abbey and explaining her thoughtlessness as being due to ignorance and lack of education: 'She never meant any harm; she didn't understand it was a secret. She isn't educated; she doesn't think clearly.' This is a point of view that we have heard expressed before by EJO. Joan suggests to Jen that, by not understanding and forgiving Susan, she is failing the 'spirit' of the Abbey. Jen, of course, finally overcomes her anger and makes things right with Susan, thus taking one more step towards Jen the understanding, who solves so many other people's problems. And another character is established in Susan Spindle, later to be Joy's devoted cook at the Hall. One incident in this story that is repeatedly retold in later books is the episode when Joy hangs out of the window to talk while she still has a temperature and thus develops pneumonia and nearly dies. But this is mainly a jolly book about two nice tomboys having adventures, while for

'You understand, girl, you will never have stopped learning.'
(*Damaris Dances*)

Abbey readers it adds to the Abbey story and shows us a developing Jen.

Damaris Dances, published by the Oxford University Press in 1940, is very much a backwards and sideways book. It was the first EJO title to be published by the prestigious Oxford University Press, which, in the 1930s and 1940s, was publishing a number of popular authors for young people. It was also the first EJO title to be illustrated by Margaret Horder, the Australian illustrator, who was undoubtedly the most distinguished illustrator ever to work on EJO's books. The skills of a ballerina are grafted onto Damaris; there was never any mention of ballet in either *Maidlin to the Rescue* or *Damaris at Dorothy's*. Why did EJO begin to take an interest in ballet at this stage and why did she decide to give one of the people linked to the Abbey a gift in this particular art?

By the 1930s ballet had become popular in England, and the success of Noel Streatfeild's first book, *Ballet Shoes* (1936), had no doubt revealed its potential as an attractive theme for girls' books. Lorna Hill in the 1940s and 1950s was to exploit this theme in conjunction with that other popular theme, ponies, while Enid Blyton is on record as having been asked by her readers to write ballet stories in the early 1950s (she refused). EJO was not so prudent, and *Damaris Dances* reveals her lack of knowledge about techniques.

Why this interest in ballet in the 1930s? According to Grove's *Dictionary of Music and Musicians*, ballet was discredited by the beginning of the twentieth century, owing to the lifeless formalism into which it had sunk. About 1909, however, an astonishing revival was apparent, the impulse for which came from Russia. The new school dated from the alliance between Diaghilev and Fokine, which produced a company that gave its first season in Paris in 1909. This company was in fact a secession from the Russian Imperial Ballet School. Efforts were made to raise the level of ballet music. The principal ballerina of Diaghilev's company was Tamara Karsavina, the principal male dancer Nijinsky, and Anna Pavlova was their contemporary. Owing to the First World War, the Diaghilev company found itself in exile, a situation perpetuated by the Russian Revolution, and began to shed some of its national characteristics.

Diaghilev died in 1929, but within two years there was in both France and England a remarkable revival in the standards of performance and production and consequently in public interest. A ballet company formed by Colonel de Basil in France, which included some of the dancers from Diaghilev's company, visited London for the first time in 1933 and gave a long and successful season. Interest in ballet in England had been fostered by the formation of the Camargo Society and the growth of the Vic-Wells Ballet, which had created a new audience for ballet. There was a tremendous amount of activity in English ballet in the 1930s—Ninette de Valois, Marie Rambert, Frederick Ashton, Alicia Markova and Anton Dolin were introducing ballet to an ever-increasing audience—and thus EJO's interest but low level of detailed knowledge at this time are easily accounted for. The Russian-French influences and the English contribution to the development of new ballets are clearly reflected in *Damaris Dances*.

The second question remains. Why did EJO select Damaris as her ballet dancer? If a talent for ballet had to be attached to an already established character, Damaris was, in fact, a fairly obvious choice. Although she had appeared in two books, she was not too old to start serious training, and early lessons in America and a continuing interest discouraged or suppressed by the aunts could account for the current situation, although the overall result does lack a certain amount of conviction.

Damaris Dances opens towards the end of term following the events of *Maidlin to the Rescue*. Damaris has returned to St Dorothea's to take matriculation and is now dancing for the girls in the dormitory after lights-out. Miss Allen, the gym mistress, who sees her dancing and who receives the explanation of early lessons and aunty discouragement, encourages her, and, when she gets to the Abbey, Damaris tells Rachel of this encouragement. The sisters agree, however, that they cannot tell Maidlin and expect her to pay for Damaris to train as a dancer. They therefore go off to Annecy as planned, for Rachel to perfect her French and fit herself to become Maidlin's secretary. Fortunately for Damaris's future, however, Annette, the daughter of their French landlady, is being courted by M Berthelot, who is a ballet enthusiast and who, having seen Damaris dance, arranges for her to go to classes.

Thus, while Rachel learns French, Damaris learns to dance, and the winter passes. In March, just as they are about to return to England and the Abbey before going on to Italy, news comes that the Cumbrian farm, Crossrigs, is to be affected by a new road, and Damaris will not be able to farm it. Back in England, Maidlin tells Rachel that she is not going to take up her duties on her Italian estates and therefore the job planned for Rachel will also disappear. During this holiday, however, Maidlin has tickets for Sadler's Wells so Rachel and Damaris go to see *Swan Lake*, *The Spectre of the Rose* and *Checkmate*, a fairly typical programme of the period and one which reflects the elements discussed earlier. Damaris is now able to tell Maidlin of her wish to dance; after much discussion, she is given full support by Maidlin and the Abbey family, and she and Rachel go off to Italy for the autumn and winter for her to continue her training.

By the time they return to England the following June, now over two years after the events of *Maidlin to the Rescue*, Rachel has written a story of which Mary-Dorothy approves, and Damaris is ready to start her career as a ballet dancer. Fortunately, M Berthelot of Annecy has a brother who is a theatrical agent in London (although this is the first time we've heard of him), and who is prepared to give Damaris an introduction to a ballet company. She is accepted as a member of the corps de ballet for a new production, *The Goose-Girl*, and thereafter the story follows a familiar pattern; dismissed from the corps de ballet for refusing to conform, she returns as the goose-girl herself when the girl who was to have danced the role falls ill. Inevitably Damaris is a great success, and the story ends on a note of triumph.

The story of the Abbey girls continues in the background, although the reader of the previous books learns little that is new. In *Damaris Dances*, uncharacteristically, there is no new person to be brought up to date on the story thus far. Instead, at the beginning of Chapter 3, necessary explanations are made directly to the reader. Thereafter, Rachel and Damaris come to the Abbey periodically and witness the continuing Abbey saga, or happenings are told to them while they are away. We learn of Maidlin's successful singing career, Rosamund's marriage to the Earl of Kentisbury—Rosamund also gives Damaris her stage name of Mary Damayris and the use of the Kentisbury town house when she and Rachel have to be in London—Joy's marriage to Sir Ivor and her departure for New York, the twins growing up and Cecily Perowne becoming the first Fire-Maker in Camp Waditaka. Cecily is quite an important background character in this book, perhaps because she can present Damaris's case convincingly to Maidlin, comparing what has happened to Damaris in her discovery of ballet to what she experienced in her discovery of music. As she says to Maidlin: 'I don't see how you can stop her, Guardian. She has the same right to go ahead that you all gave me.'

Joan and Jen, on the other hand, are not mentioned at all, and the omission of Jen seems particularly surprising in view of her role at the time of Maidlin's rescue of the Ellertons and the fact that they stay at the Grange, unnamed here, on their journey to and from Crossrigs. The omission of Jen may be due to an abridgement of the text in the Spring Books edition that we used, but it may possibly have been due to the fact that Jen is not unlike Damaris both physically and in character (fair curls and plenty of bounce), and perhaps EJO felt there was no room for them both in a book that was primarily concerned with Damaris. If the omission was deliberate, this emphasises the background nature of the Abbey and the main Abbey characters in this book.

The book's main message, however, is that Damaris is not spoiled by her success. She retains her love of home and family. Four chapters actually have the word 'home' in the title and the last one is called 'Home in the Background'; the sisters plan to have their own home eventually, near the Abbey. Damaris tells Rachel that she wants to save up so that one day they can buy or rent a scrap of land from Joy 'and we'll build a little house, just for us two, Ray …'; this is yet another example of the sisters theme in EJO's work. In *Damaris at Dorothy's* Rachel realised that Damaris was more important to her than any friend; in *Maidlin to the Rescue* the sisters planned quite separate careers, with Damaris farming at Crossrigs and Rachel becoming Maidlin's secretary; but now they come together again, and Rachel sees her life's work as mothering Damaris and writing books. This support is seen as important in preventing Damaris from succumbing to the temptations of the bright lights.

Although this was the first EJO book to be illustrated by Margaret Horder, we used the Spring Books edition printed in Czechoslovakia, which has illustrations by some far less distinguished and unnamed illustrator. There has also been some updating—the Queen's Hall, where Maidlin sings at some of her earlier concerts and which was bombed during the Second World War, has been replaced by the Royal Festival Hall. The Children's Press abridged editions of EJO's books are well publicised, but little has been said about the EJO titles published by Spring Books. During the postwar period, they reprinted books and published new titles which were sold at low prices, largely because they used printers in Czechoslovakia, where the work could be done much more cheaply than in the UK. The Spring Books editions of girls' stories were intended for a popular readership, hence the rather cheap-looking illustrations typical of the time at which these editions appeared.

As well as writing about the early exploits of the Abbey girls, EJO now produced what might well be described as a retrospective Kentisbury book, set in the summer before the events of *Rosamund's Tuck-Shop* and before the death of the young Earl of Kentisbury. *Patch and a Pawn* was published as a full-length book by Warne in 1940, but had appeared as a serial in the *Girls' Own Annual* the previous year. According to Monica Godfrey, it was lengthened for book publication. The reason for this story was two-fold: first, to show the unsuitability of young Geoffrey as an Earl and, secondly, to introduce a new

Tansy pointed with her whip to the green slopes by the lodge.
(*Patch and a Pawn*)

character for whom EJO had plans, Patricia (Patch) Paterson, cousin of Tansy's friend Roger, the doctor's son, who is on a visit from her home near Vairy Castle in Scotland.

The other characters in this story are, of course, Geoff, the young earl, his sister Rhoda, their cousin Rosalie and her brother Bill (or Geoffrey-Bill). Roger also figures and so, of course, does Tansy in her role of loyal hanger-on and errand-runner for Geoff. Bill and Rosalie are described as distant cousins, but a new adult character is added to the Kentisbury family tree. This is Lady Rosabel, elder sister of the old earl and therefore Great-Aunt to Geoff and Rhoda, and also referred to as 'Aunt' by Bill and Rosalie.

Geoff's behaviour is, throughout the book, that of a thoroughly spoiled and thoughtless adolescent. He plays stupid and sometimes dangerous tricks on visitors to the park, but is then furious when some local boys hit back with his own weapons; he shirks his duties as Earl and has to be bullied into them by Rhoda, but can be thoroughly autocratic where his own personal affairs are concerned. His behaviour is thrown into relief when seen from the point of view of Patch, the visitor, and when contrasted with that of Bill, the sailor-to-be, who is everything that Geoff is not: courteous, thoughtful, responsible and wise.

The episode of the pawn which gives the book its title is typical of Geoff's behaviour on two counts. First, he is playing the old childish trick of trailing a mysterious parcel on the ground in front of people in the park and, when they stoop to investigate it, whisking it away. Bill is disapproving and calls it childish, and Patch, wandering in the park as a visitor, sees the whole thing and climbs the hillside to confront Geoff and give him her unvarnished opinion of his behaviour, an intention to which she holds still more firmly when she discovers who he is: 'You're the new earl? ... Well, then, I think it's simply disgusting. You ought to be ashamed, all of you ...' Her forthright honesty and indignation appeal at once to Bill, who openly expresses his admiration for her—an admiration that, by the end of the book, has developed into something more.

Secondly, when it turns out that the parcel, which Roger has thrown into the lake in disgust, actually contained not merely stones but also a silver pawn from the famous chess set, first Roger and then Bill goes diving in the lake in the early morning, and when Roger insists that there is no pawn there, Geoff, in a typical fit of temper, infers that he must have found and kept it, a point of view that disgusts Bill, Rhoda, Roger and Patch. The pawn is safely returned by a lad who works on the estate, Ted Lelliott, and friendship is established between the group at the Castle and Roger and Patch when Patch helps Rhoda who has been thrown from her horse, scared by some boys flashing a mirror in the sunlight—incidentally, this is also a trick that Geoff has previously played on unsuspecting children.

This is the theme that runs through the book—a friendly group of young people continually split by some selfish or unkind behaviour on Geoff's part. There is a burglary, a fight and a mad rush to rescue against a tidal river. Time and again Geoffrey's behaviour disgusts Bill, Roger and Patch, and upsets Rhoda, whose sense of the responsibilities of her position is very high. She is conscious of her inheritance and the long line of ancestors who had tried to be worthy of their name. Rhoda's character is established in this book; we are made aware of her sense of duty and her anxiety to try and make her brother live up to her own high ideals. We also hear her views on the arrival of Rosamund's young half-brother, whose birth moves Bill one step down in the succession, and her bitterness on this subject, which has already been seen in *Rosamund's Tuck-Shop*, is in great contrast to her essential good sense.

Patch is the onlooker, representing EJO's views. Her criticism of Geoff's behaviour and, in certain cases, her refusal to have anything to do with him unless and until he apologises are the final condemnation. Since the young reader will, almost certainly, have identified with Patch (probably another reason for her introduction, it not being so easy for the average schoolgirl to identify with the daughter of an Earl), no one will have regretted the disappearance of Geoff from the scene. Patch is also established as EJO's favourite type of girl, even in her attitude to Bill's tentative proposal.

The feudal atmosphere of Kentisbury is very apparent in this book and particularly in relation to younger people on the estate: Ted Lelliott, employed in the garden, whose desire to go to sea is encouraged by Bill and discouraged by Geoff; Bob with his motor bike, who cannot control the young Earl's rash escapades; and Tom, who assists Geoff in a forbidden midnight trip on the river. In each case, their future is at the mercy of the young Earl's whims, although these are fortunately tempered by Bill's good sense. Geoff's early death is well prepared for. The motor bike is given to him for his sixteenth birthday, and there are frequent hints that he's not to be trusted on it and that he will come to some harm.

There is also an interesting tie-up with folk music, based on the name of an old inn by the river, just outside the Castle grounds. The inn is called 'The Princess Royal', which, to Patch as a Scottish dancer, suggests a dance she has learned at school. To Bill this tune suggests an old sea-song called *The Arethusa*, sung by an old man at the inn, who, in turn, tells Patch and Tansy about an Englishman who danced to it, jumping 'ever so high' with 'big hankerchiefs', one in each hand. All EJO readers will recognise a Morris dancer. This interconnection of folk melodies clearly fascinated EJO as much as it does folk scholars of today.

This is not a well constructed book but it stands as the adventures of a group of young people in the romantic surroundings of a great castle. It seems most likely, however, that EJO intended it to serve as a clear statement of her view on the responsibilities attached to rank and privilege, and it also serves the purpose of filling in some gaps, lessening any regret the reader might feel about Geoff's tragically early death and making Rhoda's capitulation to Rosamund's kindness and charm more convincing. It also fills in the background to the precious chess set, which is at the root of Tansy's later troubles.

In the following year, 1941, *Adventure for Two* was published by OUP and, like *Damaris Dances*, illustrated by Margaret Horder. This is very much a sideways book, since the events in the latter part of *Damaris Dances* are retold from a different viewpoint. Unlike its immediate predecessor, it is a very well constructed story, although Sheila's high opinion of it as one of EJO's best books may be partly due to reading it soon after its publication, at the age of twelve or thirteen. Publication by OUP gives it a certain status too.

EJO wove this story round two completely new characters, Daphne and Elsa Dale, sisters who in this case form an equal partnership. Although Elsa, the younger by a year and only sixteen, has always been in the shadow of her elder sister who is training as a dancer, once the sisters' lifestyle is threatened by the death of their aunt and a consequent shortage of money she emerges as a strong, independent character, determined to make a living and shocked at Daphne's decision to borrow money from Madame Roskova, her ballet teacher. Although the aunt does seem to have had some intention of Elsa being a support for Daphne, once she is out of the way both sisters get on and do things, and neither of them is condemned to a rather passive role as Mary Devine and Rachel Ellerton to some extent were.

When the story opens, the Dales are living in a hostel in London, Daphne training as a dancer and Elsa as a secretary. This was a time when such hostels were thriving, providing a home and safety for girls in their late teens and early twenties who were training for a career or working away from home. EJO had already drawn a picture of such an establishment in Switzerland; her London one is much more convincing. Elsa and Daphne have been brought up by their aunt in Sandylands as their mother died when Daphne was only two and their father, yet another seaman, had died soon after Elsa's birth. They have two special friends at the hostel, Irene Jones, another young dancer whose stage name is Irina Ivanovna, and Michelle Barker, who has recently lost her French mother. The girls all have flatlets near each other in a corridor that they have named 'Rainbow Corner'. Once again, EJO's preoccupation with colour is reflected in the description of the rooms.

Aunt Mary has died, and although she has left her house to Elsa, believing that Daphne has already had her share in her expensive training and hoping that Elsa will make a home for Daphne, there is no money left for them to continue their training and live in London. Elsa resolves to return to Sandylands and earn a living as best she can, but Daphne is equally firm in her intention to continue with her dancing in London. Michelle is run down and decides to accompany Elsa to Sandylands to get the benefit of the sea air; together, they fall on their feet and are soon earning enough money to keep themselves by running a ferry service, providing coffee and teas for the tourists and dressmaking. Daphne is equally fortunate, getting a job as an understudy in the new ballet of *The Goose-Girl* and then having a new ballet written for her and Irina, *Rainbow Corner.*

At the beginning of the story, the sisters are together in London; we then follow their separate adventures—Daphne in London and Elsa in Sandylands—until at the end they are together again in Sandylands when the ballet company opens its provincial tour there and the sisters' faith in Daphne's talent is vindicated in the eyes of their various friends.

There are two 'sideways' elements. The first is the link to the story of Damaris. In the second chapter Irina, who has been given a place in the corps de ballet of the company that is putting on *The Goose-Girl*, tells her friends how she has taken over Damaris's role of warning the goose girl because Damaris insisted on putting in a pirouette. Later, when Damaris becomes the goose-girl, Daphne gets the chance to practise her dances, and pleases both Damaris and Madame so much that she becomes understudy for this role. As a result of Irina's jealousy over this new situation, Damaris successfully makes amends by choreographing a ballet for Irina and Daphne which is based on a Welsh folk tale, and for which the music is composed by John Grant Grandison, the composer of *The Goose-Girl* music.

A second sideways link is introduced when Elsa is inspired to take up her career of ferryman and teashop proprietor by a suggestion from Nell Masterman and her Scoutmaster brother, who were also the first customers entertained by Damaris and Rachel at Hikers' Halt. Nell and her brother are only two of the typical recurring EJO characters who make a brief appearance to smooth the path of the heroines. Other archetypes are represented in this book by the retired Admiral who owns the land around the ferry and grants Elsa the rights to the ferry and to the cave system that she discovers, and Madame Roskova, who is a stereotypical dancing teacher. Mr Courtier, who, unusually in an EJO book, is an unsympathetic solicitor, is finally convinced by Daphne's success.

Much more interesting and original are Irene Jones and Michelle Barker, who are older and more experienced in the ways of the world than the Dales. Irene is half Welsh, half Russian; she has knocked about the theatre world, and reacts jealously to the news that Daphne is to be Damaris's understudy. Michelle is half French, half English, and gives Elsa's enterprise just the support it needs.

The location of Elsa's seaside adventure can be easily identified. Sandylands is Weston-super-Mare, which faces west, thus accounting for the splendid sunsets, and which, for long after EJO described it, was the terminus for a fast train service from London. At the southern end of Weston Bay, the land juts out to Howe Rock, at the end of a spur of land where there was an old Anglo-Saxon settlement. When we visited this area, we could hardly believe how perfectly everything matched EJO's descriptions. On one side of the river lies a headland that is the original of EJO's 'island' of Caer-Ogo. On the Weston side there is the village of Uphill, which matches EJO's village of Hillside. The land spur looks like an island because all the land around is marshy, and access to it from Uphill by road is still a distance of nine miles or so. It is an outlying crop of limestone from the Mendips, and Uphill village is now the starting (or finishing) point for the signposted Mendip Way. EJO invented the cave on Caer-Ogo but had justification for doing this in the existence of the famous Wookey Hole cave system to the south. As Elsa says to Michelle: 'If the hills round Wells and Cheddar have caves, and if the island is at end of the [Mendips], why shouldn't it have a cave too?'

We know that EJO knew this part of Somerset well since Cleeve Abbey, the model for

Elsa's Ferry at Uphill, 1991

the Abbey, lies only about twenty-five miles to the south-west, and the area of Summerton and the Seymours to the south-east. The location of Sandylands meets all the requirements of the clues offered by EJO—a seaside town on the Somerset coast, with a view across the Bristol Channel to the Welsh coast. The Welsh influence is strong, the house being called Min-y-Mor, meaning Beside the Sea, while the dog is called Mor and the cat Min.

A look at the map shows how EJO found some of her names—the bay to the north of Weston Bay is Sandy Bay, no doubt the source of 'Sandylands'. The lord of the manor who grants the ferry rights to Elsa is retired Admiral Sir Rodney Barron, a name perhaps suggested by Rodney Stoke, a village to the south-east on the way to Wells, and Berrow, a little village further down the coast.

EJO's knowledge of ballet seems much firmer in this book, although her knowledge of the examination system seems minimal and to bear more relationship to the certificate system for folk dancing than anything else, and it is surprising that Daphne, a rising ballet dancer who has been in London for some time, has never seen *Carnival*, *Checkmate* or *Façade* until she goes with Rachel and Damaris. Perhaps this is why Elsa emerges as the stronger and more attractive character of the two.

Although there is no Second World War raging, Margaret Horder's black-and-white illustrations reflect the period of publication. Elsa's slacks, which were her aunt's Christmas present, are seen as right for the sands, though she doesn't 'wear them to go to town, though heaps of people do'. *Adventure for Two* is a good novel of action and character, and interestingly demonstrates EJO's real skill in using well-established characters from other books as minor characters without lessening the pace of the story, and in maintaining the balance between interest for the reader who is in the know and information for the reader who isn't.

'There's no saying when they'll have anything more.'
(*Jandy Mac Comes Back*)

In 1941 Jandy Mac returned. The book is called, quite simply, *Jandy Mac Comes Back* and was published by Collins. The title explains the book. Having established Jandy Mac in the retrospective books and then sent her off to Samoa to marry Alec and start her family, EJO is now ready to bring her back, as she had promised, complete with daughter Joan, known in the family as Littlejan. They turn up at Joan's home without prior warning, only to find that Joan has just had another baby and is, naturally, not up to receiving visitors. This seems a singularly tactless way of doing things, but it gets the book off to a good racy start and also places Jandy and her daughter in a quandary on Joan's doorstep, ready to be rescued by the Countess of Kentisbury and carried off to her 'little house'. This is Rosamund in her new role as Countess; she also takes the place of Jen as rescuer-in-chief, for in this book Jen is removed from the scene almost as soon as she appears.

It seems strange to an adult reader, although as girls we don't remember finding it odd, that Janice should not know where to look for Jen, when she has addresses for both Joan and Joy. She and Joan admit to having been poor correspondents, but that Janice should not be aware that Jen had married Ken Marchwood and was living at the Manor takes a lot of believing. However, it is a very neat way of introducing the new reader to the Abbey circle. When Jandy has finally been reunited with Jen, Ken has a car accident in Yorkshire, and Jen rushes off to the Grange. In the next few Abbey books, Jen is away more than she is at home. All this seems a rather contrived way to place Jandy and Littlejan at Kentisbury for a time and to throw Rosamund, and later Maidlin, into prominence as representatives of the Abbey—Joy, of course, is safely out of the way in New York. Thus Jandy has a brief reunion with the Abbey but is almost immediately whisked off back to Kentisbury to be entertained by Rosamund, who sends for Tansy to keep Littlejan company. Both Jandy and the new reader can be brought up to date with the earlier events in the Kentisbury story.

This book moves quickly. Once all the parties are established at Kentisbury, and the Castle and its grounds have been described, we are launched into another Kentisbury adventure, this time a plot to kidnap the heir and hold him to ransom, a plot that is foiled by Jandy, her daughter and Tansy, thus giving Jandy a chance to repay all the kindness she has been shown by the Abbey people. This has been hinted at early in the book when Janice says: 'All the giving has been on their side. If a chance came and there was something we could do, how glad I should be.'

The kidnap plot is very weak and easily detected by Littlejan and Tansy, although they don't realise it is a plot to kidnap, suspecting instead an attempt to steal Rosamund's jewels. The actual kidnapping is very inefficient, with too much violence from the very inexpert kidnappers, and the baddies are, as usual in EJO, very unconvincing. Also, when the kidnappers have taken the young Viscount Verriton, much is made of Tansy's courage in saving Roddy, because he is the next heir. It is, after all, not a crown that is in question!

However, the book certainly establishes Littlejan as an important character. At first, and especially with adults, she seems precocious, not to say cheeky, but, in a brief meeting with the twins, she wins their respect; with Tansy, who is a little older, she shows herself to be a girl of good sense. At the end of the book she reveals that she is to stay in England and go to Miss Macey's school and so become a permanent member of the Abbey circle.

Horses and riding have a part in this book, but it is noticeable that in EJO's work they are restricted to Kentisbury and Wood End. The enthusiasm for horses that took hold of young teenage girls from the 1930s onwards never had a place in the writing of EJO. Riding remains a very upper-class pastime—unless you come from Australia.

So—here beginneth another chapter in the Abbey saga, a chapter in which the second generation is to have a leading role, and in which the stories have, generally speaking, more pace than the earlier ones, in part because matters moral and spiritual are handled in brief, telling conversations rather than in longer, more searching ones, a sign that EJO really did have her finger on the pulse of her readers.

Published in the following year, 1942, by Muller, *Pernel Wins* has no connections with any of EJO's previously published books and introduces no characters from earlier works. Although it is the story of another young girl and, in its way, a Cinderella story, to the present adult reader it appears rather as a book about holiday camps. One wonders if someone put up a holiday camp on EJO's doorstep and the book was written to help her to come to terms with it?

Holiday camps were, in fact, a pre-war invention, first appearing in the 1930s. As James Walvin writes in *Leisure and Society, 1830–1950,*

> New types of holidays sprang up; camping and hiking became popular, as did the new vogue for holiday camps, perfected, though not pioneered, by Billy Butlin. On the eve of the Second World War some half a million people annually spent their holidays in one of over a hundred camps around the country.

The setting of this holiday camp and of the happenings of the book is vaguer than in most of EJO's books, but from a few odd clues and a remark of Pernel's to the effect that 'we're miles beyond Plymouth' it would seem to be somewhere on the south coast of Cornwall.

Although a nearby holiday camp provided customers for Michelle's dressmaking skills in *Adventure for Two*, it is clear that EJO disliked these camps. In the first chapter of *Pernel Wins* she introduces Julius Joyes, the holiday-camp tycoon, as a hard-hitting business man, out to get what he wants without consideration for other people, and describes the camp's 'flaring scarlet advertisement ... in large letters on a hoarding with pictures of beflagged buildings and dance halls and a sort of glorified circus near the beach' in a way that seems like a perfect expression of the middle-class view of that sort of entertainment.

'There's a man going to the door.'
(*Pernel Wins*)

It is certainly the view of the book's leading character, Pernel Richards, returning as she believes to Quin Court, which has been her home and which, on the death of her uncle who was also her guardian, she expects to inherit. But she receives two bad shocks, the first being that her father was not the eldest son and that the Court belonged to her uncle. Furthermore, her father, an artist of some talent who had been little recognised during his lifetime, had handled his finances very badly, and her uncle had allowed his own affairs to suffer in order to clear his brother's debts. Finally, to make some reasonable provision for Pernel herself he had sold Quin Court, leaving her with an adequate income and a delightful home at the 'Look Out'—an old lighthouse and coastguard station converted into cottages. All this is quite bad enough, but the final blow is that Quin Court has been sold to Julius Joyes, who is going to build a new Joylands.

Pernel's first impulse is to leave the district as soon as it can be arranged but, learning that Julius Joyes also wants to buy the 'Look Out', she determines to stand out against him because she would 'do anything, no matter what it costs me, to spoil that man's plans'. This is a declaration of war on Julius Joyes, his camps and anything connected with him, and she does her best to keep it up. The title of the book suggests its main theme—Pernel will not really be happy until she has conquered her prejudice, the latter partly increased by a feeling of guilt because the whole affair was due to her father's mismanagement.

Julius Joyes has installed his wife and daughter at Quin Court. Judy Joyes is a girl of Pernel's own age, intelligent and well educated, who immediately sees the situation in terms of *As You Like It*, with Pernel as Rosalind and herself as Celia. The barrier between these two begins to break down when Judy begs for Pernel's help to interpret for a French girl who has arrived at Joylands in advance of her party, and Pernel's better nature will not allow her to refuse. She is further drawn to Judy when she finds that Judy is caring for her own family's Pets' Cemetery.

Julius Joyes's stepson, Marmaduke Terry, known as 'Duke', introduces himself dramatically by landing his aeroplane in the field next to the Look Out and then attacking Pernel for her prejudice against his younger half-sister. Young men who fly aeroplanes play an important part in this book, and their enthusiasm for this form of transport is very much in the mood of the late 1930s. There is even a hint of what may happen—and had happened by the time the book was published: 'And if ever there should be another war—though, of course I hope there won't be—planes are going to play a big part in it; the biggest part, perhaps.' By 1942 this statement was only too true. But if EJO could mention the possibility of war like this was there, later, a moment when she made a deliberate decision to ignore the war when it came—or were her future books already so well planned that introducing the war would have needed a complete rethink of those plans?

Duke is Pernel's sternest critic and a major influence in her victory over her prejudice, partly owing to the attraction between them, which is apparent at their first encounter. Later it is Pernel who helps him to overcome his sense of defeat and depression after a flying accident, when it is feared that he may never walk again—he does, in fact, recover.

The Rosalind/Celia relationship between Pernel and Julia is supported by a Touchstone, Pernel's friend Gwen, one of EJO's sensible, well-balanced, supporting characters like Monica Howard. Gwen sees the situation and sympathises with both sides; while she is loyal to Pernel, she has a sneaking fondness for fun-fairs and can see the argument that what provides innocent fun for so many (Julius Joyes does not allow drinking or gambling in his camps) ought not to be sacrificed for the comfort of one person. She holds the balance between Pernel and Judy and makes their friendship possible in its early stages.

Aeroplanes and the fun-fair provide the adventures: a serious crash for Duke, when Pernel goes to the rescue and saves his life, and later a fire at the flimsily-built amusement park, when Pernel again comes to the rescue and saves Judy by climbing a cliff, and so wins Julius Joyes's heart that he is prepared to close down his treasured venture to please her. By this time, however, she has conquered her prejudices and is prepared to work with Judy to develop a new aspect of the camp for people who like music and pictures and a quiet holiday.

All the ingredients for an arts-centred holiday are already there. The high quality of Pernel's father's pictures is accurately assessed by Gwen, an assessment that is confirmed by her father, an art critic. Judy sings and Pernel is a violinist of talent, the quality of her music having been enriched by her personal emotional problems. True to the EJO tradition, there are also important cats who rule the lives of their owners.

Pernel Wins is not one of EJO's best books. As a novel for older girls it was perhaps ahead of its time, but it does not seem to have been popular at the time of publication. Sheila borrowed it several times in the early 1940s but never managed to finish it. As has already been said, it has no connection with any of the books that precede it, though Gwen, Pernel and Judy do make a brief appearance in a later book. To the present-day critic it is interesting, partly for the picture it provides of the newly established holiday camps and partly for the way in which flying as a career for young men is presented—these are the young men whom the heroines will presently marry. Of course, some contemporary writers were already producing stories about young women flying aeroplanes, but nobody would expect EJO to do this—it was just not her style.

For EJO, it was important for the heroines to marry; she still had one of her Abbey heroines unmarried—Madalena di Ravarati—and so we come to *Maid of the Abbey*, published by Collins in 1943. Looking at this book at this point, the theory that has already been advanced, that much if not all of it was written long before it was published,

A song from 'In a Persian Garden'
(*Maid of the Abbey*)

becomes even more attractive. It follows exactly the pattern of *Joy's New Adventure* and *Maidlin Bears the Torch*, and returns to the theme of carrying the torch for the Abbey. Here the musical girl is Belinda (Lindy) Bellanne, who, with her sister Anne, comes on holiday to the Abbey and pays her entrance fee to the circle by rescuing Margaret from a tree and being injured in the process. She is then taken up and helped in her singing career by Maidlin. The parallel is even commented on by Maidlin when she says to Margaret: '... Aunty Gail burnt her hand saving Elizabeth from a fire ... Aunty Benneyben hurt her head and her arm saving you from a bad fall ... then Aunty Lindy comes and hurts her shoulder, helping you out of a tree ...'

The events of *Maid of the Abbey* take place during and just after the Easter before the events of *Jandy Mac Comes Back*. When the book was originally planned, EJO may even have seen Lindy as a bearer of the torch.

When Maidlin and Rosamund are discussing this matter in the penultimate chapter, which is called 'Passing on the torch', the latter actually suggests Lindy as a possibility for the role, although she adds prophetically 'someone else may appear'. However, in the end, EJO or her publisher found Lindy no more satisfactory in this respect than Gail or Benedicta.

Two mentions in the early chapters also point to an earlier date for composition. Lindy visualises singing in the Queen's Hall in London, which was completely destroyed in an air raid in May 1941, two years before the book was published, and the oratorio in which the Bellannes hear Maidlin sing is *The Dream of Gerontius*. Although this had first been performed in 1900, Elgar's death in 1934 had led to an increased interest in his work, and it is therefore likely that EJO, casting around for an oratorio in which there is an attractive contralto role for Maidlin, may have heard *Gerontius* performed in the mid-1930s. Apart from *Gerontius*, Maidlin is to perform in Liza Lehmann's song cycle *In a Persian Garden*; this choice of a work by a woman composer may be a happy accident or it may reflect EJO's interest in female achievement—probably the former, as the composer's name is never mentioned.

The references to the radio also seem rather more appropriate to the 1930s than to the early 1940s. (Incidentally, the Abbey books do throw interesting light on the developments of modern technology, as cars, radios and telephones come to be taken more and more for granted in them.)

Two other points should be mentioned in this discussion of the date at which *Maid* was written. First, it seems unlikely that, having established not only Jandy Mac but also her daughter, EJO would have gone back in time to continue Maidlin's story. Secondly, EJO may even have visualised *Maid* as bringing the whole Abbey sequence to a conclusion. The reunion of all the main characters at the May Day celebration in the final chapter— Rosamund with Tansy as her maid, Maidlin with Lindy, Joy unexpectedly back from New York and able to have twin maids, Joan, very pregnant, coming with Jansy, and Jen using one of her boys as a page, with Mirry, daughter of the very first Queen, being crowned as the 21st Queen of the Hamlet Club, would have made a splendid finale. This theory would also accommodate the speculative conversation about who will carry on the Abbey tradition of caring hospitality after Maidlin's departure.

The only evidence that does not support this theory of an earlier composition date for *Maid of the Abbey* is the fact that *Jandy Mac Comes Back* contains no references either to Maidlin's engagement or to Lindy. If the manuscript of the former were already in existence, even though visits to the Abbey are brief, in the latter it is surprising that Rosamund makes no reference to Maidlin's new-found happiness, and there is obviously a crying need for a Lindy to be a nursery governess when Littlejan and her mother visit the Hall. There are, however, references in *Jandy Mac Comes Back* to other events foreshadowed in *Maid* such as Joan's new baby.

If *Maid* was written in the late 1930s, it must have been subsequently rewritten in the light of the retrospective books. Although EJO is at first vague about exactly what has been discovered in the Abbey, she later refers to the Monk's Path, which was only discovered with the help of Jandy Mac. Susan Spindle, the cook who brings measles to the Hall and whose place Anne Bellanne takes, thus repeating the story of Ann Rowney, also first appeared in the retrospective *Stowaways in the Abbey*, which also included Joy's bad attack of measles to which reference is made by Jen. Finally, on this fascinating topic of order of composition, the fact that Maid's engagement and Lindy are not mentioned in *Jandy Mac Comes Back* may support the theory of the earlier composition. If EJO had written the whole of *Maid after* she'd written *Jandy Mac*, she would surely have found some way of removing these discrepancies—if she wrote it *before*, she could easily have overlooked it. We shall never know!

Maid of the Abbey, in its published form, is very much a book of the later period in terms of length and style, and if it were composed earlier some of the introspective or philosophical conversations may have been abridged or omitted. It is made up of two interwoven stories. Anne and Belinda Bellanne are the new characters introduced to the Abbey circle, and their arrival at the Hall gives Maidlin the opportunity to impart the essential facts about the Abbey characters and their current whereabouts. Anne, eight years older than sixteen-year-old Lindy, has had a disappointment over the failure of a cake-shop (no doubt a teashop would have been more successful) and has been on holiday to the Grange near Sheffield, but the weather was poor, and kindly Ann Rowney has recommended her and Lindy for a holiday in Joy's hostel in Whiteways. Because measles are rampant in the village, the Bellannes are invited to stay at the Hall. Lindy, who has just left school, has ambitions to be a singer, but good training is out of the question financially. The measles crisis (needless to state, the twins catch it) enables the Bellannes to prolong their stay in order to help out, and this gives time for Lindy's gift to be discovered.

Secondly, it is the story of Maidlin's romance with Jock Robertson. This is one of EJO's best and most convincing romances. Dr John Robertson, known as Jock, has taken over the role of Maidlin's mentor in Sir Ivor's absence and has conducted various performances in which she has sung. Maidlin is being courted by his nephew, who is about her age, but his proposal causes her to realise that it is the older man whom she loves, and her resulting happiness is portrayed very convincingly. One suspects that she and Jock spend the first day of their engagement in a way that EJO would have chosen—they slip into the lovely old church at Ewelme, wander on the Sussex Downs, visit Rosamund's castle and stroll in the Abbey grounds.

Jock Robertson comes over as one of EJO's more successful male characters. There is not much competition for this status. EJO created a female-dominated world, a fact that may account for some of her appeal. This is carried through to the extent of always putting the emphasis on the Queen—just as Rosamund tells Jandy and Littlejan about going to see the Queen, so it is the Queen to whom Maidlin is presented; there is no mention of the King at all.

Joy makes a brief appearance in this book when she comes back to see the twins after their attack of measles—did EJO realise what a monster she had created in Joy, and therefore shift her interest back to Joan? Not only is Joy hurtful about Maidlin's little house, but she also crosses swords with Lindy over the question of spoiling the twins, although she rapidly makes amends in both cases. *Maid of the Abbey* is an interesting book and, whenever it was written, fills quite an important gap in the story of the Abbey girls.

Elsa Puts Things Right, published in 1944, was the second of EJO's books to be published by Muller and the third to be illustrated by Margaret Horder. The format of these books published by Muller reflects the period of publication and the paper shortage—they are slimmer than previous books and on poorer paper, a wartime necessity.

Ewelme Church, 1992

Generally speaking, they have no coloured frontispiece but are illustrated throughout by black-and-white drawings of various sizes either used as chapter headings or incorporated in the text. These vary from quite definite pictures of people to very simple line drawings that are almost cartoons. They appear at irregular intervals and must have made the books fun to read. Margaret Horder was to illustrate the next five books, and a further two books that were also published by Muller, so one can assume that EJO approved of her.

The setting for this book, a Somerset town dominated by a 'long green hill' and containing the 'grey ruins of an old Priory', is easy to identify. There is another helpful clue—its heroine lives on Road Street, which causes comments from strangers to the town. There is no doubt that 'Priorsbury' is Glastonbury, which has a cross and a ruined abbey, and just south of it is the small town of Street so there is in Glastonbury a Street Road. Perhaps because the Abbey is of so much importance to her books, EJO converted Glastonbury Abbey into a Priory with nuns instead of monks, and in her description of the ruins does not mention the Abbot's kitchen, an outstanding feature of the site. She does make the point that the Priorsbury ruins are mainly of the church, and contrasts it with the Abbey at the centre of her saga:

> 'I believe there's an Abbey where you can see how the monks lived—dormitories and workrooms and refectory all complete; but they have no big church, which must have been glorious. It's gone as completely as our living-places.'

To round off this identification, visitors to Priorsbury stay at the Pilgrim's Rest Hotel, while present-day visitors to Glastonbury will do the same at the George and Pilgrims.

In spite of having her name in the title, Elsa Dale of *Adventure for Two* is a rather sideways influence in this book, but her island and cave and the ferry and the nearby town of Sandylands are all featured and, of course, are within reasonable distance of Priorsbury. The book's main character, Nancybell Morgan, lives in Priorsbury, but has connections with Elsa's village of Hillside; her mother came from there and her maternal grandfather was the old man whose death left the ferry free for Elsa. On her father's side, however, she is a direct descendent of Mistress Nanciebel, who married Blaise Morgan at the end of EJO's early historical novel.

When the book opens Nancybell has no idea of her distinguished ancestry or of her connection with the modern branch of the family, the Seymours of Summerton. To the best of her knowledge she is an orphan, living with her Aunt Poll (Mrs Paine) who had been her mother's best friend and with whom her mother had run a sweetshop in Priorsbury. Nancybell and her 'almost sister', Mrs Paine's daughter Margery, have been waiting anxiously until they are both sixteen to reopen the shop, which had to be closed because Mrs Paine was ill. A sweetshop is clearly considered quite respectable, as were the tuck-shops run by Prudence and Gail. In fact Margery, commenting that girls who work in offices tend to look down on 'shop girls', says: 'We'll be running a prosperous little business some day while those girls are still only clerks.'

Nancybell is one of EJO's lively open-air girls, reminding us of the early Damaris. She has a mop of thick brown curls and likes to go striding over the countryside in her shorts. She would have preferred an open-air job, but is quite willing to tackle the sweetshop with Margery. She is impulsive, a little too quick to react to a situation, but very much open to reason when her first outbursts have died down. But, for Nancybell, things go wrong—not major disasters nor heartrending shocks, as is the case with many EJO heroines, but good things go sour on her over and over again until she comes to believe that this is her 'bad luck' and her normal good sense and sunny temper are affected by it.

The first setback is a delay in the reopening of the shop, because Mrs Paine has used the money she had saved for doing so to help her younger sister. Then, when Nancybell thinks she can make a fortune from her photography, she discovers that a local chemist is doing very well out of one of her photographs, for the copyright of which he paid her five shillings. Something better grows out of this disappointment when her great friend Robin Farnham suggests that she should submit some prints to a well-known firm, Knights— very easily recognisable to those who are familiar with the sepia postcards by Judges that were ubiquitous in the 1930s and later, and have now become collectors' items. Knights are interested in Nancybell's talents and buy two pictures quite quickly.

Robin delivers the next blow by telling Nancybell that her grandfather's ferry has been restarted by Elsa Dale. Nancybell is quite unreasonably indignant and jealous, although it is clearly pointed out to her that she had never thought of it, and in any case her job is in the sweetshop. She works up a real hatred against Elsa, and only the threat of Robin's disapproval stops her from rushing off to confront her—she cares a great deal for his good opinion.

Her final disappointment is linked to the discovery of her connection with the Seymours of Summerton. Nancybell receives a cheque for £20, left to her in the will of her grandfather, Sir John Seymour. Mrs Paine explains Nancybell's connection to the family, and that her father had quarrelled with his own father and changed his name to Morgan (or rather, back to Morgan), but she hears of her famous ancestress and namesake only when she meets her Seymour cousins, and it is through them that her pleasure in the legacy, which makes it possible to reopen the shop at once, is spoiled.

The present generation of Seymours are Sir John's grandson, now Sir Gilbert, and his sister Annamaria, Mya for short, who are aged seventeen and fifteen respectively. Mya is a character who is never quite presented sympathetically. There is a streak of worldliness in her of which EJO does not approve, and she is used more than once as a foil for a favourite or sympathetic character. In this book she shows her good side, expressing indignation on Nancybell's behalf and wishing to be friends, but she is apt to act on impulse. It is she who leads Nancybell to understand that her legacy was a gesture of scorn and not of generosity. She also has a tendency to consider all girls of over seventeen as possible wives for Gilbert.

Sir Gilbert is not a Lord Larry or a young Earl of Kentisbury. He is proud of his title, but hates to be teased about it, very much a half-and-half—half young man and half schoolboy. He has his own dignity when it is required, and his manners are beautiful, but when he is allowed to drive the car on the sands and almost runs over a small boy he is very young and shaken, and Nancybell and Martin, the chauffeur, have to take charge. Martin, incidentally, joins the ranks of EJO's chauffeurs. Like Frost and Henderson, he not only drives the car but also takes a fatherly responsibility for the family, encouraging Mya to get over her car sickness and helping Gilbert in the matter of the accident.

Gilbert and Mya come to find Nancybell, introduce themselves and tell her the story of her famous ancestress. Nancybell is thrilled to learn that she has a real family, but this relationship turns sour when Mya reveals that the legacy was 'a spiteful, scornful thing to do'. Nancybell's good nature and sense of fairness persuade her to be friends with her cousins, but her joy over the legacy is spoiled for her and so is the idea of her new-found family.

It is all this that has to be put right by Elsa Dale. Nancybell enlists Gilbert's help to take her by car to see the ferry, where she ends up helping Elsa by taking charge of the boat in an emergency. Elsa does not realise who she is but sees that she has something on

The big car lurched over the edge.
(*Elsa Puts Things Right*)

her mind and persuades her to talk about it. When Nancybell blurts out her feeling that the ferry should have been hers, Elsa is stricken, saying: 'I can see I haven't been fair to you. I didn't mean it but I forgot you and of course you felt sore. I can never feel the same now that I know I've been unfair to you.'

Nancybell, seeing Elsa's unhappiness, can also see the point of view of those who, unwittingly, have hurt her. She is completely knocked off balance when Elsa offers to share with her, to let her have the ferry while she shows the caves, and this 'little scrap of fairness' changes everything for her. She stays with Elsa overnight and is helped to put her other problems in perspective.

From then on things come right for Nancybell; another Seymour uncle, a young brother who lives in South Africa, writes to welcome her into the family and give her a small income. She makes real friends with Gilbert and Mya, goes to visit Summerton, and yet convinces Robin that the existence of rich and titled relations does not change her affection for him.

Robin is a steady, kind and reliable young man and a suitably restraining influence on the impetuous Nancybell. He is a young farmer, training at agricultural college, and he and Gilbert get together on the subject. Margery Paine is rather a background character in this story; she is one of the quiet, sensible girls, attractive enough for Mya to consider her a possible sister-in-law, and owner of a very large amiable cat called the Pouffe, one of EJO's famous felines.

In this book the location of Summerton is still vague. The clues we have so far are that in *Mistress Nanciebel* Lady Llety calls on her way to Bristol from London, and in *Elsa Puts Things Right* it is near enough to Priorsbury and Hillside to take in both by car in a day, although the journey is long enough to make Mya carsick. The family lawyer's letter to Nancybell is postmarked Salisbury. We are given more help in later books, when Summerton again appears and becomes more significant in the saga.

With *Two Joans at the Abbey*, published by Collins in 1945 with illustrations by Margaret Horder, we come to the book which finally and firmly cemented together the mainstream and the retrospective books about the Abbey. Littlejan takes her place in the Abbey circle and from this point on becomes the focal point for the series, the younger Jansy and the Marchwood twins looking up to her, and the older generation of Abbey folk having a high regard for her

'I'm not going to stay here any longer.'
(*Two Joans at the Abbey*)

qualities of leadership and good sound commonsense; future new arrivals are likely to be seen in terms of their relationship with Littlejan.

Although Littlejan is anxious to shake off what she regards as her 'infantile' nickname and is in fact referred to as Joan or Joan-Two, it is convenient to use the name here to distinguish her from Joan Raymond, who now re-enters the series as a major character. The reasons for her long absence from this role on the centre of the stage are now easy to see. Just as Joy was too flawed a character for EJO to cope with as a permanent fixture, Joan is too perfect. As we said in our discussion of *The Abbey Girls*, she is described by Mary Cadogan and Patricia Craig as 'one of those well-behaved girls whose moral uprightness is boringly unshakeable'. Now holding the household at the Hall together while Joy is in America and Maidlin prepares for her wedding, she fills a useful and convincing rôle.

The two main events of *Maid of the Abbey* are now neatly slotted in, and their omission from *Jandy Mac Comes Back* are swiftly accounted for. Jandy says: 'I only saw Maidlin for five minutes … I saw the lovely ring she was wearing, and later I heard about her engagement from the Countess.' This works quite well, but less easy to swallow is Jansy's explanation that 'Miss Belinda had gone to Manchester for a few days', when Littlejan remarks that she'd not seen any governess when they went to the Hall and that the twins said they were doing lessons with Maidlin—it would be fair to have expected some mention of Lindy's existence at that point.

The events in *Two Joans at the Abbey* take place in the summer in the two weeks immediately following on from the events of *Jandy Mac Comes Back*. As Joan tells Jansy: 'Littlejan has been at the Castle for only three weeks.' It opens with Jandy and Littlejan arriving to see Joan and Jansy; they are on horseback, much to Jansy's envy, and at last Joan and Jandy meet again after fifteen years. Jansy immediately takes to Littlejan. and suggests that she will be Captain, Jansy her Chief Mate and the twins the crew (it is interesting to note the easy use of a seafaring hierarchy, although on earlier readings of the book both of us had tended to relate it to Arthur Ransome rather than to EJO's preoccupation with the sea). Littlejan, quite reasonably and typically, suggests that, as they'll be living in the twins' house, the twins may object to being merely crew. At this meeting Jansy drops hints about the mysterious governess, and Joan fears an older, strict governess who will inhibit their activities.

By the time Jandy and Littlejan move to the Hall, Joan is established there with her family. A need to rebuild extensively at the Raymonds' Sussex home provides an excuse for them to move to the Hall, thus releasing Maidlin to make her wedding preparations. Joan has refused to let Littlejan bring Chestnut, her pony, to the Hall on the grounds that, if she does, Jansy and the twins will want to learn to ride and that, in any case, there is no suitable accommodation for him. She promises that if a 'billet' (wartime influence on the vocabulary here, perhaps?) can be found for him in the village, it might be possible later. It is the search for a 'billet' that leads to the main action in this book.

Jandy arrives at the Hall to find a letter from Scotland waiting for her. Aunt Mary, who had brought her up and come with her on her first visit to England, and who has since returned to Scotland, is ill and the family wants Jandy to go north. Littlejan has meanwhile met Lindy, the stern 'Miss Belinda' of Jansy's mysterious hints, who provides a useful link between Littlejan and the adults and also proves to be a tower of strength when Littlejan is left at the Hall by her mother. Lindy tells Littlejan of another link between herself and the Abbey—the fact that she was at Dorothy's with Damaris Ellerton, who danced for them at night. More importantly, she tells Littlejan of how the Abbey 'used to be a holy place, filled with monks who did all sorts of good deeds, and I think the people living here now try to carry it on ... the friendly feeling'. This presentation of the Abbey as a place of sanctuary comes better from Lindy, so near in age to Littlejan and something of a newcomer herself, than it would have done from one of the older generation.

Joan now tells Littlejan the story of Bell's Farm, which is next door to the Abbey and which she thinks may provide a possible billet for Chestnut. This is the first time that Bell's Farm has ever been mentioned, but its absence from the Abbey chronicles up to this point is accounted for quite convincingly by the story of the feud between the old farmer (not a Mr Bell but a Mr Edwards) and the Abinger family. The revelation of the secret of Bell's Farm—or one of the secrets—is delayed a little while by a day's picnic outing to the site that Maidlin and Jock have chosen for their main house, The Pallant. This is at Sunrise Hill near Blackdown, which is described as being just within the Sussex border, thus being a convenient midway point between the Hall and the Castle. Much amusement is engendered by the fact that Margaret asks where the nurseries are to be, and Elizabeth referring to all the three men of the party—Jack Raymond, the Earl of Kentisbury and Jock Robertson—as 'fathers'.

The Saturday picnic over, the twins seize a golden opportunity to explore a tunnel they have found when, on the following Monday, Littlejan has gone to Kentisbury, Jansy is at school and Lindy is called away from the schoolroom to help Joan when Nelly, the twins' nurse, scalds herself. Fortunately Jansy returns unexpectedly early from school (mumps have broken out) and follows the twins into the tunnel. The twins have come up against a blocked end, and as they are trying to dig their way through the tunnel collapses behind them; this forces them on into the barn, which they instinctively recognise as belonging to the Abbey, but which has been hidden from view all these years by the evergreen ilex trees growing between the Abbey meadow and Bell's Farm. Rescued and in disgrace, the twins keep their find a secret. Jansy has been injured and there is concern for her.

Littlejan, returning from Kentisbury, gets Jack Raymond to drop her off at the Abbey, sees signs of the tunnel, goes through it into the barnyard and then manages to bring the tunnel down on top of herself on her return journey. The barn, of course, is revealed as the Abbey tithe-barn complete with a statue of the Abbot Michael. Young Mr Edwards, who has recently inherited the farm from his father, tells how the latter retained the barn when the rest of the Abbey buildings were handed back to Sir Antony. He has always wanted to give it back, and now all he asks in return is support for his two young daughters who are about to start at Miss Macey's school. The barn is claimed for dancing and a party is planned; on the eve of the party, Mr Edwards comes with news of a new find, the Abbey bell, Cecilia. Inevitably and characteristically, it is Jen who makes the connection between the hidden bell and the name of Bell's farm.

In this book Rachel and Damaris are established as 'outposts' of the Abbey. Rachel meets Jandy in London on her way back from Scotland and sees her onto the train for Wycombe. But most of all it is Littlejan who is established as a major, strong character, the heir to Jen and Rosamund. By way of contrast, the book demonstrates EJO's inability to portray strong male characters; the commanding men of the world so beloved by romantic novelists seem to be totally lacking in her work. Jack Raymond must be one of the wettest of all the male characters. However, he does acquire one distinctive skill in this book—photography. It seems likely that about this time EJO met somebody who was keen on, and good at, photography, since as an art form it is featured in two successive books—in *Elsa Puts Things Right* Nancybell was the photographer; here it is Jack Raymond who now plans and makes the *Book of Littlejan* for Jandy to take back to the South Seas.

The Abbey books had clearly reverted to being books for girls in their early teens. From now on the reader is expected to identify with Littlejan; the older generation of Joy, Joan and Jen and even the 'new Abbey girls', Rosamund and Maidlin, tend to be looked upon as adults, much older than the reader—even Jen decides not to go and play cricket.

EJO now put her writing for older girls into other characters. In a way she was a pioneer of the teenage novel that was beginning to take shape, still in a fairly innocuous way, in the late 1940s and early '50s, mainly in the form of the 'career novel' in which there was a growing interest. This trend had begun in America and was to reach a peak in the 1950s with the publication of such books as Bertha Lonsdale's *Molly Hilton, Library Assistant* (1954). EJO's view of careers, however, was somewhat limited by her own experience, having been born into a generation and class where few girls went into the professions. Her horizons seem to have been limited, and marriage still seemed the most desirable destiny for girls. Music in its various manifestations, shopkeeping and writing seem to sum up the possibilities envisaged by EJO, who was, in any case, obsessed by the view that girls whose parents could afford to support them should not take work from those who needed it.

It is music that is to the fore amongst the careers being pursued by the girls who inhabit the hostel in London that first featured in *Adventure for Two* and now reappears in EJO's next book, *Daring Doranne*, published in 1945 by Muller, with illustrations by Margaret Horder. Although the reader meets some old friends, this book introduces a new heroine, Doranne Hardie. When the story begins, she is about to leave the hostel and go to Sussex to look after her Great-Aunt Dora Anne for whom she is named, but whom she has never met and about whom, as it turns out, she knows remarkably little. Just before she leaves the hostel, she meets Pernel, Gwen and Judy from *Pernel Wins*, when they arrive to take possession of two of the rooms in the same corridor. By now Pernel and Judy are engaged and it is Gwen who plays the major role in this book, being invited to keep Doranne company after the death of her great-aunt.

Daring Doranne has a rather complex plot but basically it is another Cinderella story. Great-Aunt Dora Anne turns out to be a rich eccentric living in a modest house, and a few weeks after Doranne's arrival she quietly and conveniently dies, leaving Doranne an immense fortune and the Rainbows estate on the borders of Sussex and Surrey. Meanwhile Doranne has made friends with Maureen Dering, also known as Soupy or Mops, a lively fifteen-year-old who lives next door with her grandparents, and with Maureen's brother, Marcus, who has to come and see his sister

Daring Doranne

secretly because his grandparents do not approve of his interest in flying. Maureen and Mark suspect Great-Aunt Dora Anne's secret because Mark flies from the Rainbows aerodrome, and they have put two and two together. Through a series of events Mark is reconciled with his grandparents, his admiration of Doranne predictably develops into something more, and the story ends with a proposal of marriage.

As well as packing the book with incident—Doranne's good fortune; an incognito visit to Rainbows; Mrs Dering's illness and a mercy dash by her doctor from the Channel Islands in Mark's plane; a trip to Scotland by Gwen and Doranne; Mark's going missing on a flight; and Maureen being badly injured when she saves a Guide camp from being stampeded by a horde of horses (an echo of the episode in the short story *The Last Night in Camp*?), to mention only a few of the highlights—EJO also manages to introduce some of her many and various interests.

Dunoon, the little house in Darthington where Great-Aunt Dora Anne has taken refuge, is based on the house, Inverkip, in Worthing to which EJO and her sister moved at about this time. Darthington is Worthing, and we have identified the Rainbows estate as being at Ewhurst, a village just over the border with Surrey to the north of Worthing. There is another brief echo of the Sussex school stories at one point: Gwen comes to stay at Dunoon because Maureen turns down Doranne's invitation to do so on the grounds that she is going to spend a few days at her headmistress's hilltop bungalow and doesn't want to sacrifice what she calls 'the chance of a lifetime'.

The kind of life that Doranne leads in the few weeks before her great-aunt's death possibly reflects EJO's lifestyle at this time—walks on the downs, trips into the town for the shops, concerts and teas, the housework done by a woman who comes in daily. There is, of course, a cat—Geoffrey Ginger, 'an enormous golden person … with enquiring yellow eyes', which moves through the story and influences the development of the plot. As well as the name of the house, there are other Scottish links. The great-aunt's husband was a Scot and Dunoon is filled with landscapes of Scotland that she has painted—it is these that inspire Doranne to go on her tour of Scotland. The caretaker and gardener at Rainbows are a Mr and Mrs Duffy who speak with the broadest of Scottish accents.

There is a development of the interest in flying, which had first appeared in *Pernel Wins*. The 1930s had seen a great expansion in flying, and it was an activity increasingly reflected in stories for young people—not only in books for boys, such as W E Johns's books about Biggles, but also in books for girls, which were often stories about girls owning their own aircraft and making a living through flying. By this time W E Johns had also created Worrals of the WAAF, who had an important role to play in the Second World War. Even as late as 1945, EJO may have been keeping open her options for introducing the war into her stories. When Gwen and Doranne visit Rainbows for the first time and Mark has to be summoned to identify them to the Duffys, he hints at the possibility of a war. The girls look at him anxiously and he goes on: 'There's fear; there's an ugly chance. But it's no more than that yet … the thought of an air war appals me … I hope it won't happen.'

Maureen actually mentions Amy Johnson and Jean Batten, whose achievements had shown that flying was an activity open to girls as well as boys. Tommy Ayrton, the young airman who made a brief appearance in *Pernel Wins*, appears again as Mark's companion on the flight when they both go missing, although the promised romance between him and Gwen moves no further forward.

Although the remark about an air war made in a book published in 1945 may seem rather odd to the adult reader today, no doubt the girls who read it soon after publication assumed that it was set, like most of the other books they were reading, in the 1930s. By this time EJO seems to have been able to shut her mind to all the unpleasant aspects of life. Just as there seems to have been no question of Elsa and Daphne returning to Somerset to attend their aunt's funeral, so nothing is said of Great-Aunt Dora Anne's funeral. Doranne returns home from a day on the downs to be greeted with the news that her great-aunt 'just fell asleep'. Perhaps EJO felt about funerals what she felt about weddings—that they were a very private matter.

Most important is Doranne's use of her inheritance. Here we have yet another EJO heroine who, although she plays the violin, has no particular talent or qualifications but is determined to take her responsibilities seriously. Even before she knows the extent of her wealth, she tells Gwen: 'There's music but I mustn't use it to take engagements or pupils from people who need the money.' When she does realise it, she knows that she must face up to the responsibility. Various ideas are floated before she tells Gwen what she has decided—she will live at Rainbows with friends from London who want holidays, and organise a little orchestra that she will conduct; one wing will be used as a college for airmen and the other for a children's home. With the proceeds from the sale of the antiques, for which Doranne has little use, a model village is to be built in the park, and the house will contain a library and reading-room with a 'nice girl in charge', and a community centre! Through Doranne, EJO is creating her own version of the communities that had begun to spring up during the period between the two World Wars and which continued to flourish during the Second World War, often supported by the efforts of conscientious objectors.

Such a community fitted in perfectly with EJO's interest in crafts, folk dancing and the countryside. It is interesting to see how the ideas reflected in *Daring Doranne* parallel those in John Middleton Murry's *Community Farm* also written during the 1940s. Doranne tells Miss Stewart, her mentor at the London hostel:

'… we'll hunt for the right sort of people, who are longing for a home in the country, If they want cinemas and theatres they mustn't come; we'll be miles from anywhere.'

At about the same time, John Middleton Murry wrote:

… the countryman … does not need a cinema round the corner … I believe that the rural community can offer the rest of the country the pattern of a good life in the future.

Never mind that EJO's community was to be governed by a young benevolent despot, a far cry from Middleton Murry's socialist vision; at least her fictional community worked!

The last book of this period, *An Abbey Champion*, published by Muller in 1946, and again illustrated by Margaret Horder, is very much a 'forwards' book. Littlejan, now in her place as the focal point of the new Abbey circle, performs the task required of her,

ELSIE JEANETTE OXENHAM

that of reviving and revitalising the Hamlet Club. As we have already seen, Lynette Muir found a parallel between the Abbey saga and the Arthurian romances. *An Abbey Champion* in its very title certainly reflects that theme; Littlejan's discovery that the Hamlet Club is in danger of dying out and taking upon herself the task of reviving it is an echo of the Round Table Knights going out on their quests to perform the brave deeds demanded of them.

First of all, however, it is necessary to clear the ground. *An Abbey Champion* follows on after *Two Joans at the Abbey* and opens with the prospect of Joy's return, and Maidlin's wedding only two weeks away. However, these plans are shattered by two pieces of news: first, that Jandy Mac must return to Samoa ready to move house to Ceylon owing to a change in her husband's job. This means that she will miss the wedding and Joy's homecoming, and that Littlejan must be left sooner than was expected. This news is at once overshadowed by a message from New York that Joy is seriously ill, may not recover and that there is a new baby boy who is not expected to survive. (The lengths to which EJO will go to keep Joy out of the way!) There are two days of serious anxiety while Maidlin and Jock plan to have an earlier, quiet wedding so that they can then take the twins to New York to their mother, and the twins themselves provide a minor problem when they refuse politely but firmly to allow Joan to take them to choose new winter coats—to them this is their mother's prerogative.

Once Joy is pronounced out of danger—and the baby, of course, also survives—the twins are told the truth and everyone is kept busy with new plans. Maidlin's wedding is described in more detail than most, and we learn what happened to the piece of material that Rosamund wove and which was spoiled by ink in *Rosamund's Tuck-Shop*. Happily for all concerned, skilful cleaners had removed the stain, and the dressmakers had been able to arrange the material so that the damaged parts didn't show, so Maidlin is married in a gorgeous white-and-gold dress, giving pleasure to all concerned. It is at this wedding reception that Littlejan makes friends with Rachel and Damaris, thus being brought into contact with even the outposts of the Abbey.

When all the excitement has died down, the Abbey is quiet again, with Joan in charge at the Hall and Littlejan and Jansy going to school each day. Even Jen, who had returned for the wedding, has to rush back to Yorkshire owing to a setback in her husband's recovery. It is Joan who helps and comforts Jen in her anxiety, and it is also Joan who is the guiding hand in Littlejan's crusade for the Hamlet Club. As in the previous Abbey book, Joan fulfils her role as guide and comforter to the 'clan'.

At first Littlejan confides her disappointment in the Hamlet Club only to Mary Devine, but Mary persuades her, reminding her of the Club's motto—the question of making a right choice—to talk to Joan, who insists that she must go to Cicely Everett, the President. Joan really does direct things here; although Littlejan tries to persuade the head girl, Alison, and the reigning Queen, Mirry, to go with her, Joan has always intended that Littlejan should go on her own and admits as much, if only to herself: 'I wanted my John Hampden to go alone … But it will answer the same purpose if she stirs up the rest with her deputation; they'll realise she is the moving spirit and that's what I want.'

The problem that Littlejan has uncovered is a lack of enthusiasm on the part of the seniors, who have left things to the younger girls; the Club has come to be regarded as just an amusement for the young. Once this has been brought into the open, Cicely Everett, with her usual efficiency, sets about resolving the problem. She goes up to Cecil Sharp House to find a teacher to run a weekend school, which by this time had become an accepted way of learning folk dancing—'one of the newer ideas'.

This leads to the reintroduction of a character from earlier books—Mrs Thistleton, née Tazy Kingston, is now established in London and a lively member at Cecil Sharp House. A happy reunion with Joan and Cicely brings the new reader up to date on the Abbey circle and the Swiss connection, and during the weekend school she is a great success with the Hamlet Club. The weekend school also provides an occasion for the revival of all the Hamlet Club ceremonial, and Tazy is treated to a procession of the Queens in full regalia, plus solos from Maidlin, and the dances and the correct way to do them once again assume a real importance.

Littlejan has become a force to be reckoned with in the school, and she continues to be so, introducing Cicely's next plan, which is to revive the Folk Play. This is said to have been last produced in Maidlin's reign, but there is no previous record of such a performance in the books. It is described as a 'mix-up' of all the existing folk plays, and Tazy is careful to say: 'Don't let the girls think it's found anywhere in such a complete state.' Sheila recalls that as a young librarian in the early 1950s she received a request for a text for the 'folk' play from a local Music and Drama college, and it possible that a new interest had surfaced generally around this time. The folk play as performed by the Hamlet Club does give a very good general idea of its nature and meaning, though, naturally, nothing is said about fertility symbolism!

A final act of self-sacrifice on Littlejan's part is a repeat of Lindy's quarantining herself with the twins. Jansy develops chicken pox, and Littlejan, having already had it, keeps her company to help Joan, who has her hands full with the two younger children. In doing so, Littlejan expects to miss another dancing school and a further performance of the folk play, in which both she and Jansy have parts.

All this is leading up to the inevitable—when it comes to choosing the new Queen, there is a unanimous vote for Littlejan, who is suitably surprised and humble at being chosen but faces up to the job with enthusiasm and is hailed by all as a new Abbey Queen. Once again we have a crowning with full—and even extra—ceremonial, and her father is there to witness his daughter's triumph. There is a general feeling that with a Queen from the Abbey in charge, the Hamlet Club is no longer in danger: 'The Club will be safe now for three or four years, and then Jansy will be ready to take charge.'

But even this is not the end. The culmination of the book shows that the Abbey circle has no need of fertility dances! In the last chapter both Rosamund and Maidlin produce twin daughters, prepared for by quiet asides and their appearance at Littlejan's crowning as Queen Marigold in new white gowns and by the amused reception of Tazy's desire to teach the Club to dance 'Twin Sisters'. Rosamund suggests that it must be the influence of the Abbey 'breaking out in a new way. The Abbey likes girls, and so all its girls come double.' The naming of new babies becomes a serious matter, Rosamund beginning her series of Rose names and Maidlin's twins having Joy and Rose as their second names. Jandy Mac in Ceylon also produces a baby daughter called Cecily Rose for the Countess and the recently discovered Abbey bell.

So, by the end of this period of writing, EJO had established her new, young Abbey circle, headed by Littlejan with some of the girls from Miss Macey's school and with Jansy and the twins to complete it. The Hamlet Club had also recovered and was now as strong as ever, dancing and Queens having an important part in the story. The older generation appear when needed to give a helping hand but are, more often than not, relegated to the background and to producing babies for whom the Abbey bell can be rung and the Hamlet Club can dance Sellenger's Round.

The books are also more concise. As Monica Godfrey reveals, EJO herself had commented on this:

> I feel those early books are rather wordy and spun-out. There is probably just as much story in the modern ones but it is told much more tersely and neatly. I used to put in whole pages of what people thought. Now I let you discover it from the things they do.

Seven of the twelve books of this period were illustrated by Margaret Horder, of whom EJO definitely approved. Once again EJO was on to a winning streak, and during the rest of her writing life only three of her books did not have 'Abbey' in the title and were not directly concerned with the Abbey circle.

Chapter 9

ROBINS AND ROSES,
1947 TO 1952

By now EJO was well into her sixties, and during the remaining years of her life she concentrated on developing the story of the Abbey girls. Even those books that do not have Abbey in the title are linked to the Abbey characters. She no doubt felt—and was possibly encouraged by her publishers to feel—that she could write best about the characters that interested her most. She also assumes that the reader is involved in the Abbey story; this is particularly apparent in *Robins in the Abbey*, where most of the standard Abbey characters appear although some—for example, Jandy Mac and Maribel Marchwood—make only very brief appearances. However, EJO is still careful to fill in the story thus far for the newcomer to the series. Three EJO books appeared in 1947, a remarkable achievement especially in view of the fact that wartime shortages of paper continued for some time after 1945, although these three books came from three different publishers—Collins, Muller and Lutterworth.

Robins in the Abbey was published by Collins and illustrated by Margaret Horder. The 'robin' theme appears in four ways. Essentially, this is the story of Robin Brent and her meeting with, and marriage to, Rob Quellyn, but scenes in the Abbey invariably include mention of the friendly and faithful robin that hops about. We are also reminded that Jen's maiden name was Robins, and her new babies, twin sons, are described as 'little Robinses', meaning that they take after their mother.

Like its predecessor, *An Abbey Champion*, *Robins in the Abbey* takes place over quite a long period of time, from just after the crowning of Littlejan and the birth of Rosamund's and Maidlin's twin daughters until September of the following year. This is necessary to allow time for the flowering of Robin's romance, but one must also consider the possibility that EJO was anxious to push events along so that she could have Joy's twins as Queens before her writing career came to an end. That she had this event ultimately in mind may also account for the removal of the twins to New York at this period—this enables them to grow up off-stage. There are signs of this process beginning to happen in *Robins in the Abbey*; Margaret has already been changed by her year in New York—the result, it is said, of having a baby in the house—and Joy proposes to take them back in the autumn to continue the process. When the second Abbey bell, Michael, is found in the woods by Littlejan and the twins, Jen's immediate reaction is: 'Don't tell me the twins have found something without killing anybody, for I simply won't believe it!'

The romance of the two Robins is one of EJO's best romances so far; they are clearly destined to marry from the moment Rob Quellyn is first mentioned, but their problems are portrayed convincingly and the growth of their feeling for each other delicately described. Robin Brent, of course, was one of EJO's earliest heroines, first appearing in *The Girl Who Wouldn't Make Friends* in 1909, reappearing briefly as a schoolgirl at Wood End in

Rosamund's Tuck-Shop and subsequently as a minor character. EJO evidently has Robin's story clearly in mind because there are references here to her having been head girl at Wood End.

When the story opens, Robin is returning alone from New York to England, travelling on the same boat as Joy, the twins, the two little boys and Lindy, the nursery governess. Lindy wants to make friends with her but Robin explains that Joy resents her ownership of Plas Quellyn. Despite this, Joy does not prevent Lindy and the twins from spending their time with Robin, and when Robin arrives in Southampton to the news that her father has been injured in a Portuguese aircrash and her mother has flown out to him, Joy's better feelings come uppermost and she offers Robin a temporary refuge at the Hall so that Robin becomes another seeker of sanctuary at the Abbey.

'Cinderella has gone home to the Abbey—
she left her slipper behind.'
(*Robins in the Abbey*)

Robin—and the new reader—hears the full story of the Abbey, the Hall and the Manor. While she is there, Joy receives a letter from Ivor telling her of the talented Rob Quellyn, aged about twenty-five, who can both paint and compose. His father, Ivor's father and Robin's godfather were cousins. Rob's father had gone out to New Zealand, and Rob, roaming around the South Seas after his father's death, had met Jandy Mac in Samoa and decided to come home to look up his relatives. On hearing of his existence, Jen immediately suggests: 'Couldn't the Robins marry? The heiress and the representative of the family.' Joy replies fairly briskly that she's already thought of that!

Rob Quellyn arrives with Sir Ivor during a Hamlet Club party, and immediately notices Robin, saying to Joy: 'There's a pretty girl …' Robin sees him and leaves the party hurriedly for her bedroom in the Abbey but, like Cinderella, leaves behind one of her red dancing shoes, which Rob brings back to her the next morning. Both immediately see that the other has something they would like, but Robin thinks: 'I'm not going to marry the Prince, even though it would change my name to Quellyn', while Rob says to himself: 'The Prince doesn't marry the Queen, just to get the kingdom.' (It is typical of EJO that she thinks in terms of Queens and Princes, rather than Kings and Princesses!)

Later the same day Robin hears that her parents are coming home to Quellyn and she must go to meet them there. Soon after, Rob visits Quellyn and they spend happy days going about the Lleyn Peninsula. The following May Robin comes to the May Day crowning and sees Rob; although he doesn't speak to her, she realises that she loves him. He disappears from the party and she expects him to come to her in the Abbey the next morning; he doesn't appear, however, and on the Monday morning a noncommittal message comes in a letter to Littlejan. Bitterly disappointed, Robin returns home to Quellyn. It is only the death of her father and her mother's illness that finally cause Rob to come to Quellyn to propose to her, and the book ends with the Robins coming to a Hamlet Club party shortly after their marriage and escaping from Sellenger's Round in the traditional way.

Four people play a major role in furthering this romance. Pride of place must go to Littlejan, whom Robin meets soon after her arrival at the Hall:

> On a terrace stood a slim girl of fourteen … She ran down the steps to the lawn and came to meet the stranger with no trace of shyness—only an eager desire to make her feel at home.

Thus Robin first sees Littlejan as a person offering sanctuary to someone whom she's never met. It is Littlejan who gives Rob the red dancing slipper, telling him that he'd better be the Prince and return it to Cinderella. She then keeps the Robins informed about the doings of each other; it is she who receives the news of Rob's exhibition, who tells Robin that he is going abroad, and who tells Rob of the death of Robin's father (although, in fact her letter is too late—Rob has already had 'an odd feeling' and come home), and both the Robins quite rightly pay full tribute to Littlejan's part in their romance.

There is, however, a limit to what a schoolgirl, even though that schoolgirl is Littlejan, can do. Robin's mother is also helpful; she comes over as a very real person, which may be a reflection of her central role in *The Girl Who Wouldn't Make Friends*, and is full of sensible and supportive advice, saying to Robin:

> 'If you cared for one another, I hope neither of you would be so weak and silly as to think of what people would say. You know nothing about love, Robin, or you'd realise that other people and their opinions simply don't matter one scrap.'

which must be about the most sensible statement EJO ever made on this subject. Mrs Brent also speaks to Rob, telling him that if the right man for Robin should come along 'I hope … he'll have the pluck to look beyond her inheritance and tell her what he feels for her.' After Rob leaves Quellyn, she comforts Robin and suggests that 'he cares too much'. Then, after Robin's brief visit to the May Day celebrations, when she sees but does not speak to Rob and returns home to tell her mother: 'It's been a mistake. He doesn't care.', her mother persuades her that his strange behaviour can only be explained by the fact that he *does* care.

Mary-Dorothy is another helpful adviser, recommended by Littlejan, who comforts Robin and later counsels Rob to ask Robin to marry him. Jen, despite a long absence in the middle of the book, also plays a part in the developing relationship, finally arriving at just the right moment to reinforce Mary's advice and say she's glad that he's 'going to swallow the castle at last'.

Jen's character comes through clearly in this book, apart from her involvement in

Robin's story. She reacts with all her old enthusiasm to the finding of the Abbey bell, she is the one who takes Robin to the Abbey and later shows her round. By now, of course, EJO was a very experienced writer, and the main Abbey characters were well established and could be relied upon to speak and act in characteristic ways. Joy's resentment of Robin is all too believable, even though it has never been mentioned in previous books, as is the way in which her generosity surges up and conquers when necessary. She does not approve of Robin's plan to share the Quellyn estate with Gwyneth. She is also unkind to Jen, saying thoughtlessly 'It's a good thing you're going away.', but immediately repenting 'Why can't I learn to think before I speak?'

However, *Robins in the Abbey* does have touches of untypically poor workmanship—a sign perhaps of advancing years? Why does Robin not meet her parents and travel back with them to Quellyn? Joy says that she is helping Robin to get a passport, but Robin has just come back from New York and must already have one, and is certainly not an inexperienced traveller needing Joy's help and support to the extent suggested.

In this book, too, EJO was carried away by her enthusiasm for twins and for babies in general. As Geoffrey Trease commented in *Tales Out of School*:

> The normal incidence of twins in Britain is … something like one case in eighty live births. The incidence in fictional families is closer to one in two.

He was, of course, writing well before the advent of fertility treatment! It is this book that is responsible for much of the following critical comment about EJO in Mary Cadogan and Patricia Craig's *You're a Brick, Angela!*:

> Rosamund's most startling feat is to have twins twice within ten months … The [grown-up] Abbey girls engage in an unspoken competition to outbreed one another … Baby-loving Jen goes one better than the others; she has twin boys.

Rosamund does indeed produce a second pair of girls ten months after the first, although her anxiety to produce a large family quickly is explained by her concern for Geoffrey's continued well-being, and the book concludes with Jen's feat. In addition Cicely produces Shirley Rose, Joan has Jillian Rose, Mrs Thistle has Tazy Rose, and there are two little Roses in France as well as Cecily Rose in Ceylon—at least Jen can't give her two boys 'Rose' names. As Maidlin says: 'They all like to say—"She has the Countess of Kentisbury for her godmother!"' Pity the poor godmother, Countess or not, if she's expected to remember all their birthdays.

There are other points to mention about this book. It is clear that *Margery Meets the Roses* was planned or even written by this time since Rosamund refers briefly to the discovery of the 'new family of cousins'. We also learn that Robin's friend Gwyneth marries her childhood friend, Ivor Lloyd, another seaman, and there are hints of a Bobbibach. In this book, too, we are given details of the complete sequence of Queens, a number of whom seem to have spent their time considerably training as nurses or governesses to service the Hall, the Castle and The Pallant! The ground is also prepared for Jansy's election as Queen. Early in the book, Littlejan announces to the older generation her plans for Jansy to be Queen. Later Jansy is upset when she has been teased and taunted by the other girls, but Littlejan arranges for Jansy to teach the Club a new dance, saying: 'I want them to feel she counts … is worthwhile.'

EJO's view of marriage is clearly presented in this book; she believes that marriage is something to be worked at. The women appear to lead very independent lives and are not criticised by their husbands for their Hamlet Club activities, nor for their loyalty to, and involvement with, friends and relations. They seem to call the tune for what would seem to be the important things in life—a good example of this is to be found in *An Abbey Champion* when the decision to send Andrew, John and Tony away to school is taken. Joan tells Jansy: 'Aunty Jen has always meant to send Andrew and Tony to the prep part of a very good school in York; her brothers went there, and she wants her boys to go too; and Uncle Ken agrees with her.' Where did Ken and his brother go? One would have expected him to want to send his sons to *his* old school!

At the same time, the need for wives to support their husbands is emphasised. Joy must go with Ivor to New York, Maidlin must entertain for Jock, Rosamund must look after Geoffrey, Jen must leave her children and accompany Ken on his world cruise. Does this kind of partnership reflect the real-life or wished-for partnerships of EJO admirers, and is this one of the reasons for her appeal?

Also published in 1947, *The Secrets of Vairy* came from Muller, with black-and-white illustrations by Margaret Horder, but this time they are larger, three-quarter-page pictures, and there are none of the small chapter-headings and insertions that are so attractive in the earlier books. This book has no direct Abbey connections, but it is closely linked to the Kentisbury story. It was an unusual story for EJO to produce at this period, going back in time and off at a tangent, and, unlike earlier books of this type, there is no indication in the way of short stories that it was written much earlier. One possibility, though unsupported by any evidence, is that EJO was happy with, and interested in, the romance of Bill Kane and his Patch, and might have written other books about them if she had had the time and energy.

The timing of the book is exact:

> It was now August; the year before Patch had spent her Easter holidays at Roger's home in Sussex and had formed a close relationship with Bill and his sister Rosalie and with their cousins at Kentisbury Castle, the little Earl, Geoff and his sister Rhoda.

Later in the book the Earl of Kentisbury says that he and Rosamund have been married for six months, so in Kentisbury terms it comes after *Rosamund's Tuck-Shop* and before *Rosamund's Castle*, and in the Abbey timescale before *Jandy Mac Comes Back*.

The Secrets of Vairy

The Secrets of Vairy also represents a return to EJO's favourite Scottish setting—the west coast with its lochs and valleys and high hills, the area about which she wrote so well in many of her earlier books. This could be another reason for writing it: as a nostalgic return to an area that she loved. In fact, when we explored this part of Scotland in 2001 we discovered that Vairy Castle occupies the same site as Morven in *Holiday Queen*, which in reality is occupied by Knockderry Castle on the eastern shore of Loch Long.

On the face of it, *The Secrets of Vairy* is an adventure story with all the right ingredients—a romantic Scottish castle, missing papers, jewels and a mystery about a previous Earl of Kentisbury—but it is also an account of the developing romance between Bill Kane and Patch Paterson, and provides a further opportunity for EJO to present her own ideas on the subject of marriage.

The book opens with Bill and Roger arriving to spend the summer holiday with the Patersons. The Bill–Patch situation is introduced almost at once, a sign of its importance. Bill tells Patch that he has something important to discuss which affects her as well. Patch doesn't want to talk about it, but is interested and involved in spite of this.

Then comes the mystery. Patch has a friend with her, a pretty, golden-haired Scots girl whose full name is Christina Rosalin Macdonald. Patch explains that she comes from the next loch, where Vairy Castle is situated, and that the name 'Rosalin' has been a tradition in her family: 'About a hundred years ago she had a great-grandmother who was called Rosalin, and the name's been in her family ever since.' Bill is intrigued at the idea of a Kentisbury rose-name turning up in a family living so close to Vairy, the Scottish seat of the Kentisbury family, and wants to know more. The last Kane to live at Vairy had been old Lady Rosabel, whom Rhoda and Rosalie had gone to visit during the happenings of *Patch and a Pawn*, and her great friend and companion had been Rosalin's Aunt Kirsty, who is still alive and who could perhaps help.

Having established the mystery, we hear about Bill's problem. Old Lady Rosabel has left him her money and he is now a rich man and does not need to go into the navy. He could, in his own words, 'go to Oxford and mess about for a year or two. I might get a degree, and again I might not. Then build a house, get married and settle down.' (This is a neat, expurgated picture of the Oxford 'playboy' of the period.) Bill wants Patch's views on the subject. Patch can see what's coming and is unwilling to be involved; she reminds him that she is still at school, not yet eighteen and asks him not to 'hustle' her into being 'grown-up' before she's ready. In this she reminds us of Jen, refusing to take Ken seriously, but Patch is more mature and sensible than Jen was. She *has* considered the possibility of marrying Bill and faced up to the prospect of being a sailor's wife. Now she is horrified at the idea that he should do nothing serious because he has inherited money. She asks incredulously: 'And do nothing for the country or the world?'

Bill points out that making a home and raising a family does add 'something to the world', but they are finally in agreement that he must first go into the navy and be trained. Later on he can leave, but 'you'd be ready if you were wanted', Patch reminds him. This is, in part, a parallel to the views of the young airmen in two earlier books, but is also an expression of the between-the-wars view of the army and navy—it sounds strange in a book published so late in the 1940s.

This discussion and the decision that is made reflect the point that EJO has made many times before, that those who have money should give of themselves to help others—in this case Bill should give his time and service to his country. What is also important in presenting EJO's view of marriage is that Bill consults Patch before making up his mind, and that what she says influences his decision. As he says, he does not want to wait until he is thirty to get married—and neither does Patch, who admits her agreement, although she still reacts violently to teasing as the story continues. Bill has to be rather firm with Roger on the subject.

The mysterious papers are the next matter of interest. Rosalin and Patch tell the boys about a box of papers, treasured by Lady Rosabel and referred to as 'bills'. Everyone thought they were old bills kept as souvenirs by an old lady whose mind was wandering, but Patch, now that she knows Bill is Lady Rosabel's heir, has tumbled to the fact that what the old lady meant was 'Bill's', papers for Bill. These papers have gone missing, and Bill, once he hears Patch's idea, is anxious to find them. Rosalin's Aunt Kirsty seems the best person to ask, but Aunt Kirsty is ill and mustn't be bothered.

At this point the villain of the piece is introduced—Rosalin's Uncle Jeffery, come back from Canada and already a doubtful character. His name, its spelling and the fact that it too is a family name cause Bill to suspect a definite connection with Kentisbury. The Kentisbury name was spelt in this way until the 'old Earl' changed it because 'his father, Jeffery Kane, was a thoroughly bad lot, and we think he wanted to forget him'. Bill is more and more convinced that an earlier Kane has behaved badly to some ancestress of Rosalin's.

A further indication of the Macdonald connection with Kentisbury is provided when

Knockderry Castle, 2001

Rosalin produces a piece of family jewellery, a collar-necklace of garnets with seven pendant stones, which Bill recognises at once as a version of the Kentisbury 'dog-collar'. These necklaces are traditionally given to Kentisbury brides at their wedding, a custom dating back to the gift of a diamond one from Henry VIII to a Kentisbury girl who scorned his attentions.

It seems obvious that Aunt Kirsty could be of help in all these mysteries, but Aunt Kirsty has been badly upset by a letter from Uncle Jeffery and cannot be seen. The young people search in vain, but so does Uncle Jeffery, and when he comes to threaten Rosalin he finds himself faced by a determined Bill Kane. We do learn a little more; Uncle Jeffery is convinced that the early Jeffery had actually married Euphemia (Phemie) Macdonald—the common ancestress of himself and Rosalin—and *he* thinks the stones in the necklace are rubies. Bill's presence disconcerts him, and in a later interview Uncle Jeffery adds a further question—was the man who married Phemie the Earl or not? It appears there is some doubt. He is once more discouraged by Bill, who explains that the succession to Kentisbury can only be passed through the male line. If the early Jeffery and Phemie had a daughter, as is claimed, the Macdonalds have no claim to Kentisbury.

Aunt Kirsty recovers, the papers are found and given to Bill, and the whole story of Jeffery and Phemie is now made clear. He did marry her but later regretted the marriage. However, while he was away in London, Phemie died, and her irate father told him that the child had died too, so he was free to marry a rich wife. The problem is that he had told the Macdonalds that he was not the Earl but a cousin who had taken the place of the rightful young Earl, killed in a duel in Italy. Investigating after Phemie's death, the Macdonalds had gone to London, seen the Earl and recognised him as Phemie's husband, although he denied the whole story. So the doubt remains. If *that* Jeffery was not the Earl, but an impostor, then the title of the present Earl of Kentisbury is in doubt. And if *this* proves to be false, then the real Earl of Kentisbury is Bill himself, descended from a younger brother.

The prospect does not appeal to Bill, nor to Patch, but innate honesty compels Bill to decide to go to Kentisbury and speak to the present Earl. He is even more convinced of the necessity when they learn that Uncle Jeffery has gone away, possibly en route for Kentisbury, with blackmail in mind. In fact he has not actually left, and a message from him has lured Bill and Patch into the ruins of the old Castle of Vairy, where they are trapped and almost buried by a collapse of stonework, possibly induced by explosives— Uncle Jeffery was a miner. However, they escape, and Bill catches the next train to Kentisbury, where he is delighted to find that the story is already known and that Phemie's husband was indeed the Earl.

All this mystery and excitement provide a background and contribute to the development of the romance of Bill and Patch. Bill is very sure of what he wants, and Patch's doubts are only really due to her feeling that they are too young to make definite decisions. In their conversations they show that they have very definite views on the relationship between husband and wife. Bill discusses important questions with Patch, and Patch insists that difficulties as well as pleasures must be shared. There is one difficult moment when Bill insists on reading Aunt Kirsty's papers himself, before he shares them with the others, and Patch flares out at him in temper. She recovers herself quickly enough and apologises.

This is the most detailed of EJO's romances, even more detailed than that of the

Robins. Patch and Bill discuss their present and future at great length and express their views very clearly. The difference between the two romances lies in the fact that, right from the start, Patch and Bill have no doubt about the other's feelings. Bill comes over as a modified male chauvinist—he insists on his right to protect 'his girl', but does allow her to share problems, within limits, and respects her need to take her time. Patch, in turn, while insisting on her independence, finds happiness in the feeling that she has Bill's strength and support behind her.

Rosamund and her husband appear in the two penultimate chapters, when Bill learns that he is not, after all, the Earl of Kentisbury. At this stage there is no mention of a prospective baby for Rosamund, although Bill insists it would be a good idea. Both the Earl and the Countess warn Bill against 'unsuitable attachments', but they are agreeably impressed by what he tells them about Patch. They are also interested in Rosalin, and Rosamund talks of inviting her to Kentisbury later on—there is, however, no mention of this visit in later books.

There is another interesting fact about Christina Rosalin that is never mentioned in this or any other book—she must be related to Jandy Mac and Littlejan. In *Schooldays at the Abbey* Jandy had told Joan and Joy that her grandfather Fraser was factor for the Earl of Kentisbury at Vairy. In this book, Rosalin's Aunt Kirsty is being looked after by the Misses Fraser, and Patch explains to Bill that their father was the factor at Vairy and 'they're very slightly related to Rosalin, for her uncle who went to Australia married a Fraser girl who had gone out there from Vairy'.

The Misses Fraser are surely Jandy Mac's aunts whom she goes to visit in Scotland and Jandy must be the daughter of the marriage described by Patch; since she married a Fraser cousin, there is an undoubted link here of which EJO could have made something. Imagine Littlejan's delight on learning that she has a very distant connection with Kentisbury! The complication of these relationships may have overwhelmed EJO at this point, and it seems possible that she had neither the time nor the energy to pursue this line, however interesting. What characterises *The Secrets of Vairy* is the fact that it is a romantic adventure with Kentisbury connections, but it provides several possibilities for other books that EJO might have written. As it is, Bill and Patch make further brief appearances as we hear of their marriage and their production of the inevitable twins.

The new characters and events described in *Margery Meets the Roses*, which was also published in 1947, add to the Kentisbury

'Everybody's helping,' Nanta cried gleefully.
(*Margery Meets the Roses*)

family tree, and at last we have a final version. This book came from the Lutterworth Press, formerly the Religious Tract Society, and was dedicated to Elinor Brent-Dyer 'with love and all good wishes', a response to Elinor's dedication of *Seven Scamps* to her, twenty years previously. The Margery of the title is our old friend Polly Paine, now on her own after her mother's death and the marriage of her friend Nancybell to Robin Farnham. The Roses represent a new and hitherto unknown branch of the Kane family, whose advent was mentioned briefly in *Robins in the Abbey.*

Elsa Dale makes a brief appearance at the beginning of *Margery Meets the Roses*, and is the catalyst for the events. Margery, with Nancybell married and their shop about to be pulled down to make space for road improvements, has to decide what to do next and has come to Elsa for advice. Margery's decision to give half of her compensation money to her mother's sister, now in America, just as her mother had so often helped that same sister out, is a good example of the 'thick' texture given to EJO's work by the interweaving of books and characters.

Elsa briskly suggests to Margery that she should investigate the possibility of opening a shop in Doranne Dering's new community at Rainbows, of which she knows through her connections with the London hostel, where Daphne still lives. The idea appeals to Margery, who feels that she needs to remove herself from Gilbert Seymour's orbit; he still wants to marry her, but she knows that such a marriage could not work. Elsa also tells Margery about Daphne's visit with Damaris to Kentisbury, where she had seen the first twins, Lady Rosabel and Lady Rosalin. Thus Margery hears of the Kanes of Kentisbury and their tradition of 'Rose' names for the girls of the family.

Doranne is delighted to welcome Margery to Rainbows, and on her first visit of inspection, as she travels on the bus from Dorking, Margery meets the black-headed, dark-eyed twins who call themselves Araminta (Minty) and Amanda (Mandy) Rose. She also encounters a young man, David Woodburn, whom they call 'Wild Man of the Woods', and who is said to have been 'making eyes at Virginia', their elder sister.

There are four girls in the Rose family. Virginia, whom Margery first sees teaching a country-dance class, is the eldest, serious and responsible. Mandy and Minty are totally irresponsible, outspoken—'revolting' is one of their favourite words—and keen on horses and boats respectively. They are not characteristic EJO heroines, being neither competent and reliable organisers (Elsa, Margery, Littlejan) nor artistically gifted (Maidlin, Joy, Damaris); it is not surprising that they soon disappear from the centre of the stage, and after their appearance in this book, to which they are fairly central, are only referred to in passing. The youngest sister, Atalanta (Nanta), who is fair and blue-eyed like Virginia, is totally absorbed by music and by her admiration for Virginia.

There is obviously some mystery about the girls; their mother was American, and after her death their father had sent them to live with her sister, who had married a Scot, in Edinburgh. At her death they had come to London so that Virginia could study the violin at the Royal Academy of Music, and the authorities there had recommended her to Doranne when the latter was looking for a violin player for her small resident orchestra.

Doranne and Margery wonder whether Virginia is in love—Mandy and Minty have revealed that Virginia has seen a man she likes at a country-dance party, 'frightfully distinguished, like a prince in disguise'. Margery wonders if there is some family secret and notices that Virginia, welcoming her to Periwinkle Place where she is to spend the night on

THE KANES OF KENTISBURY FAMILY TREE

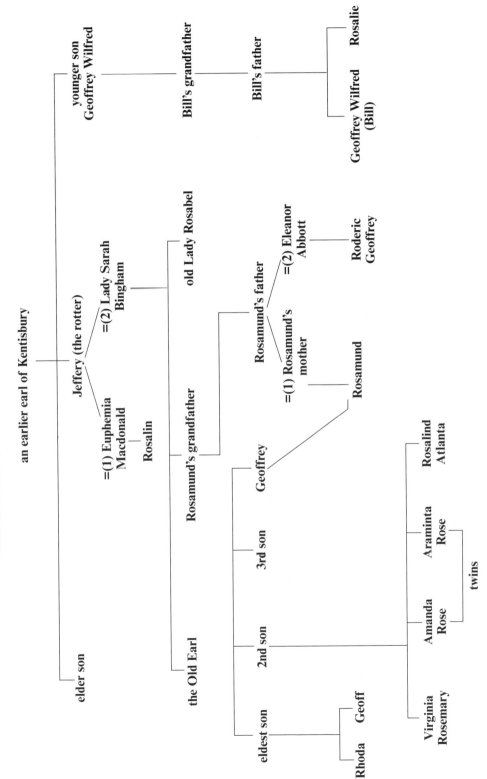

an earlier earl of Kentisbury

elder son

Jeffery (the rotter)

=(1) Euphemia Macdonald

Rosalin

=(2) Lady Sarah Bingham

old Lady Rosabel

younger son Geoffrey Wilfred

Bill's grandfather

Bill's father

Rosalie

Geoffrey Wilfred (Bill)

Rosamund's grandfather

the Old Earl

Rosamund's father

Geoffrey

3rd son

=(1) Rosamund's mother

=(2) Eleanor Abbott

Roderic Geoffrey

Rosamund

2nd son

eldest son

Rhoda   Geoff

Amanda Rose

Araminta Rose

Rosalind Atlanta

twins

Virginia Rosemary

her first visit to Rainbows, receives her 'with the gracious manner of a duchess inviting a guest into her castle'.

Both Virginia's problems are solved during the course of the story. The 'prince in disguise', of course, is Gilbert Seymour. Even before Margery finally leaves Priorsbury, Mya, via Elsa, has warned her that Gilbert has seen 'this girl somewhere and without even speaking to her he knew she was the only girl in the world for him'. Gilbert assists Margery in her move, and as they are driving to Rainbows he tells her that the name of his unknown love is Virginia. Margery promptly puts two and two together and thereafter helps the romance along. When Virginia runs away on the day of the removal when Gilbert appears, Margery points out that this is a good sign: 'If she's afraid of liking you, for some extraordinary reason, or afraid that you're going to like her, then of course she'd run away.'

Virginia seems anxious to avoid Gilbert, and Margery guesses that this is owing to the family secret. She manages to establish that at least it isn't insanity or illness, and she reassures Gilbert, saying that it's just a matter of time as the secret is apparently nothing bad or 'even very serious'. There are various hints; Nanta explains that there's something Virginia 'won't tell anybody. But she says she couldn't get married without telling.', and there is talk of marriages being illegal. These hints lead Margery to speculate, and the penny drops when she recalls Elsa's words about the Kentisbury Rose names. Without hesitation she goes to Periwinkle Place and says: 'Are you related to Lord Kentisbury's family?' Mandy explains that their father was the second son, who had a row with his father, went to the United States and let the family think he was dead. After the death of the young Geoff, although he never knew it, he was Earl for a week—hence his four daughters have titles. Virginia is ashamed of the fact that she has rudely rejected the present Earl's offer of help, but tragedy in the village—an accident to Doranne who is thrown from her horse—persuades Virginia to reveal her true identity. As Lady Virginia Kane she will have authority in the eyes of the community.

Meanwhile, Margery's own romance with David Woodburn has been flourishing. During her first visit to Rainbows they make friends over an injured bird, and when she misses her bus he takes her to the station and they have time to enjoy coffee together. When she moves into Cherry Tree Cottage, David makes friends with Pouffe, her cat, whose trials and tribulations in making the move from Priorsbury to Rainbows are described in such detail that one feels EJO is writing from close observation. David is a kind of Wildlife Park Warden, who also takes photographs of birds for books, and it subsequently transpires that the lawyer of the Rose girls in Edinburgh is his uncle, who has asked him to keep an eye on the sisters. Thus David, although not of the same social standing as Gilbert Seymour, is established as the right person for Margery to marry, and it is David and Margery together who persuade Virginia to reveal her true identity.

They tell her that she must use her title and come forward to lead Rainbows while Doranne is out of action. When she points out that she can't just suddenly claim a title, they go to Kentisbury to seek the Earl's help. They meet Rosamund, resting after the arrival of the second set of twins three weeks previously. She is interested in the relationship of David and Margery and helps things on a little. On the way home David tells Margery that she had asked him about 'you and me, Polly Paine. I told her—not yet, but I hoped someday.' Margery's response is to clench her hands under the rug and reflect that she had never felt like this about Gilbert. The book ends with her engagement to David.

Meanwhile the Earl has come to Rainbows, met the family and been to the post office, as the centre of village gossip, to introduce his nieces in their proper names, after which Virginia has been able to restore the sagging morale at Rainbows by giving the villagers a pep talk. Gilbert has turned up and taken her and Nanta for a run to the sea, much to the satisfaction of Martin, the chauffeur, who approves of Virginia as much as he had disapproved of Margery.

Margery Meets the Roses shows the signs of careful planning. It is set at a period that runs concurrently with part of *Robins in the Abbey*, and it is possible that the two books were being written at the same time. Rosamund's rejection of the name 'Rosalind' for one of the second twins appears in almost identical terms in both books. EJO has here created yet another set of girls thrown on their own resources. Critics of books for young people have frequently commented on the ruthless way in which parents are removed from the scene so that the young people can get on with their lives, but in EJO's books the incidence of parents dying rather earlier than might have been expected seems statistically high. Parents get a very raw deal; one of them at least is despatched at a very early stage, and the second in what must surely be early middle age—Margery's widowed mother, for example, has been neatly disposed of between *Elsa Puts Things Right* and *Margery Meets the Roses*. As far as the Kanes of Kentisbury are concerned, for some reason and quite unnecessarily, EJO introduces a third son, who died unmarried, between the father of the Roses and Geoffrey.

The reader of this book also learns a little more of the philosophy behind the creation of the Rainbows community. There is mention of the damage to the trees that have had to be cleared to make way for the homes and the landscape is described as 'a scene of desolation, raw and new'. Doranne is apologetic, Margery horrified and Gilbert critical, looking 'round with loathing at the tree-stumps and the bare patches'. Incidentally, although Doranne's model village is clearly in the area of the real-life Ewhurst, there is no trace there of a model community—whether it is based on a real one is a matter for debate. For Doranne, concerned as she is that everything should be in good taste, the general good is more important. If trees have to be felled to provide space for good housing, then that is unfortunate but high-quality houses must come first. Similarly, Virginia would like to concentrate her attention on the really good dancers, but Doranne insists that all those interested must be catered for. The beauty versus usefulness conflict is clearly set out.

This well-planned book carries the story of some of EJO's favourite characters further; it has plenty of action and two romances, and also continues to explore some of EJO's favourite ideas—the community life, marriage and the importance of making a contribution to society. Her love of colour schemes comes out in the importance of the turbans (very much a head-dress of the 1940s) that the twins wear, and in the names and furnishings of the cottages at Rainbows.

A Fiddler for the Abbey was published by Muller in 1948 and illustrated by Margaret Horder. The 'Abbey' in the title marks it as one of the mainstream Abbey books, though by rights it should have been called *A Fiddler for the Hamlet Club*. The fiddler in question is young Rosalind Kane (Nanta), who was introduced in *Margery Meets the Roses*, and who is of the right age to join the new, revitalised Club. The book opens as *Robins in the Abbey* closes, with the meeting of the Hamlet Club to welcome the newly-weds and the arrival of Jen's boy twins. At this meeting Rosamund invites the Club to dance in the

A Fiddler for the Abbey

quadrangle at Kentisbury Castle. Monica Godfrey tells us that the English Folk Dance Society did once dance at Arundel Castle, thus giving EJO a real-life precedent, but the Kentisbury dance party is also important to the Abbey story. In the course of the proceedings all Rosamund's children are shown off to the Hamlet Club, and we are prepared for an interesting little incident in a later book when Cicely, the President, expresses surprise that Roddy calls Rosamund 'Mother'. It also provides an opportunity for Rosalind to meet Littlejan.

The Club's need of an accompanist is revealed at the opening party when Margia Lane tells Rosamund that she has to go into hospital for observation. This seems an appropriate moment to consider Margia, who has been very much in the background since her first appearance in *Girls of the Hamlet Club*. She has been there when needed, to play for the Club (with occasional help from Cecily Perowne and Maribel Marchwood), to design and make the Queen's train and to paint watercolours of the Abbey. We assume that she has continued to live quietly, perhaps with the sister who was ill in the earlier book, painting in her beloved woods and making enough to live on. She is only about five years older than the first Hamlet Club girls—Cicely, Miriam and Marguerite—so it looks as though Margia is being temporarily removed, EJO-style, to make room for a new fiddler.

In *Margery Meets the Roses* Rosalind was presented as a girl with two enthusiasms, music and her sister Virginia. An attempt was made to widen her horizons and give her a more practical interest by helping Margery in her sweet shop. Now Virginia is to be married, and, although the plan was for Rosalind to live with the newly-weds, there is also Mya to be considered—not that Mya is not prepared to welcome Rosalind with enthusiasm, but the two are temperamental opposites. In EJO terms, Mya is worldly and commonplace, and Rosamund is afraid that too much Mya will be bad for Rosalind, saying that the latter will be run by Mya and will give in 'for the sake of peace; and she'll retire inside herself and build a secret life and live in it'. This remark is made at a family conference held at The Pallant, which, by introducing the under-twos of all the families except Jen's, gives the new reader the background to the families and their ex-Hamlet Club nurses. Rosamund's remark is the cue for Mary Devine to explain the danger of such a secret life and to illustrate it by her own experience. Maidlin comes up with the solution: 'Turn her over to Marigold.'

No 'turning over' is necessary. As has already been said, Littlejan and Rosalind meet during the dance at Kentisbury and make friends. From then onwards the book is mostly concerned with the doings of the Hamlet Club, the important members being those centred on the Abbey, Littlejan and Jansy; the present Queen, Jean Guthrie; and Rosalind, asked to help out by playing for the Club at a private weekend school organised by Littlejan to bring new members up to scratch in the dances. As a result of this weekend, two seniors, Tessa and Phyl, new to the school and to the Club, are also involved with this inner circle based at the Abbey. EJO now has a nice nucleus of girls to support Jansy and carry the Club forward until Joy's twins are ready to be Queens.

Before this, however, Rosalind has to meet the Abbey circle. She comes to stay at the Hall to play for the weekend school and is introduced to the Abbey, which of course appeals to her imaginative nature. The Abbey spirit is explained to her by Jen, who says: 'The Abbey takes hold of some people and tells them things.' Obviously Rosalind is going to be one of those for whom the Abbey has a special role—she is in fact seeking sanctuary from Mya, whose influence might have sent her in the wrong direction. She talks about friendship to Mary Devine, who says that one of the nicest things about friends is that 'you can't have too many of them', which is clearly a sentiment that EJO shared. Mary talks to Rosalind about her own writing, and here she must surely be the mouthpiece of her creator when she says that her books give her a lot of fun first: 'I only share them with other people. If they weren't fun for me, I think you'd find them rather dull.'

The weekend school gets off to a good start but then seems doomed to collapse as Littlejan is rushed off to York where her small brother is being operated on for appendicitis. This, of course, is designed to throw Jansy into prominence. Deprived of Jean's support as well, she and Rosalind go to tell the girls the school is off and end up running it themselves, with Jansy giving detailed and helpful guidance to new dancers, and Rosalind ably supporting her with her music. This is the final step needed to establish Jansy as the Club's choice for the new Queen, although she is not told of their decision until the following February. In the meantime Rosalind, having made friends and become involved with the Hamlet Club, decides that she would like to go to Miss Macey's school as a cookery student, once Virginia is married to Gilbert—a decision that is applauded by adults and girls alike and, as well as solving her own problems, gives the Hamlet Club a new fiddler on the spot.

This book is a return to the old theme of a newcomer to the Abbey being helped and absorbed into the family circle. There is a special hint of nostalgia here, in repeated references to Rosalind's likeness to Rosamund, but in this book we are almost entirely concerned with the new generation. Rosamund, Mary and Jen play their part, but it is Littlejan and Jansy who extend the Abbey spirit towards Rosalind. Many old ideas are here treated in the new 'taut' way: the Abbey spirit, the question of loyalty between old Hamlet Club members—Joy will not leave Queen Bee in New York when she is taken ill with typhoid—and the problem of *why* serious accidents occur. This last question is discussed by Mary Devine and Rosalind, after which Rosalind says: 'I'll take something home with me, when I go away from here'—a sentiment EJO would have liked to, and sometimes did, hear from her readers.

Guardians of the Abbey, published by Muller two years later in 1950 (was the two-year gap a sign that EJO was slowing down a little?) and also illustrated by Margaret Horder, is, like the previous book primarily concerned with Rachel and Damaris Ellerton, a 'parallel' book. Many of the events in it take place during the period of time covered by *A Fiddler for the Abbey*. It goes back to the time just after the folk-dance school in the October of Queen Jean's reign, rescued by Jansy and Rosalind, and then pushes events a little further forward to the July following Jansy's coronation when Joy arrives home from America.

As a reward for Jansy's efforts in saving the school and as compensation for Littlejan's worry over her brother Alan, Joan has suggested that Mary-Dorothy should take them and Rosalind to see Mary Damayris in her new ballet. The story opens with Littlejan practising 'Bacca Pipes' in the Abbey ruins, and she is briskly introduced:

> She was nearly sixteen, ex-May Queen at the big school in Wycombe; her name was Joan Fraser, but she was known as Marigold, from her choice of flower and colour as Queen, or as Littlejan, to distinguish her from her godmother, an older Joan, the owner of the Abbey.

The seed of this particular Abbey book is sown in the next paragraph when Littlejan reflects that Mrs Watson, the Abbey caretaker, is 'getting past the job'.

At the performance that night, Damaris, leaping to save Daphne Dale from being hit by falling scenery, is badly injured. She refuses to entertain the possibility of returning to the world of ballet unless she can be as good as she was before the accident. She and Rachel are offered sanctuary at the Abbey, and the fact that Mrs Watson is taken ill and can be pensioned off makes it possible for them to take over the responsibility of the caretaker's job, appropriately enough since Mrs Watson is their aunt.

Although this story is essentially about Rachel and Damaris, Littlejan is very much a key figure and events are frequently seen through her eyes. The story opens with her dance in the Abbey; she is present when Damaris is injured, and her immediate reaction is that Damaris's action is 'the bravest thing I ever imagined'. She also puts into words the possibility that Damaris might recover but not be able to dance any more. Littlejan is at the Abbey on the day when Rachel and Damaris move in, is present when the idea of the Abbey garden is born, and generally maintains a central role.

Rosalind is also a key character—the trio of Littlejan, Rosalind and Jansy, with their differences in age, appearance and background, seems to have appealed to EJO. Rosalind conveniently provides a means of filling in the background to Rachel and Damaris and Maidlin as she has to be told that Mrs Watson is their aunt; she comments that Mrs Watson is 'not the sort of aunt you'd expect a great dancer to have', not the most tactful of remarks but no doubt included to reflect what some of the readers might be thinking.

Jansy, the third of the trio, also plays a vital role in events. When Littlejan goes to the Abbey to give news of Damaris to Mrs Watson and finds that she's been taken ill, Jansy has the presence of mind to use the Abbey telephone to alert the Hall to the situation. Although she sometimes appears to be Robin to Littlejan's Batman, her quick intelligence and real ability are always emphasised. It is Jansy who sparks off the idea of turning the Abbey meadow into the

We'll see where the steps lead.
(*Guardians of the Abbey*)

Abbey garden by showing Damaris a group of golden crocuses in a sheltered angle of the gatehouse wall. There are descriptions of the party at which Jansy is chosen as Queen in both *A Fiddler for the Abbey* and *Guardians of the Abbey*. In the latter Rachel slips into the barn in time to see Marigold stand on a chair to make the announcement, after which:

> Jansy was up on the chair, thanking the Club and saying it was still a long time to May, and if they changed their minds in the interval she would quite understand.

In *A Fiddler for the Abbey*, this same speech had been reported directly:

> 'And it's still a long time till May; you've been in a great hurry this year! If you change your minds before the end of term I shall quite understand,' Jansy said pluckily.

In *Guardians of the Abbey* the reigning Queen Jean is scarcely mentioned. The younger generation is represented by Littlejan, Rosalind and Jansy, and, although many readers must identify with Littlejan, Rosalind serves as a model for the more artistic, introvert reader and Jansy as one for the slightly younger but able reader.

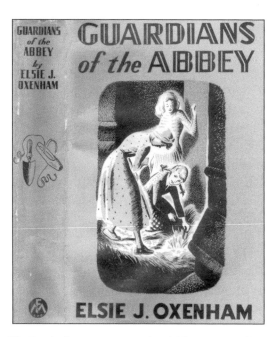

However, this novel is really concerned with continuing the story of Damaris and Rachel who, once Damaris was successfully established as a dancer, had become 'outposts' of the Abbey. As soon as Damaris is injured, the possibility that she will not be able to continue her career in ballet is mentioned. Even before this, the fact that Mrs Watson's career as the Abbey caretaker is coming to an end has been hinted at. The day that Mrs Watson is taken ill, Rachel turns up at the Abbey to see her aunt, and she immediately claims the job and says that only that morning Damaris had suggested to her that as Aunt Ann must be getting past the work, perhaps they could come and take care of the Abbey.

During this visit, the idea of Rachel as 'guardian' is born; not only do Jansy and Littlejan let her guide them round the Abbey and say that she 'passes with honours', it is also clear that, with her career as a writer launched and her love of story-telling, she will be an ideal guide. Mary is doubtful whether Damaris will settle, and her doubts prove to be fulfilled. At the beginning of February, Damaris and Rachel move into the Abbey, and although at first the novelty of their new surroundings keeps Damaris going, it is soon obvious that she needs something more to occupy her. Jen suggests that she might help with her children, but Rachel doesn't see that as the answer; she can't do teas as that would be competing with people in the village; she weeds the Abbot's garden, but there isn't much to do.

Here, however, lies the solution to the problem. When Jansy shows her the crocuses, the idea of Damaris turning the Abbey meadow into a garden is born. Damaris has found the job she needs: 'Something to do for the Abbey—a big thing to add to it, to make it even more beautiful.' Although the adults have some doubts about the idea, Littlejan produces Ambrose's book to prove that the meadow used to be a garden where he met Jehane, and this discovery finally wins Joan over to the idea. Once work has started, the aim is to create the garden in time for Joy's return from New York in July, and the story finishes with her arrival, her genuine delight in the garden (much to the relief of her peer group who are only too well aware of Joy's ability to be hurtful) and Damaris's ringing of the bells—'Joy had come home'.

Although this is a fairly short book, its taut construction enables EJO to explore many of her favourite themes and ideas. Littlejan and Jansy are taken to visit Rainbows, to give them 'something new to think about', so the reader once more hears all about the concept of Rainbows. Rosalind explains how Mrs Dering inherited the estate and wanted to share it, and that the three things 'she liked best were music and home and friends, so she decided to give those to people'. EJO yet again emphasises the 'scene of desolation', and this suggests that the community must have been based on a development of which she knew, although it has not so far been identified.

EJO's love of cats is seen yet again. At Rainbows the visitors are introduced to Margery Paine's cat, Pouffe; later Maidlin brings two kittens to the Abbey, promptly named Miss Nigger (not yet a politically incorrect term) and the Angel. EJO's love of beauty and colour is, of course, reflected in the creation of the Abbey garden. Right from the start, its making is seen as the positive creation of beauty. Littlejan asks Damaris to include the lobelia that Jansy will choose for her flower when she is Queen; orange marigolds are planted for Littlejan herself; Maidlin contributes lilies, Rosamund roses. There is also the image of Rachel as a young novice, wearing a monk's robe made from the 'yards of soft white material' given to her by Joan. ('Is it a wedding dress?' Damaris asks.)

Much is also made of the change in the rooms of the Abbey which become home for Rachel and Damaris—the preferability of the bare stone walls to the pink-washed walls so much liked by Aunt Ann, the colour now provided by curtains, cushions and the pottery contributed by Jen. In this book, EJO is able to dispose of a character who must have been something of an embarrassment to her for many years—Ann Watson. Maidlin as her niece was just about plausible, although when Maidlin develops into one of the central characters of the saga there seem to have been some complications, but to bestow on her two more nieces who are clearly from a different social background was perhaps stretching implausibility too far. This must surely be why Aunt Ann dies instead of being allowed to live in honourable retirement; EJO had had enough of this ambivalent character, whom Jen unkindly calls 'a little old black rag-bag'.

One important new character is introduced. Sir Robert Duncan, the great surgeon, happens to be at the ballet the night Damaris is injured, and he becomes very much involved in her future. Old characters make brief appearances. Cicely visits the Abbey with her son Dickon, and romance for Jansy and Dickon, who are about the same age, is hinted at, not for the first time. Daphne Dale marries a rich American, whose gift of money makes many of Damaris's ideas for the garden possible, while her sister Elsa is to marry Rodney Barron, son of the old Admiral from whom she rents the ferry. We hear again of

Joy's Madeline Rose, and there is news of Robin Quellyn's Bobbibach in the last chapter.

The Abbey is extended again. When Damaris visits Joan she overhears the 'Rainbow Corner' music on the radio and is upset by it; as a result of this Joan gives her the key to a little room off the refectory stair, the 'Abbot's Lodge', and this is later found to open into a staircase leading up to the Abbot's oratory.

More important, though, are the philosophising—which arises from Damaris's accident—the discussion of marriage and the careers and methods of writers. When Damaris questions God's wisdom by asking why she, who had tried to save Daphne, should be so badly injured, Rachel talks to her and points out that we don't know why accidents happen, but God can help us to make the best of things. This sound philosophy is frequently expressed in girls' stories of the twentieth century and can perhaps be best summed up as the 'Pollyanna' spirit, a term taken from Eleanor Porter's heroine who demonstrated it as well as anyone. At an early stage, Sir Robert says that there is no point in anyone lying around fainting and weeping; Mary says 'if it's the end of one career … it will be the beginning of another'; and when Damaris eventually leaves the nursing home, Madame tells Rachel that there may be 'something waiting for Damayris which she can only find by going to look for it'. Later Joan discusses the Hamlet Club motto with Damaris and suggests that she's the first who's had to accept the second part of the motto, 'not to be', and carry on in spite of it.

EJO's evident belief that girls should marry is emphasised in *Guardians of the Abbey*, frequently through Madame, who herself had left the stage for twenty years of home life. She tells Rachel: 'Girls should marry and they are happier so.' When Daphne, whose career has been saved by Damaris's sacrifice, then gives it up for marriage, this is seen as making things easier for Damaris—proof of the fact that marriage is much more important than a career.

It is interesting that of all EJO's main characters in the Abbey books, only Mary and Rachel, the writers, remain unmarried. Did EJO feel that although girls should normally marry, a writer might remain single with honour, for her books are her babies? (Nobody, of course, marries and remains childless.) Just as Mary appeared to be her mouthpiece in the previous book, so here we perhaps learn something of EJO's methods from Rachel— in many of her books EJO must have been pushing forward a little at a time to see what would happen next to her characters. This method sometimes led to problems (for example, the role of Ann Watson) but they are largely overcome by EJO's ability to go back and make her reader believe in the longstanding existence of something which has never previously been mentioned. There are two good examples of this in *Guardians of the Abbey*—the Abbot's Lodge and the mention of the Abbey garden in Ambrose's book. This ability, of which there are many examples, also helped to give EJO's books the richness that must account for much of their appeal.

It was ten years since EJO had published a retrospective Abbey book, but now three appeared in three years, the first picking up the story where she had left off in *Stowaways in the Abbey*. It is interesting to note that all three were illustrated by Frank Varty, who also illustrated the annual stories set in the same period which were discussed earlier. The first of these was *Schoolgirl Jen at the Abbey*, published by Collins in 1950, the same year as *Guardians of the Abbey*. Joan, Joy and Susie Spindle have all recovered from the measles. Mrs Shirley plans to take Joy away to the seaside to 'get braced up before the winter', and

It was a small metal box, rusted and discoloured.
(*Schoolgirl Jen at the Abbey*)

Jandy Mac announces her return to the Abbey for one last visit before she goes home to Australia. The whole situation is neatly set before the new reader in the first chapter, when Jen is invited to spend one more long weekend at the Hall before going home to Yorkshire for the summer holidays. Already in this first chapter we are made aware of Jen's admiration for Joan and of the hospitality exercised by the Abbey and the Hall, in the persons of Joan and Joy.

The idea of the Abbey as a place of sanctuary, where those in need of help will find it, is at the very heart of this book. Two people appear on the scene needing help, and in each case the help given requires some form of self-denial on the part of those giving it. There are also new discoveries made in and about the Abbey, and Sir Keith Marchwood and Susie Spindle, introduced in the previous book, both make appearances in this one. The events take place in a relatively short period of time, beginning at the end of the summer term and ending in the first few weeks of the autumn term, with a long gap while Jen is away at her home in Yorkshire.

It is easy to think of alternative titles for this book, *The Abbey Sanctuary* being one of them, but as Jen has either a part to play or a definite opinion to express in every episode in the book, it is clear that, as in *Stowaways in the Abbey*, EJO was reviving an interest in a very popular character who had taken something of a back seat in the later books, and was providing for her readers more stories of Jen's lively early years.

The opening incident concerns a large elm tree that shades the Abbey gatehouse; this has become diseased—Dutch elm disease—and has to be cut down. Jen is disposed to be sentimental, but Joan, while sympathising, does not allow her to give way to this and points out the dangers of infection to other trees and even an improvement to the view of the Abbey.

While saying goodbye to the tree, Jen meets the first of the story's refugees, a young girl called Lavinia (Vinny) Miles, who is a member of the Miles family of King's Bottom Farm. Her father and brothers emigrated when she was a child and left her with an aunt who remained in service at the farm. Then the aunt died and Vinny had stayed on at the farm, really because she had nowhere else to go. Her situation reflects almost exactly that of Eilidh in *A Princess in Tatters* but, in this context, seems much less credible. Vinny, too, is sad about the tree because she has happy memories of the drill classes that Joan used to hold for the village children when she lived in the Abbey, and as they compare their sorrow, Jen learns Vinny's story. Jen's ready sympathy is aroused and she rushes off to tell Joan and to see if something can be done for Vinny.

The second Abbey fugitive announces himself dramatically. Joan and Jen, alone for one night, are having a picnic supper in the Abbey when Jen, who has gone off for a walk, rushes back in a panic, announcing that she has seen the ghost of Ambrose, the lay-brother who lived in the Abbey after the dissolution of the monasteries. It is, of course, no ghost—EJO does not go in for ghosts—but an old man called Boniface Browning, the former guide to the Abbey whose retirement had paved the way for Mrs Shirley and the girls. He has been living with a son in Birmingham but, homesick for the village and the Abbey, has come for a holiday, and on this particular evening has deliberately allowed himself to be shut in when the Abbey is closed for the night.

Jen's solution for Boniface is that he should stay and live in the Abbey, looked after by Ann Watson, but she does not realise what this would mean to Joan—the loss of her privacy in the Abbey once it is closed to the public. Joan also sees this as a solution but hates the idea of never having the Abbey to herself. However, the Abbey spirit wins; the Abbey welcome 'to old and tired folk must be upheld'. In typical EJO fashion, the story's threads are drawn together when it is discovered that Vinny is Boniface's great-niece, not so strange a coincidence in a small village.

Discoveries in the Abbey usually involve accidents, but in this story the accident merely serves to keep Jen still long enough to appreciate what is to come. She is hurt when the tree is cut down as she rushes to save Vinny, who is in danger of being crushed as it falls. Jandy Mac arrives in time to support Joan through the anxiety until it is known that Jen has come to no serious harm.

While Jen is resting after her accident, she has two visitors, each bringing a book that adds something new to the story of the Abbey. Sir Keith Marchwood has found a book of drawings done by Katharine, the wife of Peregrine Abinger, who lived at the Hall in Ambrose's time. Vinny has also got an old book, the diary of a young girl called Jane Miles, the daughter of the highwayman who hid his loot in the Abbey, which she has brought as a gift for Jen. This book also contains a map, much like the earlier ones, said to show the hiding-place of something 'that would bring luck'. It takes the girls some time to decipher this, but in the end Jen has a bright idea that leads them to Ambrose's rosary, yet another treasure for the Abbey.

Meanwhile Joan, with Jen's help, makes plans to send Vinny to join her father and brothers in Canada, who are happy to have her and who send money for her passage. However, she cannot make the journey alone; fortunately, it turns out that Boniface also has a great wish to go to Canada, where he has a married daughter, and this seems to simplify matters.

It is while these plans are being made that Susie Spindle has a small role. She becomes sulky and difficult, jealous of Vinny who seems to be getting all the attention, especially from Jen, whom Susie much admires. It is not difficult to make Susie see sense—Vinny is going away and will probably never come back, while she, Susie, is to stay on at the Hall. Susie expresses her own private ambition: 'I'd like to be cook some day'; she is encouraged to learn all she can and told there's no reason why she can't become cook when the time comes. As we know, her wish is to be fulfilled. Susie, Vinny and Boniface are all examples of the fact that EJO was at her least successful when handling characters from working-class backgrounds. In fact, to a modern reader, the whole tone of this book is thoroughly condescending and patronising. For the EJO enthusiast, it is only saved because the central characters are Joan, Jen and Jandy Mac.

There is a final problem, caused by Boniface, who panics at the idea of taking the great trip to Canada with only young Vinny as a companion. The girls continue with their plans, hoping that he will change his mind, but the problem is finally solved by Jandy Mac, who elects to travel back to Australia via Canada and the Pacific, thus seeing the protégés safely to their families. This is seen not as a great sacrifice but at least as a giving-up of personal comfort, as she would really prefer to go all the way by sea and must now cross the Atlantic second class instead of first.

Joan and Jandy here represent the wise and careful caring element, Jen the enthusiast who must be restrained and taught to think before she acts, while Joy, in her brief appearance, is at her least attractive, lacking in sympathy and understanding. Perhaps this is why she does not play a large part in this adventure, and perhaps also her earlier character had been recalled by EJO when she was writing the previous book. A further reason for EJO's return to writing retrospective Abbey books may have been a revival of interest in the Abbey itself. In *Guardians of the Abbey* she had the discovery of the Abbot's Lodge and the recalling of the story of Ambrose and Jehane, and it may be that this had prompted the two further additions to the Abbey story that come to light in *Schoolgirl Jen*.

The condescension and patronage that are so obvious in *Schoolgirl Jen* are to be seen again in *Strangers at the Abbey*, published by Collins in 1951. Judged as a contribution to the Abbey saga, this is a disappointment; considered apart from that context, it looks much better. The action takes place in the summer term following the events of *Schoolgirl Jen*—thus, once again, the cold months are ignored. Nesta is crowned Queen Honesty early in the book, and the story culminates in the end-of-term fête which includes a procession of the Queens, a demonstration of singing games by a group of children trained by Jen and a performance of *As You Like It*. Catering for a young readership, it is much more of a school story than the majority of the Abbey books and follows the typical pattern of the new girl who is at first a misfit but gradually learns to conform, and who also scores successfully, in this case with a brilliant performance as Jaques. It does, however, differ from the typical school story in that Rykie, the new girl, is never seen from the inside but only observed through the eyes of Joan, Joy and Jen, and as such, is a far from sympathetic character.

As a retrospective book, *Strangers* belongs to the period of time that lies between *The Girls of the Abbey School* and *The Abbey Girls Go Back to School*, written thirty years earlier. Looked at in terms of its chronological time, two elements in particular jar on the reader—the preoccupation with the world of films, centred on Hollywood, and Joy's acquisition of a new car. By 1951, when the book was published, the passages about the films and Hollywood would probably seem quite oldfashioned to the reader, but in 1921 they would just not have been possible (a salutary reminder of how quickly the cinema as popular entertainment rose and fell). In *The Abbey Girls Go Back to School* Joy has only quite recently acquired a motor-bike and sidecar, but obviously in a story published in 1951 someone of her means would be expected to have a car.

Rykie Reekie, a name that reflects EJO's increasing delight in odd names, is not only a stranger to the Abbey; she is also a stranger, by character, to the Abbey girls, who exclaim in horror when she arrives beautifully made up and with her hair permed; they are horrified at the way in which she tries to grab the part of Jaques in the school play—and succeeds—and they are most concerned that she will let them down. She also commits the ultimate crime of attempting to steal one of the Abbey jewels. By contrast, Joan, Joy and Jen are portrayed as clean-living, honourable and generous, which they are, but they also tend to come over as somewhat mean-minded and positively rude at times. Joan and Joy, for example, do not hesitate to comment on Rykie's appearance almost as soon as they meet her—Joy calls her a 'figure of fun', and Joan says: 'The sooner you get home and clean yourself up the better.' Jen, sitting between Joan and Rykie in the back seat of the car, tells Joan: 'I think she looks horrible.' EJO's snobbishness also comes over loud and clear—Rykie's red nails are said to be like those of 'shopgirls'.

'Oh! Joan, stop him!' she shrieked.
(*Strangers at the Abbey*)

The impending arrival of fourteen-year-old Rykie, short for Frederica, provides an excuse for fifteen-year-old Jen to be invited to stay at the Hall for the summer term so that the two schoolgirls will be company for each other and can cycle into school together, since Joan and Joy have now left school. Rykie is the younger daughter of Mrs Shirley's sister; Belle, the elder, goes off to Hollywood and only appears at the end of the book. The other 'stranger' of the title is Angus, their older stepbrother, who conspires with Rykie to steal one of the Abbey jewels. He is earning his living at sea (naturally) but is a gifted violinist, and his crime is seen to be the result of his frustration at not having the lessons and encouragement that he merits. His existence, although hinted at in the opening of the book, is not revealed to the Abbey girls until he is discovered, with Rykie, at dead of night, carrying out the theft of the Abbey jewels—Rykie's intention was that he should take just one, to cover the cost of her fare to Hollywood, but, seeing them, Angus is tempted to take more.

The characters of Joan, Joy and Jen can be developed little—this is perhaps one reason why they sometimes appear snobbish and mean-minded. EJO has to content herself with hints of the future to come, such as Joan's daughter being named Janice and becoming the Lobelia Queen. Mrs Shirley appears frequently in this book and is consistently portrayed as a fragile 'little old lady'. Even if she did not have Joan until she was 35, which seems unlikely since Joan is an only child, she would in fact be only in her mid-fifties by the time of *Strangers at the Abbey*. This fragility is also emphasised in the short stories set in this same period; in *Mistakes in the Abbey*, for example, Joan is sleeping in her mother's room so that she can ply her with cups of tea throughout the night.

The elder sister, Belle, is portrayed rather unsympathetically before she actually appears, but then comes over as the most attractive of the three Reekies; by this time, EJO's attitude to the Reekies seems to have mellowed, a mellowing that is reflected in the reactions of Joy, Joan and Jen. When Belle eventually appears, she is married to Terence Van Toll, whose father owns a chain of cinemas in the United States; she has thus become Belle Van Toll (wisely she decides that in future she will be known by her full name of Isabella). Their arrival with an offer to take Rykie with them to Europe means that Rykie has to make a choice—to give up the trip or let the school down. She shows that the Abbey spirit has had its influence by deciding to give up the trip, and is applauded by Terry and Belle, as well as by her new friends and relations.

In these later retrospective books, of course, EJO was becoming increasingly handicapped in her plotting and ability to introduce new characters. Over ten years earlier she had started to write the retrospective books with a real purpose in mind, a purpose that had been brilliantly achieved by the creation of Jandy Mac. It had also been possible to absorb Susie Spindle into the Abbey household, but now EJO had reached the stage when she really had to dispose fairly permanently of any new characters that she introduced— so Vinny and Boniface emigrate to Canada, while Belle and Rykie depart for America, never to return.

Selma at the Abbey, published by Collins in the following year, 1952, not only follows on in time almost immediately after *Strangers at the Abbey* but also has events which arise directly from the previous book. On the other hand, it is a very different type of story; not so obviously intended for younger readers, it is in fact a romantic love story and one with a theme much used at an earlier period by writers of adult novels—that of the clever/rich man choosing a bride from a lower class than himself and having her educated to become his partner. In a book for schoolgirls, romance or no, this theme is very tenuous but is nonetheless present.

In *Strangers at the Abbey* Joan and Joy, sympathetic to Angus Reekie's musical aspirations and understanding his feeling of frustration at not being able to get the proper training, sold one of Lady Jehane's rubies and gave the proceeds to be used on his behalf. Their

Dark daughter of the Vikings.
(*Selma at the Abbey*)

236

kindness and generosity have impressed him so much that, when he is in need of help and advice, it is to Joan and Joy that he comes. Angus wants help for Selma, 'his girl', as he calls her, although he is twenty-one and she is only sixteen. Selma has had a good education but is now working in a shop in Glasgow; her mother and her Swedish father (her name is Andersson) are both dead, and her only relative is a stepfather with whom she does not get on.

What Angus wants for Selma is the undefinable 'something' of which he is aware in the Abbey circle. He talks about the need for her to meet all kinds of people and move in all kinds of society when he becomes a famous violinist, but Mrs Shirley expresses what he really means: 'Angus wants sanctuary for his distressed sweetheart and he has come to the Abbey for help.' So, once again, the idea of the Abbey offering sanctuary is positively expressed. (In passing, one cannot help observing that at this point in Abbey time the Abbey girls lived in a rather narrow world, and it would be some time before they themselves became accustomed to meeting all kinds of people and moving in all kinds of society, but never mind.)

Joan, Joy and Mrs Shirley appreciate his feeling for Selma and, understanding, agree to invite her to the Abbey for a visit, but not until Joan and Joy have given him motherly and fatherly advice, respectively. Despite their personal feelings about getting married (at this stage Joy thinks it must be 'an awful bore'), Joan warns him to go slowly with Selma, who is still rather young to accept so complete a commitment, while Joy advises him not to think of marriage until he has made a good start with his career. Inevitably, at Angus's request, Jen is sent for to stay at the Hall and be friends with Selma, thus assembling all the Abbey's forces to deal with its newest guest. There is a certain amount of anxiety in case she turns out to be another Rykie, but the Abbey is prepared to cope, even in that eventuality.

Selma is not another Rykie, however; she is a very real and rounded character from the same stable as Patch Paterson—in fact they have quite a lot in common. Much is made of her Swedish ancestry, Joy having already christened her 'dark daughter of the Vikings', and she is certainly possessed of a love of adventure and new things, and is excited and puzzled to receive an invitation to stay with strangers in the south of England. Her first ideas and enthusiasms are very well presented—to a Scottish girl of that period a visit to England must truly have been a voyage into the unknown.

At this early stage Selma's feeling for Angus is just a strong liking, and she gets rather annoyed when her friends refer to him as her boy-friend, but just before she leaves for England Angus confesses to her the story of his attempted theft of the jewels and, in her sympathy for him and their sharing of this secret, she is aware of a stronger bond between them. As she explains to him:

'It makes us belong more than ever, because we both know and we feel the same about it, just terribly sorry it nearly happened, but so frightfully glad it didn't quite. And we know it could never happen again. It's a sort of secret joining us together ...'

Like Patch many years later, Selma's family background has fallen away from her, and her understanding with Angus makes her feel safe and secure.

Unlike Rykie, Selma fits into the Abbey circle, makes friends with Jen, explores with Joy

The dormitory at Cleeve—'Each window has a recess with a little seat ...'—1991

and goes to Joan for support and advice. For Mrs Shirley she has a slightly awestruck reverence—once again, Mrs Shirley is presented as much older than she really is. Angus describes her as 'the perfect grandmother, but rather a grand lady too'. And Angus is two years older than Joan and Joy!

Selma also sees what Angus has seen, that she needs a broader cultural background if she is to support him in his future career, and she is very willing to accept any support the Abbey people will give her. Joy widens her musical horizons and Joan, rather ineptly, tells her what books to read. It is also rather surprising that Joan, when trying to help Selma modify her Scottish accent, is so vague about the correct uses of 'shall' and 'will' for which, at that period, there were still definite rules. There is, however, one very nice touch, when Joan explains that 'You only say "I will" when you want to be very emphatic.', and Joy suddenly appears outside the window and says: 'Or when you're getting married.', to which Joan retorts: 'That is a time for being very emphatic.'

Jen's role in this book is a rather smaller one. We are told that she makes friends with Selma, but although Selma goes to school with her, and dances with the Hamlet Club, Jen's most important part seems to be the unthinking revelation to Selma of the fact that Angus had asked Joan and Joy to invite her to the Abbey. Joan manages to smooth things over, showing Selma that Angus was paying them a compliment and that Selma herself need not be ashamed, thus helping her to appreciate Angus even more. But Jen is disgusted with herself: 'I've always thought people who hurt other people were the absolute limit and now I've been and done it myself.' Perhaps regular readers of EJO were relieved to know that the quality of understanding, so prized by her characters and especially visible in the older Jen, had to be acquired over the years.

We have not yet seen the last of Lady Jehane's jewels. Since Angus's abortive attempt to steal them they have been kept at the Hall, much to Ann Watson's relief. Now, while Angus is staying at the hall for his birthday, yet another attempt is made to steal them. Angus himself surprises the burglars and in trying to prevent their escape, his arm is broken—deliberately.

Angus has now fully expiated his earlier attempt to steal the jewels, and the Abbey adopts him completely. The real thief turns out to be yet another renegade Watson—Alf, come home from America—Ann Watson really does not have any luck with her relatives. Alf is pretty inept and ends up taking refuge in the Abbey, but he is not the kind of person to whom the Abbey gives sanctuary; his aunt reveals his presence to Joan and he is handed over to the police but, at Angus's request, not prosecuted.

The danger to Angus, and the fear that after his arm has healed he will not be able to play again, reveal to Selma the depth of her own feelings. When, at the end of the book, her Swedish relations write and ask her to go to them, she insists, desperately, on becoming engaged so that she does not have to leave Angus. In the end both he and Selma go to Sweden and return to a happy ending. Terry Van Toll, Angus's American brother-in-law, has rescued a famous violinist from a blazing car, and as a reward come help and lessons for Angus who, with Selma, leaves for America as so many Abbey sanctuary-seekers have done. Jen laments this, but Joan very sensibly points out that: 'We should be overcrowded if they all stayed … People have to go, they'd never get on in the world if they stayed in this quiet place.'

The Hamlet Club is there in the background in this book. Selma dances with them (pointing her toes!), and in the last two chapters Queen Beatrice (Beetle) is elected and crowned. Also, in Chapter 33, Littlejan is born and her nickname explained. Altogether *Selma at the Abbey* is a much better book than its predecessor, a well-rounded story, a happy little romance with enough Abbey background to please EJO's regular readers. In the person of Selma, it reintroduces things Scottish—another of EJO's enthusiasms. In the earlier chapters Selma and Angus take boat trips down the Clyde from Glasgow, and Selma's description of the beauty of her native scenery and her soft Scottish voice (no Glasgow accent) remind us of the many earlier books with Scottish settings.

In this five-year period EJO had published eight books that, between them, gave more breadth of background to the Abbey and to Kentisbury, introduced important new characters, notably Rosalind Kane, and set events moving towards what seems to have been her ultimate goal. By now Rachel is established in the Abbey as its Guardian, Joy and the twins have returned from New York, and the Hamlet Club has been well and truly revived, while the retrospective books have added depth to well established scenes and characters.

Chapter 10

WORDS AND MUSIC,
1952 TO 1959

By 1952 EJO was in her seventies, and her earlier production rate, not surprisingly, had slowed down somewhat. The smaller output may also have been due in some part to changing patterns of publishing for children and young people in the 1950s, and her books may have become less attractive to publishers. EJO's six remaining books, published between 1951 and 1959, were all concerned with the Abbey or, in the case of *New Girls at Wood End*, the only one which does not have 'Abbey' in the title, with a character, Robin, who had by now become very much part of the Abbey circle.

The themes that dominate these last books reflect EJO's own interests but do not necessarily complement the plots, which probably reflect the demands of the publishers. 'A school story please?' the publishers probably asked. EJO met their request to some extent but also continued to pursue the themes that interested her and, as she believed, her readers. Her books did not meet the requirements of the 'career' stories that were extremely popular in the 1950s. Few of her characters have careers in the accepted sense of the word—too many of them are in the situation of Benedicta, who says: 'I haven't any real job and I've not had enough training to get a good one.' The career stories were also providing innocuous teenage romances for the kind of audience for which EJO wrote, so she may well have been under pressure to write school stories suitable for the ten- to twelve-year-olds of the early 1950s.

EJO herself was undoubtedly anxious to push events forward to the point when the Marchwood twins could be chosen as Queens, an event foreseen soon after their birth when, in *The Abbey Girls at Home*, Maidlin tells Joy that the girls of the Hamlet Club are saying 'we're going to have twin Queens some day, as soon as ever they're old enough'. EJO was also preoccupied with three ideas—the role of the writer for girls, music in its various manifestations, and babies. By this time her self-image was probably that of a sympathetic and efficient person who had made a successful career out of writing for girls; she still liked to put this kind of person into her books, and in these later works Mary-Dorothy, the mainstay of so many Abbey crises, is being replaced by Rachel, also a writer, a conjuror with words. EJO, quite correctly, saw her books as being helpful to the adolescent girl, and, through Mary and Rachel, she extended this role at a personal level.

Music, in various forms, had always been of interest to EJO. Joy's musical gift has been handed on to her twins and some of their crisis situations now arise from this. Damaris, the dancer, reflects another aspect of this musical interest, while Rosalind (Nanta Rose), a central figure in the final sequence of Abbey novels, is another fine musician.

One hesitates to add such a different theme as 'babies' to those of 'words' and 'music', but by this time EJO was obsessed with babies, not only handing them out liberally to all those of childbearing age but also going into considerable detail about their care, and giving one small schoolgirl in *New Girls at Wood End* an outsized maternal instinct. Mabel Esther Allan was very critical about this obsession, commenting in a letter written in 1983: 'What I always found so incredible was the way she seemed to think one only needed to desire twins to get them … also always smiled at some references to keeping cocks and hens. She appeared to think an equal number was required.'

Rachel in the Abbey, published by Muller and illustrated by M D Neilson, appeared in 1952, the year before the publication of *Selma at the Abbey*. It carried forward the story of the second generation of Abbey girls, and in it Rachel emerges as a kind and helpful counsellor—EJO was into counselling long before it became a fashionable and specific job in education and social work—to carry on Mary-Dorothy's role for the younger generation. As the 'Abbot' based in the Abbey she holds the story together, but it is as much concerned with the affairs of Benedicta Bennett, who reappears after an absence of four years; of Damaris, recovering from her accident; of Jansy, the reigning Queen; and of Rosalind, thrust into a more prominent role with the departure of Littlejan.

… wearing a white gown like a monk's robe …
(*Rachel in the Abbey*)

Rachel in the Abbey starts at the point at which *Guardians of the Abbey* finishes, late in the July afternoon when Joy returns home from New York, and comes to an end on the day, the following May, when Rosalind is crowned as the twenty-fifth Queen of the Hamlet Club. The story opens with the return to the Abbey of Benedicta Bennett, whose arrival makes it possible to bring up to date a reader who may have missed out on recent events, or to set the scene for a newcomer to the books. In the opening paragraph Benedicta is reacting to the Abbey garden that is, of course, new to her. The final sentence of this paragraph mentions the flowers that represent the schoolgirl trio—Jansy, Littlejan and Rosalind—in describing the path winding among the flowerbeds edged with lobelia and marigolds with lavender bushes amongst them.

Rachel combines three roles—she is the caretaker or guardian of the Abbey, she is a successful author and she is counsellor to the younger generation—and all three roles are emphasised in the second chapter where, the scene having been set in the first, she is introduced to the reader and the trio come to consult her. This first consultation is fairly low key. Littlejan feels they are in the way at the Hall now that Joy has come home, and wants to take refuge at the Manor; unwisely, they do not take Rachel's advice, and this incident may well have been included to emphasise Rachel's development in the course of this book that bears her name. In the final chapter, Damaris tells her: 'You're needed here. All those girls come to you for help, and they'll come again, often.'

Benedicta, having been a pupil at Wood End School, is well equipped to become Damaris's assistant in the garden and is thus on the spot to take over her job when, at the end of the book, Damaris makes a complete recovery and plans to return to the ballet. In the meantime she joins the counselling team at the Abbey, and is injured a second time when she prevents horses from the farm next door from damaging the Abbey garden, thus reinforcing her position in the Abbey circle.

Since the story starts in July, school is virtually over for the summer. The summer holidays, which Rosalind spends with her sister while Jansy and Littlejan stay near Plas Quellyn, are glossed over fairly quickly, everyone's whereabouts being reported to Benedicta by Damaris when the former returns to the Abbey to take up her job as assistant gardener. Before the new term can begin, however, there is a crisis when Littlejan is called away, collected by her father who wants to take her back to Ceylon. Interestingly, everyone assumes that Littlejan will be distressed by this and is taken by surprise when Littlejan, although regretful about leaving to some extent, is delighted at the thought of seeing her mother and baby sister. Her departure marks the end of Mary-Dorothy's reign as counsellor; on her last evening she comes to see Mary-Dorothy and tells her: 'It's a big bit of the house, this brown room, and talking to you is a big bit of—of our life here.'

In the next chapter Joan, talking to Benedicta in the Abbey, learns that people come to Rachel 'to be helped', preparing the way for the scene at the very end of the book when Damaris tells her sister that she's needed much more at the Abbey, 'among all those kiddies and schoolgirls'. The private nature of these consultations is emphasised. When the twins go to Rachel, Jansy confidently tells Rosalind that Rachel will tell them all about it afterwards. The older and more sensitive Rosalind says 'I don't believe she will', and, indeed, at the end of the session Margaret tells Rachel: 'Anything we tell you in the Abbey is a secret.'

Why is Littlejan, the central figure in the most recent Abbey books, called away halfway through this book? One reason is that EJO may have felt that she had now got too many major characters; Littlejan would certainly have overshadowed the Marchwood twins in a way that Rosalind and Jansy don't. Another is that the way had to be open for Rosalind to prove herself in order that she might be chosen as the next Queen. With Littlejan present, the storm in the teacup at school would probably not have blown up at all or would have been sorted out at a very much earlier stage—as it is, it is quickly settled. Littlejan's departure is therefore necessary for very practical reasons of plot and characterisation, although it does also provide just the kind of crisis situation much loved by EJO. Her return, however, is anticipated so that neither the Abbey folk nor the reader are totally bereft of this attractive personality. It is Mary-Dorothy who says: 'I expect you'll come back, perhaps to take the Cookery course.'

The given reason for Littlejan's departure, of course, is a baby—Jandy, it seems, has caught the Abbey baby fever, and her long-time companion and family nurse needs to return home to the islands. In *Rachel in the Abbey* Joy's latest baby and Jen's feat of producing twin boys are still a novelty. Benedicta tells of Gail's baby, Penelope Rose,

Damaris tells Benedicta of Robin Quellyn's Bobbibach, Janet Joy is born to Jandy in Ceylon, Maidlin produces a boy, John Paul, Virginia produces Nancybell Rose as a birthday present for Rosalind, and Jen scores again by producing a third girl, named Barbara (with its meaning of 'stranger' because she is fair rather than dark) Rose.

At this point Jen does admit that the expense of educating so many children has made them stop to think! Rosamund even explains why she isn't having another baby yet, telling Benedicta that it was 'rather a strain having the girls so close together and they [the doctors] say I must wait till the tinies are at least two before I think of having another'. However, by the end of the book the two years are up, and she announces that she can begin thinking about 'that little brother'.

If EJO was being pressured by her publishers to write school stories, the school element in this particular book is fairly small. Margaret and Elizabeth Marchwood go to school for the first time. The first school crisis, however, does not involve them directly but does provide an opportunity for Rosalind to demonstrate qualities of leadership. A new head, Miss Raven, had been appointed to succeed Miss Macey at the beginning of the previous term; she has now decreed that the older girls are to wear skirts rather than gym tunics when the weather turns cooler, an edict that does not find favour with some of the seniors. The other bone of contention is that she is said to have sacked Mademoiselle, and has appointed an English person, Miss Verity, to teach French instead. The older generation of Abbey girls are in favour of both these changes that seem to have caused a storm in a teacup, and with Rosalind and Jansy to bring and support their views to the school, the rebellion soon collapses.

They climbed the stony track.
(*A Dancer from the Abbey*)

Rachel tells them that the Hamlet Club 'should back up the new Head through thick and thin', and Rosalind is encouraged to follow in Virginia's footsteps by talking to the Club and encouraging the members to do just this.

This theme of reaction to the ideas of a new headmistress is a well-worn one of school stories, but in EJO's book it is turned on its head to some extent, just as the theme of the misfit had been in *Strangers at the Abbey*. Miss Raven enjoys a total victory and the rebellious element never really stood a chance.

It is also interesting to note once again EJO's attitude to the French language. Comment has already been made on the fact that first Biddy and then Rachel are sent to France to learn French when one would have supposed that Italian would be rather more useful to a person destined to be secretary to an Italian heiress. French is evidently regarded by EJO as an essential accomplishment, but the attitude of her heroines hardly reflects this, although in this latest book Damaris does actually manage a few words of French to Benedicta. The schoolgirls seem to believe that a mademoiselle is a better teacher of French, although revelations about this particular mademoiselle's ability to keep order perhaps explain the generally low standards achieved by Jen and her peers!

The twins meet their first personal crisis at school when Elizabeth, the cello player, is welcomed to the school orchestra more enthusiastically than Margaret, who plays the violin. Rachel, consulted by the distressed twins, can see the situation clearly. Margaret is accustomed to playing in a trio with her mother at the piano and Elizabeth on the cello, and it is obvious that Margaret, standing in the front with her violin, has felt herself the leader of the trio. Now Margaret's dream was 'shattered; Elizabeth was the important one; she herself was merely "another fiddle"'. Rachel consoles Margaret with the thought that if she learns to play with the orchestra, and works hard, she may one day be the leader of the orchestra.

In *Rachel in the Abbey* there are several illustrations featuring Rachel, including the frontispiece, which shows her with tourists, and another in which she is wearing her white gown 'like a monk's robe', but it is the dustjacket illustration that best demonstrates the direction the series is taking; it shows Rachel in front of the Abbey gatehouse with two young girls, presumably Jansy and a twin, clinging to her arm.

A Dancer from the Abbey, published by Collins in 1953, follows on immediately after *Rachel*, which ends with Rosalind's crowning as the Lavender Queen; it opens on the morning of the following day, appropriately enough in the garden that Damaris created and which she is about to leave to take up her career as a dancer once more.

According to a letter dated 18 January 1953, the publishers apparently wanted to call this book *The Abbey Girls at the Ballet*, which EJO thought 'utterly meaningless and inappropriate'. *A Dancer from the Abbey* can fairly be described as yet another example of EJO's habit of turning an accepted contemporary idea on its head. As the title that was finally agreed suggests, it is much concerned with Damaris's return to her chosen career as a dancer, but its theme is rather that of career versus marriage, and in this case marriage wins. To give EJO her due, the point is made that in some cases, such as Maidlin's, it is possible to combine marriage with a career, but a ballet dancer has special problems (or had, fifty years ago) and can only do so if she marries another dancer. This, of course, we know to be untrue, but EJO was for keeping things simple.

The man in Damaris's life turns up in the opening line. He is part of her dancing life and of the musical life in which Joy has been involved since her marriage to Ivor Quellyn. Brian Grandison is the son of John Grant Grandison, who wrote the music for the ballet *Rainbow Corner*; he has just returned from South Africa and arrives at the Abbey anxious to meet Mary Damayris. He is, clearly, much attracted to Damaris at their first meeting, and the main theme of the book is the conflict between their romance and Damaris's return to the stage. Brian recognises this and admits his feelings quite early on, but Damaris takes longer to accept that she cares for Brian at all. In fact, the sequence of reaction is: Brian admits he loves Damaris; Damaris is jealous when it is suggested that Brian may care for Benedicta; Brian agrees to keep away; Damaris realises that she cares more for him than for her dancing. Once they are engaged, apart from one temperamental panic on Damaris's part, it is Brian who suffers from doubts and she who is confident in her decision to make a triumphant comeback and then give up her dancing career for marriage.

Interwoven with this main storyline, and sometimes arising from it, are other stories reflecting EJO's main concerns at this period. Rachel's role of Abbot and her career as a writer are both developed further: Brian comes to her for help in handling her more temperamental sister; Jen herself comes, and later sends two small girls to be comforted; and later Rosalind, now the reigning Queen, comes for advice and help in the matter of Tessa as the possible new Queen. Tessa 'fools about' and is considered unreliable, a preparation for an incident in a later book.

From a school story that Rachel invents to amuse the two small girls comes another development in her career. So far she has only written for adults but, on Mary's advice, she now seriously considers a book for girls. In the course of a conversation about writing between Mary and Rachel that, again, gives EJO's readers a little more insight into the life of a writer, Mary says:

> 'I've never dared to think I could help grown-ups; I doubt if I could even amuse or interest them. But it has seemed worthwhile to try to influence girls and children for good, by amusing them and catching their interest. Girls are the grown-ups of the future. They may keep something of what is put into them while they are fresh and receptive. I've believed it is more worthwhile to write for them than to try to write novels.'

This credo is interesting and leads one to speculate—was EJO Mary or Rachel? *Did* she at some point consider writing adult books or is this a statement of her earliest beliefs?

Rachel herself gets help and advice from Mary, not only in the matter of her writing, but also in the separation from Damaris when the latter goes back to the world of ballet. The importance of Rachel's role in the Abbey has already been emphasised, and this is repeated, but Mary reminds her that she has her own work and that the secure, peaceful background of the Abbey is best for her writing.

The music theme is, of course, inherent in Damaris's return to the ballet, but all the musical threads come together at one point in the book where Joy holds a musical evening when all the musicians of the Abbey circle perform, Damaris dances, and the party ends with a little gentle folk dancing.

There are the inevitable babics—Maidlin has a son and Rosamund a second son—but it is the slightly older children who come to the fore in this book. Benedicta witnesses an important moment when Rosamund's young brother, Roddy, who has always called her 'mother', now realises that there is a difference between himself and the other children, and wants to know why. We have been prepared for this in a conversation between Rosamund and Cicely in *A Fiddler for the Abbey*—EJO obviously had it all worked out well beforehand.

Jen's eldest daughter, Rosemary, known as Brownie, goes to school, thus giving us a voice among the juniors for the school crises to come. Jen is anxious about Rosemary, who is a shy child and has been too much at home, but Rosalind, as Queen, solves this problem by asking Rosemary to look after yet another shy, frightened junior, Hermione Manley, known as Myonie Rose. Hermione is the daughter of a lesser-known Queen of the Hamlet Club, Queen Clover; Anne Manley has been recently widowed and has come to live in Wycombe with her mother so that she can send her daughter to her old school. She is immediately taken up by the Abbey circle, especially by Rosamund, for whom, without her knowledge, Myonie Rose had been named. Before the book's end she has a baby boy, giving her something to live for, in true Abbey tradition.

Brian Grandison provides the reason for a recap of the Abbey families and a recital of past events. Ken Marchwood's African interests are used as an excuse to keep Brian around; when Jen hears that Brian has just returned from South Africa, she says: 'You must meet my husband. He lived there once and I think he's left part of his heart in Kenya.' Thus, we are reminded that Ken, as well as Andrew, had lived in Africa and that he gave up his plans for a future there when he inherited the Manor—something which we have no certainty that Andrew would have done! But Jen, much earlier, had said that she had no wish to live in Africa—another example of the husband falling in with his wife's wishes, rather than vice versa. Again, the distinction between East Africa, of which Kenya was part, and South Africa is conveniently blurred, but this blurring was probably not uncommon amongst those British people who had no direct links with either place at that period.

True to tradition we also have a new discovery for the Abbey. At the farm next door, Benedicta and Brian find the font from the old Abbey church, which is being used as a drinking trough for the dogs. A reminder of EJO's interest in folklore comes when the farmer, John Edwards, explains that his grandmother, who is nearly a hundred years old, remembers a family tradition handed down from generation to generation that 'the Old One who lived in the gatehouse had it put there'. The 'Old One', of course, was Ambrose the lay-brother—it is a nice idea, but seems rather unlikely!

Brian's other excuse for staying around the Abbey and its three attractive residents is a further development of EJO's interest in gardens, first shown in *The Tuck-Shop Girl*, carried further in the creation of Wood End School and brought to its peak in Damaris's creation of the garden for the Abbey. Brian's suitability as a husband for Damaris is further increased by the fact that he has inherited a house at Ambleside with a big garden that has possibilities as a market garden. Not only will Damaris return to her beloved fells, but she will also be able to continue with her secondary career. The house is called Heather Garth— EJO has always attached importance to the names of houses. This one will remind Damaris of the Abbey and gives significance to the bunch of heather Brian sends her on the night of her return to the stage.

The school element is here very much in the background, apart from Rosemary's friendship with Myonie, the choice of Tessa for the next Queen, and the encouragement of cricket practice for the twins and for Rosemary, who has inherited her mother's expertise as a bowler.

It is, however, the marriage versus career theme that dominates the book, placed beside the idea that a great artistic gift must not be used selfishly but shared with the world, and also, subtly hinted, the idea that a writer does not need marriage and children, the latter always a necessary ingredient in EJO's marriages. Rachel stresses that she has no intention of marrying and is given the old ring that Ambrose made for Jehane, as a symbol of her 'marriage' to the Abbey. Earlier in the book, talking with Rachel about Damaris, Mary says:

'… she would be wrong to deny her gift its full expression just for ease and comfort; to settle down at home and enjoy herself. She couldn't do it. But if she loved some man, I'd say she was right to give up even her dancing for him. I'd think it was wrong to let her career spoil the happiness of two lives.'

It is significant that, despite the title, this book ends not with Mary Damayris's triumphant return to the theatre but on the following day when Damaris, in her shorts and jumper, greets Brian in the Abbey garden and reassures him that he is more important to her than the ballet.

The beginning of *The Song of the Abbey*, published in 1954 by Collins, overlaps the ending of *A Dancer from the Abbey*, published in the previous year. It seems likely that the opening sequence, at least, had been planned out by EJO while she was still engaged in writing *A Dancer from the Abbey*; as we have seen, there are hints in the latter of Tessa's irresponsibility, which has discouraged the girls from choosing her as Queen. With Rachel's encouragement, Rosalind talked to Tessa, and the following January Tessa became Queen-elect. The next day, as Rachel and Jen are sitting on cushions in the rose window of the sacristy (as has already been observed, it is always summer at the Abbey) and discussing Tessa's choice of colours and flowers, Jen tells Rachel that Rosalind's Cookery Course will be over in March. These two elements—Tessa's tendency to be irresponsible and the fact that Rosalind will finish her course at the end of the Spring term—come together to make up the first part of *The Song of the Abbey*, which is rooted in the doings of the school and the Hamlet Club, possibly in response to the publisher's requirements.

A Dancer from the Abbey ends the day after Damaris's triumphant return as the goose girl and the fairy; at the beginning of *The Song of the Abbey*, the reader is taken

They walked through the garden.
(*The Song of the Abbey*)

back to the day prior to the eagerly awaited performance. As the catalyst to the events that are about to be described, EJO revived one of the few unreformed and certainly the most memorable of her villains, Carry Carter. Carry's unspeakable behaviour to Joy in *The Abbey Girls* has never been completely forgotten, perhaps because she is so unusual a character in EJO's work. There have been occasional references to her behaviour, and in the retrospective *Strangers in the Abbey* the generous attitude of Aileen Carter, a cousin, is seen as unexpected from a Carter.

Everyone who is anyone in the school seems to have a ticket for the performance at which Damaris will make her comeback—except Tessa, who would have hated being left out in any circumstances, and who feels particularly upset because she will become Queen in May. It is only March, but she thinks that someone who is about to be Queen certainly ought to be there. Moreover she knows that her mother would be happy for her to go, but unfortunately her mother is away and the aunt who is temporarily in charge regards ballet as 'unsuitable for a schoolgirl'. Even more unfortunately, Tessa meets Carry Carter (now calling herself Caroline) and this proves to be her undoing.

When Carry offers her the opportunity of going to the performance after all (Carry had been intending to take a young relative and so has two tickets), Tessa cannot resist taking it, her wish to be there on this glittering occasion over-riding any sense that she is behaving dishonourably. Carry Carter, despite her sophisticated appearance and manner, seems to harbour some childish feeling that by taking Tessa to the theatre she will be getting back at the Hamlet Club and all the misery it caused her so many years before. So Tessa goes to the ballet and has her enjoyment, but quickly repents, partly because she meets Miss Raven, the Headmistress, at the theatre and the latter assumes that Tessa's aunt has relented at the last minute. Tessa's better side comes to the fore and she confesses to Miss Raven.

Rosalind is now tested. Miss Raven will only consent to Tessa's being crowned in May if Rosalind will stay on for the summer term to take the lead and give Tessa more time to develop a proper sense of responsibility. The reader knows that Rosalind is looking forward, not so much to leaving school, but to spending the summer with Virginia who is expecting another baby in the autumn. Rosalind must thus make a sacrifice to help the Club out of its difficulty. Rachel, who has been consulted before Miss Raven puts forward the solution that has been suggested to her by Miss Verity, has assured Rosalind: 'There will be a way; there always is … I don't say it will be easy … you'll have to go ahead and see what you can make of it.' Once the proposal is made, Jansy points out that Rosalind 'can't forget the motto! "To be or not to be"—oh, Nanta Rose! You'll have to stand by the Club!' and, of course, Rosalind does.

In this book she becomes predominantly 'Nanta Rose' again. She tells Rosamund: 'It's no use, Aunt Rosamund. They won't call me Rosalind … They keep mixing us up.', and it may well be that EJO was beginning to feel overwhelmed by all her Roses too, particularly as Rosamund makes frequent appearances in this book. Perhaps for the same reason, Joy's little girl becomes 'Maidie-Rose', although at the end of the book Patch is allowed to name her girl baby 'Rosella Rose', which seems a shade excessive!

Once Tessa's affairs are settled, there is an interlude in which Damaris, preparing for her marriage to Brian Grandison, talks to Rachel about her bridesmaids and reveals that she is planning to bring Rosalind and Brian's young cousin, Derek, together, explaining that it 'would be so suitable … he's a rising young composer … It would be marvellous for Derek to have a beautiful and talented violinist for a wife!' The developing romance between Derek and Rosalind forms the central part of the book; as the title, which is also the title chosen by Derek for the piece of evocative music that he is inspired to compose about the Abbey, for Rosalind to play, shows, this is very much Rosalind's story.

However, an important minor event brings the reader up to date on the story of Patch Paterson and Bill Kane. It is while Rosalind is acting hostess at Kentisbury in her aunt's absence that Patch and Bill reappear, having married in Glasgow the previous day. Patch's family life has suddenly crumbled beneath her when her widowed father remarried and she has summoned Bill who has promptly married her so that he can provide her with a home. The Kentisbury household offers Patch a refuge when Bill, now a Naval Lieutenant, has to return to sea, gives her a training in childcare (although she has already been looking after her baby brother, just as Rosamund had done), and the end of the book sees Patch and Bill the triumphant parents of a set of mixed twins, Roger (after Patch's cousin) and Rosella.

It is interesting to remind ourselves at this point that only a few of EJO's characters—and they are on the periphery of the stories—pursue successful academic careers; EJO seems to have had a rather low opinion of university and college courses for girls, if the words that she puts into Patch's mouth are anything to go by: 'I went back to college; there seemed nothing else to do. But I couldn't work; I was reading history, and it just didn't seem to matter.' The only career for women is to be a wife and mother, and EJO pressed her characters into this role ever earlier. Even Jansy, who is one of her comparatively few characters said to be academically able, is, at fifteen, looking to the day she will marry Cicely's Dickon, although she does think that perhaps she will go to college first.

Rosalind's observation of the obviously very happy, newly-married Patch and Bill turns her thoughts in the direction that makes it possible for Damaris's matchmaking plans to bear fruit. She is nineteen and she has seen many happily married couples at the Hall and in the Abbey circle. Derek, like so many of EJO's heroes, falls for his destined bride as soon as he sets eyes on her as she follows Damaris up the aisle. (Not surprisingly in this essentially matriarchal society, Maidlin gives Damaris away, just as Mary-Dorothy had given Jen away at a previous Abbey wedding.) Back at the Manor, where the reception is being held at Jen's insistence, Derek asks Rachel to introduce him to Rosalind. EJO now makes a distinction between Rosalind and Jansy—they can no longer be seen as schoolgirls together. Derek is in awe of 'Lady Rosalind', but greets Jansy as 'Miss Pigtails', although her presence serves to make their initial conversation easy and lighthearted. Rosalind is thrilled to meet a real composer, music gives him the entrée to the Abbey circle, and, although he is warned not to go too fast with Rosalind by both Brian and Rachel, the romance develops steadily through their mutual interest in music.

Rosalind agrees to play his sonata for violin and piano, with Joy taking the piano part, during a weekend at the Hall. Derek, there for this reason, is shown round the Abbey by Rachel and immediately conceives the idea of a 'romance', putting the stories of the Abbey into music. From the first Rosalind is seen as a means of promoting Derek's career as a composer, and this idea, first mentioned by Damaris, is echoed by Virginia when she sees the way the wind is blowing, commenting 'she'd be the making of him in his career'. Rosalind herself is almost the last person to be aware of the developing romantic relationship between them.

The first performance of *The Song of the Abbey* forms part of a concert by the musicians from the Abbey circle—Maidlin sings, Jock plays his viola, Dr Grandison contributes some piano pieces, and a small orchestra accompanies *The Song of the Abbey*, which is a great success. Interestingly, Maidlin's plea that Lindy should sing is turned down—'too many novelties at one time'—and thus we have a hint that Lindy's story has still to be completed.

It is after this concert that Rosalind says she would like to get to know Derek better. He is invited to Summerton by Virginia, and soon after Rosalind's twentieth birthday he arrives in a car and, after a series of outings, asks her to marry him. The events of this book take place over a period of a year, during which Rosalind moves from being a schoolgirl to being a successful violinist and an engaged woman.

One of the things that brings Rosalind joy is the fact that they are going to live at Rainbows. Again, the brief description that appears in this book suggests that it was based on a place known to EJO. Rosalind tells her sister that it's 'beautiful now! ... trees have grown and it doesn't look bare and ragged any more ... every garden has those double flowering cherry trees ... It looks quite lovely.' The story ends with the idea that Derek may some day write a *Song of Rainbows*.

The music theme is very obvious in this book since it forms the central core of the plot. As far as babies are concerned, there are not only Patch's twins, who arrive pretty promptly, but Virginia produces an heir for Summerton, Charles Geoffrey, and Damaris, almost as soon as she is married, is joyfully anticipating 'Raimy', to be named for Rachel and Maidlin. We learn that Polly Paine, now Woodburn, gives birth to Margery Rose, and in the November copies of Rachel's first book, described as her 'first baby', arrive from the publishers. Thus, once again, EJO suggests that authors do not marry and that their books are their 'babies'. (This is rather ironic since it has been demonstrated over and over again elsewhere that the one thing a mother at home with her children can do, if she has the gift, is the writing of books.)

One incident in *The Song of the Abbey* that sticks in the throat a little is the 'squashing' of Carry Carter. Carry has not been able to get a ticket for Damaris's farewell performance, and rather unwisely she seeks Joy's help. Joy is gratuitously pompous and then boasts of her behaviour to the twins, Jansy and Rosalind. This may be characteristic of Joy, but it ill becomes an Abbey girl who has been given so much, and contrasts strangely with the kindness shown to Tessa and her friend, Phyl. Damaris, who has felt herself to blame for Tessa's downfall, is only too pleased to let Rosalind and Jansy invite them to inspect the wedding presents; gladly, Tessa and Phyl come, bearing wedding gifts, just as they are delighted to be invited to Rosalind's first concert performance. They are the fortunate ones who are accepted by the Abbey circle and provide a contrast to the rejected Carry, although they are still very much outsiders, not part of the magic inner group.

The twins, now fourteen, continue along their path of destiny to become joint Queens, although their immaturity still puts them amongst the younger schoolgirls. They are bridesmaids for Damaris, present bouquets at the concert, and attend both the performance at which Damaris makes her comeback and her farewell appearance, and Margaret plays for dancing. They show something of their earlier self-importance when they ask Derek to include the Abbey cat, Rory, in his music, but also show some mature judgment in choosing the cat rather than themselves, which is Margaret's first idea.

The return of Littlejan is anticipated. Her absence is regretted in the Hamlet Club crisis at the beginning of the book when Rosalind wails: 'If only Marigold would come back!' When Rachel's first book is published, Jansy plans to buy a copy to send to Littlejan, saying: 'She can read it on the voyage home, if they start soon.' But spring comes, Rosalind becomes engaged about a year after the Hamlet Club crisis, and Littlejan has still not returned. She, the twins and Lindy are all characters about whom there is more to be told.

In a letter of 20 December 1954, EJO showed that she was dissatisfied with the production of this particular book. There is a misprint (two lines reversed) on page 15, and she was critical of the frontispiece: '... they ought to be in wedding garments and Derek most certainly is not. They were coming back from the wedding dance in the barn. But I daresay nobody will think of that. He does not look dressed to be the best man!'

EJO's next book, *New Girls at Wood End*, was not published until 1957. Admittedly, EJO was not getting any younger, but there were also problems of delay in publication. Monica Godfrey reveals that:

> Originally it had been accepted as two short books for girls by a new publisher, but after two years both were returned because the firm which had accepted the pair was unable to publish them after all ... Four more years passed before Elsie found another firm to accept the two manuscripts which she then had to amalgamate to make one normal-length book.

It was finally published by Frederick Books (F Muller in association with Blackie). Combining two short books seems to have given EJO some trouble, but the final result is perfectly reasonable. In a letter written to an unknown correspondent on 11 January 1956 she says: 'I'm afraid Muller wants the book shortened a good deal. The two half-size books put together are too long so I am cutting out what I can and not adding anything.' In a later letter of 4 March 1957, she added: 'I don't think anything has been cut out except unnecessary explanations where the second story joins on.' It is clear from the earlier letter that EJO did not find the publisher's suggestions either helpful or relevant: 'I believe his people criticise just to show their own efficiency(?) and to keep me in my place. I don't believe he read the book himself.'

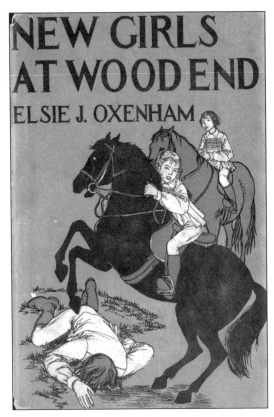

New Girls at Wood End has no illustrations, but the dust jacket was designed by Margery Gill. It is dedicated to EJO's great-nephews, although it tactfully hopes that 'they will read and love books', since they are unlikely to have wanted to read this one. The jacket blurb describes it as 'A junior school story by a well-known author', and it certainly seems to be aimed at a younger age group, probably a deliberate attempt to write for younger girls at the behest of the publisher to whom she had originally intended to offer it. But it is also a natural progression from her interest in the younger girls at the Wycombe school.

In time it is a retrospective book, following on from *Rosamund's Castle* and continuing the story of Wood End School as well as of Robin Brent, who is now the Head Girl. Robin seems to have been a favourite of EJO's—Monica Godfrey tells us that she said: 'I was so glad to find Robin in the story. It's pleasant to meet an old friend.' Benedicta also appears and, as the book is about Wood End School the gardening theme is well to the fore. Perhaps it was the return of Benedicta and the making of the Abbey garden that had turned EJO's thoughts back to Wood End when she was planning a book for younger girls.

In order to make this possible a change had to take place because Wood End was originally established to take only girls of fifteen and over. Now it is to have juniors, and we learn that this was planned for in the rebuilding after the fire that occurred in *Rosamund's Castle*. The first juniors are five in number, and they have all been accepted for special reasons. They include Miss Rainey's niece, Janine, and her goddaughter, Jean-Ann (a lovely play on names which is typically EJO), two sisters, Bridget and Moira, and a girl on her own, Diane, who is the eldest of the five. The existing seniors do not regard the advent of the juniors with much favour, but Robin is kind to them and wins their respect and admiration. Some of the sickly sentimentality has gone—Robin does not kiss her 'babes' goodnight, and although Miss Rainey asks for a kiss from her goddaughter and her niece, she is, in agreement with Janine and Jean-Ann, a headmistress most of the time.

In general, the book is about the escapades of the juniors and the reforming influence of the school on a sixth junior, Brenda Branden, who is added to their company. There is also the question of what makes a good leader. Diane, the eldest junior and their elected captain, proves to be too easily influenced. Janine, who has more character and more good sense, is a better influence on the younger ones, and though at first she refuses to take on Diane's job she is, at the end of the book, persuaded by Robin that it is something she must do for the sake of the school. Janine and Bridget, discussing the younger ones, especially Brenda, work out for themselves the value of the training the school provides for those whose ideas are not yet 'fixed', and come to the conclusion that they also, as elders, must play a part in this. It is EJO's familiar thesis of the influence of the older girls on their juniors, but presented in a more modern way.

Even in a school story, the 'baby' theme is not omitted. Lisabel Durrant, now Lisabel Courtney, returns to the school to fill in as gardening mistress, bringing her baby daughter Lisabel Rose with her. Once again, the girls' attitude is much less sentimental, although many of them are genuinely interested in the baby. Jean-Ann, a quiet, shy child, who reminds us a little of Elspeth Abbott, becomes the baby's chief admirer, is allowed to help with her and is therefore of great assistance when Lisabel is hurt in a riding accident. Jean-Ann efficiently changes nappies, mixes a bottle and feeds the baby, while the academic ladies stand back in helpless admiration! Her newly acquired skills give Jean-Ann a new confidence and win the respect of her contemporaries.

There is a central incident in which the juniors, when out of bounds picking bluebells for Robin's birthday, happen to witness a road accident. Some time later, when the school is listening to the news on the radio, a police message is broadcast, asking for witnesses to the same accident. The older juniors then have the excitement of being interviewed by the police and find that this is not at all a frightening experience. Something very much like this happened to Stella during her schooldays, and possibly EJO knew of a similar occurrence and, apart from making an exciting incident in the plot, hoped that it would reassure other small girls in the same situation.

It is not difficult to guess at the content of the two shorter stories from which this one was produced. Chapters 1–19, which include the arrival of the new juniors, the accident and the arrival of Brenda, make one neat whole, confirmed by the ending of Chapter 19, when Moira says with delight: 'And then we sha'n't be new girls at Wood End any longer … for Brenda will be much newer than we are.' This leaves us with the last nine chapters as a book in themselves, covering the arrival of Lisabel, the riding accident, the problem of looking after the new baby and the question of the best choice for junior captain.

Like *New Girls at Wood End*, *Tomboys at the Abbey* appeared in 1957, albeit under the Collins imprint, and is another retrospective book which does not quite fit into this last period of EJO's creativity. Although there is a certain amount of musical interest in the background, neither of these books really reflects the prevailing 'words and music' interest of this period, and in *Tomboys* there is no hint at all of the 'baby' theme which dominates most of the other books, including the Wood End title, at this time.

For the Abbey fan, *Tomboys at the Abbey* slots neatly in at the end of the other retrospective books and, immediately before *The Abbey Girls Go Back to School*, which must open in the following Autumn term—in fact Jen's unexpectedly early departure from school is foreshadowed in her remarks to Jack. *Tomboys* opens with the May Day celebrations at which Beetle is crowned as the latest Hamlet Club Queen, wearing her 'gaudy train of striped red, green and yellow', an event that was also described in the final chapter of *Selma at the Abbey*.

In the tradition of the later Abbey books that it is always summer at the Abbey, the events of *Tomboys* all take place in the summer term, beginning with the May Day crowning and ending with the summer fête. It must be one of the weakest of the Abbey books, due partly, perhaps, to EJO's declining powers but also to the restrictions caused by the need to slot it into such a small space of time. One cannot help feeling that the keen Abbey book

The room was in wild confusion. 'We're celebrating,' Jen explained.
(*Tomboys at the Abbey*)

reader, who were eagerly awaiting the advent of the latest instalment must have been very disappointed. Basically it is the story of Selma's Swedish cousin, Gudrun Palmgren, who comes to seek Joan's help in realising her ambition of becoming a Shakespearean actress.

Jen and Jack are living at the Hall. Jack's parents have moved to London so she is to be a boarder for this last term before she joins them. Jen has therefore decided to sacrifice

Hamlet Club activities during this summer term and play cricket (remember, we are back in the period when the younger girls were not allowed to play cricket as well as dance with the Hamlet Club), so that she can see as much as possible of Jack. To compensate, the two girls have been invited to live at the Hall, and they are therefore the first people to meet Gudrun, who has stayed overnight with Mrs Puddephat in the village.

Gudrun, who is nineteen although she looks younger when she first arrives at the Abbey, has come to London with her uncle (yet another sea captain), who is on a business trip, and has taken the opportunity, when he was called away to Manchester, to seek out the Abbey girls, of whose kindness she has been told by Selma. Her problem is that her grandmother with whom she lives (like so many other EJO heroines, she is, of course, an orphan) does not approve of her ambition to become an actress. Although she cannot approve Gudrun's action in deceiving her uncle, Joan is very sympathetic, and Gudrun, who has already spent a year at drama school, is offered elocution lessons with Miss Cameron—admittedly, she does need to improve her English if she is to act Shakespeare. Fortunately, Miss Cameron can do better than this and introduces her to a small touring company, the Nonesuch Players (whose name, of course, delights Joan and Joy), which specialises in Shakespearean productions. Grandmother is won over to Gudrun's viewpoint on her deathbed by the news that Gudrun is also to marry her cousin Karl, and on the day of the summer fête Joan receives a newspaper cutting telling of Gudrun's success as Viola, when one of the cast has been rushed to hospital for an emergency operation.

Thus *Tomboys at the Abbey*, despite its title, includes a romantic interest. Gudrun is loved by her cousin Karl, also a seaman, and, without too much difficulty, she comes to love him in return and they become engaged. This developing relationship gives EJO an opportunity to reflect a new view of marriage. Bluntly, Joy points out that Gudrun would be expected to give up her career when she marries, but Karl would be free to go to sea, leaving Gudrun at home, and would only come back to her between voyages. At the end, the two young people have agreed that each will pursue their chosen career. Karl tells Joan, Joy, Jen and Jack: 'It must be the same for both of us.'

All this, of course, takes place in the course of one term, and the relationship between Gudrun and Karl develops very quickly. Gudrun is called away to see her dying grandmother and Karl arrives to escort her back to Sweden. When they return to the Abbey shortly afterwards, she tells the other girls that 'some day, when he has passed his exams and I've had my first part in a real play', they will be engaged. Karl becomes a little less progressive in his ideas when he is actually faced with the reality of Gudrun joining the Nonesuch Players, but the appearance of the short, stout and bald manager and his motherly wife convinces him that Gudrun will be well looked after. Even as far as Gudrun is concerned, an incredible amount happens in about ten and a half weeks!

Did EJO, in view of her chosen title, originally intend *Tomboys* to be just a story of the four girls having fun in the Abbey and making new discoveries, and then put in Gudrun's story in order to give the plot some substance? Alongside the main plot is the discovery of more bits of the Abbey but these discoveries seem rather feeble. Joy tells Jen and Jack that the Hall used to be called 'Holyoake House' and challenges them to discover the reason for this—a holy oak, a hollow oak or perhaps an oak, covered with holly? It turns out to be a hollow oak, hiding the entrance to yet another tunnel, this time leading to the cloister garth. But the hollow oak may also have been a holy oak and Jen finds a drawing of

Ambrose planting the oak tree, reminding them that they had laughed when they first saw this, saying: 'Ambrose had taken to gardening in his old age'. The finding of this tree and the adventures in the tunnel (inevitably Jen and Jack are plunged into danger when the hollow oak falls over) are a means of bringing about a reconciliation between the two younger girls, who have had a misunderstanding over Jen's refusal to reveal the hiding place of the Abbey jewels.

The book displays EJO's fascination with jewels—the ruby that has been sold to pay for Angus's music lessons comes back to the Abbey as the old lady who had bought it had willed it back to the Abbey, her imagination captured by the story behind it. A pearl brooch is made for Gudrun to match her engagement ring, and brooches are also made out of the bits of the hollow oak for Jen and Jack. We can also observe EJO's fascination (it might almost be called an obsession) with the sea and with all things Scandinavian. In passing, it is interesting to observe that Swedish actresses were not unknown in the heyday of the cinema—by the 1950s Greta Garbo was a legend and Ingrid Bergman at the height of her career—and EJO could well have mentioned this. However, by this stage in her career, EJO was well aware of the dangers of linking fictional elements too closely to reality.

Joy's music is present in the background; her musical gifts contrast strangely with the enthusiasm with which she enters into the tomboy antics of Jack and Jen—apple-pie beds, a silent serenade, midnight feasts and pillow fights. Because the book has to fit into the sequence, characters can only be more of what they are already; they cannot develop. Joan is serious and responsible, Joy is blunt and unthinking, and Mrs Shirley is much loved and fragile. Susie Spindle appears briefly to reinforce the band that performs the silent serenade. The book does give EJO an opportunity to make references to the bad-tempered and unfriendly Mr Edwards at the farm next door, and also to tell some of Anne Manley's (we never learn her maiden name) earlier story. She appears as a shy, new girl of eleven, whom Jen suggests to Joan as a substitute maid when Jen wants to play cricket during the summer term. Inevitably, future events are foreseen:

> They would have been still more amused if they could have foreseen that seventeen years later, Jen's nine-year old daughter would be comforting Anne's shy little girl of eight years old, on her first day at school.

Anne also describes the colour and flower she would choose if ever she were to be chosen Queen: 'Clover … pink clover … And white clovers round the edge of the train, and some four-leaved ones for luck.'

Despite the restrictions of time, EJO errs only in two matters—she forgets that Jen grew tall after her accident and refers to her as 'tall' Jen, and, as has been noted before, she has Joy confidently driving a car while six months later the motor-cycle and side car is to be a novelty.

At the summer fête, on the penultimate page, Jen says to Joan: 'I thought at first it was going to be Jack's term, but now I believe I shall think of it as the Gudrun term.', to which Joan replies: 'I rather thought it was going to be the Tomboys' Term.' This neatly sums up the book, but it is perhaps the tomboy pranks which most of all make this story such a disappointment.

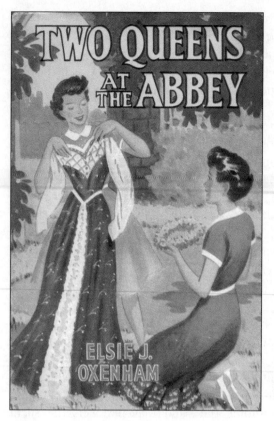

Some of the content of EJO's last book, *Two Queens at the Abbey*, published by Collins in 1959, the year before she died, has been obvious for some time; what is remarkable is the way in which she draws together all possible threads in her Abbey saga as well as achieving what has been, since their birth in *The Abbey Girls at Home*, the ultimate high point in the story, the crowning of Joy's twin daughters as Queens of the Hamlet Club. Their path to the throne, however, is not all plain sailing.

Two Queens at the Abbey opens as *Song of the Abbey* closes, and they must to some extent overlap. As the final chapters of the latter concentrated on Rosalind and her romance, the affairs of the Hamlet Club at that period have not been chronicled previously, and the reader needs to be brought up to date. *Two Queens* opens when Phyl (of Tessa and Phyl) has just been chosen as the Hamlet Club's next Queen, and the Marchwood twins are disappointed. With a little help from Rachel, still the Abbey 'adviser', they reason the matter out and come to realise that they, and in particular Margaret, are lacking in some quality requisite for a Queen.

In Chapter 2 we are given a hint that Phyl, whose full name is Phyllida—an echo of Phyllida Merton, perhaps—may not live up to the high standard required of a Queen of the Hamlet Club. Phyl herself says that she sometimes gets 'worked up over music … and nothing else seems to matter. I wouldn't mean to neglect the Hamlet Club, but I might not be able to help it.' And early in the term she begins to make muddles over dates of meetings and so on, and is not prepared to give up her own pleasure for the sake of the Club.

In the meantime Margaret is faced with a typical Abbey 'choice' situation. She is chosen to be leader of the school orchestra, a post she has long coveted, but the position matters desperately to Jennifer, the other candidate. When Margaret learns how much it means to Jennifer, after a silent struggle with her own feelings, and supported but not influenced by Elizabeth, she relinquishes the position in Jennifer's favour and earns the respect and admiration of the rest of the school. Her sacrifice is rewarded—after the end-of-term concert, Jennifer leaves the school and Margaret becomes the leader of the orchestra.

It is interesting that one of Margaret's anxieties is whether her mother will be annoyed that she should give up the leadership of the orchestra in favour of Jennifer. In fact, Joy is approving and supportive, saying: 'I'd have been proud to see Margaret lead the orchestra, but I'll be much more proud to see her playing under Jennifer. I'm glad and happy that she's been so brave.' It is Ivor Quellyn, the twins' stepfather, who voices disapproval and is firmly silenced by Joy. Perhaps Joy shows in the best possible light because in this book she stands at the centre of the Abbey circle, if only because she lives on the spot, with the Abbey in her back garden.

As her year of office continues Phyl shows little sense of her responsibilities as Queen. A crisis comes when she fixes a date for a Hamlet Club dance on an evening when she herself is going to a concert, and no former Queen is available to direct proceedings. From the Club members comes an appeal to the twins to run the party, which they do with great success, thus confirming their suitability as Queens. In February the decision is made, the colours and flowers are chosen—the Buttercup and Daisy Queens—and arrangements for the Coronation put in train. There is one more obstacle, clearly designed to enable yet another thread to be drawn in, when Margaret gets chicken pox and the crowning has to be postponed. But this is so much in the tradition of the Abbey stories (how often has illness on the part of the twins been used to develop a

The twins were running the party.
(*Two Queens at the Abbey*)

particular plot?) that it is quite acceptable here. The penultimate chapter of the book describes the ceremony, leaving the final one for recapitulation.

Not content with the twin Queens, EJO was determined that there should be one grandchild for the Abbey girls before their story ended. Just as Jandy Mac was introduced in a retrospective book to provide an older girl when a new generation was needed, now it is Littlejan who returns to the Abbey at nineteen, after an absence of nearly three years. She announces that she is married but her name is still Fraser, though her husband, Len, is no relation to her own family—this seems an unnecessary complication. Predictably, he is connected with the sea, having been the radio officer on her father's ship, and is now about to join an expedition to the Antarctic. This, as with the expedition undertaken by Lexa's parents in *A Holiday Queen* so many years before, shows that, although she ignored the war and many of the social changes that took place afterwards, EJO was at least aware of some contemporary events, in this case the Commonwealth Trans-Antarctic Expedition led by Sir Vivien Fuchs in 1955–58. The fact that Len will be away on his expedition for two years has brought Littlejan back to the Abbey so that she can go 'back to school'. She does just this but it is not long before she is overtaken by motherhood and produces a son, John Lennox.

Littlejan's wish for a house near the Abbey gives EJO the chance to add one more bit— an unused plot of land, very suitably sited, turns out to have been the old Herb Garden and, as usual, she manages to convince the reader that it has always been there. All goes well with Littlejan until just after her baby boy is born, when the news comes that her husband has been heroically involved in a serious accident in the Antarctic. It is not easy to understand the reason for this particular disaster, unless it is to provide one more chance for EJO to express her own personal view on why such things happen. This theme has already occurred in the book when Jansy and Dickon Everett discuss the reasons for the death of Dickon's sister, Shirley Rose. Littlejan, plus baby, eventually flies out to Australia to cheer Len in hospital, but all of them return to England just in time for Littlejan to be present at the twins' coronation.

Rosalind's wedding provides a suitable interlude in the course of the book, and before the story ends we hear that she is also having a baby. There are still plenty of babies to arrive, and just before or during the course of this book new ones come for Jen (no 9!), Maidlin, Rosamund, Damaris and Robin.

Belinda Bellanne is another character whose story is revived and brought to what is, for EJO, a happy conclusion. As Littlejan sails up the Channel in Chapter 2, Lindy's first major concert is being broadcast—a great success—and we later learn that she is to fulfil her ambition to sing in *Elijah* with Maidlin. Lindy is all set for success, but she has a problem in the person of a persevering elderly admirer called Sir Konrad Abrahams. It is surprising that in 1958 EJO was allowed by her publishers to have a character like this in her book. He is like the typical 'nasty man' in a novel of the 1920s or '30s: rich, fat and distinctly unattractive, pursuing young girls with offers of 'the best of everything'. Lindy is his immediate object but apparently 'any girl will do if she's young and fresh and attractive'. He spends his money lavishly in the world of music, trying to gain favour in that particular society and access to pretty young girls.

For the 1950s he just isn't real, and there is an unpleasant undercurrent that does not escape the modern reader and did not escape many of those who read the book when it was first published. The name 'Konrad Abrahams' has distinct Jewish overtones. Regina Glick, Jewish herself, and an admirer and collector of EJO's books saw this when she read the book on publication. As she told us:

> 'When I read *Two Queens at the Abbey* I was disturbed by the portrayal of Sir Konrad Abrahams which, I felt, hinted at an anti-Semitic attitude on the part of Miss Oxenham, though there had never been even the remotest hint of this in any of her books. As I had corresponded with her for about fifteen years and she had found books for me and lent me books, I felt I could mention this to her. She replied immediately, assuring me that Sir Konrad Abrahams was not meant to be Jewish— and that many nationalities had biblical names.'

It is difficult to understand how EJO could have been so naïve or so innocent as not to realise the implications of such a character with such a name, although it is true that, with her complete exclusion of the Second World War from her books and the lives of her characters, she retained the standards and social rules of the 1920s and '30s; for example, much is made of Littlejan's married status to provide a 'chaperone' for Lindy. There is also no hint of any sexual motive in Sir Konrad's chasing of young girls—but neither is there any mention of marriage!

In an attempt to avoid 'Sir K' (as he is referred to), Lindy and Littlejan take refuge in

Maidlin and Jock's bungalow, Step Down, one of EJO's little 'dream houses', which now becomes a welcome sanctuary for Lindy. Happily, a solution to Lindy's problem appears in the shape of Jock's nephew, Donald Robertson, last heard of in *Maid of the Abbey*, when he was seriously paying court to Maidlin and was cut out by his uncle. At some point in the earlier book Jock did actually suggest 'we'll marry him to your little soprano' and, after a confrontation between Donald and Sir K, Donald and Lindy become engaged.

Jansy Raymond, although too young for a real romance, and in spite of the fact that she is expected to go to college, perhaps even university, being the first Abbey girl to be academically inclined since Miriam Honor, has her 'understanding' with Dickon Everett pretty well confirmed, after spending six weeks with the President and her family on a cruise.

This final book must be assessed on two counts. Taken purely as a story for girls published in 1959, it is very much behind the times. Only six or seven years later a book about an unmarried pregnant schoolgirl was to be published for young people! *Two Queens at the Abbey* is very contrived, with a particular aim in view, and can hardly have attracted a new reading public. But for readers of EJO and followers of the fortunes of the Abbey girls, it brings all the loose threads together and leaves everyone comfortably settled down for the future. In a radio programme, *Stop the Week with Robert Robinson*, broadcast on Saturday 2 June 1984, just as we were coming to the end of writing our original study, it was suggested that the appeal of the girls' school story—Angela Brazil and the like—was its presentation of a safe, ordered, fantasy world. Although not school stories, EJO's Abbey series provides just that.

Chapter 11

CONCLUSION

I n November 1984, just as we were preparing to write the final chapter in our original study, a first edition of *Girls of the Hamlet Club* was offered for sale in the Bookmark Phoenix Catalogue at what we then felt must be a record price of £32.50. This would have proved a very sound investment since prices have soared in the last twenty years, helped by an increasing number of collectors with more money to spend and no doubt encouraged by buying and selling on the internet. The chances of finding a bargain in a charity shop or secondhand bookshop nowadays are almost nil—most people who have anything to do with secondhand books are well aware of the prices that the rarer titles, especially if they are in good condition and have dustjackets, can command.

The relatively high prices that were being asked for some titles, such as *Girls of the Hamlet Club* and *Joy's New Adventure*, twenty years ago were undoubtedly due to the fact

that some of the key books in the Abbey series were published in fairly small print runs and therefore had a rarity value. Many of the Abbey books, on the other hand, were reprinted in great quantities and were therefore easy to find and relatively cheap to acquire. The collector, hooked on collecting through the readily available titles, was then prepared to pay high prices to obtain the more elusive volumes. For some collectors, the problem of missing titles was solved by the purchase of photocopies, but many people wished to upgrade the titles they already had and were prepared to pay high prices for copies in good condition. All this is still true, and the price of good copies has risen steadily over the last twenty years; nowadays, the growing number of collectors includes some who want not only the best copy they can buy but also variant editions.

The establishment of the *The Abbey Chronicle* and the Elsie J Oxenham Appreciation Society in 1989 led to the publication of two hitherto unpublished manuscripts by EJO. Three such manuscripts were evidently rejected by her publishers; two of these were discovered by her niece, Wendy Dunkerley, and were published with the support of members of the Society. These were *A Divided Patrol*, the fourth book about Jinty, and *Deb*

Leads the Dormitory, the third story about Deb Lely, and discussed earlier along with the other books about Jinty and Deb. The third was an historical novel set in Elizabethan times, *The Lily Maids of Meddyn*, but this remains unpublished; the title seems to suggest a Welsh setting, but the rest is speculation.

The existence of *The Abbey Chronicle*, *The Abbey Guardian* (Australia), *The Abbey Gatehouse* (New Zealand), *Friends of the Chalet School*, *The New Chalet Club Journal*, *Serendipity*, *Souvenir* and *Folly* has also helped to create an interest in collecting authors such as EJO, Elinor Brent-Dyer, Dorita Fairlie Bruce, Violet Needham and other writers of girls' stories whose books were published in the first half of the twentieth century. Their pages provide a way of publicising new books in the field, and the specialist publishers Girls Gone By are providing a very useful service by republishing titles such as *Rosamund's Castle* and *Margery Meets the Roses* in attractive editions with introductory notes, but as these go out of print they too are likely to be offered for sale at premium prices.

Those of us who were schoolgirls in the early 1940s had a special problem as far as EJO's books were concerned. In the case of Elinor Brent-Dyer and Dorita Fairlie Bruce, copies of their books usually contained a complete list of the other titles in the series, and one could therefore search for them in libraries, bookshops or amongst friends. Because EJO's books came from so many different publishers, few of them listed more than two or three other titles, and one had no idea of how many Abbey books there were, or of their reading order.

Although there is no proof of the fact, observation suggests that EJO's books have been even more eagerly collected than those of her contemporaries, and her popularity is undoubtedly due to the fact that many of her other books link into the Abbey story, albeit, in some cases, rather tenuously. The interlinking of characters and events gives a special texture to her stories, as well as providing the appeal of a long-running soap opera for the reader and that of a treasure hunt for the collector.

From man's earliest days the fairy tale has been an essential part of popular entertainment, while since the end of the eighteenth century and the rise of the modern English novel, the Gothic novel has enjoyed continuing popularity. EJO combines the more attractive elements of both in many of her books. We have commented several times on EJO's use of the Cinderella story. In fact, a better term might be the 'fairy-tale princess motif'. Sometimes the princess has fallen on evil days, usually seen in terms of poverty (Eilidh Munro, Joy Shirley), but sometimes she is already in comfortable circumstances when she comes into her kingdom (Robin Brent, Rosamund Kane), and sometimes, even, she is already established in that kingdom when the story begins, but must learn how to cope with her responsibilities (Lexa Stewart).

As Nicholas Tucker wrote in an article in *New Society* in November 1973:

> The real focus of fairytale attention remains the Princess herself, whether she is the victim of traumatic christenings, the object of doting love (or jealous hatred), the recipient of portentous omens, or the cause of ardent courtship.

In the same article, he points out that it is difficult to think of any more appealing literary image than the fairy-tale princess. This was a secret upon which EJO stumbled early in her literary career, and she continued to make use of it until the end—the fact that her princesses enjoy the title of Countess or Queen is neither here nor there.

Attention in EJO's books tends to focus on the very rich and the very poor—the landed gentry on the one hand, their servants, or the people to whom good can be done, on the other, just as the fairy tale is concerned with the high-born (kings, queens, princes and princesses) and the humble (the poor woodcutter or maidservant). In the tradition of the fairy tale, EJO was able to carry off certain anomalies or near impossibilities which would certainly not worry her readers. Although there are no magical rings, nor pumpkins that turn into coaches, the stories often leave the impression of such magic in the reader's mind.

EJO took the fairy tale one stage further—towards the Gothic romance. EJO's great houses—Plas Quellyn, Castle Charming, Kentisbury Castle and Gracedieu Abbey—are all the very stuff of Gothic romance. One is, incidentally, reminded of Catherine Morland's reflections, when she goes to stay at Northanger Abbey and is able to compare the reality with the stories that she has read about 'abbeys and castles, in which … all the dirty work of the house was to be done by two pair of female hands at the utmost'. In EJO's houses, as in the Gothic romance, there is little evidence of the staff that must have been necessary to run them. House servants, gardeners, chauffeurs are only mentioned when they are essential to the plot. Workmen and gardeners must have been there to contribute to the upkeep of the Abbey, but one is never conscious of anyone except Ann Watson, the Abbey girls or, of course, the occasional intruder.

The way in which the girls come into fortunes and cope so beautifully with their new affluence is pure escapism—it is interesting to note that the two boys who enjoy the same good fortune—Lord Larry and Geoff, the young Earl of Kentisbury—are absolute disasters in the situation. EJO's heroines look forward to a life 'happy ever after' and in many cases the reader witnesses it. The fairy tale goes on.

In most of her books EJO painted on a very broad canvas, and few of them, in fact, have a single heroine. The role is often shared, even when the title suggests otherwise. Rosaly is not the central character in *Rosaly's New School*, for example, and Robin and Gwyneth share the central position in *The Girl Who Wouldn't Make Friends*. Although EJO is concerned with the high and the low, she does manage to give an impression of the wider world in which the characters move. Her books, therefore, have the attraction of an unsophisticated and relatively untroubled 'comédie humaine'.

Against this wider landscape, EJO skilfully manipulates her characters. Although she had a strong sense of place—and most of her settings can and have been identified—she soon gave up any attempt to place events in time. A few of the earlier books are tied to the period of the First World War, and of course there are the two historical novels, but in general she ignored world events, and this is particularly obvious as so many of her books were written in the period leading up to and during the Second World War—a parallel with Jane Austen's ignoring the Napoleonic Wars does not seem inappropriate here. Only in a couple of books does EJO even hint at the possibility of the Second World War—and this in books that were published when it was nearly over. This timelessness meant that she could revive Robin Brent, last seen as a twelve-year-old in 1909, as a teenager in 1937. However, the books do tend to reflect, if only in general terms, the period at which they were written. As has been observed, the main problem caused by this cavalier treatment of time is in references to transport. The first fifty years of the twentieth century saw more technological changes in terms of personal transport (carriages and carts to cars and aeroplanes) and communications (the advent of the telephone and radio) than in the whole history of mankind before 1900, and these were changes that could not be ignored.

It is only when one reads the books in the order in which they were published that one begins to realise how skilfully EJO built on her characters and places. In her very last book, *Two Queens at the Abbey*, she was able to add a herb garden to the Abbey treasures in a convincing manner, but there are, as has been shown, many earlier examples of this skilful grafting. Rosamund's aristocratic connections are not mentioned until long after Rosamund is a well established character. EJO's most notable achievement in this respect, however, is the creation of Jandy Mac and her insertion into the Abbey story; her only real failure was her inability to build Damaris's early ballet training into Damaris's story before *Damaris Dances*. Although plot construction and character motivation were not always sound, EJO can be commended for the way in which all her books work as individual titles. The recapitulation necessary to put the new reader fully in the picture is cleverly done. Although she whets the appetite for other books in the series, she does not make them essential to an understanding of the story. In this respect she outclasses Elinor Brent-Dyer, who frequently has her characters talking about events and incidents in past books in a way that is not really necessary to the story currently being told.

The bibliographical problems posed by EJO's work are very much a reflection of the period during which she wrote. For much of this time children's books were not very highly regarded, and, although these books appealed to girls in their teens, they were essentially children's books. Publishers tended to behave in a very high-handed way, buying copyright outright and then making changes without informing, or consulting with, the author. Good public-library provision for young people was not widely developed until the 1950s, and in the 1920s and 1930s was distinctly patchy. EJO's books were published to be bought by individuals rather than by institutions, although some of her titles did appear in the lists of recommended books published by the Library Association in the 1920s, *Books for Youth*. At 2/6 or 3/6 a volume, they made good Christmas and birthday presents. Up to the 1940s, magazines, annuals and collections of stories—the famous 'bumper' books—formed the staple reading diet of many young people, and, as we have seen, many of EJO's books originally appeared in this way. Many children's books were published without the date of publication being indicated in the book; although it is possible to date most of the novels from the British Museum Catalogue, the same is not true of the annuals and collections.

The fact that the market for children's books until after the Second World War, which marked the beginning of the development of both public children's libraries and school libraries, was composed of individuals rather than institutions also accounts for the cheap Seagull editions and the abridged editions issued by the Children's Press, both of which were published by Collins. The Children's Press books were also a response to the advent of mass paperbacks for children around 1960—although Puffin Story Books began to appear in 1941, they had the children's paperback market to themselves for twenty years, and their emphasis was very much on quality rather than on popular books. However, there was still a demand for hardback books from adults buying for presents or prizes, and from libraries on limited budgets, and the series of hardbacks published by the Children's Press and a few other publishers found a ready market. These were also a godsend to young keen readers, who could buy hardbacks at pocket-money prices.

The way in which books are published at any given period to some extent accounts for the way in which authors write. As far as EJO is concerned, the whole situation is confused by the fact that EJO's books were not necessarily published in the order in which they were written, nor in the form in which she originally wrote them, again a reflection of the prevailing conditions of publishing for the young. Coincidentally, the modern 'golden age' of children's literature is said to have begun in 1960, the year after the publication of EJO's last book.

Girls who read many of EJO's books when or soon after they were published are now in their seventies and eighties; even girls who read *Two Queens at the Abbey* soon after it was published are now in their fifties. Some of them may have held or may hold positions of power and influence; many are mothers and grandmothers. Since EJO wrote for, and must have been widely read by, girls in circumstances not far removed from her own—middle-class girls, with much the same moral and social code, who would continue their education until they were seventeen or eighteen, who might go on to college or into one of the very limited number of professions open to them—what kind of ideas was she putting forward which they might absorb at a very impressionable period of their lives?

EJO had a very clear philosophy that emerges strongly from her work. She encourages an optimistic view of life—one should not be dissatisfied with the way things are; one should expect things to work out for the best; one should make a positive contribution to society; and, most important of all, when faced with a choice between two courses of action, one must choose the right course, the one that will be best for the community in which one lives. This philosophy is reflected in the two themes that emerge from EJO's books—survival and sanctuary represented by 'island' and 'abbey'—which we have noted in our discussion of all EJO's books. One survives through optimism and finds sanctuary in a happy ending. This may be an over-simplification, but it's not a bad approach to life!

In EJO's work, there is a curious mixture of socialism and snobbery. She was a great admirer of John Hampden and the Puritans. She loved the idea of the community, although her communities tend to be run by a benevolent despot rather than a committee. Her ideas about arts and crafts, gardening, folk dancing and the Welsh and Gaelic languages sit as happily in the early twenty-first century as they did in her lifetime. Her books even reflect the leisured society into which more people moved during the course of the twentieth century. She emphasises the need to share beautiful things and good fortune. She sees the girls' organisations—Camp Fire and Guides—as forces for good because they encourage girls to seek better things for their children.

At the same time, her heroines are frequently snobbish about the accents and tastes of those less fortunate than themselves. In not criticising this behaviour, EJO was reflecting pre-1939 attitudes and the great divide that existed between girls who lived protected lives and those who went out to work in factories or as domestic servants as soon as they left school at fourteen.

The careers chosen by EJO's characters tend to be in the arts (ballet, theatre, music, writing), but she also had a high regard for cooking and shopkeeping, although a surprisingly low one for teaching. Her most adventurous choice was gardening, a career in which women are still rarely to be found in senior posts and in which the largest training institution at Swanley was apparently not open to women until 1939. If girls needed to have jobs, EJO emphasised the need for proper training—Rosamund goes off to train in cookery, Lisabel and Rena in gardening and so on. There is, of course, Lexa's mother who goes off with her husband to explore the South Polar region before 1911. This is an area where few women have ventured until comparatively recently, and a memorable television programme,

The Worst Place on Earth, shown early in 1985, showed that even the formidable Mrs Scott did not accompany her husband thither.

The attraction of the girls' school story was that it created a miniature world in which the female could dominate and fulfil a positive role. EJO went one step further in creating a female-dominated world, an adult society in which women seem to have great freedom but usually marry and have children, and thereafter have a loyal duty to husband and children. Few of her heroines pursue careers once they are married. This reflected contemporary thinking when the books were written; in many professions, up to the outbreak of the Second World War, young women were required to resign on marriage. This was true of teaching, local government and the Civil Service, for example.

EJO seems to have been strongly influenced by an idea that presumably did prevail amongst the reasonably well-to-do middle classes in the 1920s and early 1930s—that girls who did not need to work should not take jobs from those who did. We would have thought that a much more common reason for not training girls for careers was that it was thought to be a waste of money, when they would marry and leave them at an early stage. However, whatever the reason (and EJO's reason may have been more logical for her purposes, as, if she'd set up a conflict between a girl and her parents, it would have had to have been resolved somehow in the girl's favour), the role of girls was generally seen as helping at home until such time as they married; if they did not marry, they looked after their parents and did good works.

Perhaps because she herself did not marry (and had no desire to do so?), EJO seems to have had a very simplistic view of courtship and marriage, even allowing for the fact that she was writing for girls in their teens. Those men destined to marry into the Abbey circle fall in love the moment they set eyes on their prospective bride; sometimes they are ousted by a rival, in which case they are seen not to have been in earnest in the first place, so that nobody is really hurt. The women usually profess not to be interested until the moment when they finally give in gracefully. Only Joy seems to suffer any doubts and pangs about the intentions of her future husbands— significantly, perhaps, she is the only one who marries twice.

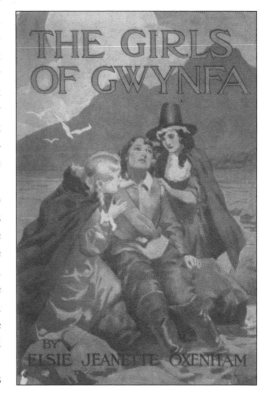

Of EJO's main characters, only a handful do not marry; marriage was regarded as women's true destiny, even though many women in the 1920s and 1930s could not marry because the men who would have been their husbands had been killed during the First World War. At the same time, during the two World Wars women did step in and take over many roles, so the female-dominated society that EJO portrayed was not a complete fiction.

EJO is much stronger on the relationships

between her female characters and particularly on those between sisters, which presumably reflects her own experience. Some of her most attractive and successful characters are the mature female observers—Marjorie Rogers in *Dorothy's Dilemma*, Ruth Devine, Monica Howard and Jandy Mac. Married, her heroines become powers behind the throne—Jen with Ken, Rosamund with Geoffrey. Although girls do not generally inherit titles, and many of EJO's heroines have no brothers to inherit the estates, some odd things do happen—Robin's acquisition of Plas Quellyn is perhaps explicable, but why does Jen, rather than her brothers, inherit the Grange? Very realistically, and perhaps accidentally, EJO recognised that money provides freedom, and most of her central characters either have it or get it. While EJO could never be considered a campaigner for women's rights, she never doubts that a woman is perfectly capable of running a large estate or able to bring up a child alone, while her heiresses do not allow themselves to be browbeaten by their lawyers.

Of course EJO can be criticised—for her obsession with twins, for her ruthless disposal of parents (at least the fact that many of the fathers are seamen preserves them from the fate of the early death met by so many of the mothers), and for her insularity (she is good on England, Scotland and Wales, but fails to make much of her Swiss and French settings, as can be seen only too clearly when one looks at what Elinor Brent-Dyer made of the idea that she apparently took from EJO—an English school in a foreign setting). The twins and the seafaring males occur over and over again, as do the Scandinavian names and the cats.

Those early books designed as full-length novels, rather than those which first appeared as serials or were cobbled together from shorter stories, undoubtedly represent EJO's best work in their loving and detailed descriptions of the countryside, their convincing characterisation and their properly constructed plots. Her later books, and particularly those written after the early 1940s, seem to have been affected by the demands and requirements of her publishers, although the attraction of the Abbey saga no doubt kept her young readers and caused mothers—and grandmothers—to introduce her to their daughters, not always successfully. Everyone has their own particular favourites—perhaps the book that introduced them to the Abbey chronicles, or one that was read at a time when it seemed to have something special to offer, or one set in a place known to the reader.

How much of EJO herself is reflected in the character of Mary Devine? Were her early creative efforts, like Mary's, disparaged by her father? *Goblin Island*, although about young people, seems to have been written for the adult reader. Did early reactions to her work cause her to move into writing for young people, a field in which she was not competing with her father? Did she live in a dream world peopled by her creations? Was she, like Mary, in danger of losing touch with reality? Perhaps she was fortunate to live in an age when girls were not expected to pursue conventional careers, where middle-class homes had at least one domestic help, and where there was time for writing—and a market for it. Few people can now contemplate making a living out of writing in the way that EJO and many of her contemporaries did.

Whatever lies behind the story of EJO and her work, she certainly managed, through her stories, to bring many hours of pleasure to countless readers. As Jessica Mann wrote in *Deadlier than the Male*, 'where the collective enthusiasm of a large number of readers is aroused, it is fair to declare that the personality of the writer echoes, and his work expounds, a more than individual passion'. EJO created and wrote about people and events in a way that inspired a very corporate passion.

Postscript

FROM SCOTLAND TO SUSSEX—AND A DIVERSION TO ANNECY: THE GEOGRAPHY BEHIND EJO'S BOOKS

These notes are based on visits that we have made since 1990. First, we must pay tribute to Eva Löfgren, who taught Sheila the art of researching and looking at sites used by girls' writers during a visit to Dorita Fairlie Bruce country in the 1980s, to all the contributors to *The Abbey Chronicle* who have written about these places, and to the people to whom we have talked over the years and who, in some cases, have accompanied us to sites, especially Chris Keyes, Gillian Priestman and Doreen Litchfield. We have given the year in which we visited each place—things may have changed since, although we found so much that hadn't changed since EJO knew the places that any major changes seem unlikely.

Scotland

EJO had very close links with Scotland; her mother was Scottish, her parents were married in Greenock and her maternal grandmother had a holiday house in Dunoon. She spent many of her holidays on the west coast of Scotland, where she set some of her early books and also sited Vairy Castle, the Scottish home of the Kanes of Kentisbury.

During our visit to Scotland in 2001, we explored the area that EJO loved and knew best, approaching it via the road up the west coast and passing through Inverkip, the name that was given to the house in Worthing that EJO shared with her sister Maida. North of the Clyde lie, from east to west, Loch Lomond, Gare Loch, Loch Long, Holy Loch, Loch Striven, Loch Riddon and Loch Fyne, all of which feature in her books.

Loch Lomond, an inland loch, becomes the Loch Avie of *Goblin Island*—it has several islands, and their real names and those of places on its shore are echoed in EJO's fictional names; Innis Beg (Inverbeg), Balmona (Balmaha), Ben Aan (Ben Eich) are all in the right place in relation to Luss (Lios). In *Schoolgirls and Scouts* Jill Colquhoun says 'my Loch Avie is a lake', different from the other nearby lochs that are 'bits of the sea running up amongst the hills'.

To the west of Loch Lomond lies Gare Loch, the loch by which Patch Paterson lives. In the first chapter of *The Secrets of Vairy*, Roger and Bill arrive near the head of the loch to be rowed across to Craigard by Patch and Christina Rosalin. There is mention of the smoke of nearby towns and shipbuilding yards, a reference to Helensburgh and Glasgow, and of the large estates and mansions surrounded by trees alongside the loch. One of these estates must be Glenleny, to which Elspeth Buchanan had travelled in *Schoolgirls and Scouts* some thirty fictional years earlier.

On the other side of the hills on the western side is Loch Long where Morven in *A Holiday Queen* and Vairy Castle occupy the same site on the eastern shore—in reality, Knockderry Castle on the Rosneath Peninsula. When we were there, the Castle appeared to be uninhabited—not a ruin but surrounded by thick undergrowth and looking much like the castle of the Sleeping Beauty. The Knockderry Hotel next door is a splendid survival of Edwardian splendour, and EJO must have surely visited it during her Scottish holidays; it would have been an inviting place for tourists in the early part of the twentieth century, served by the steamers which ran regular services around the lochs. EJO, accustomed to the steamer service, seems to have been unaware of how long it takes to reach places by road. From Knockderry to Dunoon by steamer would be a short and easy journey but it is about fifty miles by car!

Dunoon, frequently mentioned in *A Holiday Queen*, stands on the Firth of Clyde, near the entrance to Holy Loch, which is also the Loch Shee of Dorita Fairlie Bruce's books. Both EJO and DFB mention a little loch on the A815 between Dunoon and Sandbank (DFB's Lochside). In *Daring Doranne*, Doranne admires a picture painted by her aunt who says: 'That's the lochan—the little loch, near Dunoon, just across the water from Inverkip. The water-lily loch, some people call it.'

Loch Striven, which comes next—and the head of which is passed on the B826 from Sandbank to Loch Riddon—seems of little interest even today, but in *Schoolgirls and Scouts* Eilidh Munroe says to Elspeth '… don't you think Loch Striven, up there, is very beautiful?' as they pass the mouth of it on the day that Eilidh brings her yacht to carry Elspeth and her siblings off to her home on Loch Ruel. Loch Ruel is the name EJO gives to Loch Riddon in *A Princess in Tatters*, in which Eilidh is living with the Maclachan family on a farm near the head of the loch, almost certainly on the eastern side. We drove down the western side to Tighnabruaich, surely the Innistraive of *A Princess in Tatters*. EJO probably used a little poetic licence in her descriptions of sailing trips, with more water being covered in the time allowed than would have been possible in reality. From Tignabruaich, we turned west to the shores of Loch Fyne, on the western side of which stands Inverary Castle, the home of the Dukes of Argyll. Ruth Allen has suggested that this might be the model for Vairy, although it's in the wrong place. It is square with pepperpot towers and certainly has the 'white turrets' of Vairy. As EJO had appropriated the splendours of Arundel Castle for Kentisbury, it seems likely that she would requisition Inverary for Vairy, the fictional name echoing the real one.

The Lake District

The Lake District, having been 'discovered' by Wordsworth and some of his fellow poets, was well established as a place for holidays by the early twentieth century. EJO must have visited it, and is not the only writer to have made use of its landscape in fiction. It features in her work mainly in connection with Maidlin and her cousins, Rachel and Damaris. We had two unexpected bonuses on our trip there in 1993. The first was an exhibition at Abbot Hall in Kendal of the sketches made in 1952 by Ivor Hitchens for a mural at Cecil Sharp House, which portrayed Morris dances, the Horn Dance, a May Queen and country dancers and musicians of all kinds. We also visited Brantwood, the Lakeland home of John Ruskin, where there was an exhibition of the robes worn by the Queens at the

Whitelands College ceremonies, from which EJO may have taken ideas for the Hamlet Club.

From near Penrith we took the A592, which runs down one side of Ullswater, and then went over the Kirkstone Pass. In *A Dancer from the Abbey* Rachel walks from Crossrigs, the Ellerton farm, to Ullswater and plans to come back this way. We felt sure that Hikers' Halt was on what is now a narrow but well-made road that leads from the top of the Kirkstone Pass down into Ambleside. We found a possible site for Crossrigs, guided by a description early in *Maidlin to the Rescue*. After Rachel and Damaris have been sitting on the hill above Windermere, they come down to the road and face a 'long tramp' home. Turning their backs on one town (Ambleside?), they go along the side of Rydal Water, pass through another small town (Grasmere?) and then pass from Westmoreland into Cumberland. On one side of the road, the A591, is Helvellyn, 'towering above the fells', and a track goes off to Grisedale Tarn. Later in *Maidlin to the Rescue* Jen and Maidlin go to look at Crossrigs, and Maidlin recalls that the farm is 'just over the boundary line'. This fact is reinforced by the account of Rachel and Damaris's visit in *A Dancer from the Abbey*. Grasmere is much as it is described in *Maidlin to the Rescue*—the church, the graves of the Wordsworth family and the place with a garden by the river 'looking across at the church'. We were amazed, however, to find a Baldry's Café, and had our coffee there—presumably 'Baldry' is a local name.

Yorkshire and Derbyshire

Yorkshire is a large county and EJO made use of three distinct parts of it—the north-eastern area around Saltburn, Whitby and Goathland; an area further inland centred on Harrogate, and the southern part to the west and north of Sheffield. We visited the Yorkshire sites on two different occasions, combining the parts around Goathland and Harrogate in 1996 and visiting the area north of Sheffield in 1993.

North Yorkshire is the setting for *Rosaly's New School*, *At School with the Roundheads*, *Finding her Family* and *A School Camp Fire*, all published between 1913 and 1917. It is an area rich in abbeys and traditional folk dances, and EJO obviously knew it very well. One of her brothers went to school in York and another worked with the Beach Missions, which may have been reasons for her visits to the area. Moving further inland for *A School Camp Fire* was perhaps due to the fact that this coast was bombarded by the Germans during the First World War; Harrogate has been a popular spa town since the late nineteenth century and is somewhere that EJO might well have visited. We made our base at Goathland, which nowadays is famous for the restored North Yorkshire Railway and for the ITV soap opera *Heartbeat* and its spin-off, *The Royal*. We spent a day exploring Goathland itself. At Beck Hole, we found the site of the old station and the stepping stones where Rosaly and Andrew first meet, and we climbed the 'long green slope', which, as Rosaly tells him, is the original railway track from Beck Hole to Goathland, and found the road junction, near to which there was still plenty of room to build 'a new school'. As we looked across the valley, we could see a house that could have been 'Moorside Manor'. Despite today's tourists in search of *Heartbeat* connections and the railway, Goathland would no doubt seem familiar to EJO with its 'grey church across the wide road with sheep cropping the turf under its walls'. One of the significant incidents in *Rosaly's New School* takes place when Ronald misdirects Malvina and her party to Egton Bridge station instead of the station at Goathland. Thanks to the preservation of the railway, both still exist.

Another day was spent in Saltburn, the home of the Allerbys in *Finding Her Family*, and, as the fictional Redburn, the site of the school in *At School with the Roundheads*. We drove across the moors along the 'white road' mentioned in both books, with views of the 'heather-clad uplands' and 'wide-sweeping moors'. We paused in Castleton, where Polly and Pinky drank ginger beer before they turned back, and where Brenda lived. In Saltburn we saw the famous 'jewel' streets, the Victorian letterbox in Milton Street, where Audrey posts a letter, the station, the convalescent home that becomes the school in *Roundheads*, the Halfpenny Bridge (or the site of it — the actual bridge has gone, but the toll bridge on one side and the Zetland hotel on the other are clearly visible). At the public library we were able to read P D Moore's history of Glenhow School, which existed at the time when EJO knew Saltburn and may have inspired her to create her fictional boys' school, even though she sited it in a convalescent home at the other end of the town. We spent time down on the beach where Brenda, Audrey and Hazel mount an exhibition, telling the story of St Hilda's Abbey at nearby Whitby. The cliff lift from the beach to the upper town still flourishes. We visited 'Old Saltburn' down by the sea, which Audrey points out to Hazel, with its 'white cottages' and 'our only public house'. Staithes and Whitby, which both feature in *Finding Her Family*, are easily accessible, but our visit to Staithes was cut short by an accident and a consequent encounter with a doctor, and as we are both Yorkshirewomen we know Whitby and St Hilda's Abbey well, so did not visit them on this occasion. We were particularly grateful for all the work that Kate Kirman and Jennifer Hignell had done in Saltburn as it enabled us to see much more than we would otherwise have done.

Our journey back to Wales took us past Fountains Abbey and Studley Royal, both of which are visited by the girls in *A School Camp Fire*, to Brimham Rocks, which are described in great detail: 'And there's one place where there are hundreds of them, all together, all with names ... Druid's Altar ... the Idol ... the Yoke of Oxen ... and the Lover's Leap and the Pivot Rock and the Dancing Bear.' EJO may well have exercised a lot of poetic licence in this book, for her descriptions of a reservoir like 'a shimmering lake', 'low green hills' and 'the quiet grey town in the dale' would fit various locations in the area around Harrogate, which is the local shopping town, but Brimham Rocks are unique!

In 1993, on our way to the Lake District, we went to the Yorkshire of Jen and Rocklands. It was an easy journey through Derbyshire, and there we stopped on Froggatt Edge, which EJO knew through staying with friends in the area. There are several of these 'Edges' in this part of Derbyshire and the adjacent part of Yorkshire, and quite near to Froggatt Edge is Eyam, the Derbyshire village famous for the well known Plague story that EJO used in *Mistress Nanciebel*. Eyam now has a museum that tells the story of how the Plague was brought to the village and how, organised by the rector, the villagers managed to contain it and prevent it from spreading to other local communities.

Bolsterstone, the village of Rocklands, is in Yorkshire, almost on the border with Derbyshire, and lies about ten miles north-west of Sheffield. It is still a small windswept grey-stone village, quite unspoiled, and must have seemed a very attractive place to the rich Yorkshire industrialists who built imposing houses, large enough to accommodate a small school, at the end of the nineteenth century. One of these houses was Waldershaigh, the home of Ribby, the little boy who corresponded with EJO and who was the inspiration for Wriggles, the invalid boy, while his home became Rocklands. We met Primrose Lockwood and Margaret Perry, the daughter of Ribby's nurse, Violet Ellis, for lunch, and afterwards we all went to look at Ribby's grave. Below the ridge on which Bolsterstone stands is the valley of the reservoirs, one of which was being built in *Jen of the Abbey School* and for which 'Tin Town' had been created to house the workers. Some of the features mentioned in the books, for example 'the ornamental tower, like a castle', can still be seen, although the shacks of Tin Town have been replaced by the small modern town houses of Ewden.

From Bolsterstone, we went to Penistone, the original of Stonecliffe, the town where the dancing competition takes place in *Jen of the Abbey School*. We found an impressive array of late nineteenth/early twentieth-century municipal buildings, including a hall (now a cinema), council offices and a Carnegie Library, but nowadays it probably isn't quite such an important town as it was a century ago.

Sheila had always thought that in staying at The Grange, near Sheffield, en route from the Abbey to the Lake District, Jen and Maidlin had gone out of their way, but, when we'd done the journey from the south ourselves, we could see that in the 1930s, before the advent of motorways or even really good trunk roads, it would have been a sensible way to travel north.

Wales

EJO used a fairly small part of this fairly small country as the setting of some of her early books. From the top of Aran Fawddwy, one of the mountains that she frequently mentions, it is possible, on a clear day, to see most of the area, much of which lies in the Snowdonia National Park and has changed comparatively little since EJO wrote about it; the roads are slightly wider and better surfaced, but the landmarks to which she refers are still there. EJO wrote about the areas around Lake Bala and Criccieth, and the Lleyn Peninsula, which together now constitute one of the most Welsh areas of Wales, and where the Welsh language is widely spoken. Although it is still possible to get from London to Pwllheli by train as Robin did, it is not by the route that she probably used, as the line that used to run from Ruabon to connect with the Cambrian Coast line was closed in 1964.

However, some of the former railway lines have been restored as tourist attractions, and the Bala Lake Railway, which runs for about five miles along the southern side of the lake, is one of these. It is more than likely that EJO got her first inspiration for the setting of the Torment books as she travelled along this line; they could even have been written on the basis of observation from the train, reinforced by the use of local maps and guidebooks.

Tygwyn, the home of Antonia and Marsaili, is easily identified. Glan-y-Llyn, meaning 'on the shores of the lake' or 'lakeside', is the only house that fits EJO's description. Once the summer home of Sir Watkin Williams Wynn, one of the great landowners of North Wales, it is now an outdoor pursuits centre. The fictional school was sited on the opposite side of the lake, near the village of Llangower. The remains of the 'private' halt and the jetty can still be seen, and nearby there is 'a green point', a piece of land jutting out into the lake, and still unoccupied, which could have accommodated the school building fairly comfortably. The town of Bala, referred to in the books as 'the junction town', lies at one end of the lake and the site of the boatyard where Sadie's grandfather runs his business is probably that still occupied by a boatyard when we first visited the area in the 1980s. The walks, the cycle rides, the drives and, above all, the spectacular views described in the Torment books are all there to be enjoyed today.

In October 1990 we visited Criccieth and the Lleyn Peninsula, a beautiful area with relatively unspoilt villages, wonderful views, beaches and bays. It is no wonder that it inspired five of EJO's earlier novels, and that she dwelt lovingly on names like Porth Neigwl, Yr Eifl and Porthdinllaen. *The Conquest of Christina* is set in and around Criccieth, and the places EJO mentions are easily traceable. The views that Christina enjoys from Black Rock Sands are still the same, and her ride through Criccieth to Llanystumdwy, through the town, past the station (mainline trains still stop here) and the Castle. can be followed. The mansion of Plas Glyn-y-Weddw, the house with the ornamental pleasure gardens, to which Christina promises to take the children, can be visited too. We also went to look at Llyn Mair, a lovely and unspoilt lake below Tan-y-Bwlch station, and recalled EJO's description: 'The railway ran along the top edge of the cup and away down in the bottom lay a little round lake, gleaming white in the sunlight and holding up a mirror to the dark trees behind.' The train still operates here as part of the Festiniog railway, and nearby are Ffestiniog and Blaenau Ffestiniog, the old slate-quarry villages, where David Jones has to go to work when the family fortunes fail.

Pwllheli, where Robin and other EJO characters arrive by train, also still has a train service, being the terminus of the Cambrian Coast line. Beyond there, we visited Abersoch, where Blaise Morgan in *The Girls of Gwynfa* had a house, and enjoyed the same views as Sylvia of Sarn, but could not reach Cilan Head, the site of the caves where the girls of Gwynfa find refuge. The road to the headland was barred by barbed wire, which we weren't dressed to cope with. However, we had the beach at Porth Neigwl or Hell's Mouth to ourselves and could look south to Cilan Head. We also visited the fifteenth century church at Llanengan to which the Gwynfa girls sometimes went on Sunday mornings.

Visiting the area revealed something that we'd not anticipated—just as Morven and Vairy occupy the same site in Scotland, Robin's Plas Quellyn and the Madryn Castle of *Mistress Nanciebel* share the same site in Wales. There was an old Madryn Castle, the home of Colonel Thomas Madryn during the Civil War, which was higher up the hill than the one built in 1830 as a romantic, baronial-style mansion by the Jones-Parry family, and which, judging by the photographs, may well have inspired EJO's descriptions of Plas Quellyn in *The Girl Who Wouldn't Make Friends*: 'A great gray house covered with ivy, with long, narrow windows, turrets, battlemented walls, and an imposing doorway, it was more her idea of a castle than a dwelling ...' This, in turn, was pulled down in the 1960s, and all that remains is the original seventeenth century gatehouse, ruined and covered in plants and bushes. Like Robin and her mother in *Robins in the Abbey*, we walked on the turf of the headland above Porthdinlleyn, which lies along the shore, a 'gray hamlet crouching on the sand at the foot of the cliffs' just as EJO describes it; there is one impressive stone house which, although it is not white, may have been the inspiration for Moranedd.

Nearby Nefyn still dreams of its celebrated seafaring past. Like Nanciebel we saw herds of black cows: 'From the opposite bank, across the stream, and straight towards her, came a great horrid monster ... behind it came a crowd of others, swinging tails like bell-ropes, all black, and fierce, and shaggy ...'

In all the 'modern' EJO stories set in the Lleyn, the characters at some stage go to Beddgelert; in *Sylvia*, the Berringtons take the three young people there to tea, Christina's troubles begin with an ill-fated trip there; and it is one of Robin's favourite places, to which she makes a point of taking Rob Quellyn. So, finally, on our way home, having stood under the shadow of Snowdon on the shores of Llyn Cwellyn, from which EJO took the Quellyn family name, we rounded off our trip with lunch at Beddgelert.

This part of Wales may seem very isolated from the rest of Britain, but it must be remembered that, at the time when EJO knew it, Lloyd George, a dynamic politician who became Prime Minister and who had been brought up in Llanystumdwy, lived and practised as a lawyer in Criccieth. It seems possible that EJO's journalist father knew Lloyd George, and the Dunkerleys may well have visited Madryn Castle, which belonged to another MP around the turn of the century.

The West Country

On our way to Somerset in 1991, we met in Cheltenham to explore the sites described in *The Abbey Girls Go Back to School*. Appropriately, Stella arrived by train, and soon afterwards we were parking Sheila's car at Cheltenham College, the boys' public school that is the 'college' where the English Folk Dance and Song Society summer school was held in the 1920s:

> The great gray college, the reddening creeper and yellow roses, the double rows of wide perpendicular windows, the great doorway, the tower and little turrets, the beautiful chapel at the side, the wide gravel drive …

It was all just as EJO describes it, even to the yellow roses, although it was a bit early for reddening creeper. It was the school holidays, although a language school was in progress, but we ventured inside and were greeted by the helpful school secretary who took time to show us some of the rooms. When we enquired about 'the great hall' described by EJO, she was sure that it must be the present Refectory, for which she didn't have a key, but a very helpful Hall Porter did, and so we were able to see it with 'the honour tablets in the walls … with open vaulted roof and stained-glass windows'. Everything that made Joan feel she was dancing in the refectory at the Abbey was there.

Back in the car we drove down Shurdington Road, where Tormy overtook an exhausted Jack running back to get help after the accident. We spotted Naunton Park Road, and eventually negotiated a one-way system to arrive outside the Naunton Park Council Schools, established 1909. The buildings face on to a wider-than-normal piece of road, with lots of room for the Pixie to put her class through *Upon a Summer's Day* while waiting for the caretaker to arrive with the key.

We drove up onto Cooper's Hill, which has been suggested as the spot where Joan and Cicely went to talk about their young men, and we looked west to the Malvern Hills and compared the view with the description in the book—the green downs behind us, Cheltenham and Gloucester at our feet, the wooded hills of Birdlip and Leckhampton to our left and, beyond the Malverns, the fainter Welsh hills. It was just possible to see the silver streak of the Severn and the square tower of Gloucester Cathedral, as EJO must have done.

The base for our exploration of Somerset was Wells, where Sheila's sister lives. We'd both been to Cleeve before—Sheila had visited it without ever realising that it was the original Abbey of the books—and we've been since, but on this particular trip we had it more or less to ourselves in perfect Abbey weather. *The Abbey Girls* serves as a useful guide to the Abbey. We stood in the cloister garth and identified the places that have become so familiar to so many through the books—the Refectory with its beautiful roof, the Chapter House, the Sacristy with the rose window now sadly bereft of tracery, and the Monks' Dorter. We recalled images from the books: Joan and Joy dancing their minuet, Rachel in her white robe, and Jen disappearing down the tresaunt.

Not far from Cleeve is the site of Elsa's ferry which features in *Adventure for Two*. Having spent many holidays in the area Sheila had some years previously reached the conclusion that it was just west of Weston-super-Mare, which became EJO's Sandylands. We followed the coast road from Burnham-on-Sea through Berrow and Brean to where it comes to an end at Brean Down. This is a green ridge with a white limestone outcrop, stretching out into the sea and down to marshes on its western side. As we walked up the path to the top of the ridge, we saw a sign reading 'Ferry' pointing away to our right. The view from the top seemed almost familiar; in front of us was the wide sweep of sand described in both *Adventure for Two* and *Elsa Puts Things Right*, and across the sands were the hotels and pier of Weston. We were pretty sure that we were standing on Elsa's island of Caer-Ogo. Everything fits perfectly—in Sheila's opinion, it is one of the most exciting EJO sites.

The ferry sign revealed that it only ran on Sundays and Bank Holidays, so we drove the long way round, via the A370, to Uphill (EJO's Hillside) and found signs pointing to the beach. It was late afternoon and we drove the car right down onto the sands. The view fits EJO's description in *Adventure for Two* perfectly: '… long shining wet sands, stretching for miles, a distant sea, a huge blue arch of sky, a great green hump of an island …'. We followed the path to the ferry across fields and mudflats until we came to the river; the tide was out and there seemed to be only a trickle of water, but there were large warning notices that the mud is treacherous and that the river channel cannot be crossed on foot! The present ferry is not a rowing boat, as Elsa's was, but a pull-ferry on a chain. Brean Down is not an island, but the ferry provides a useful short cut for walkers. So much for the reality in 1991. What EJO created to fit into this distinctive landscape are Elsa's bungalow, although it seems unlikely that such a building in this position would survive for very long, and the Caer-Ogo cave system.

Inland lies Glastonbury, fascinating in its own right even without the Margery and Nancybell connection. As we've said in the main text, there is no doubt that EJO's Priorsbury is Glastonbury; the most significant change that she made was to replace the abbey by a Priory of nuns, possibly to make a better contrast to *the* Abbey. In *Elsa Puts Things Right* Nancybell actually compares it to the Abbey: 'I believe there's an Abbey where you can see how the monks lived—dormitories and work-rooms and refectory all complete; but they have no big church … it's gone as completely as our living-places. I'd rather have our church even if it's only a shell'. A visit to Glastonbury with a copy of *Elsa Puts Things Right* is definitely recommended.

Oxfordshire and Buckinghamshire

It's over fifty years since Sheila first tried to visit High Wycombe for its Abbey-book connections. She was staying with an aunt and uncle in a London suburb; a car trip was proposed, and Sheila tried to negotiate for High Wycombe but was thwarted (they went to Oxford instead). Although her exploration of the High Wycombe area was somewhat delayed, this early experience demonstrated two things—that, living in west London, the Dunkerley family would have been able to visit the Chilterns frequently, and that Oxfordshire is not far away.

At last, in 1992, we were able to explore it together. We stayed in a little village outside the town, and on our first day decided to follow the route that Cicely takes in Chapter 15 of *Girls of the Hamlet Club* when she sets out to visit her friends. We drove into Wycombe and took the A404, turning off on the B474 through Tylers Green to Penn, where Marguerite lived. EJO described Penn as 'a long, straggling' village, and it was still this in 1992, but 'very picturesque' would seem a more appropriate term. We visited the church, which lies at one end of the village, where Marguerite took Cicely to see 'the brasses of the Penn family—the row of little boy figures in their quaint costumes and of little girls in ruffs and hoods and long skirts, all with folded hands or holding Bibles, ranged behind their parents in order of height'. From Penn we went on to Beamond End, a real hamlet with just a few houses and a duck pond, and then to Penn Street, where we walked a short way into Penn Wood to find that EJO's description is still true: 'Long aisles led into the wood, with heavy shadows giving an impression of mystery … shafts of sunlight playing on the grey-green trunks and mysterious silence everywhere.' Although EJO, for the most part, used real placenames in this book, she invented that of Darley's Bottom, important in the early Abbey books as the home of Dorothy Darley and the site of the barn where the girls danced, which appears to be where Flowers Bottom is in reality.

We visited Great Kimble Church, with its John Hampden associations. It is easy to miss Green Hailey, where Miriam lived, but Whiteleaf village and Whiteleaf Cross are easy to find. Once one knows that Chinnor is 'Whiteways', the village to which EJO translated Cleeve Abbey, it is easy to find evidence to support this view. Ideally, one should approach Chinnor along the B4009 from the Princes Risborough direction, and choose a day when there is perfect Abbey weather. Part of Chinnor is industrialised, but the older part of the village on a warm and sunny afternoon in June is just as one imagines it. When we were there it was very peaceful, and, as we wandered round, two ladies in garden-party-style straw hats stopped their car to enquire if we were waiting for a lift to the Mothers' Union Strawberry Tea—it was like stepping back in time.

EJO must have visited Chinnor and realised that it would be a perfect setting for the Abbey—far enough away from the hamlets mentioned in *Girls of the Hamlet Club* not to have been mentioned there but near enough for the Hamlet Club girls to go there on one of their rambles, and for girls from there to walk, cycle or go by train to school in Wycombe. In 1992 there was still plenty of room for the Abbey and the Hall in an area slightly above the village, to the right of Keens Lane as one goes up towards the Bledlow Ridge. In the older part of the village there are a few old cottages, although some of the larger houses have disappeared. One could imagine that in the 1920s there would have been plenty of places to accommodate Joy's good works. In the Chinnor library we found a typescript compiled in 1929 by the members of the Women's Institute, which said that 'In the farmyard of Keane's Farm, a beautiful Tudor farmhouse stood' and that it had been demolished about fifty years previously. It's interesting to note that 'Keane's Farm' had become 'Keens Lane' in the meantime, the kind of mutation that is sometimes mentioned in EJO's work.

From Chinnor we drove through Princes Risborough and Monks Risborough, and Stella spotted the Whiteleaf Cross, where we sat on one of the arms to look at the view so well described in *Girls of the Hamlet Club*: 'miles of flat country, meadows, hedges, golden woods, glistening water … one little town with a pointed spire … and another even smaller … with an ancient square tower'.

High Wycombe itself must be very different from the town as EJO knew it—we were there on a quiet evening but Sheila has been back since, and, although there are many interesting things to see, it has a one-way road system and several multi-storey car parks, and at certain times during the day the traffic is horrific. Even on a quiet evening it had a rather shut-in feeling, and we could appreciate how 'stuffy' Jen must have found it after the bracing air of the Yorkshire moors. But, considering how near they are to London, the Chilterns are relatively unspoilt away from the main roads.

We spent some time in West Wycombe, coming down to it along the Bledlow Ridge and spotting the 'tower and ball of West Wycombe Church' that Joy saw as she walked to Wycombe along the hills—we went to look at the golden ball and the church at close quarters. Nearby, at the bottom of the hill on which the church stands, there is an entrance to the caves, the existence of which helps to legitimise all those underground passages around the Abbey. Broadway End, the home of Cicely's grandparents, is almost certainly on the site of Chequers, but for obvious reasons we couldn't visit this!

We also went to look at Hampden House, as Mabel Esther Allan—who taught there in the 1940s, when it was a girls' school—had suggested that the interior had been the inspiration for the 'great square hall', oak-panelled, with a wide staircase at one side and a fire burning on the 'great open hearth', that Joan and Joy first see when they go to tea with Cicely. Unfortunately we couldn't check this as there was nobody around from whom we could seek permission. In the 1990s it was being used as offices and looked very private.

From the Chilterns we were going to Cleeve, and en route we fitted in a visit to Ewelme to look at the lovely old church to which Jock took Maidlin after they became engaged. Ewelme seemed half-asleep in the midday sunshine; with its Chaucer and Henry VIII connections, it is another EJO place that is well worth a visit in its own right.

Surrey and Sussex

Sussex was probably the county that EJO knew best of all, and, although we've not done a mathematical check, we have the impression that more of her stories have associations with Sussex than with any other part of the United Kingdom. She went there for family holidays as a child, there may well have been outings there from her home in Ealing, and in 1922 she, her parents and three sisters all moved there to live. To get there they would have travelled many times through the more rural parts of Surrey, and at times in EJO's work the boundary between Surrey and Sussex is somewhat blurred. Somewhere along the route must be the so far unidentified Rayley (or Rayleigh—both appear) Park, Joan Raymond's home, and The Pallant, the house that is built for Maidlin and Jock after their marriage.

The Surrey places that are used by EJO are distinctive—Farnham, Abinger Hammer, the Silent Pool, and the site of Rainbows village—and the first three may well have been visited by the Dunkerleys before they moved to Worthing.

Farnham pottery plays a part in those books set after Joy, Joan and Jen have left school, and is first mentioned in *The Abbey Girls in Town* (1925). It seems likely that EJO had recently come across the Pottery herself and wanted to share her pleasure in the blue, green and golden-brown pots with her readers. We decided to visit it on our 1998 trip and found it quite easily in Wrecclesham, a suburb on the south side of the town. Although there was a 'closed' sign outside, we wandered round the back and met a senior member of staff who showed us round and told us something of its history. From the street it looks much as it must have done in the 1920s, and there were interesting features from that early period—for example, the splendid toilet block, roofed with curly green tiles left over from those supplied for the British Residency in Rangoon. The business, which was set up by Absolom Harris towards the end of the nineteenth century, had been kept going by the sale of surplus land. In 1998, the buildings had just been taken over by a Trust, which then leased those required for current production back to the firm. Nowadays terracotta pots are produced in quantity, but there are examples of the pottery that EJO loved, and others can be seen in the excellent Farnham Museum. (Farnham, incidentally, is also the basis of Dorita Fairlie Bruce's Maudsley in the books about Nancy Caird.)

The next morning we went in search of Rainbows. All the evidence in *Daring Doranne* and *Margery Meets the Roses* points to its being in that part of Surrey and Sussex which lies between the A24 Dorking to Horsham road to the east, the A281 Guildford to Horsham road to the west and south, and the A25 Guildford to Dorking road to the north, with the Sussex Downs and Worthing to the south. Ewhurst somehow sounded right, although it's in Surrey and Rainbows is said to be in the northern part of Sussex; nor could we persuade the Ewhurst postmaster that Dorking is their local town, although things have probably changed since the Second World War with the growth of Crawley.

Ewhurst is still an attractive village of the kind that EJO loved. There is no model village, but the hills rise to the north, and there is plenty of woodland that would have had to be cut down to make room for Doranne's Rainbows. While exploring the hillside we accidentally got into someone's drive, and while turning round we had a breathtaking view, gazing down, as Doranne and Gwen did on their first visit to Rainbows, 'to the village ... and then across miles of green country to the blue Sussex hills'—a clinching moment indeed.

We visited Abinger Hammer and the Silent Pool on our way home from Worthing in 1997. They are much as EJO must have known them. She may well have taken the family name of Joy's grandfather and the Hall from the former, which was a centre of the iron industry in the seventeenth century, and certainly the clock, depicting a smith at his trade, would have stuck in her mind. She would also have loved the peace, romance and mystery of the nearby Silent Pool.

EJO's Sussex stretches from Chichester, which appears as Eldingham in the Ven and Gard books, in the west to Rottingdean, the village of *The School of Ups and Downs*, in the east. In between there is plenty of room for a number of fictional schools, for Arundel Castle, which has a starring role as Kentisbury Castle, and for the South Downs that feature in many of the stories set in this area.

We explored some of this area in 1997, staying in Worthing with Chris Keyes and meeting up with Gillian Priestman. Together we went first to Pagham and Bognor Regis, the area in which the Ven and Gard books are set, going to look at the lagoon, one of the girls' favourite meeting places. We also wandered round the settlement of bungalows that are basically old railway carriages, still going strong eighty-plus years after EJO described Pro Tem, the bungalow that belonged to Barbara Holt. We were lucky enough to be invited into one of them, which consisted of two carriages placed at right angles to each other, with an extension to accommodate a bathroom and a verandah.

We'd both been to Arundel Castle before, so we concentrated on looking at specific places nearby, having lunch at the Black Rabbit, the pub that becomes the Princess Royal in *Jandy Mac Comes Back*, and walking along to Swanbourne Lake which features in *Patch and a Pawn*. It is here that Roger and Bill dive to try and find the missing pawn; above lies the path with the cave where the young people sit and from where Geoff plays tricks on local children, and higher still is the ridge along which Jandy is riding when she sees the happenings in Campers' Cove when baby Hugh, the heir, is snatched. The River Arun, down which the kidnappers take the two young children and Tansy by boat, flows into the sea at Littlehampton, which becomes 'Littleton' in *Jandy Mac*.

In Worthing itself is Inverkip, the house that EJO shared with her sister Maida, and which becomes 'Dunoon' in *Daring Doranne*. On the outskirts of the town is The Conifers, the house where their father, John Oxenham, lived. Worthing and the area around are rich in Camp Keema connections: a teashop frequented by the girls near the pier; Lancing Ring, one of their meeting places; and High Salvington windmill, where they had tea, which was also the starting place for Marian and Peggy Mason when they set out to explore the Downs behind their new home. Both Chanctonbury and Cissbury Rings feature in the Camp Keema stories, and in *The Abbey Girls Play Up*, as Maribel and Rosalind are driving from Maribel's home in Worthing to pick Cecily up, they suddenly spot Chanctonbury—'Oh—Chanctonbury! I always want to curtsey!' says Rosalind. We even found the old toll-gate house from which some of the girls catch a bus back to the town after the break-up of Camp Keema.

A site has not yet been found for the school in the Camp Keema books, but The White House School of *Dorothy's Dilemma* is quite easily identifiable, still intact and beautifully preserved as a Bowling Club on the sea front. The church at nearby Sompting is also easily recognisable as the subject of one of the essays that causes the dilemma of the title, and the Downs, with their rings and dewponds, are also featured in this story.

St Margaret's of the Deb books is in this area and includes incidents that take place at what are obviously Chanctonbury Ring and Lancing Ring, while Lancing College, the nearby boys' public school, becomes Waring College, one of the few boys' schools to play an important supporting role in EJO's books.

Washington, the village of the Rose and Squirrel and of Woodend School, is still a charming little place a few miles north of Worthing. We've visited this on other occasions, but we'll never forget the exact date of our 'official' visit during the Worthing trip since it was the day that Diana, Princess of Wales, was killed in the Paris car crash. As we didn't hear the news until teatime we were still quite shell-shocked when we went to have dinner in the pub there, the flag flying at half mast above us.

The School of Ups and Downs, set in Rottingdean, which we visited in 2000, was the first book that EJO set in Sussex; Rottingdean lies further east and must have been known to EJO before she moved to Worthing—not surprisingly, since at the beginning of the twentieth century it was a community of writers and artists. It lies a couple of miles to the east of Brighton, which is thinly disguised as 'a fashionable watering place'. On the coast road from Brighton, one first passes Roedean, the famous girls' public school founded in 1885, which may have given EJO the idea of creating a boarding school in the area. The geography of Rottingdean, now a small town with a village atmosphere, its church, and the artist Sir Edward Burne-Jones, are central to the plot of *The School of Ups and Downs* so we've discussed it fully in the main text. But—be warned! A lot depends on the way you arrive there and on the weather that prevails during your visit. When we visited it in 2000 we drove along the coast road from Brighton, and at first sight it looked most unattractive, but it was a cool, rather grey day when we arrived and there were few visitors around. In 2003 Sheila went again about the same time of year and came into it from the north, which is a much better approach, but it was a hot sunny Friday and the place was packed with tourists!

This is one of the problems of this type of exploration—it's important to have a very positive attitude, but we've had a lot of Ray–Waring luck on our trips and wish you the same. A good road atlas will help you find our various routes quite easily although we have on occasion invested in local Ordnance Survey maps. More detailed accounts of these visits are listed in the bibliography, page 303.

And an Annexe about Annecy

Annecy is the only foreign EJO site on which we can offer the experience of a visit. In 1994 Stella went to this attractive French resort, which EJO must have been to many years ago and which she chose as a setting in which to explore self-discovery, where Maidlin took on her first big responsibility, Damaris danced, Cecily camped, and the Camp Mystery was solved. The other of the 'we' here is Joan Newey.

When Maidlin goes to look for Biddy in *Biddy's Secret*, she arrives by train at Aix-les-Bains, so we went to look at the station where we saw the TGV, the French high-speed train, on which Maidlin would certainly have travelled if it had been around at the time. Aix was a popular spa in Victorian times, patronised by Queen Victoria herself.

In *Damaris Dances* there is a good description of Annecy which mentions 'the arcades above the shops, giving shelter from the blazing sun, the narrow streets and the canals, the curious red-roofed church towers, the open-air market, the mountains all around and the deep green of the lake ...'. They are all still there, as enchanting as they must have been for EJO—and for Rachel and Damaris. We stood, as Maidlin did, in the little public garden by the lake, and while sailing on it recognised the mountains mentioned by EJO: Tournette, Parmelan, Dents de Lanfon and the Semnoz.

One day we took the lake steamer and went to Talloires, the site of *The Camp Mystery* and an idyllic spot in which to spend a quiet summer afternoon. Like Maribel and the Guides we disembarked and climbed the steep street to the centre of the village. At least two streams run alongside the narrow streets under old stone bridges, just as EJO describes them, and on the day of our visit the village was very much a small local community. It was Mothering Sunday (later in the year than ours) and roses were being handed out to all the mothers, so we were able to sit by a fountain, enjoy our picnic lunch and watch the parade of families, escorting mums and grandmas, carrying flowers and pâtisseries in fancy boxes, and greeting each other.

In *The Camp Mystery* Gina talks about Talloires as 'a queer brown village ... a waterfall and an old bridge' and EJO describes 'chalets hung with creepers and climbing roses ...' with 'wooden outside stairs, big balconies and overhanging eaves'—we saw some chalets that answered this description perfectly. The Roc de Chère, which is mentioned frequently and to which Rosalind takes Gina and Cecily for a picnic, is a great craggy promontory stretching out into the lake, and this is now a nature reserve. We found a municipal camping site rather farther from the village than EJO sites the camp of St John's and St Mary's, but it was an ideal site for a camp and no doubt the spot that EJO had in mind— and telescoped the distances. The Château to which Astrid rows with Gina and John is unmistakeable—this is the Château de Duigt.

There can be no question that EJO knew and loved Annecy and the area around. The descriptions in the books are so vivid and so recognisable, and she conveys her own affection for it so well, that it was like revisiting a well known and well loved place.

Publishers' note: in the maps which are shown on the following pages we have not only included every place mentioned in this Postscript but have also attempted to show all those mentioned in the preceding chapters. The index map on page 281 is a guide to the subsequent regional maps, and in addition to the one of Southern England there are detailed maps of London, Somerset and Sussex.

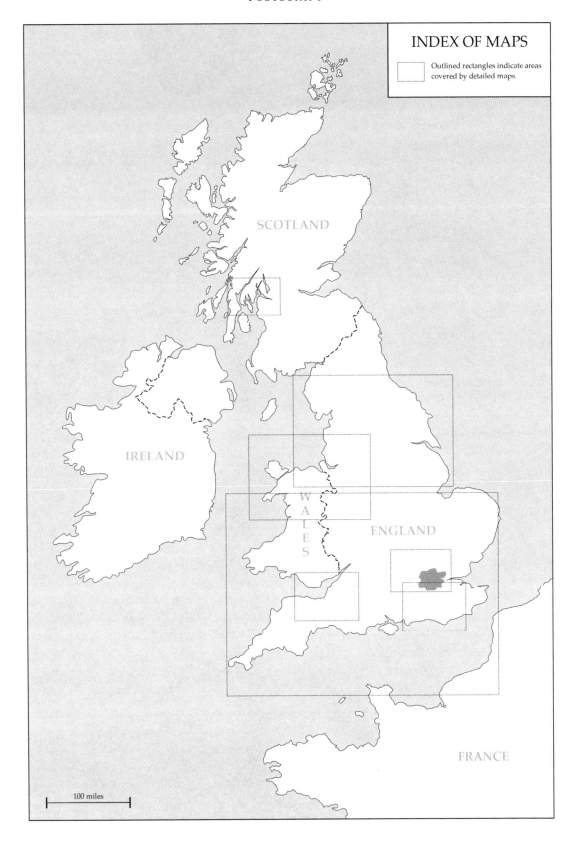

INDEX OF MAPS

Outlined rectangles indicate areas covered by detailed maps.

SCOTLAND

IRELAND

W A L E S

ENGLAND

FRANCE

100 miles

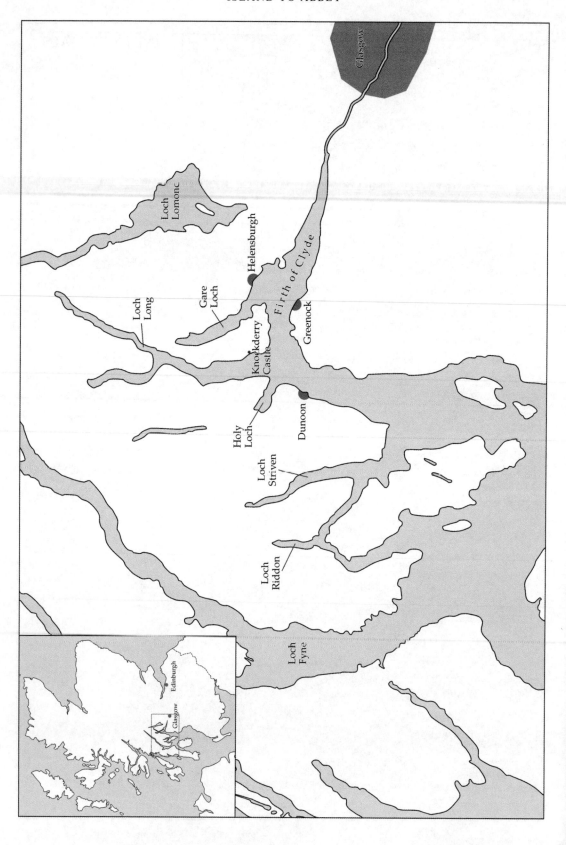

Glasgow

Loch
Lomond

Helensburgh

Firth of Clyde

Loch
Long

Gare
Loch

Greenock

Knockderry
Castle

Dunoon

Holy
Loch

Loch
Striven

Loch
Riddon

Loch
Fyne

Edinburgh

Glasgow

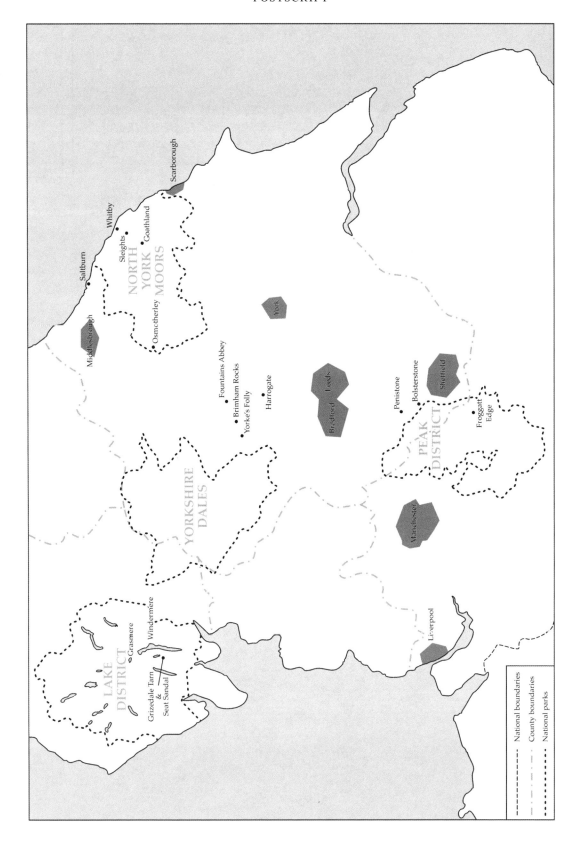

National boundaries
County boundaries
National parks

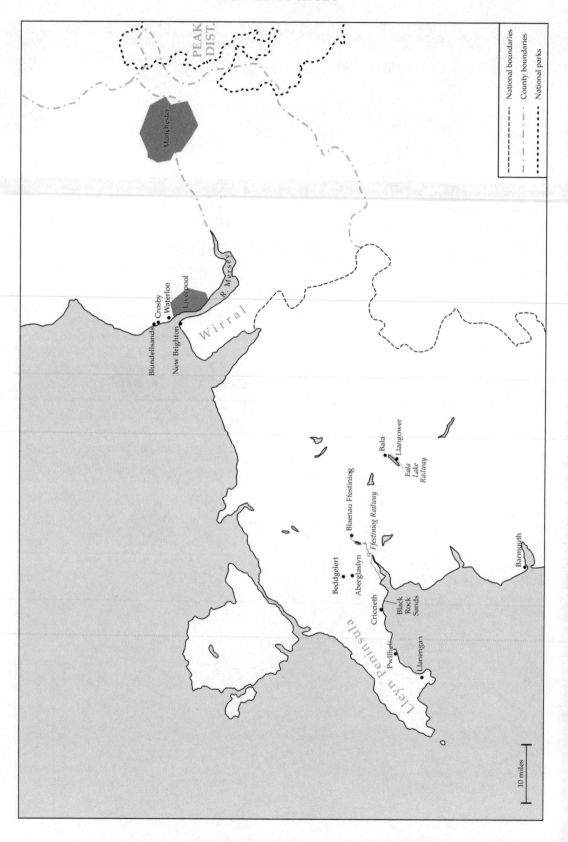

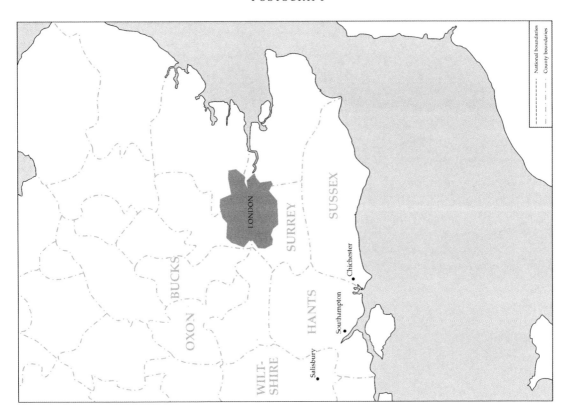

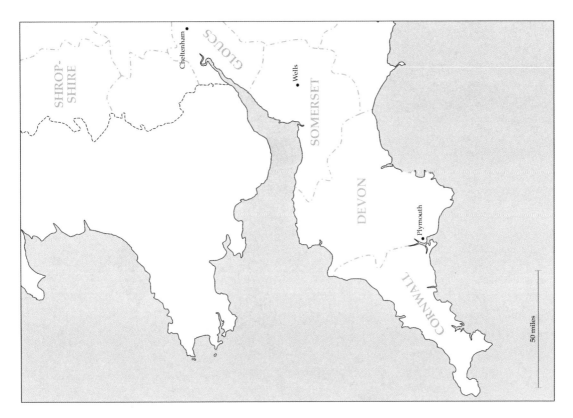

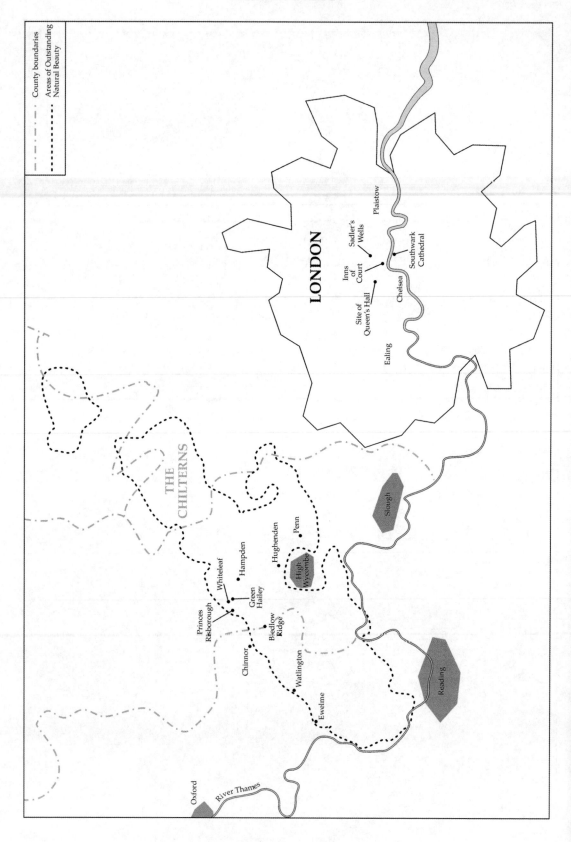

County boundaries

Areas of Outstanding
Natural Beauty

LONDON

Plaistow

Sadler's
Wells

Inns
of
Court

Southwark
Cathedral

Site of
Queen's Hall

Chelsea

Ealing

THE
CHILTERNS

Slough

Penn

Hughenden

Hampden

Whiteleaf

High
Wycombe

Green
Hailey

Princes
Risborough

Bledlow
Ridge

Chinnor

Watlington

Reading

Ewelme

Oxford

River Thames

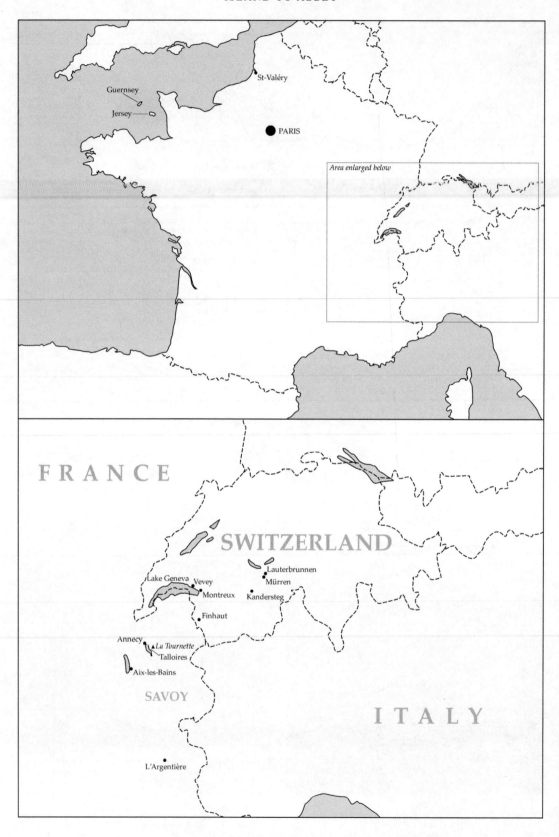

Little loch near Dunoon, 2001
(Scotland)

Tignabruaich, 2001
(Scotland)

Kirkstone Pass, 1993
(The Lake District)

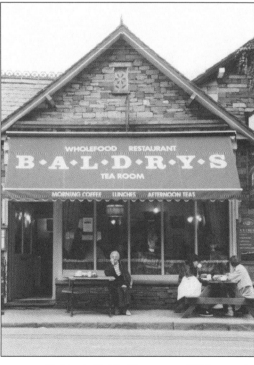

Baldry's Café, Grasmere, 1992
(The Lake District)

Site of Rosaly's new school, Goathland, 1996
(Yorkshire and Derbyshire)

Egton Bridge Station, 1996
(Yorkshire and Derbyshire)

One of the 'jewel' streets, Saltburn, 1996
(Yorkshire and Derbyshire)

Brimham Rocks, near Harrogate, 1996
(Yorkshire and Derbyshire)

Ribby's grave, Bolsterstone, 1993
(Yorkshire and Derbyshire)

Ewden village, 1993
(Yorkshire and Derbyshire)

Municipal Hall, Penistone, 1993
(Yorkshire and Derbyshire)

Tygwyn, Lake Bala, 1990
(Wales)

Llyn Mair, Tan-y-Bwlch, 1990
(Wales)

View from the train across Lake Bala,
Llangower, 1990 (Wales)

The old gatehouse, Madryn Castle, 1990
(Wales)

Porthdinlleyn – 'a gray hamlet … at the foot
of the cliffs', 1990 (Wales)

Cheltenham College – 'a beautiful hall …
stained-glass windows', 1991
(The West Country)

Cheltenham College '… honour tablets on
the walls', 1991
(The West Country)

Naunton Park School, Cheltenham, 1991
(The West Country)

Cleeve Abbey, 1991
(The West Country)

Cleeve Abbey, 1991
(The West Country)

Brean Down—the island of 'Caer-Ogo'—1991
(The West Country)

Glastonbury Abbey, 1991
(The West Country)

The George and Pilgrims, Glastonbury, 1991
(The West Country)

Whiteleaf Cross, 1992
(Oxfordshire and Buckinghamshire)

Interior, Chinnor Church, 1992
(Oxfordshire and Buckinghamshire)

Duck pond at Beamond End, 1992
(Oxfordshire and Buckinghamshire)

Hampden House, 1992
(Oxfordshire and Buckinghamshire)

The owl over the doorway of the kiln,
Farnham Pottery, 1998
(Surrey and Sussex)

Farnham Pottery on display in the museum,
Farnham, 1998
(Surrey and Sussex)

The Silent Pool, Abinger Hammer, 1997
(Surrey and Sussex)

The clock at Abinger Hammer, 1997
(Surrey and Sussex)

Railway carriage home, Pagham, 1997
(Surrey and Sussex)

The courtyard at Arundel Castle, 1997
(Surrey and Sussex)

High Salvington Windmill, Worthing, 1997
(Surrey and Sussex)

The Bowling Club, Worthing, 1997
(Surrey and Sussex)

Sompting Church, 1997
(Surrey and Sussex)

Stained-glass windows by Burne-Jones,
St Margaret's Church, Rottingdean, 1997
(Surrey and Sussex)

Les Dents de Lonfon, Lake Annecy, 1994
(France)

Canals and red roofs, Annecy, 1994
(France)

HAMLET CLUB QUEENS

This is the list of the Queens that we produced in 1985 at the time of our original study. It follows the order given in the description of the procession in *Robins in the Abbey*, and we noted only one discrepancy—in *A Dancer from the Abbey,* Jen exclaims: 'Clover! The Queen after Maidie-Primrose.' Since 1985, there has been much discussion in the pages of *The Abbey Chronicle*, and no doubt elsewhere, about the Queens, the order in which they came, and what we are told about those who reigned between Maidlin, the Primrose Queen, and Mirry, the Forget-Me-Not Queen. The Queens from Ivy to Heather reigned during the period when the Hamlet Club is scarcely mentioned in the Abbey books, and had to be created retrospectively.

It is interesting to note how the names of the Queens change in style. At first the emphasis is on colour, then from Barbara to Maidlin on flower names which match the girls who take them. In the interim period wild or large flowers predominate, and then, finally, the emphasis is very much on flowers to which the Queens-elect can point in the garden.

For those who want further information about the Queens, a more detailed list appears in Appendix 1 of Monica Godfrey's *The World of Elsie J Oxenham and her Books* (Girls Gone By, 2003), pp 262–266.

White Queen	Miriam
Golden Queen	Cicely, President of the Hamlet Club
Strawberry Queen	Marguerite
Green Queen	Joy
Violet Queen	Joan
Blue Queen	Muriel
Silver Queen (Honesty)	Nesta
Striped Queen	Beatrice
Wild Rose Queen	Barbara
Red Rose Queen	Rosamund
Beech Brown Queen	Jen
Primrose Queen	Maidlin
Ivy Queen	
Clover Queen	Anne (later Manley)
Bluebell Queen	
Poppy Queen	
Gray or Garden Queen	Gracie Gray
Hyacinth Queen	
Lilac Queen	
Heather Queen	
Forget-Me-Not Queen	Mirry (Miriam's daughter)
Marigold Queen	Littlejan
Rosemary Queen	Jean

Lobelia Queen	Jansy
Lavender Queen	Rosalind (Nanta)
Lupin Queen	Tessa
Wallflower Queen	Phyllida
Buttercup and Daisy Queens	Elizabeth and Margaret

'Queens of Whitelands' exhibition, 1993

BIBLIOGRAPHY

The Social Background

These books were helpful in throwing light on the society in which EJO wrote and on ideas in which she was interested. They were found mainly by chance; in no sense was a serious literature search undertaken.

Avery, Gillian. *The Best Type of Girl: A history of girls' independent schools.* Deutsch, 1991.

Bridges, T C & Tiltman, H Hessell. *Master Minds of Modern Science.* Harrap, 1930; revised edition, 1934.
> This book contains chapters on Baird, the Curies, Einstein and others. Chapter 18 is 'Dr. Sunshine: how Dr. Rollier founded the most wonderful school in the world'. Rollier was a Swiss doctor who established a school at Leysin, Switzerland; he used sunshine as a cure for tuberculosis and his ideas were well known by the time EJO wrote her Swiss books.

Clarke, George. *The Later Stuarts.* 2nd edition. Oxford University Press, 1956. (*The Oxford History of England*, Vol 10).

Community in a Changing World. A record of outlook, experiment and activity issued as a successor to the book *Community in Britain* by the Community Service Committee, 1942.
> Craft, music, simplicity, emphasis on rural life—these ideas, which obviously appealed to EJO, were an essential part of the community idea, but her communities were led by a young girl, as a benevolent despot, rather than a democratic committee.

Freeman, Winefride. *Guide Book to Arundel Castle,* n.d. Published at 1/- with 22 illustrations at the period when EJO probably came to know Arundel Castle, and possibly used as the basis for her Kentisbury.

Gilyard-Beer, R. *Cleeve Abbey, Somerset.* HMSO, 1960.
> This is the official guide. There are more up-to-date editions, but this was the one that we happened to use.

Grove's Dictionary of Music and Musicians. 5th edition, edited by Eric Blom. 9 volumes, 1954, and supplementary volume, 1961. Macmillan.
> An invaluable reference source for the music, folk-dance and ballet elements.

Massingham, Betty. *Miss Jekyll: a portrait of a great gardener.* New edition. David & Charles, 1973.

Murry, John Middleton. *Community Farm.* The Country Book Club, 1953.

The Story of the English Folk Dance and Song Society. Revised edition. EFDSS, 1974. (Leaflet no 12).

Walvin, James. *Leisure and Society, 1830–1950.* Longman, 1978.

Children's Literature

These books are about children's literature generally; some of them mention EJO specifically.

Allen, Mabel Esther. *Ragged Robin Began It and Other Articles about Old Girls' Books.* Published by the author, 1993.

Auchmuty, Rosemary. *A World of Girls.* The Women's Press, 1992.

Auchmuty, Rosemary. *A World of Women: Growing Up in the Girls' School Story.* The Women's Press, 1999.

Auchmuty, Rosemary & Wotton, Joy, editors. *The Encyclopaedia of School Stories.* Vol 1: *The Encyclopaedia of Girls' School Stories*, by Sue Sims & Hilary Clare; Vol 2: *The Encyclopaedia of Boys' School Stories*, by Robert J Kirkpatrick. Ashgate, 2000.

Avery, Gillian. *Childhood's Pattern.* Hodder & Stoughton, 1975.

Cadogan, Mary. *Chin Up, Chest Out, Jemima!: A Celebration of the Schoolgirls' Story.* Jade Publishers, 1989; revised edition, Girls Gone By Publishers, 2004.

Cadogan, Mary & Craig, Patricia. *You're a Brick, Angela!: The Girls' Story, 1839–1985.* Gollancz, 1976, reprinted with postscript, 1985; revised edition, Girls Gone By Publishers, 2003.

Carpenter, Humphrey & Prichard, Mari. *The Oxford Companion to Children's Literature.* Oxford University Press, 1984.

Chevalier, Tracy, editor. *Twentieth-Century Children's Writers.* 3rd edition. St James Press, 1989.

Crouch, Marcus. *Treasure Seekers and Borrowers.* Library Association, 1962, reprinted with amendments, 1970.

Eyre, Frank. *British Children's Books in the Twentieth Century.* Longman, 1971.

Fisher, Margery. *Who's Who in Children's Literature.* Weidenfeld & Nicholson, 1975.

Freeman, Gillian. *The Schoolgirl Ethic: The Life and Work of Angela Brazil.* Allen Lane, 1976.

McClelland, Helen. *Behind the Chalet School: A Biography of Elinor M Brent-Dyer.* 2nd edition. Bettany Press, 1996.

Trease, Geoffrey. *Tales Out of School.* 2nd edition. Heinemann Educational, 1972.

Tucker, Nicholas. 'A Proper Princess', *New Society* 8 November 1973, pp 328–330.

Watson, Victor. *Reading Series Fiction: From Arthur Ransome to Gene Kemp.* RoutledgeFalmer, 2000.

Watson, Victor, editor. *The Cambridge Guide to Children's Books in English.* Cambridge University Press, 2001.

EJO: Her Work and Family

Cadogan, Mary. 'A Rival for Angela Brazil', *The Birmingham Mail,* 4 December 1980.

Daily Telegraph, 2nd January, 1981. 'Joan's New Line of Business is Old Books'.

Godfrey, Monica. *Elsie J Oxenham and Her Books.* Autolycus Publications, 1979.

Godfrey, Monica. 'Elsie J Oxenham and Her Schoolgirl Stories', *The Book and Magazine Collector* 8, 1984.

Other articles about EJO appear in Numbers 51, 145 and 198 of *The Book and Magazine Collector.*

Godfrey, Monica. *The World of Elsie Jeanette Oxenham and Her Books.* Girls Gone By Publishers, 2003.

Muir, Lynette. 'Fifty Years of the Hamlet Club', *The Junior Bookshelf* 30 (1) 1966, pp 19–23. Reprinted in Mary Cadogan's *Chin Up, Chest Out, Jemima!* (revised edition).

Oxenham, Elsie Jeanette. *Ribbie's Book: "Give My Love to the Stars",* compiled and edited by Olga-Lock Kendell & Ruth Allen. The Abbey Chronicle, 1999.

Oxenham, Erica. *J.O.: A Life of John Oxenham.* Longman, 1942.

Oxenham, Erica. *Scrapbook of J.O.* Longmans, Green, 1946.

Peck, Joan. *Elsie J Oxenham: A Chronicler of the Folk Movement.* EFDSS Magazine, 1980/81.

Shelley, Noreen. 'Marvellous letters from Margaret: A Tribute to the late Margaret Horder, Illustrator'. *Reading Time,* July 1979, pp 12–15.
    Although this article does not mention EJO, Margaret Horder was arguably one of the most distinguished illustrators to work on EJO's books, and this is an excellent source of information about her.

Thompson, Allison. *Lighting the Fire: Elsie J Oxenham, the Abbey Girls and the English Folk Dance Revival.* The Squirrel Hill Press (Pittsburgh, Pennsylvania), 1998.

The following articles, describing our explorations of EJO sites in more detail, have been published in *The Abbey Chronicle*. They are listed in order of publication as we felt this might be most helpful for readers.

'*EJO's Wales, Part 1*', *Abbey Chronicle* 6, September 1990, pp 4–6.

'*EJO's Wales, Part 2*', *Abbey Chronicle* 8, May 1991, pp 5–9.

'*The EJO Trail Continues—into Somerset*', *Abbey Chronicle* 10, January 1992, pp 2–7.

'*EJO Journey 1992: From Chinnor to Cleeve*', *Abbey Chronicle* 13, January 1993, pp 3–10.

'*Yorkshire Moors and Lakeland Fells*', *Abbey Chronicle* 16, January 1994, pp 9–15.

'*Annecy*', *Abbey Chronicle* 18, September 1994, pp 5–8.

'*In the Steps of the Roundheads, Rosaly and Hazel (not to mention K.K. and J.H.)*, *Abbey Chronicle* 25, January/February 1997, pp 46–52.

'*Abbey Girls in West Sussex*', *Abbey Chronicle* 28, January 1998, pp 42–53.

'*Where is Rainbows?*', *Abbey Chronicle* 31, January 1999, pp 47–50.

'*Ups and Downs in One of the Deans*', *Abbey Chronicle* 37, January 2001, pp 15–19.

'*Lots of Lochs: EJO's Scotland*', *Abbey Chronicle* 40, January 2002, pp 51–56.

Books and Short Stories by EJO

As these are dealt with chronologically in order of publication in the main text and can be traced by title through the index, this part of the bibliography is arranged by series, with titles in reading order. Titles of short stories appear thus: *'Adventure in the Abbey'*, while books that connect from other series are shown thus: [*Jen of the Abbey School*]. As we have shown in the text, there are discrepancies, and we do not claim that our solutions are the right ones!

For more information see the lists in Monica Godfrey's *The World of Elsie Jeanette Oxenham and Her Books.*

The Abbey Books

Girls of the Hamlet Club, 1914.
The Abbey Girls, 1920.
The Girls of the Abbey School, 1921.
Schooldays at the Abbey, 1938.
'Adventure in the Abbey', 1955.
'Mistakes in the Abbey', 1956.
Secrets of the Abbey, 1939.
Stowaways in the Abbey, 1940.
Schoolgirl Jen at the Abbey, 1950.
Strangers at the Abbey, 1951.
Selma at the Abbey, 1952.
Tomboys at the Abbey, 1957.
The Abbey Girls Go Back to School, 1922.
[*Jen of the Abbey School*]—the events in this take place before and after those in *The Abbey Girls Go Back to School.*
The New Abbey Girls, 1923.
The Abbey Girls Again, 1924.
The Abbey Girls in Town, 1925.
Queen of the Abbey Girls, 1926.
The Call of the Abbey School, 1934—consists of the first 9 chapters of *Queen.*
The Abbey Girls Win Through, 1928.
The Abbey Girls at Home, 1929.
The Abbey Girls Play Up, 1930.
The Abbey Girls on Trial, 1931.
The Girls of Squirrel House, 1932—consists of first 12 chapters of *Trial.*
Biddy's Secret, 1932.
Rosamund's Victory, 1933.
Maidlin to the Rescue, 1934.
Joy's New Adventure, 1935.

Rosamund's Tuck-Shop, 1937.
Maidlin Bears the Torch, 1937.
Rosamund's Castle, 1938.
Maid of the Abbey, 1943.
Jandy Mac Comes Back, 1941.
Two Joans at the Abbey, 1945.
An Abbey Champion, 1946.
Robins in the Abbey, 1947.
A Fiddler for the Abbey, 1948—the events in *Fiddler* and *Guardians* overlap.
Guardians of the Abbey, 1950.
Rachel in the Abbey, 1951.
A Dancer from the Abbey, 1953.
The Song of the Abbey, 1954.
Two Queens at the Abbey, 1959.

The Kentisbury Books

Patch Paterson is the chief protagonist in the two books that are concerned mainly with filling in the Kentisbury story.

[*Rosamund's Victory*]—introduces the Kanes of Kentisbury.
Patch and a Pawn, 1940.
[*Rosamund's Tuck-Shop*]
The Secrets of Vairy, 1947.
[*Margery Meets the Roses*]

Rocklands

A Go-Ahead Schoolgirl, 1919.
Tickles, or The School that was Different, 1924.
Jen of the Abbey School, 1927—consists of *The Girls of Rocklands School*, 1930, *The Second Term at Rocklands*, 1930, which is made up of *'Jen's Presents'* and *'Treasure from the Snow'*, and *The Third Term at Rocklands*, 1931.
[*The Abbey Girls at Home*]—Betty McLean reappears.
[*Rosamund's Victory*]—Rena Mackay and Lisabel Durrant reappear.

Damaris and Rachel Ellerton

Damaris at Dorothy's, 1937.
[*Maidlin to the Rescue*]
Damaris Dances, 1940—some events are also described in [*Adventure for Two*].
[*Guardians of the Abbey*]
[*A Dancer from the Abbey*]
[*Rachel in the Abbey*]

The Camp Keema Story

The Crisis in Camp Keema, 1928.
'*Freda Joins the Guides*', 1931.
'*Camp Keema Finds a Guardian*', 1928.
'*The Last Night in Camp*', 1928.
Peggy and the Brotherhood, 1936.
[*The Camp Mystery*]—includes '*The Watchers on the Lake*' and '*The Missing Link*'.
[*The Abbey Girls Play Up*]

Robin Quellyn (née Brent)

The Girl Who Wouldn't Make Friends, 1909.
[*Rosamund's Tuck-Shop*]
[*Rosamund's Castle*]
New Girls at Wood End, 1957.
[*Robins in the Abbey*]

Nancybell, Margery, Daphne and Elsa

These characters are all first seen in the Priorsbury/Hillside area of Somerset. Their fortunes are eventually linked into the Abbey books through Daphne and Margery.

Mistress Nanciebel, 1910.
Adventure for Two, 1941.
Elsa Puts Things Right, 1944.
Margery Meets the Roses, 1947.

The Torment Books

The School Torment, 1920.
The Testing of the Torment, 1925.
A Camp Fire Torment, 1926.
[*The Abbey Girls Go Back to School*]—Torment meets the Abbey girls at the school.

The Swiss Set

The Two Form-Captains, 1921.
The Captain of the Fifth, 1922.
[*The Abbey Girls Go Back to School*]—Tazy and Karen join the summer school.
The Camp Mystery, 1932—includes '*The Watchers on the Lake*' and '*The Missing Link*'.
The Troubles of Tazy, 1926.
[*Patience and Her Problems*]
[*The Abbey Girls Play Up*]—Cecily reappears in this.
[*An Abbey Champion*]—Tazy reappears in this.

The Scottish Set

Goblin Island, 1907.
A Princess in Tatters, 1908.
A Holiday Queen, 1910.
Schoolgirls and Scouts, 1914.
The Twins of Castle Charming, 1920.
Monica Howard also appears in *Finding Her Family*.

The School of Ups and Downs

The School of Ups and Downs, 1918.
Patience Joan, Outsider, 1922.
Patience and Her Problems, 1927—Patience meets the Swiss Set.

The Ven and Gard Books

The Junior Captain, 1923.
The School Without a Name, 1924.
Ven at Gregory's, 1925.
Peggy Makes Good, 1927—contains '*Christmas Quarantine*', '*Peggy Plays a Part*' and '*The Bungalow Baby*'.
Ven appears in *The Troubles of Tazy,* Barbara Holt appears in *Patience and her Problems* and Sadie Sandell reappears in *The Camp Fire Torment.*

The Jinty Books

The Tuck-Shop Girl, 1916.
The Reformation of Jinty, 1933—contains '*Jinty of the Girl Guides*','*The Honour of the Guides*', '*The Guides and Roger*' and '*One Good Turn*'.
Jinty's Patrol, 1934.
A Divided Patrol, 1992.

The Deb Books

Deb at School, 1929.
Deb of Sea House, 1931.
Deb Leads the Dormitory, 1992.

Free-standing Books

The Girls of Gwynfa, 1924.
Expelled from School, 1919.
The Conquest of Christina, 1909.
Rosaly's New School, 1913.
At School with the Roundheads, 1915.

Finding Her Family, 1916—Monica Howard from the Scottish Set appears in this.
A School Camp Fire, 1917.
Dorothy's Dilemma, 1930.
Sylvia of Sarn, 1937.
Pernel Wins, 1942.
Daring Doranne, 1945—Pernel and Judy reappear at the beginning of this. Gwen plays a
    larger part, and Doranne's model village, Rainbows, takes its name from the 'Rainbow
    Corner' part of the hostel where Daphne Dale lives in *Adventure for Two*. Doranne and
    Rainbows later appear in *Margery Meets the Roses*.

Free-standing Short Stories

'Dancing Honour', 1921.
'Honour Your Partner', 1923—set in same school as *'Dancing Honour'*.
'Muffins and Crumpets', 1926.
'Dicky's Dilemma', 1927—possible link with *Dorothy's Dilemma*.
'Helen Wins', 1934—seems to be set in same school as *'Dicky's Dilemma'*.

Index

The Index covers the text of Chapters 1–11 and Postscript, and the photographs on pp. 289-98. All titles, illustrators and publishers of books by EJO are indexed, as are all illustrations and photographs. Places are indexed selectively – if a specific place cannot be found in the Index, look under the appropriate county or region e.g. Yorkshire, Lake District. Page numbers in italics refer to illustrations.

FURTHER INFORMATION

Societies
There are four flourishing Abbey societies in Australia, New Zealand, the UK and South Africa. Each of the first three produces a quarterly or tri-annual A5 magazine.

The Abbey Girls of Australia (newsletter *The Abbey Guardian*)
Details from: Cath Vaughan-Pow (editor), PO Box 136, Jesmond, NSW, 2299, Australia
e-mail: editor@abbeygirls.com

The Abbey Gatehouse (New Zealand) (magazine T*he Abbey Gatehouse*)
Details from: Barbara Robertson (editor), 39D Bengal Street, Wellington 6004, New Zealand
e-mail: born.robertson@xtra.co.nz

The Elsie Jeanette Oxenham Appreciation Society (UK)
(journal *The Abbey Chronicle*)
Details from: Ruth Allen (membership secretary), 32 Tadfield Road, Romsey, Hampshire SO51 5AJ, UK
e-mail: abbey@bufobooks.demon.do.uk
website: http://www.bufobooks.demon.co.uk/abbeylnk.htm

The Abbey Chapter (South Africa) (no magazine but group meets regularly)
Details from: Rose Humphreys, 3 Egret Street, Somerset West 7130, South Africa
e-mail: dogrose@ballmail.co.za

Elsie Jeanette Oxenham website
There is also an excellent website to be found at
http://home.pacific.net.au/~bcooper/popular.htm

Girls Gone By Publishers

Girls Gone By Publishers republish some of the most popular children's fiction from the 20th century, concentrating on those titles which are most sought after and difficult to find on the secondhand market. Our aim is to make these books available at affordable prices, and to make ownership possible not only for existing collectors but also for new ones so that the survival of the books is continued. We also publish some new titles which fit into this genre. Authors whose books have already appeared, or will be published in 2006, include Margaret Biggs, Angela Brazil, Elinor M Brent-Dyer, Dorita Fairlie Bruce, Gwendoline Courtney, Monica Edwards, Antonia Forest, Lorna Hill, Clare Mallory, Violet Needham, Elsie Jeanette Oxenham, Malcolm Saville and Geoffrey Trease.

We also have a growing range of non-fiction titles. Those already available, or to be published in 2006, include a new edition of the seminal work *You're A Brick, Angela!* by Mary Cadogan and Patricia Craig, and books about Elsie Oxenham (*The World of Elsie Jeanette Oxenham and her Books* by Monica Godfrey, Antonia Forest (*The Marlows and Their Maker* by Anne Heazlewood) and Monica Edwards (*The Romney Marsh Companion* by Brian Parks).

For details of available and forthcoming titles, and when to order the latter (please do not order any book until it is actually listed), please either visit our website, www.ggbp.co.uk, or write for a catalogue to Clarissa Cridland or Ann Mackie-Hunter, GGBP, 4 Rock Terrace, Coleford, Bath BA3 5NF, UK.

Biographical Note

Stella and Sheila, both educated at Yorkshire West Riding grammar schools, met on their first day at the University of Leeds when they were on the same table for dinner at their Hall of Residence. After graduating in 1951, they trained as librarians together and both went to work for the West Riding County Library. They had both read EJO's books as schoolgirls and had developed an interest in folk dancing, but it was some years before they discovered their common interest in EJO and first Stella, then Sheila, began to collect EJO's books seriously. They both moved into teaching, Stella teaching French in Loughborough, having taken time out to have a daughter, and Sheila teaching librarianship in Birmingham, as a result of which she wrote a thesis, subsequently turned into *The Blyton Phenomenon,* for an M.Phil. After this was completed, they decided to write a study of EJO's books and the rest is history. They are both interested in local history, music, theatre and travel, all of which have complemented their research into the work of EJO.

Sheila Ray, left, and Stella Waring on a bridge in Wales

Cover

Front, clockwise from top left: dustwrappers of *The Girls of Gwynfa, Two Queens at the Abbey, Patience Joan, Outsider, Reformation of Jinty, Goblin Island* and *The Two Form Captains.* Centre: EJO and one of her brothers.
Back, clockwise from top left: Cleeve Abbey, Madryn Castle, Stepping Stones at Goathland, Arundel Castle, Knockderry Castle and the Burne-Jones windows at St. Margaret's Church, Rottingdean. Centre: EJO aged about 13.

The EJO photos appear by the permission of EJO's niece, Wendy Dunkerley, the dustwrappers by courtesy of the publishers and the photographs of the EJO sites are from the collection of the authors.